Jolson: The Legend Comes to Life

JOLSON

The Legend Comes to Life

Herbert G. Goldman

NEW YORK / OXFORD   OXFORD UNIVERSITY PRESS
1988

Oxford University Press

Oxford   New York   Toronto
Delhi   Bombay   Calcutta   Madras   Karachi
Petaling Jaya   Singapore   Hong Kong   Tokyo
Nairobi   Dar es Salaam   Cape Town
Melbourne   Auckland

and associated companies in
Berlin   Ibadan

Copyright © 1988 by Herbert G. Goldman

Published by Oxford University Press, Inc.,
200 Madison Avenue, New York, New York 10016

Oxford is a registered trademark of Oxford University Press

Library of Congress Cataloging-in-Publication Data
Goldman, Herbert G.
Jolson : The Legend Comes To Life / Herbert G. Goldman.
p.   cm.   Stageography: p.   Filmography: p.   Radiography: p.   Discography: p.
Includes index.
ISBN 0-19-505505-5
1. Jolson, Al, d. 1950.   2. Singers—United States—Biography.
I. Title.
ML420.J74G6   1988
782.81′092′4—dc19
[B]   88-4222   CIP   MN

2 4 6 8 9 7 5 3 1

Printed in the United States of America
on acid-free paper

To the memory of my loving grandfather,
Max Goldman
(September 20, 1902–September 27, 1958)

Preface

This book might well be called *The Best of Jolson*. God, but there was so much that I cut. The original manuscript was between two and three times the size of the final draft. There was additional data on Jolson's family, more reviews and critiques, information on various lawsuits and trials (in 1926, attorney Arthur Driscoll asked Al if he knew Jake Shubert. Jolson said he did. "I've even slept with him"), and many more (documented) anecdotes. Jolson enthusiasts and collectors will be disappointed at the limited references to Al's commercial records, but this book is about Jolson's life *as he lived it,* and recordings, for the most part, were a mere sideline of his professional activity.

I did the best I could, given the fact that Jolson has been dead for well over thirty-five years and that the two people living today who knew him best, Ruby Keeler (Al's third wife) and Erle Galbraith (his widow), did not choose to abet my efforts. Ruby, who suffered a burst embolism in 1974, did not return my letters. Erle answered my one letter, and was gracious when I phoned, but declined to offer a substantial contribution.

The research took more years than I would care to admit, and I probably acquired enough knowledge to meet the requirements for several Ph.Ds. in American theatre history in the process. I went through every issue of *Variety* published from that illustrious trade paper's inception in December 1905 until Mr. Jolson's body was finally laid to rest at Hillside in September 1951. Other theatrical publications, like the *New York Clipper,* the *New York Dramatic Mirror,* and *Billboard* (the same publication that now restricts itself to the popular music and video fields), were combed for the years of Jolson's stage career. I even consulted numerous daily papers in the cities Jolson played *en tour,* etc., in order to obtain numerous specifics. And I interviewed more than twenty-five people, speaking to an additional two hundred in the process.

Just as the recordings in *The Jolson Story* were made up of many different "takes" pieced together to form one magnificent sound-track, so this book is the result of painful editing and rewrites. At least twenty drafts were done of the first chapter. It took time to find the proper way to tell the story, and I finally decided on a modern, fast-paced, direct style. *Jolson: The Legend Comes to Life* is neither an exposé nor an "affectionate look" at Jolson in the manner of, say, John McCabe's *Mr. Laurel and Mr. Hardy*. I have tried to portray Jolson as he was—no mean feat in itself.

Since I wanted both the writing style and the format of this book to reflect and emulate its subject, I cut out all footnotes and contented myself with general "chapter notes" at the end of the text. Nothing in this book has been imagined. In some instance, I have relied on second-hand accounts in order to reconstruct important scenes in Jolson's life. (For example, Jolson's 1919 telephone conversations with Henrietta Keller, his first wife, were taken from an interview with Jean Carlson, Henrietta's friend and confidante.) Everything is from one good source or another—cross checked for accuracy to the greatest possible extent.

Most printed references to Jolson are loaded with inaccuracies and half truths, with an occasional lie thrown in for malicious measure. My search for the true facts and the true Jolson took me into many cities, many libraries, and many homes. At the end, I felt that I had captured Al as greatly as he'd captured me so many years ago—as if I, in the role of Captain Ahab, and Jolson, as Moby Dick, had finally harpooned each other and vanished in the mists.

Let me thank those people who graciously allowed themselves to be interviewed: the late Samson Raphaelson, Kitty Doner, Julia Rooney, Manny Mannheim, the late George Jessel, the late May McAvoy, the late Ben Lyon, the late Marian Nixon, Pearl and Stan Fried, the late Patsy Kelly, Teresa Flax Goode Kaplan, Ethel Flax Brown, Marvin Cantor, the late Pearl Goldberg Sieben, Irving Caesar, Doris Vinton, the late Kitty Gordon, the late Matty Malneck, Dorothy Wegman Raphaelson, Carol Bruce, Marjorie Olsen, the late Mrs. Leon "Beanie" Dworkin, Jean Carlson Sidman, George Jolson, Gertrude Yoelson Sollod, Ray O'Brien, and the late Joseph Meyer.

My deepest thanks go to Helen Gurley Brown, who graciously allowed me to quote passages from "The Jolson Nobody Knew" by Harry Akst as told to Ernest Lehman, an article that originally appeared in the February 1951 issue of *Cosmopolitan*. I am likewise indebted to Sid Silverman, grandson of Sime, the founder of *Variety*, for permission to draw numerous quotes, large and small, from *Variety*, which covered Al's career so well for more than forty years. The letter to the Shuberts near the end of Act I, Scene 5, is quoted with permission of The Shubert Archive. My thanks to Professor Brooks MacNamara and Maryann Chach.

I also thank those who, in various ways, made it possible for this book to be written and, finally, finished. People like Rochelle M. Balter (whose help could not be measured), Eleanor DiMaio, Anna Marie Gubitosi, Gerald Bordman, Greg Gormick, Will Jordan, George Nestor, Otis R. Lowe, Larry Kiner, Patrick Hawkins, Nat and Joan Loubet, and Miles Kreuger, president of the American Musical, Inc., the world's most respected authority on film musicals and musical theatre. My deepest appreciation to Leona Capeless, and to Rachel Toor, Joellyn Ausanka, and Sheldon Meyer, vice president of Oxford's Trade Book Division, a man of vision and a gentleman of taste.

Special thanks must go to Edward B. Greenbaum, who provided me with wisdom, counsel, friendship, and a patient ear during the years it took to research and write this book. I also thank his wife, Dorothy, and their children, Eve-Lynn and Matthew, for putting up with countless hours of telephone conversations, and Jolson, Jolson, more Jolson, and, for good measure, Al Jolson, those long years.

My very special thanks to Ronald J. Fields, whose sound editorial advice helped this author through the final rewrite. Ron, my friend, you are the greatest. Enough said.

It seems odd to me, having spent twenty-five years as a Jolson fan, that most people under the age of thirty-five today have little idea of who Jolson was. His films, of course, have not been shown on TV in the last fifteen years, due to their obviously dated (and frequently inferior) quality, their black-and-whiteness, and the fact that Al appears in blackface in every movie he appeared in save for the dreadful *Say It with Songs*, his cameo in *Hollywood Cavalcade*, and the flawed but interesting *Hallelujah, I'm a Bum*. The situation is not likely to change, but I can hope that many, having read this book, will have a new respect for Jolson as an artist. If *Jolson: The Legend Comes to Life* does that, it will have served its original purpose.

Well, it's finished. Good night, Al. It's been mostly terrific.

New York   HERBERT G. GOLDMAN
January 15, 1988

Contents

CONTENTS

Jolson: The Legend Comes to Life

"You're on, Mr. Jolson"

"Swanee, how I love ya, how I love ya, my dear old Swanee."

The late 1960s saw the beginning of a vast nostalgia boom in response to the great social upheavals taking place in American society. Slender "coffee table" books on the "Films of . . ."—various Hollywood stars never considered anything but mediocre by their contemporaries—flooded the market, and Ruby Keeler emerged as the "Queen of Nostalgia" when her 1930s Warner Bros. films enjoyed a following that fluctuated between cult and camp.

Lost in the shuffle of old radio transcriptions, "duped" films, early TV kinescopes, and vintage sheet music covers were the kings and queens of the live theatre before World War II. Especially Al Jolson.

The man contemporary critics called "a genius" was crucified in any number of books—personally ("an ego who walked and talked like a man"), artistically ("a mass media figure whose blaring of the title "Mammy" somehow captivated a generation of Americans"), and even socially ("his blackface routine was an insult to black people"). At best, he was ignored.

Like a dark and omnipresent cloud, however, Jolson's talent, as well as his legend, continue to hang over the imaginations of critics. The passage of time demands a new look at the man billed as "The World's Greatest Entertainer."

It is not easy. Jolson has been dead for more than thirty-five years, and it has been over forty-five years since his last appearance in a Broadway show. Contemporary critics claimed that his films and radio appearances totally failed to capture the dynamic, almost supernatural appeal of his stage appearances, and a cursory glance at what survives only serves to confirm the opinion.

But to three generations, Al Jolson, comedian and "mammy" singer of the 1910s and '20s, typified the dreams that made up Broadway—the "spirit of after 8 p.m. above Forty-Second Street, when a million incandescent lights fired Manhattan's lane of light and the

3

hum of the restless taxi cab was in the air." There was a primeval quality about Jolson that even his own contemporaries were not able to unravel. About the best those thinning ranks of people who were privileged to see him on the stage can tell us is "the man was magic." Their eyes glisten.

He was a musical comedy star—a belter of songs tailor-made for his dynamic personality and an infectiously funny sketch comedian in the grand tradition—and, to some extent, the makeup—of the *commedia dell'arte*. ("No one funnier than Mister," said his on-and-off-the-stage companion Kitty Doner.) It is probably wiser, and more accurate, to compare him to Bert Lahr than to Frank Sinatra.

On the stage or off it, Jolson mugged almost incessantly, walking with a peculiar trot that made his torso shift, and talked with what John Crosby called an "odd style of speech wherein he managed to eliminate consonants almost entirely." He was only five-foot seven, and not really handsome—possessing a large head with gleaming, eager, deep-set eyes that could turn hauntingly dramatic in a song. His voice, described as "leathery" and "a perfect blend of ringing brass and amber warmth," is probably the most imitated, parodied, and emulated in history. Jolson on the Winter Garden runway, fingers flittering together as his voice went into a high register in "April Showers," or belting out George Gershwin's "Swanee" with his gloved fists clenched, was an unforgettable experience.

He worked in "blackface," often singing songs about his southern "mammy" with a passion that endeared them to sophisticated Broadway audiences. Critic Gilbert Seldes, writing in the '20s, thought that Jolson's blackface was "so little negroid that it (went) well with diversions in Yiddish accents." But the image of him singing "Mammy" in *The Jazz Singer,* famed as the first talking picture, eventually transcended all of Jolson's other fame.

The Jazz Singer assured Jolson's immortality, but his talents were not suited to the movies, and his popularity declined in a succession of poor pictures with banal scripts and maladroit acting. Release of *The Jolson Story,* the tremendously successful film biography starring Larry Parks, revived his career in 1946, but Jolson was never personally popular with many of his colleagues. Moody, unpredictable, and sometimes cruel, Al Jolson was one of the most disliked men in the theatrical profession. Known as the biggest egotist in show business, Jolson could not stand competition, and, it seemed, lived only for applause.

The onstage Jolson seemed to love his audience. The offstage "Jolie," as his colleagues called him, seemed to love only himself. A

Jew, he never went to services and prayed but once a year. That was when he chanted *Yahrzeit* for his mother.

Naomi Yoelson, a Lithuanian Jewess born around 1860, was the real "mammy." She died when Al was eight, but she remained his leading lady—the unacknowledged mistress of his failed private life and of his stage career.

He loved her deeply. He probably loved no one else.

ACT ONE

Naomi

The real "Jolson Story" began with a scream.

The place was Washington, D.C., just before sundown on Wednesday, February 6, 1895. Asa Yoelson, an eight-year-old Lithuanian immigrant in knickers, ran up the steps to the Yoelson apartment, where his mother had lain ill for weeks. She was pregnant, with a host of complications that had never been explained to him.

Now she was screaming, the final agony upon her as a doctor tried in vain to stem her bleeding. Asa pushed open the door and saw his mother. Naomi Yoelson was still screaming. Her eyes were open, but she seemingly looked through her young son with no sign of recognition.

Asa Yoelson would never be the same again. He grew up in that moment—probably as much as he would ever grow up. Al Jolson, for all his tough, earthy exterior, would remain an emotional child for the rest of his life—a self-assured braggart who was terrified of being alone, a sentimentalist with a heart of gold who made life miserable for most of those around him, and a lothario who chased, conquered, and, in turn, ignored young women. In short, a man-boy, full of seeming contradictions and haunted by the spectre of his mother's death.

Roots

"Early life? Well, very early in life I was born in Russia and named Asa Yoelson. That's what they tell me. Personally, I don't remember it. I bet I was left in a basket on the doorstep. I'm Skeezix for all I know. There's nothing much to tell about me."

A l Jolson was a Jew, probably the first man of his faith well known as a Jew and idolized by the American public. As befits the man who made the song "My Mammy" famous, he was born in a log cabin—not in the rural southern U.S. but in Seredzius, Lithuania, a small, predominantly Jewish village a few miles west of Kaunas.

The facts are simple enough. Al Jolson was born Asa Yoelson, the fifth child of Rabbi Moshe Reuben Yoelson and his wife, Naomi Cantor Yoelson. The other Yoelson children were Rose (1879), Etta (1880), Hirsch (later known as Harry, 1882), and a baby girl, name unknown, who died in infancy c. 1884. Al was probably born on or about May 26, 1886. The year may have been 1885, and the exact date is uncertain.

Seredzius consisted of one dirt street bordered on both sides by wooden houses, two synagogues (one was used for holidays, the other for regular services), a Russian Orthodox church, a few small tradesmen's shops, and a tavern. The Niemen River ran alongside the village and was the chief source of recreation for its people. It was a village not unlike those described in the tales of Sholem Aleichem. But Naomi Yoelson, Al's mother, not Tevye the Dairyman, was the central character in Jolson's childhood.

When Al, or Asa, was only four years old, his father left Seredzius for America. Rabbi Yoelson planned to put down roots quickly and then send for his family, but it took almost four years for him to get established. Naomi raised the family in Seredzius—a "single parent" in all practical respects.

Asa was his mother's favorite child. He was the baby, named after her father, Reb Asa Cantor, president of the great synagogue in Keidan and one of the wealthiest Jews in the Baltic States. Naomi, Reb

Asa's only daughter, was better educated than most Jewish women of the period. When Asa reached the age of six, she had him given violin lessons and encouraged him to practice with tales of the fabled Steinway Hall in New York City.

Al needed all the encouragement his mother could give him. In childhood, as in later life, he was an active and mercurial individual—not the kind who likes to practice on the violin. (He would later become known as a ferociously hard worker in rehearsals.) Al's earliest ambition was to be a doctor; he liked the way that "Dr." Cohen (the village medial practitioner, an ignoramus with no degree who began practicing because he liked the idea) had cured his older brother of a case of indigestion.

Asa was the center of his mother's world. It was the beginning of an egocentricity that would finally emerge as a gargantuan ego.

Naomi Yoelson was, from all accounts, a remarkable and personable woman—one of those people who can take a chicken and, by dint of personality, make everyone around feel like they're at a banquet. It took all her reassurances, however, to convince her younger son that going to America was not the end of the world after Moshe's letter—with the magic word, "Come"—arrived early in 1894.

Rabbi Yoelson had finally secured a good position in America—head of the Talmud Torah Congregation in Washington, D.C. The girls were in their teens and Hirsch was a gawky twelve-year-old. Children seldom like being uprooted, and Asa, who had only a dim memory of his father, did not want to leave Seredzius. Naomi did her best to assuage his fears, but Al always remembered the trip to America as a "terrible" experience.

The trip itself was typical of those endured by eastern European immigrants. Naomi, Rose, Etta, Hirsch, and Asa left Seredzius for Kaunas in a hay wagon on a cold night in March, 1894. Several changes of trains brought them to Memel, the harbor, where they took a steamer to Liverpool, England. It would be a few days before their ocean liner sailed for America, so Naomi took a room in a cheap boarding house. The boys had had a language tutor in Seredzius, and, since they spoke a little English, Naomi reluctantly allowed them to explore the city. Asa inevitably wandered away from his older brother and got lost. Hirsch returned to the boarding house without him.

Naomi's nerves were shot. Not knowing English, she felt helpless, and she was terrified of losing Asa. She blamed Hirsch for her baby's disappearance, and Al's older brother never forgot the way his mother berated him that day. A Liverpool policeman brought Asa back an hour later, but Hirsch was already starting to resent the way Naomi favored Asa. In time, this same resentment would mature into a bitterness that Al's own death would not entirely erase—a bitterness akin to Salieri's feelings toward Mozart.

They sailed for America on the *Umbria* the following day and arrived, seasick and disheveled, at Ellis Island on April 9th. Asa became frightened when his mother broke away and ran to a strange man. The man was Asa's father.

Naomi, Rose, and Etta all wore shawls on their heads, and Hirsch had on long trousers—never seen on twelve-year-old American boys in 1894. Their father, already accustomed to the smarter look of people in America, just looked at them and said, in English, "I'm glad it was night when you come."

Then he took them down to Washington by train.

Their new home was a set of rooms above Barnes' Flour & Feed Store at 208 4½ Street in the Southwest quarter of the city. The next few months proved to be a difficult period of adjustment. The boys were enrolled in the Jefferson Public School on Sixth Street, while Naomi and her daughters struggled with a new language, new methods of housekeeping, and new ways of dealing with merchants.

Moshe endeavored to reimplement religious instruction. A cantor as well as a rabbi, his training involved singing in addition to prayer and study. Moshe's original ambition was to be an opera singer— this in contrast to the usual portrait of him as a hater of the theatre. Having little patience with more modern methods, he propped open his sons' mouths with matchsticks to ensure that they would project properly. The method was effective but uncomfortable, and both boys disliked it. Washington was interesting, but Seredzius seemed like a long-lost paradise when Asa and Hirsch had to pray, study, or sing with their father. The seeds of a rebellion were soon planted.

They were in the country for about nine months when Naomi was confined to bed. Rose and Etta—mostly Rose, the eldest—ran the house and took care of their mother. Unaware of just how ill his mother was, Asa spent most of his time outside the house with Hirsch, selling papers and exploring the new city.

Shortly before sundown on Wednesday, February 6th, Asa arrived home from Hebrew School. He was alone, Hirsch having remained at the synagogue to practice for his Bar Mitzvah. Asa, who heard screams as he came near the house, ran up the stairs and pushed open the door to his parents' room. It was then he saw his mother, sitting up in bed with her eyes open. She was still screaming, and the doctor pushed him from the room.

For a minute, he walked nervously around, compulsively touching the furniture his mother had touched many times before. Then the screaming stopped and he ran back into the room—in time to see the doctor pull the sheet over his mother's head.

According to what Al later said—on one of the few instances he spoke about the subject—he just turned and ran. For an hour, he remained in a deserted alley, staring into space and trembling. When he finally returned home, the family was in his parents' room. Moshe, his voice choking, told his children that God had taken their mother to an "even better land" than America.

The funeral was held within twelve hours, in accordance with strict Jewish law. Then the plain pine coffin was put into a dark carriage and driven across the Potomac to the Talmud Torah Cemetary in Anacostia. Asa did not have any dark mittens, so a pair of Rose's black stockings had been drawn over his hands. It was very cold, and Asa dabbed at his eyes with his stocking-covered fists, determined to keep back the tears. Never, something in him vowed, would he accept his mother's death.

Many years later, the scene would be reversed, and Al Jolson, his face blackened with burnt cork instead of whitened by the cold and wearing white gloves, not black stockings, on his hands, would drop to one knee before his "mammy."

> "I'm a coming . . . I—I hope I didn't make you wait.
> "Mammy, mammy, I'm coming.
> "Oh, God, I hope I'm not late."

Then he would interpolate the lines, those special lines—not in the song as written—that he wished he had said when his mother stared straight through him.

> "Mammy, mammy, look at me.
> Don't you know me?
> I'm your little baby."

The song would be his trademark, but that was far in Asa Yoelson's future.

He remained dry-eyed during the *shivah,* the Jewish period of mourning for the dead. When the *shivah* was over, Hirsch noticed that his younger brother often sat on the edge of his bed and stared— as if still sitting *shivah.*

In many senses, Jolson would sit *shivah* for his mother all his life. And because his mourning was never completed, he continually experienced deep loneliness. When Naomi died, he thought that his own life had ended. He needed love, but it was not forthcoming. From now on, he felt, the love his mother had given him would have to come from somewhere else—from outside of the family. And it would have to be fought for.

He was only eight years old.

Asa was withdrawn for the next seven months. What jarred him back into the real world was a trip into make-believe—the theatre.

Not that the great actors of the day would have considered Al Reeves' Famous Big Company part of "the theatre." The striptease was not yet a staple of the burlesque world, but Reeves, "The World's Greatest Banjoist and Comedian," as he billed himself, was considered the most risqué comic of the 1890s. He worked in blackface when Asa and Hirsch Yoelson saw him at Kernan's Lyceum Theatre in Washington, delighting his audience with comments on the best features of each individual chorine's figure. Reeves was not a particularly good banjo player, but his "big finishes" brought prolonged applause. As it faded, he would exclaim, "Give me credit, boys."

Jolson often credited Reeves with giving him his start in show business—a psychological, if not factual, truth. Reeves was Jolson's idol and, in some respects, his model. The Jolson of the 1910s and '20s was a more sophisticated, more dramatic, somewhat more subtle, version of Reeves.

Al Reeves touched a special chord in Asa Yoelson. Had he reminded him directly of Naomi, the boy would probably have shut his mind to Reeves and withdrawn almost totally. As it was, Al Reeves was magic. He was unlike Asa's mother save in one respect. Like Naomi, who could take a chicken and make everyone feel they were at a banquet, Reeves took his third-rate banjo playing and made everyone feel they were at a truly memorably performance.

Reeves, and the magic world of theatre he personified, gave life back to nine-year-old Asa Yoelson. His mother's last look at him and her death were traumatic experiences from which he would not totally recover. But after he saw Reeves and discovered the theatre,

Jolson's thoughts, aims, needs, and life were channeled. At the age of nine, he had found a new life in the theatre, and a new source of love in the sound of applause. All previous memories were submerged, buried. From now on, he had but one goal—to perform.

Asa was no longer withdrawn. He and his brother Hirsch became Al and Harry Joelson in the months that followed. "As Asa and Hirsch," Harry recalled, "we were Jewish boys. As Al and Harry, we were Americans: friends and brothers to all other boys, whether they were black or white, Jews or Gentiles, Republicans or Democrats."

The truth was far less lofty; the new names allowed the Joelson boys to hang out with a street gang. "We were really tough," Al remembered just a year before his death. "We carried iron sticks on ropes for protection against each other. Yes sir, I mean iron."

Harry was thirteen, trying to assert his independence and resentful of the way his father was trying to re-establish discipline after years of absence. Al's resentment of the "old ways"—prayer, study, and devotion—doubtless went much deeper, since they stemmed from Moshe's—and God's—perceived failure to save his mother. For the remainder of his life, until his father died, Al largely turned his back upon religion. Jolson never denied his Jewishness; he never denied God. But he tended to ignore them.

By the end of 1895 the Joelson boys were in full rebellion—staying out with the gang instead of coming home after school, getting into fights, running afoul of their sister Rose, and otherwise coming into conflict with the ideals of their father. Carrying iron sticks attached to ropes for "protection" was not Rabbi Yoelson's idea of how good Jewish boys ought to behave.

Since their misbehavior had not started until after Naomi's death, the rabbi assumed what his sons needed was a mother. His congregation also needed a *rebitzen,* and he, still a relatively young man, needed a wife. He wrote to Peri Yoels, Naomi's second cousin in Seredzius, asking for the hand of her daughter, Chyesa, in marriage. The marriage was agreed to quickly, and both Peri and Chyesa left for the United States.

The Yoelson children all remembered Chyesa—Hessi, as they called her—having lived across the street from her and Peri, a loud-voiced woman whose own husband had died a few years earlier, in Seredzius. She was part of a dead past that Al had buried with Naomi—one he did not care to be reminded of again.

Al had little say in the matter. Moshe Reuben Yoelson and Chyesa
"Hessi" Yoels were married by Rabbi Moshe Rosenberg of the Agu-
das Achim Congregation on Sunday, March 29, 1896. Moshe was
thirty-eight; Hessi was twenty-six—only nine years older than Rose.
Trouble was inevitable.

Harry could not tolerate the way his father had written to the old
country for a wife instead of "solving his problem in the American
way." Al's own feelings ran much deeper; he thought his mother
had been dealt the final insult—being "replaced" by another woman.
He spent all the time he could outside the house—hawking papers,
peddling watermelons, and, sometimes, getting into trouble.

Al Jolson's career really began in the summer of 1896, when the
Joelson boys, who had attracted attention with their singing of "The
Star Spangled Banner" at the Jefferson School, became street entertainers at the urging of their friends. They spent the early evenings
singing for the congressmen and other high officials who sat on the
veranda in front of the Hotel Raleigh sipping tall, cool drinks. Popular songs like "Sweet Marie" and "The Sidewalks of New York"
brought a shower of nickels from the appreciative politicians, but
the old songs—"When You and I Were Young, Maggie," "Oh, Dem
Golden Slippers," and anything by Stephen Foster—made them throw
dimes and quarters.

Those informal performances gave Al Jolson his first taste of applause and the indescribable thrill of knowing he had pleased his
listeners. Al and Harry had learned harmony and were especially
good at "Listen to The Mocking Bird," in which ten-year-old Al
would whistle. Another street performer, a black youngster who
danced, often teamed up with them.

Black kids did not go to Jefferson, since the schools in Washington were segregated, but the Joelsons had at least a few black friends
besides their sometime partner. Among them was a boy who borrowed Al's new bicycle—his only noteworthy possession—without
asking permission. Al flew into a rage, demanding the bike be returned. The kid then brought it back with the front wheel broken,
and the hysterical Al went for his throat.

"I never want to see you again," Al screamed as his brother dragged
him off. Within a few days, however, he had cooled off and was
ready to be friends again.

Al was frequently like that—furiously angry at one moment and
then ready to forget. But he seldom said, "I never want to see you
again." It was the ultimate "Jolson curse."

The Joelson brothers became theatre habitués, using the dimes thrown at them by congressmen to purchase tickets to shows at the National, Washington's leading theatre, where the top New York attractions played *en tour*. The nearby Academy of Music specialized in comedy, melodrama, and an occasional "musical extravaganza." The Bijou was confined to melodrama, while Allen's Grand Opera House gave the National stiff competition with its "class" productions and revivals. The only burlesque theatre was Kernan's, but the boys saw every show that played there after the Yoelson family moved to 482 School Street, a house surrounded by a tall white fence. (Once, Al scaled the fence to go to a burlesque show, came down on a broken liquor bottle, and cut his foot. He carried that scar for the rest of his life.)

Al and Harry were now far more Americanized than their father, and Moshe tended to see their theatre-going as a facet of their misbehavior—especially when they ran off to see shows on *shabbes*. On one occasion, Harry got what he later described as "a hearty whipping," and Moshe demanded that their tickets for that evening be surrendered. When he refused, Moshe locked the boys in their room and went to the synagogue without them. Al and Harry escaped by sliding down the drainpipe that ran down the side of the house close to their window. They were still at the burlesque show when their father returned home.

Moshe locked the window, but left the front door unlocked against his sons' return. Unable to open the window, and not knowing of the unlocked door, the boys spent the rest of the night on a pile of hay in a nearby livery stable.

Moshe Yoelson was not an ogre. He regarded the popular theatre as something for *zuliks* ("loafers"), but his attitude in that respect was not much different from most eastern European immigrants. Nor did he insist that his two sons be cantors. (The idea that Al and Harry were the first sons in six generations not to be cantors was a myth inspired by *The Jazz Singer*. Moshe's father, Meyer, was a dealer in boots and shoes.)

The boys made a steadily wider break with the rest of the family in the months that followed. They smoked, played hookey with increasing frequency, and became increasingly difficult for Moshe to control. The last straw came when Hessi gave birth to a son, Emil, in May 1897. Al was no longer the baby of the family, a fact which served to drive an even wider wedge between Hessi and Naomi's children.

The girls now joined their brothers in rebellion. Etta, who liked

sitting in a window seat with a good book much more than she liked
housework, had a fight with Hessi and then wrote her Uncle Chaym
(a brother of Naomi), asking for a job in his dry-goods store in
Yonkers, New York.

Etta's departure gave Harry all the inspiration he needed. Al's older
brother was considered the "black sheep" of the family, a bad influence on his younger brother. If the boys angered their father, Harry
invariably received the worst part of the punishment. Hessi, in particular, saw Al as "Asikla," the same tot she had known in Seredzius
who could do no wrong. It seemed to Harry as though Al could
smile his way out of anything. And he was probably right.

At the age of fifteen, Harry left home with little more than ten
dollars in his pocket. He did not tell Al where he was going, but,
after a month, a postcard arrived at the Yoelson home saying he
was on his way to being "a big businessman." The postcard read
"New York," so Al made plans to go there and find Harry. Al was
then eleven. He had never traveled alone, but the idea of a trip to
New York held no terrors for him. America was *his* world—not his
father's—an ego identification that gave him confidence far beyond
his years.

New York City had been built from the southern end up, and
entertainment was still centered in the Bowery in 1897. Cheap melodrama flourished in "ten-twent'-thirty" theatres filled with patrons
from the lower classes. There was vaudeville, with houses like the
famous Tony Pastor's and Keith's Union Square—both located "uptown" on Fourteenth Street. Burlesque shows flitted in and out of a
number of houses, like the Gotham, Miner's, and a half a dozen
others. Dime museums, offering freaks, wonders, and a host of acts
that later found their way onto the coming vaudeville chains, were
scattered through the poorer marketplaces. The Bowery, in short,
was the place for a young performer—especially one with no experience, very little money, no friends, no job, and no real salable act
or talent.

Al knew the Bowery was where he would find Harry. He wandered through the streets for a long time before he saw what looked
like Harry standing in front of a bakery window with his nose pressed
to the glass.

Harry, it developed, was not quite the "big businessman" his
postcard had implied. Broke and hungry, he was forced to take Al
to their Uncle Chaym's house in Yonkers. The boys even had to
hitchhike their way up there.

Harry went back to New York the next day with two dollars from his uncle. Al himself remained in Yonkers for a few days, and his sister brought him down to the dry-goods store once or twice before she sent him home to Washington. One time, Etta found him in the alley—standing on some empty packing cases and singing for a bunch of kids.

It is tempting to say that the last vestiges of Asa Yoelson, the terrified small boy from Seredzius, vanished in the next few months, but the truth is that Al Jolson remained a terrified small boy all his life. At the same time, he possessed all the naive confidence that symbolized turn-of-the-century America, and the trip to New York only served to whet his appetite for adventure.

A short time after he returned to Washington, the not-yet-twelve-year-old Al ran away with a fourth-rate carnival called Rich & Hoppe's Big Company of Fun Makers. In a later interview, Al claimed to have been lured away by the show's candy-puller.

Al was given a spot as a singer and provided with a full-dress suit. A tablecloth was tied around his waist in place of a cummerbund. The mysterious candy-puller took whatever money Al made and "invested it." While with Rich & Hoppe, Al called himself "Harry Joelson," thinking, with somewhat schizophrenic logic, that his elder brother's name would make him seem a little older.

Contemporary theatrical trade sources make no mention of Rich & Hoppe's Big Company of Fun Makers, and it is tempting to speculate about the anonymous candy-puller who gave Al his first taste of show business. The Rich & Hoppe Company folded after a few weeks, the candy- puller disappeared, and Al returned home.

Al and Harry, who had finally returned from New York, obtained jobs as singing waiters on one of the excursion boats on the Potomac that summer. Sometimes, they would entertain at Snyder's Place down near the Navy Yard, where "you could get a huge schooner of beer and a dish of crabs for a nickel." The boys had long since ceased to worry about keeping kosher.

It was at this time that Al first played before his favorite audience, the U.S. serviceman. The Spanish-American War was on, and the Joelson brothers performed for the Soldiers at Fort Myer and other camps around the D.C. area in their spare time. The war ended in August, and a regiment known as the Fifteenth Pennsylvania Volunteers was ordered back to Middletown. Al, already more adventurous than Harry, went along on the same train.

The Volunteers liked him, and he became their mascot. Al stayed in Middletown until the troop disbanded in September. He was in Harrisburg on October 3rd, when the Walter L. Main Circus came to town. Al applied for a job and was hired as an usher, "water boy," and singer. At the age of twelve, the Lithuanian-born immigrant was acting out the typical American fantasy—running away from home to join the circus.

The Main Circus, then in its fourteenth year, was one of the best-known shows in the eastern part of the country. The show in the big tent was made up of two parts. "Before the last attraction in the ring," remembered Al, "the band would stop playing long enough for the ringmaster to step to the platform and announce: 'Ladies and gentlemen, the performance is now but half over. I wish to call your attention to the vaudeville and concert which follows the main show. We will offer for your indulgence some of the world's most noted variety entertainers, among them Master Albert Joelson . . .' "

Al claimed to have been introduced as the "champion buck-and-wing dancer of the United States," but he had not yet developed his eccentric dancing, and, in all likelihood, his main job with the circus was as an usher. "After the performance at night I helped pack up, and then carried water for the ponies and drove a wagon to the train. Circus life . . . was the most fascinating and at the same time the most difficult means of livelihood imaginable."

Most of the accounts of this part of Al's life say that he was stranded in York, Pennsylvania, when the circus folded, but contemporary trade papers show the Main Circus completing its seasonal tour on schedule at Burton, Ohio, on October 22nd and returning to winter quarters in nearby Geneva. In any case, Al found himself alone with little money. He took a train to Baltimore, where the Gerry Society, a reform organization, found him working in a bar. When Al refused to give his name, they brought him to St. Mary's Industrial School for Boys.

St. Mary's was not a reform school, but neither was it merely an orphan asylum. It was most accurately described, in its own day, as a "home for wayward youngsters"—truants, runaways, and petty offenders whose parents had placed them in St. Mary's because they did not know what else to do with them. There were few child welfare organizations in the 1890s, and a boy might also be referred there by the courts.

The boys' time was completely regulated, with regular hours for classes, study, sleeping, chapel—whether or not a boy was Catholic—and work. Al's job was in the laundry, feeding shirts through a wringer.

"They didn't let us smoke," he recalled, "so I got a plug of tobacco from an iceman. It didn't taste so good, but a fella couldn't sleep right if he didn't pull some kind of fast one on the Brothers." That was just routine. What stamped Al as a problem were his attempts to escape. They took away his privileges, and he retaliated by refusing to work or study. He got into fights with other boys. Once he hit another kid while they were coming out of chapel, and they slapped him into solitary confinement.

Al could not stand confinement. He looked out of the window, saw the other kids at play, and started yelling. One of the Brothers finally looked in and saw that he was red hot and perspiring. The doctor was summoned, Al was found to be running a temperature, and "then," as he remembered, "they *had* to let me out."

They took him to the infirmary, where a more stringent examination uncovered a "tendency towards tuberculosis." Al knew about TB—the "Jewish mumps" that had killed more Hebrew children than the pharoahs. He panicked and gave the Brothers his correct name and address.

Moshe soon arrived to bring him home.

Hessi and Rose wept, Moshe gave his usual talmudic lecture, and Al, amazingly, behaved himself for the next six months. He was thirteen, and did not return to school. Neither did he run away from home. This was the first in a series of "settling down" moods Al would fall into at certain times—periodic cravings for a "real life" that alternated with his need for excitement. These moods would last a few months, and then disappear.

Looking at the total situation, one cannot help thinking that Al's father was a very tolerant, long-suffering man. Harry was seventeen in 1899, and had not attended school in three years. Neither he nor Al had regular jobs, although both "hustled" for money in various ways and had what must have seemed to any neutral observer as rather vague ambitions about "the show business"—even if they were obsessive in Al's case. Careers as rabbis for either one was absolutely out of the question, as was any other profession. Moshe thought, or hoped, that they could learn "respectable" trades—like tailoring— but he never pressed the matter and seems to have been perfectly willing to let his sons choose their own ways of earning a living.

The rabbi, though, regarded the popular theatre as something less than "respectable," and certainly nothing to be compared with his own long-gone ambitions regarding grand opera. He called ragtime, for example, "loafer music."

Early in the fall, Al was hired as a supernumerary (a non-speaking background person in a play, comparable to an "extra" in a movie) for *The Children of the Ghetto,* Israel Zangwill's dramatization of his own novel, which opened at the National Theatre in Washington on September 18th. It was a controversial play, dealing with Jews and questioning their own talmudic law.

Rabbi Yoelson soon heard about the play and was shocked to learn his son was in it. Moshe demanded that he quit, and Al, who was getting twenty-five cents a performance, did as he was told.

Harry, in the meantime, took a job as a peanut vendor in the Bijou, now a burlesque theatre. Sometimes, he got Al into the balcony for free.

The Little Egypt Co. was the attraction at the Bijou for the week of December 18th. Its olio—the vaudeville acts between the two burlesque skits—consisted of Virginia Seymour, Fannie Fields, Emery Marlow, Arnold & Gilmore, Mitchell & Love, and a twenty-four-year-old singer in blackface known as Eddie Leonard.

Leonard later became famous with songs of his own composition like "Ida, Sweet As Apple Cider" (1903, later appropriated by Eddie Cantor) and "Roll Dem Roly-Boly Eyes" (1912). At the Bijou, his big song was "I'd leave Ma Happy Home for You" by Harry von Tilzer and Will Heelan. It was a popular number, and Leonard urged the audience to join him in singing the chorus.

Headliners usually had a couple of "stooges" in the audience to start the singing. Leonard had no one, but Al opened up with his boy tenor, and helped Eddie finish to a big round of applause.

A surprising number of kids broke into show business that way, but Al turned down Leonard's subsequent offer to travel with the show and "stooge it" for him at every performance.

Harry later remembered their father as having Al "under his thumb" at that time, but there is no really clear explanation as to why Al refused Leonard's offer. It was, however, a decision that he soon regretted. A few months later, Al decided to go to New York and make a real effort at breaking into show business. The year was 1900.

Any attempt to comprehend Al Jolson's career must begin by understanding that "show business" and "the stage" were virtually synonomous before World War I. The entertainment business at the turn of the century was very different from what it would be eighty years later, and provided steady work for many more people. There was no television, where one group of actors could perform for an audience of more than a hundred million at one time; no radio, no movies, not even any listenable phonograph records. There was only live performances: plays, musicals, burlesque, minstrels, carnivals, and circuses employing an estimated 40,000 performers.

Actors could be found *en tour* in virtually any town—an immediately recognizable part of Americana, yet a race unto themselves, without roots, save in their profession, and without friends, save for one another. Male vaudeville actors wore loud clothes and talked as though they were onstage. Female vaudevillians often appeared on the street in stage makeup in an era when most women wore little or no makeup at all. If Conan Doyle's Sherlock Holmes, probably the most popular literary figure of the day, could tell a man's profession at a distance of ten paces, he could probably have pointed out an actor from three blocks away.

It was far easier to break into vaudeville than it would be to get on network TV eighty-five years later, but the major circuits only booked sure-footed talent with a fair amount of seasoning in "small time" vaudeville or burlesque. But in 1900, Al Joelson had no more chance of getting into real show business than he would have had of running for governor. He was simply too young.

Al was going on fourteen, but he looked like twelve, and the law forbade employing musical performers younger than sixteen years of age. He haunted booking agents' offices for about four months without success, but made some friends among the out-of-work actors who crowded the benches in Union Square—friends who would prove valuable to both the Joelson brothers in the next three years.

Al saw his first horse race on this trip—Kinley Mack winning the Brooklyn Handicap at Gravesend over favored Ethelbert on May 26th, his fourteenth birthday. He started going to prize fights as well, and few major contests over the next fifty years would fail to find Al at ringside, throwing punches in the air as he got caught up in the action.

In bad weather, Al stayed in his room at the Trafalgar Hotel at 115–117 East Fourteenth Street—next to the famed Steinway Hall his mother had described to him in Seredzius. He had no illusions of performing there, but he would walk by Tony Pastor's Theatre and curse the marquee because the billing for the headline act was not AL JOELSON.

The Dewey Theater was across the street from the Trafalgar, and Luchow's—the "Stork Club of the Nineties," where Diamond Jim Brady, Lillian Russell, and other celebrities were treated like visiting royalty—could be seen from Al's window. When it rained, Al stayed up in his room and listened to the Luchow orchestra play "Sweet Sixteen," the music traveling upward through the rain.

The picture almost seems romantic. It was actually a bitter, lonesome time for Al, who soon fell into arrears at the Trafalgar and was forced to sleep in a wagon near the East River. He caught a bad cold before long, coughing so horribly that one of his actor friends in Union Square suggested that he go to the free Bellevue Clinic on Twenty-eighth Street.

A doctor at the clinic treated Al for TB, drilling a small indentation in his back and draining him of fluid. When he had recovered from the blood loss and the damage to the bone, an intern came and gave him a prescription. Al was told he would be dead in six months if he did not get the medicine and take it.

Al went to the dispensary. The medicine itself was free, but the bottle was ten cents.

He turned and left the clinic. Al did not die in six months, but his left lung became infected. The resulting bad spot on that lung would plague him until it was finally cut out—almost forty-five years later.

Shortly after he left Bellevue, Al showed up at Weber and Fields' Music Hall on Twenty-third Street and tried to get a job as a chorus boy in their new show, *Fiddle Dee Dee*. Al was not hired, but he got a chance to see Fay Templeton rehearse a new song with the chorus called "Ma Blushin' Rosie."

The song probably made Al think of his sister, Rose. But it was probably exhaustion, hunger, and illness that made the now ragged teenager slip between two railroad cars and ride home to Washington, D.C.

Harry, still working at the Bijou, sneaked Al into a balcony seat for a performance of the Victoria Burlesquers during the week of October 8, 1900. The chief performer was a "French chansonette" named Agnes Behler. That she had never been to France was not deemed of importance. Her big song was "My Jersey Lillie," by Harry von Tilzer and Arthur Trevelyan. "Aggie" was just starting on the chorus when Al joined in from the balcony. "My Jersey Lillie, with eyes of blue. No other lily can equal you . . ." Miss Behler had not asked the audience to sing with her, but Al Joelson was not above gate-crashing his way into show business.

Al went backstage after the performance and told William Eversole, the company manager, of his previous experience with the Rich & Hoppe Show and the Walter L. Main Circus. "My Jersey Lillie" had finished to good applause, and Al looked like he would make a good foil for Aggie, who—luckily for Al—had worked with two other stooges earlier that season.

Will Eversole insisted upon speaking to Al's father before he would give the boy a job. Eversole convinced the rabbi that his son would be watched over by himself and other members of the company, pointing out one married couple in the show's backstage retinue.

Rabbi Yoelson gave his consent, but had a change of heart a few days later—after Al and the Victoria Burlesquers had left Washington for Providence. Harry was still living at home, and the family, predictably, blamed everything on him.

The Stooge

"Fortunately, we knew nothing about vitamins—or we probably would have starved."

HARRY JOLSON

There is no way of tracing Al Jolson's first sexual encounter with any degree of certainty. *Mistah Jolson,* Harry's self-serving autobiography, makes mention of a "forbidden" street in Washington—"where painted ladies stood at doors to display their wares to men seeking romance"—but Al may have been a virgin when he joined the Victoria Burlesquers. If he had engaged in sexual intercourse, it most certainly had been with a prostitute; Al was still disturbingly naive concerning women.

He soon became infatuated with Grace Celeste, one-half of the "sister" act of (Viola) St. Clair and Celeste, a feature of the Victoria Burlesquers' olio. Grace was fairly tall, quite shapely, and, predictably, years older than the fourteen-year-old Joelson.

He started buying her cigarettes out of his five-dollar-a-week salary—cigarettes the hardened burlesque actress accepted for three months before Al talked himself into believing she was "his" girl. The inevitable quarrel ensued, Grace laughing at his naiveté and finally telling him what he could do with his cigarettes.

Al had put the burlesque actress on a pedestal, and he was deeply wounded. He stayed away from women for the next three years and, for the rest of his life his interest was in "sweet" girls—women who would mother him when he needed sympathy or affection and then return dutifully to domestic chores—women quite the opposite of Grace Celeste and much more like Naomi.

The company spent Christmas Eve in Springfield, Massachusetts, a Christmas Al later remembered as the worst ever. "It was a cold, blustery night. No heat at our third class hotel. Business was very poor. People had better things to do on Christmas Even than attend burlesque shows.

"I suppose the rest of the company felt the same way. At any rate, I was thoroughly miserable and unhappy. I can see myself—a kid singer warbling questionable songs for a meager living, and dreaming of footlight fame. Not in good standing at home, either.

"I have a peculiar dread of loneliness. It's inherent, I suppose—a rooted dislike of being alone. And I was never so alone as on that holiday eve, sitting in a cheerless hotel room—cold, depressed, and trying to decide what I was going to do."

Al was on the verge of quitting when the show reached New York in January 1901. His brother Harry, who had left home and was now employed as a singing waiter at a beer hall on the edge of Chinatown called Callahan's, cheered him somewhat when he brought his fellow singing waiters to hear Al sing "Last Night as the Moon Was Shining" at the Dewey Theatre. What really changed Al's mind, however, was when Fred Moore, the company electrician, asked him to be his partner in a singing act.

Frederick Ernest Moore, a rotund Irishman of twenty-eight, and his wife Lillian already had been made Al's unofficial "guardians" by William Eversole. Fred and Lillian often sneaked Al into their hotel rooms on the road, where Mrs. Moore's home cooking provided a welcome change from nickel beers and free lunch counters. Al told Fred of his humiliation with Grace, and Moore agreed with his decision not to continue as a "stooge." "Illustrated" singing acts, with scenes projected on a screen, were popular in vaudeville, and Fred's experience as an electrician made the use of stereoptican slides a very small problem. The team of "Master Joelson and Fred Moore" was born.

Joelson & Moore made their initial appearance in the olio of the Victoria Burlesquers at Miaco's Trocadero Theatre on Chicago's State Street on March 31, 1901—the first time that Al Joelson received billing. In the meantime, Fred wrote managers for summer bookings. It paid off, and when the show closed for the season, Joelson & Moore played the Ramona Pavilion in Grand Rapids and Lake Michigan Park in Muskegon.

They returned east in July, Fred and Lillian having left their daughter Kitty with relatives in Pleasantville, New Jersey. Al stayed in New York with Harry, who managed to get him a temporary job as a singer at the Bohemian Concert Hall on Twenty-ninth Street.

Neither Al nor Fred wanted to spend more than one more season in burlesque. Fred spent his vacation typing letters, hopeful that his contacts would get them bookings in vaudeville. But nothing happened, and Joelson & Moore were back with the Victoria Burlesquers when the show reopened at the Bijou Theatre in Paterson.

For the first time, the later famous "Jolson ego" flowered. Al had been a little shocked, but certainly not outraged, when he found out that the handsome men and beautiful female acrobats in the Main Circus were really middle-aged people behind tons of makeup. But the "cruel" treatment he had received from Grace and the rest of the Victoria Burlesquers had begun to disillusion him regarding actors. More and more, he built a wall of ego, a hard crust protecting the emotional man-child at the center.

Except for isolated moments of depression, Al was carefree, happy, and—almost—content. He was fifteen, on his own, and "one of them there show folks" traveling around the country between New York and the Middle West. He was learning, too—from dialect comedians like John Reid and Ella Gilbert, whose sketch, "The Maid and the Mick," was a feature in the olio; from Aggie Behler, from Fred, and almost every dancer, low comedian, and singer in the show he did not hate. Al learned all the fundamentals needed to become a "pro"—the proper way to come onstage; the proper way to exit; how to take applause; how to end a song so that the audience applauded. These arts, like a hundred others, have since disappeared, but they were essentials when live theatre flourished. And burlesque, in those days, was the theatre's training ground.

Master Joelson and Fred Moore left the Victoria Burlesquers to join Al Reeves' Famous Big Company in March 1902. Al now had the opportunity to study Reeves up close—his walk, his mannerisms, his inflections, and the picture of self-confidence that he projected. Al may have been excited to be working with his idol, but Reeves probably could have taken or left the young Joelson.

"He was a good boy," Reeves said almost thirty years later. "Al never drank or smoked. Just a good kid. I predicted he'd go far." Reeves, of course, had made no such prediction, and young Joelson certainly smoked as hard as his sixteen years enabled him to do.

Al and Fred were with the Reeves show for eight weeks before they left it to go into vaudeville. Fred's letter writing had finally paid off, and Joelson & Moore took the following ad in the June 7, 1902 issue of the *New York Clipper*.

AT LIBERTY FOR NEXT SEASON
MASTER JOELSON AND FRED MOORE

Song Illustrators.

Introducing Master Joelson, the Phenomenal Tenor, with Victoria Burlesquers past two seasons. This week, Keith's Union Square; week of 9, Keith's, Boston; week of 16, Keith's Philadelphia; week of June 23, open. Gorman's Parks to follow. Both play parts. Mr. Fred Moore is an experienced union electrician. Address As Per Route.

The advertisement did not help, and when September came, the only booking Joelson & Moore got was a week at Casto's Theatre in Fall River, Massachusetts. When that was over, they went back to their old stomping ground, the Columbia burlesque wheel, joining Lawrence Weber's Dainty Duchess Co. in Philadelphia.

They were with the Dainty Duchess show for five months, planning to try vaudeville again that summer, and seemingly unaware that Master Joelson's days as a boy tenor were extremely numbered. In March 1903, Al's voice began to break, and Joelson & Moore were fired by the Dainty Duchess management in April.

The Moores were almost glad. Lillian had been extremely worried about Kitty, and Fred had had his fill of being a performer. They moved back into their home in Pleasantville, taking Master Joelson along with them.

The thought that he would never sing again drove Al close to insanity, and his sullen, morose attitude made life hard for the Moores. The only clear alternative to singing was returning home to Washington and having Moshe set him up in business. It was the one thing young Al Joelson dreaded.

He sulked around the Moore house for the next few weeks before he gave up and went back to Washington. Reality had, however temporarily, won out over magic.

Moshe, although not vindictive, was relieved that his son's "stage madness" was finally over. It was not, of course, and never would be. Al would eventually return to the theatre—a little sooner if the opportunity arose, but a little later if it didn't.

The opportunity came soon enough. Within weeks of Al's return, his brother Harry drove up in a hansom, fashionably dressed and smelling of bay rum. The infamous "black sheep" of the family had finally "made good."

Nine months earlier, in August 1902, the manager of a burlesque show called The Brigadiers had hired Harry to sing and play the Emperor of Ireland in the closing travesty. Harry watched his money, saved three hundred dollars, and had now come back to Washington to "show" his father.

But Moshe Yoelson would not feel foolish. He refused to acknowledge Harry's success and predicted dire consequences for him if he stayed in "the show business." What Moshe really feared was that his elder son would encourage Al to give the stage another try—which is exactly what happened.

The Brigadiers had given Harry a modest taste of success. He fancied himself a comedian, and Al jumped at the chance to be his straight man in a vaudeville sketch. The Joelson brothers were soon entrained for New York, leaving Moshe, Hessi, Peri, and the six-year-old Emil far behind.

The boys used the train ride to outline their act. It was possible, in 1903, for young performers to eke out a living in burlesque or small-time vaudeville with hackneyed, unprofessional material. The Joelsons' contribution to this genre of unpublished dramatic litera-ture was "The Hebrew and the Cadet," with Harry as "Mr. Cohen," an East Side ghetto Jew of the type popularized by Joe Welch, and Al as "Meyer," a cadet, the young "straight" man.

The sketch was crude by any standards, the Joelsons having stolen most of the lines from old burlesque acts. A short excerpt follows:

MEYER   You are a monkey.

COHEN   A monkey! Did you call me a monkey?

MEYER   Sure I called you a monkey. Don't you know what a monkey is?

COHEN   (perplexed, after a pause) No, I don't know vot a mon-key is. Vot is a monkey?

MEYER   (with a wink to the audience) Well, a monkey is a fine person. Everybody knows what wonderful people mon-keys are.

COHEN   (beaming) Vell! Sure I am a monkey. Vot is more, I vant to tell you dhat mine brudders und sisters is monkeys, mine fadder and modder is monkeys, and all of mine ancestors vas monkeys.

The sketch ended with Al going off stage in a military walk, while Harry followed in an awkward, loose-jointed shuffle, his head bob-bing like a duck's.

The Joelsons took a room in a medium-priced boarding house on Fourteenth Street, secured props and costumes, and had pictures taken at the White Studios. Fred Moore's typewritten letters had resulted in Keith bookings, so they bought a typewriter on the installment plan.

The free and easy world of show business in the first two decades of the twentieth century can best be understood by one of George Burns's stories. "When I was seventeen, I used to sit in the Fitzgerald Building, which was the headquarters for small-time booking agents. One day, a guy came out and asked where he could find Charley Pride. I said, 'I'm Charley Pride,' and he handed me a contract for a week's engagement at the Dewey Theatre for 'Charley Pride and his Wonder Dog.' I got myself a piece of beef, caught a small dog, went on stage at the Dewey with the dog under my arm, and did my songs. Went over big."

Almost anybody could get on and get a try-out—"anybody," it seemed, but the Joelsons. Al looked younger than his years—closer to fourteen than seventeen or the twenty he sometimes pretended to be. Bookers refused to even look at "The Hebrew and the Cadet."

Harry and Al got no place until a friend advised them to rent a "rehearsal room" at the Harry von Tilzer Music Publishing Co., where they could be seen by agents, bookers, and other "right people." The Joelsons rented the rehearsal room, but rapidly ran out of money. The boys soon had to hock their baggage, costumes, and, finally, their props. They ultimately fell into arrears at their boarding house.

The Joelsons might have been forced onto a park bench if one of their new friends had not suggested the Academy Hotel at 119 East Fourteenth Street. The Academy was owned by Henri Courte, a Frenchman who loved actors. The boys gave Courte their friend's name and were given a small room. No advance was needed.

Henri Courte is just one example of the easy-going, frequently indulgent spirit which, along with far more frequent work, made actors' lives comparatively easy in the early 1900s. "More than once," Al recalled, "Mr. Courte would call me into his kitchen, which was homelike and a living room, like most French people's kitchens, and he'd have me sit down and eat with him. He'd take a big knife and whittle off slices from a long loaf of French bread, and I'll always remember how good it tasted . . . (Courte) was awfully good to the actors, and I know a lot of them beat him out of money after he helped them.'"

Harry later remembered " 'busking around' to raise enough money for doughnuts and coffee . . . We toured the East Side restaurants and asked permission to sing a couple of songs in the hope of in-veigling a few tips from reluctant patrons. . . . It was not easy to get a job busking. In many places, we were simply given the bum's rush without comment. Usually, we applied at places where we knew the boss or the head waiter. We told our tale of woe and asked permission to sing. The regular singing waiters despised the buskers, but the bosses believed it was good business to give the patrons a change of act. Few words were lost, whether we were given a job or tossed out into the gutter."

Things began to break in August, when Ed Keller of the William Morris Agency got them a three-day engagement at P. H. Morrison's Music Hall in Rockaway, Queens, at eighteen dollars—nine dollars apiece, minus expenses. Harry von Tilzer lent them the money to get their costumes out of hock, and "The Hebrew and the Cadet" made its debut in Rockaway. Harry thought the act went over well; Al thought they were "rotten," and suggested that they stay away from the theatre until just before they had to go on for the evening show. "If they don't see us before we get onstage," he shrewdly reasoned, "there won't be time for them to cancel."

Al was showing a trait Harry later labeled as "a tendency to underrate himself." It was really self-recrimination. No member of an audience, no critic, would berate Al Jolson for a bad performance more than he would castigate himself. Al was an instinctive artist and, like most good performers, knew when he had given a bad performance and was morose until he had vindicated himself by giving a good one.

The Joelsons were not canceled in Rockaway; they were promoted to a better position on the bill, and other bookings followed. The boys played a week at Henderson's Music Hall in Coney Island, and wound up having to walk back to Manhattan. They were booked for the gala opening of the Odeon Theatre in Baltimore, only to be canceled prior to the first performance. (The Odeon burned down several months later.) Then they did their act in the olio of a new burlesque show called The Mayflowers, which folded after three weeks.

These misfortunes were followed by a lucrative engagement at Charles A. Brandenburg's Arch Street Museum in Philadelphia. This was a dime museum, not a vaudeville theatre, and the Joelsons had to give their act twelve times a day. The week's pay—fifty dollars—failed to make doing "The Hebrew and the Cadet" any less monotonous, and the Joelson boys decided to switch parts at one performance. "We knew the lines," remembered Harry, "but Al got all mixed up on the names. He was so accustomed to calling me Cohen that he couldn't switch to Meyer."

Ike Bloch, the stage manager, bawled them out, but Al said that they knew what they were doing. "We've put on our act in all the Keith houses," he lied.

A large sign was put up backstage the next day: "Don't tell us what you done at Keith's. Do it here!"

Ed Keller got the Joelsons three consecutive weeks in Casto's theatres in New England in November. Then the well ran dry, and Al and Harry were out of work for so long that even Henri Courte was unable to keep them. Luckily, they still had friends among the actors. Comedian Joe K. Watson was always willing to share his room on Twelfth Street, and many actors took advantage of his hospitality. "As many as possible piled into a bed," remembered Harry, "and the others slept on the floor."

Watson never asked for money in return. Al gave him a job as a writer on his C.B.S. radio show more than thirty years later.

By the end of January 1904, Al and Harry had been out of work for eight weeks. They still made the rounds of bookers, but their real struggles were the day-to-day ones—where to get enough to eat. They *knew*, with all the naive confidence of young performers, that things would get better in the spring.

And then, they got a job. It was only February, but, to them, the long winter of 1903–04 was over.

The Joelson Brothers joined the "Spider and the Fly" Burlesquers in Brooklyn. The "Spider and the Fly" show was not on the Columbia wheel, but enjoyed good bookings due to its affiliation with the Sparrow Amusement Co. of Montreal. The Joelsons signed a contract calling for thirty-five dollars a week.

After two weeks, they were transferred to another Sparrow show, "Little Egypt's London Gaiety Girls," and played what seemed like an eternal string of one-night stands in Pennsylvania. The company did not pay their hotel bills, and the Joelsons were very interested when Cliff Grant, the manager, told them of a way that they could supplement their incomes. Song books were available in quantity from the Charles K. Harris firm for a penny apiece. Al and Harry could sell these books for ten cents each between the acts and split the profits with the company.

The books were what were nominally sold, but what made the Charles K. Harris songs—"After the Ball," "The Organ Grinder's Serenade," "Last Night as the Moon Was Shining," etc.—so appealing to burlesque patrons was the free picture of "Little Egypt" given away with each copy. It was printed on thin, wavy paper, and "Little Egypt" seemed to do a "hooch" dance when a lighted match was rotated behind the picture. One Pennsylvania town arrested the Joelsons for tampering with the morals of the community. Their fine was paid, and "The Hebrew and the Cadet" continued with the Little Egypt company until the last week in April, 1904, when the show played a week at Brooklyn's Unique Theatre, and a representative of the Sullivan, Harris & Woods office offered them forty dollars weekly to appear in a new show, *The Errand Boy,* the following season. It looked like their first real break.

Rehearsals for *The Errand Boy* were not due to begin until late June, so the Joelsons joined the "Spider and the Fly" company's stock troupe at the Theatre Royal in Montreal immediately after the Little Egypt show closed for the summer. That engagement ended after Harry got into a fight with a big stagehand over a chorus girl and Al joined in with both fists to defend him. Al's "rescue" of Harry helped to end a petty feud between the brothers, who had not been speaking for several days over dressing room space. It also got them fired.

The undaunted Joelsons showed up for *The Errand Boy* rehearsals three weeks later. *The Errand Boy* was just another in a series of shows starring Billy B. Van as a hapless, cheerful, trod-upon stock character named "Patsy Bolivar." Van had just concluded a long season in another "Patsy" show entitled *Bolivar's Busy Day,* and his overworked condition, the high-strung constitutions of the Joelsons, and the lack of air-conditioning all played a part in what followed.

Billy B. Van staged his own shows. At one point, early in rehearsals, he told the principals that they could leave, but ordered the chorus to remain. Al and Harry prepared to go, but Van yelled for them to "stay and rehearse the choruses." Al, insulted, informed him that the Joelsons were not chorus boys. More words followed, and the Hebrew and the Cadet walked out of the theatre—conveniently forgetting to return the twenty-dollar advance they had received from Sam H. Harris, one of the producers.

Al and Harry Joelson were back where they had started—out of work again.

Their next job was with Dixon and Bernstein's Turkey Burlesque Show. A "turkey" show was one that booked independently, "picking up," in the manner of a turkey, any bookings it could get. (Hence the line in Irving Berlin's song: "Even with a turkey that you *know* will fold.") The Joelsons had reached the bottom rung of show business.

They were not there long. Neither Henry (Noise) Dixon nor Freeman Bernstein would give the starving brothers an advance, so the Joelsons pawned their typewriter—on which they still owed almost the full purchase price—had a meal, and jumped the show.

Ruddy-faced Pat Casey, who later became general manager of the Vaudeville Managers' Protective Association, got the boys a week at Berkshire Park in Pittsfield, Massachusetts, where his brother Dan ran summer vaudeville. Three weeks of unemployment followed before the Joelsons played a return engagement at Henderson's in Coney Island. It was now September 1904—more than a year after their first booking as The Hebrew and the Cadet.

Many names have cropped up in discussions of Al Jolson's rise to fame: Al Reeves, Agnes Behler, Lew Dockstader, Arthur Klein, and the Shuberts, to name just a few. But Reeves himself did nothing to advance Jolson's career, and Al's job as Aggie Behler's stooge led, ultimately, nowhere. Lew Dockstader hired Jolson in 1908—after Al had established himself on the Sullivan & Considine vaudeville circuit. Art Klein and the Shuberts came in even later.

The real hero of the Jolson career was "Prof." Ren Shields, a special material and songwriter ("In the Good Old Summertime," "Come Take a Trip in My Airship," etc.) with an office on Thirty-fourth Street in New York. Among Ren's many friends in the theatrical profession was Joe Palmer, a Yiddish dialect comedian and singer who had been with the Casino Four until stricken with locomotor ataxia early in 1903. Now thirty-two, Joe was confined to a wheelchair, and had to be washed, fed, dressed, and helped onto toilet seats. His friends in Union Square—including Al and Harry—took turns helping.

Some of the actors suggested Joe team up with Al and Harry, an idea Joe liked well enough to mention to Ren Shields. Ren then made the boys an offer: if they would team up with Joe and promise to take care of him, he'd write the three of them an act—for free—and help them to get started. It was a great offer, and the Joelsons quickly accepted. Shields wrote the sketch—a good one—in about ten days. It was called "A Little of Everything," the title taken from *A Little of Everything,* a summer revue on the New Amsterdam Roof Theatre.

Al and Harry read the script in Shields' office. Ren had placed the action in a sanitarium, with Harry as the doctor, Joe as the suffering Jewish patient, and Al as a wisecracking orderly.

Never having seen the Joelsons work, Ren Shields had made Al, not Harry, the comedian. The brothers protested, but little could be done. Joe had to remain in his wheelchair as the patient, Al looked too young to be the doctor, and Ren wasn't about to write them another act. It would be a lot easier for him to get two other starving "hams" (Shields' term) to do the act with Palmer.

Joelson, Palmer & Joelson in "A Little of Everything" made its try-out debut in the Sunday concert of a New York burlesque theatre in October 1904. Al was terribly self-conscious in his new role of comedian, and nearly sunk the act. They rehearsed for two weeks more and, largely on Ren Shields' name, were booked for a week at Keeney's Theatre on Fulton Street in Brooklyn. Al, however, still lacked confidence until James Francis Dooley, a blackface monologuist on the bill at Keeney's, suggested that he do his part in blackface. Wearing burnt cork, he told Al, was like wearing a mask. You looked, and *felt,* like a performer.

It worked. Al tried blackface at the next performance, and there was an air of spontaneity about him, as if the actually *enjoyed* his work. The nervous, monotoned, self-conscious kid of just two weeks before was gone, his place taken by an impudent and joyous harlequin with traces of Al Reeves in his performing make-up.

The harlequin—that mysterious figure of the ancient pagan rites who later found his way onstage by way of the *commedia del l'arte*— was just one influence on blackface. The other was, of course, the black man. Although the medium was later vilified for insulting the black race, Jolson's blackface was probably more of a theatricalization than a caricature. The medium allowed him to show pluck and daring—an *élan* visible in the harlequin but also traceable in the black man's cultural approach to entertainment, sports, and striking back, where possible, at white society and the subservient role it forced him to assume. In time, the blackfaced Jolson would display an *élan* on the Broadway stage no other performer—black or white— would dare exhibit.

Blackface would remain a mask for Jolson all his life. The best sound film of Jolson singing is the footage of him singing "live" (as opposed to lip synching) in blackface. There is a magic to his work in blackface that he never captured *sans* burnt cork.

The spelling of Al's name now underwent a change. Joelson, Palmer & Joelson wanted to have cards printed, but found the name "Joelson" was too large for the design they had in mind. At the suggestion of the printer, Al and Harry dropped the "e" out of their name.

"Al Jolson" had arrived—and in more ways than one.

The Journeyman

"It was neither a good nor a bad voice, but it had incredible sincerity. It was stirring, pulsating . . ."

JESSE LASKY, *I Blow My Own Horn*

The world of vaudeville that Al Jolson entered in late 1904 rested on theatre "circuits"—Keith, Orpheum, Sullivan & Considine, and several others—each consisting of a number of theatres in different cities with perhaps six acts on each weekly bill. An act rotated through the theatres until it had played the entire route, after which it might be booked along a different circuit. Each act had separate bookings, which meant a vaudeville performer might find himself on the bill with different acts from week to week.

An "act" might be a sketch, like the Joelsons' "A Little of Everything," a juggler, acrobats, or "animal acts," like Swain's Rats & Cats. The "headline" act, which appeared in the next-to-last slot on the program, was usually a favored, well-established act, or, possibly, a star like Nora Bayes. McIntyre & Heath, Eddie Leonard, Blanche Ring, and Julian Eltinge were the big vaudeville stars of 1904.

The acts traveled from one city to another on trains. Show business, perhaps more than any other business in the early 1900s, depended on the railroad. It was a world particularly suited to Al Jolson, who craved motion all his life—and applause to temporarily take all self-doubts away.

The team of Jolson, Palmer & Jolson was "sure fire" from the moment that Al put on blackface. Late in November 1904 they opened a week's engagement at Keith's Theatre in Philadelphia, and a good report from house manager Harry Jordan led to a ten-week contract to play S. Z. Poli's theatres in New England at ninety dollars a week. Throughout this time, Al was improving—trying out his lines and bits of business on hotel desk clerks, waiters, and other "nonprofessionals."

The team continued in the East until mid-June, and spent the summer playing parks. In July they hit the big-time: the Orpheum Circuit, with first-class theatres stretching from the Midwest to the Pacific coast, signed them for a four-month tour at $125 a week plus train fare.

They dressed and ate in style now, and stayed in good hotels. Al saw San Francisco's Barbary Coast, with its opium dens, and seriously gambled for the first time in his life. Every type of vice was readily available in "Frisco" in those days before the earthquake, and Al seems to have indulged in most of them. Pearl Goldberg Sieben, who knew Jolson well in 1940, said the only time that Mr. Jolson ever hit her was when, seeing him gaze into space, she asked him if he smoked marijuana. He slapped her in the face, but gave no answer.

In November 1905, Jolson, Palmer & Jolson opened a week's engagement at the St. Charles Orpheum Theatre in New Orleans. Both Jolson brothers were anxious to visit the city's famous red light district, but someone had to stay with the disabled Palmer.

Al and Harry had another of their violent arguments, in the course of which Al kicked a hole through Harry's brand new derby. Later, Harry said that he would stay with Joe that night if Al agreed to pay for a new hat. Al, who had the temper of an eight-year-old, refused.

Harry, who had stood all that he could of Al's behavior, proposed that they split up the act. Al readily agreed, and Harry walked out, leaving the act—and Joe Palmer—to his younger brother. Al and Joe revised the sketch and resumed their tour of the Orpheum Circuit at the Grand Opera House in Indianapolis as "Palmer and Jolson."

This was a transition period for Al, who sometimes experimented with the slow, deliberate kind of humor that had made Bert Williams famous. Al sang Williams' theme song "Nobody" at the Grand, and the Indianapolis *News* said he made "a big hit." As the weeks went by, however, Jolson speeded things up, laying the foundations for the fast-paced and sure-footed character who would be seen later at the Winter Garden.

Al and Joe spent most of their time going over new songs and material. Jolson's voice had settled—a stirring baritone that could go up for tenor notes or down into a bass—and he spent hours learning comedy songs, like "Everybody," which remained in his repertoire until the 1910s. He also learned some ballads—like the new "My Gal Sal."

At the age of nineteen, Al was pretty much the Jolson that the world would know—a "man's man," willing to try anything, a sentimentalist, an extrovert with the enthusiasm of a small child, and a moody cuss who alternated between braggadocio and self-deprecating pessimism.

He was emotionally immature in many ways, but the "Jolson ego" was almost fully developed. Al had little trouble dealing with the man's world of his young manhood—telling little lies to stage managers, asking for big raises, and letting people know he was aware of his own worth. Girls, however, were a different story. Despite his later reputation as a lothario, Jolson was markedly unsuccessful with the opposite sex until after his first marriage. Al stayed away from romance for a long time after his humiliation at the hands of Grace Celeste. When, at nineteen, he resumed his amorous pursuits, his interests were in "cute" girls—petite and sweet looking, if not always sweet. Al's first girl friend of this type was Josie Rooney, youngest daughter of Pat Rooney I, great clog dancer of the 1880s. Josie and her sister, Julia, were on the bill with Palmer and Jolson at Chicago's Olympic Theatre in December 1905.

The Rooney Sisters were a typical dancing "sister" act, with Julia as the sparkplug and seventeen-year-old Josie as the beauty. Al introduced himself to Josie in the lobby of the Sherman Hotel, took her to dinner, and two days later asked the stunned girl to marry him.

Josie said that she would have to ask her mother, who naturally refused permission. Al had unknowingly impressed her sister Julia more than Josie. More than seventy years later, Julia remembered Al as a "nice looking boy" and wondered why Josie had not given him more serious attention. Julia even wrote a song for Al entitled "Roll Dem Great Big Beautiful Eyes."

Al and Josie had a fight before the week was over. "See, they used to have these little scraps," remembered Julia. "You know, back and forth like that. But Al was a sweet guy. He wasn't the fighting kind. *She* was the fighter.

"Al begged (our older sister) Mattie and he begged me to have Josie speak to him, to make it up with him. But it was because they were so much in love with one another. It was just jealousy—kid like, you know."

Mattie and her husband, Clayton Kennedy, patched the lovers' spat by taking them to dinner, but Josie's interest in Al had already waned. Al could not accept it. Four months later, after his first booking as a single, he took a quick train from Lansing to Detroit and called Josie.

"Josie, honey. It's me, Al. Look, I just got in from Lansing, and was I a hit! Joe and I open in Toledo tomorrow, and I have to meet him in Chicago in a few hours. But we can have supper now. I'll meet you in your lobby."

"Oh, Al," said Josie. "I'm so sorry. I have a date with a student tonight." She hung up the receiver.

It was an ironic disappointment. Al had bought a college prep cap just the day before.

Jolson did not get over that rejection for some time. He told Boston drama critic Elliott Norton about it in 1940.

Al's pursuit of the young girl continued. He placed an ad in the June 16th issue of *Variety* giving "Best Regards" to the Rooney Sisters—coyly adding that he would see "J" in California—but any chance he might have had with Josie had already vanished.

Al had now been smitten, and hurt, twice—by Grace Celeste and by Josie. He would be more careful, cynical, and calculating in the future—disguising his pursuits of girls by playing the role of a show business big shot. He never told a girl he loved her, only that she was "just right" for a certain role in a stage show or movie. Josie Rooney, who later claimed Al told her she was "the only girl he'd ever loved," had taught young Jolson a painful lesson in the never-ending battle of the sexes.

Al and Joe Palmer, who stayed with his sister on Prairie Street when they were in Chicago, had completed their tour of the Orpheum Circuit and were now playing smaller theaters in and near Chicago for the Western Vaudeville Managers' Association. They now had a new act, called "The Hebrew and the Coon," with Joe the "Hebrew" and Al the "Coon"—the euphonic, if outrageous, term for black characters then in use on vaudeville stages and in popular songs. The new act rested on Al's shoulders, providing him with excellent training wheels for his future career as a single.

That year, 1906, was very important in the history of American vaudeville. Twenty-five men, whose interests practically embraced the variety field in the United States, formed a trust called the United Booking Office under the leadership of B. F. Keith, a former circus pitchman, and his general manager, E. F. Albee. One of the few willing to oppose the UBO was William Morris. In March 1906, three months before the UBO was publicly announced, he made plans for an "opposition" circuit, and former trumpet player Jesse Lasky opened a Morris office at 167 Dearborn Street in Chicago.

Lasky and his assistant, Arthur Fabish, saw Palmer and Jolson at Chicago's Majestic Theatre on a Monday afternoon and signed them to a contract in their office the next day. Lasky's autobiography, *I Blow My Own Horn*, claims Al was more interested in a checkered suit that Jesse had lying in an open box than he was in signing the contract. Jolson finally asked Lasky if he would sell him the suit.

"Oh, all right—take it," Jesse said. "It cost me sixty bucks."

"I'll send you six sawbucks out of my first week's salary," Al promised. Then he took the suit and left.

"I never saw the money for the suit," Lasky recalled. "I reminded Al of it years later, while we were playing golf at the Hillcrest Country Club.

" 'Forgot it completely,' he said, but offered to play a match for it right then and there. I wound up losing my suit for the second time."

In 1943, when Lasky produced *Rhapsody in Blue* for Warner Bros., Jolson appeared as himself, singing "Swanee," *gratis,* as a tribute to Gershwin and a favor to Lasky, his old friend.

The Morris Circuit folded after Palmer and Jolson had played four weeks in midwestern parks. It was a catastrophe for Al and Joe, since breaking their other contracts to go with the Morris organization had caused them to be blacklisted by the WVMA, Keith, Orpheum, and other UBO affiliates. There were not many other circuits left.

Luckily, there were a few. Chris O. Brown of the Sullivan & Considine Circuit gave Palmer and Jolson a Pacific Coast route starting in Butte, Montana, on June 23rd. In the meantime, Al accepted two more bookings without Palmer: the Crystal in Detroit and a return in Lansing, where he had played a fill-in date six weeks earlier.

Shortly before they were to leave for Butte, Joe told Al he had decided to retire. Joe said he was tired, that his family was setting him up in the laundry business in Chicago, and that he'd had his full of vaudeville.

The sad truth, however, is that Palmer felt that he was holding Jolson back. It took a lot of reassuring, but he finally persuaded Al to go ahead without him.

Joe Palmer did not stay in the laundry business very long. After a few months, he was teamed with the young L. Wolfe Gilbert (future writer of songs like "Waiting for the Robert E. Lee" and "Ragtime Cowboy Joe") in an act about two Civil War veterans. When that act failed, Joe teamed up with Billy Saxton before declining health forced him to retire again in 1908. Joe entered a Muskegon sanitarium in 1909, but left it after eight months and tried to get back into show business with Lew Johnson in an act called "Cohen & Sons." His illness worsened, and, by 1913, Joe was living at 2208 Harrison Street in Chicago, supported by his brother and by checks sent by his former partner, Al Jolson.

Joe Palmer died on July 29, 1916.

Jolson was a hit in Butte. His act consisted of a monologue interspersed with comedy songs like "Good Advice," "Everybody," and one or two more. Al was not a polished monologist, but his mugging was hilarious. (One reviewer said his "facial contortions alone would win a medal for fun making.") He had learned to whistle with two fingers, and special "stunts in scale climbing" were a special feature of his twenty-minute "turn."

Al's costume consisted of white socks, a dark, ill-fitting suit with a red bow tie, brown gloves, and a jagged-brimmed straw hat that sat on top of his head. Jolson was billed as a "singing comedian," but he was funny even before he opened his mouth.

The Sullivan & Considine Circuit raised his salary several times, and Al was making seventy-five dollars by the time he reached San Francisco in September. It was a different city from the "Frisco" that Al had seen the year before. The famous earthquake and fire had destroyed old San Francisco, every theatre burning to the ground except one vaudeville house called the Chutes, which operated in conjunction with a small amusement park.

The first man to pick up the pieces was David J. (Pop) Grauman. Two weeks after the disaster, he and his son Syd (later famous as the owner of the Chinese and Egyptian theatres in Hollywood) pitched a circus tent and started running vaudeville. The Graumans called their tent the National, affiliated themselves with the Sullivan & Considine Circuit, and, as practically the only show in town, made money.

In September the Graumans began construction of a wooden theatre building on the same site as their tent. Since they sold out almost every show and were reluctant to suspend performances, they had their new theatre built right over the tent—with performances in progress.

The beginning of the "Jolson Legend" can be traced to Monday, October 1, 1906—the day Jolson opened at the National. Probably the truest account of what happened was one published in the *New York Clipper* several years later. During one of his performances, the workers' hammering almost drowned out Al's big voice. Reacting quickly, Jolson climbed off the stage, mounted a chair, and did his act in the middle of the audience. The hammering continued, but it made no difference. Twenty-year-old Al Jolson had turned the handicap to his advantage, and the audience was on his side completely.

Jolson's songs, humor, and impromptu adaptation made a deep impression on a city that had undergone a recent holocaust. His spunk, his *élan*, in an era of convention, were refreshing—and magnetic. There was something almost sexual about the way he related to an audience—as if a beam of emotional energy reached out and left each listener with the feeling that Al was performing for him and nobody else.

By the end of that week, Jolson was "made" in San Francisco. It was as a cock-sure show business professional—not the eager adolescent who had courted Josie Rooney—that he met Henrietta Keller, the young woman who would become his first wife.

Al's next booking was at the Bell Theatre in Oakland. The program consisted of the professional Sullivan & Considine acts and amateurs from Bothwell Browne's dancing school in San Francisco, billed as the Bell Minstrel Maids.

One of the Minstrel Maids did a "highland fling" in kilts. She was cute, with strawberry blonde hair, sparkling blue-green eyes, and very pronounced Scandanavian features. The highland fling did not fool anyone, but it provided Al with a glimpse of her attractive legs. "I went for her legs," he later said. She also had a shy and rather captivating smile.

The girl, eighteen-year-old Henrietta Keller, may have been shy, but she accepted when the young, dynamic blackface comedian and singer asked her out to dinner. Al rented a car for the occasion and took her to a first-class restaurant.

Al, "held over" for two more weeks at the Bell, soon met Henrietta's parents—her mother, Sefani, a woman with a heavy Danish accent, and Conrad, her father, a former Danish sea captain who had looked with disapproval at Henrietta's going to her cousin Bothwell's dancing school. Browne was a well-known female impersonator in vaudeville, and Capt. Keller's lack of enthusiasm for the theatre was exceeded only by his absolute disdain for Jews.

Al continued courting Henrietta in spite of these apparent drawbacks. He was an exciting fellow now, all the more so since his stage work had made him a minor hero in the San Francisco-Oakland region. Al had reached the stage where he could charm young women, and the way that he could "be himself" at certain moments made him seem even more interesting.

Jolson wanted to get married right away, but Conrad Keller's objections kept things at a standstill for almost a year. Al's career continued in the meantime.

Al worked in and around central California for the next four months, and the first "Jolson imitators" appeared. They mimicked his leathery voice, his rolling eyes, and the way he moistened his lips. Al even gave an "imitation of his imitators" during one of his engagements at the National.

Until he entered films and radio in the late 1920s, Jolson was identified as a comedian rather than as a singer. His jokes were rarely funny, but he made audiences laugh. "Good evening, ladies and gentlemen and everything you brought with you," he would say. Mothers of the early 1900s often went to vaudeville shows with their sleeping babes in arms—infants who would often wake and howl in the middle of the bill. Al once ad libbed "Not now, papa's working," when that happened. His timing, then as later, was impeccable, but his effervescent spirit got the laughs.

Al often went to Coffee Dan's, at Powell and O'Farrell in the heart of San Francisco's rapidly rebuilding theatre district. There were no stairs inside Coffee Dan's—just a chute that customers of both sexes slid down to enter the fun-filled downstairs. One old-timer, William Walsh, remembered Jolson getting up on a table at Dan's and singing "maybe twenty songs." Al got some of his best experience at Coffee Dan's, especially in playing to "trade" audiences in the "San Francisco style" of highly charged informal entertainment.

Jolson stayed at the Continental Hotel in San Francisco which, according to Joe Laurie, Jr.'s *Vaudeville,* "wasn't run like a hotel, but like a 'fun house.' It was no surprise to have a juggler wait on you (paying off his tab) and maybe juggle a few plates before he served you. Somebody was always playing a joke on someone, and (co-owner) Aloysius Shanley was the instigator of most of them."

Al often played cards with a group of small-time actors. He preferred their company to that of stars, and once told William Walsh that he could "learn more from talking to a small-time actor than from people like Ethel Barrymore," who, he maintained, "had it made before she ever stepped on a stage." A 1904 graduate of the School of Hard Knocks, Jolson was extremely bitter about nepotism in the theatre.

Al completed his tour of the Sullivan & Considine Circuit on December 22nd and spent the following ten weeks accepting outside engagements at the Chutes and Wigwam Theatres in San Francisco and the Franklin Theatre in El Paso. He then went back to Chicago, where he "cut up touches" with old cronies, bragged about his success in California, and let it be known he was "At Liberty" after forty weeks as a "coast defender."

What Jolson really wanted—and what his success should have entitled him to—was a contract from the Orpheum Circuit, now even more established as the "class" of western vaudeville. The blacklist ruled that out, but Al was still the golden boy of the Sullivan & Considine Circuit, and Chris Brown offered him a raise to $150 a week for twenty-six weeks in the Midwest and on the Pacific coast. Al signed—he had few options—and opened at the Bijou Theatre in Lincoln, Nebraska, on April 1, 1907.

He spent the next two months in the Midwest, garnering reviews (the Minneapolis *Journal* reported he "swept all turns out with his comical stunt" and the Duluth *News* said he was "in a class by himself" as an entertainer) and plastering *Variety* with hard-sell ads typical of the era. ("AL JOLSON . . . You don't know him? . . . You will!") Al could play in a town once and be received back like an old friend on a return engagement. He played a return date at the Star Theatre in Seattle in July and received what the Seattle *Post-Intelligencer* described as "a big hand when he first appeared." Al was recalled thrice.

Jolson had trouble with his voice that summer—the beginning of the vocal troubles that stemmed from his bout with tuberculosis in 1900—and spent several weeks in the Olympic Mountains of Washington. He wrote to Henrietta frequently, and by the time his voice returned in August, she had agreed to become his wife.

Al Jolson and Henrietta Keller were married in a civil ceremony in Oakland on September 20, 1907, with Al's friend dancer Dick Fitzgerald as the witness. Al had already paid $750 for a cottage on Sunny Slope Avenue in Oakland, but the newlyweds moved into the Continental Hotel within a few days.

Al had discovered he could not live in a house. To Jolson, a house symbolized the world he had left behind in the 1890s—a family, a father, a stepmother, and other reminders that his own mother was dead.

Al completed his second tour of the S. & C. Circuit in Oakland ("Jolson has returned and he is funnier than ever," said the *Tribune* critic. "It's a roar from the minute he pokes his head out from the wings and says, 'I'll be there in a minute.' ") on October 12th and played a week at the Empire Theatre in San Francisco. His success there led Sam Harris, manager of the Wigwam, to offer him $350 for a two-week engagement.

Jolson had great talent—even genius, some have argued. He also had great nerve, despite the doubts that plagued him, and that nerve was responsible for part of his success. Al told Sam Harris he would take nothing less than $500—$250 a week, the salary of many stars in 1907. Sam almost threw him out of the office, but gave in after a few days. Al got his $500, and the deal made Al Wilson's column in *Variety*.

Al had wanted to play parts in melodrama ever since he had seen the "thrillers" at the Bijou in Washington, D.C. He got his wish when David Grauman acquired an interest in the Globe, San Francisco's leading melodrama playhouse, and hired Walter Sanford as producer. Jolson joined the company as "principal comedian."

Al was with the Sanford Players for five weeks, beginning on November 11th in *Behind the Mask*. Jolson did not have a part in that play, but he entertained between the acts "in his popular singing and monologue turn," as Rube Cohen reported in *The Billboard*. Al had a small part in *His Terrible Secret* (also known as *The Man Monkey*), a "weird, startling drama of mystery," but it was in *The Great Wall Street Mystery* that he showed to best advantage. "Al Jolson, the popular comedian of the company, appears as the comedy Hebrew," noted the San Francisco *Examiner,* "and laughter is hearty while he is on the stage."

Jolson was a great comedian, but the only way he could express emotion on a stage was in a song. A modern actor might conclude that there was something the matter with his "sense memory." Al seemed especially ill at ease in love scenes, and his failure in that line would later hinder his career in films.

Another one of Jolson's faults (or virtues, depending on one's outlook) was his great use of profanity. Al could swear for what seemed like minutes without once repeating himself, and even Harry, no great verbal saint himself, admitted that his brother could "make the air blue" when he was cross or excited. ("He knew all the four-letter words that were ever invented.") Henrietta finally cured Al of swearing in her presence with the same trick that Mark Twain's wife had used on him. When Al came into their hotel room one day cussing over something that had raised his ire, she cut loose with a string of invectives that brought him up short. He stared at his wife in disbelieving silence, and then gasped, "You little swearing doll."

He never cut loose in front of her again.

Al went back to vaudeville after his stint with the Sanford Players, playing two weeks at the Victory Theatre in San Francisco. During Al's engagement at the Victory, a vaudeville friend of his, Sam Sidman, moved into the Continental with his bride of a few days, Jean Carlson. Jean, as it happened, was a friend of Henrietta's.

Sid and Jean were on the floor below the Jolsons. In the morning, Henrietta would put coffee on and call for Sid and Jean when it was ready. Then the two sets of newlyweds would sit and talk—Al and Sid about show business, Henrietta and Jean about the things they had in common—theatre, dancing, and good books. Both women were voracious readers.

Al was Al: he jumped around, got excited about everything, and seemed legitimately happy. He had his career, he had his wife, he had friends, and, at twenty-one, looked capable of going places. It was early January 1908, and the new year seemed to hold promise.

On January 11th, the day before Al left to play a week's engagement in Los Angeles, Harry Jolson arrived in San Francisco.

Harry's career had been only moderately successful since he had walked out on Al and Joe Palmer. His idea had been to do a single act about a young wisecracking Jew, but the act, "The Ghetto Sport," soon proved a failure. Early in 1907, Harry took a page from Al's book and began to work in blackface. He got steady work in Keith vaudeville in the East, but was nowhere as acclaimed—or highly paid—as Al was in the West. The brothers had met briefly in Chicago in 1906, patching up their differences from New Orleans, but were soon carrying on a new feud, via mail, over billing.

Harry, who billed himself as "The Operatic Blackface Comedian," objected to Al's occasional billing as "The Blackface with the Grand Opera Voice" and threatened to report him to the White Rats (a variety artists' union) and the Comedy Club.

Al said he did not "give a single damn" if Harry belonged to fifty clubs, expressing his opinion of them in four-letter words. He said he would do what he pleased, and that Harry and his fellow members could "all hang." He closed the letter, "Well, so long and good luck and be a good boy. Your loving brother, Al."

Harry's arrival in San Francisco sparked a far more serious quarrel. He had heard about Al's marriage to a *shiksa* and was furious. Harry was not religious, but he felt a Jewish identity was worth keeping, and the brothers almost came to blows.

The elder Jolson brother's trip to San Francisco was an attempt to cash in on Al's popularity in the Bay Area by the Western States Vaudeville Association. On January 13th, while Al was still in Los Angeles, Harry opened at the Empire in San Francisco. "Though Mrs. Tom Thumb was featured," wrote Al Wilson in *Variety*, "Harry Jolson was the real drawing card, due, perhaps, to the success attained by his brother, Al, on the coast as a monologuist. There were frequent verbal requests from the front for his brother's material, and Harry had to struggle hard to maintain his individuality." After two more weeks of what he later termed "odorous comparisions" of Al and himself, Harry canceled his bookings and left California.

Al followed his engagement in Los Angeles with an equally successful one in Denver before going to Chicago for more bookings. He was still *persona non grata* to the Keith and Orpheum circuits, but Ed Carruthers booked him for ten weeks on the Interstate, the "Circuit of the South." Al opened at the Grand Opera House in Nashville on February 24th.

Jolson later claimed to have observed a certain reticence in southern audiences until he took off his gloves for his whistling encore, "showing my white hands." But the most important thing about this tour was Al's so called "discovery" by Lew Dockstader, star and sole proprietor of Lew Dockstader's Minstrels, the leading show of its type.

Johnny King, one of Dockstader's end men (so called because the old-time minstrels sat in a large semi-circle, chief performers at the ends), had announced that he would not renew his contract for the following season. Lew needed a replacement, and Will Oakland, the company's famous counter-tenor (reputed to have the highest male singing voice in show business), suggested Al.

Jolson was not aware of the situation when the Minstrels came to the Capital Theatre in Little Rock on April 7th. Al himself was on the bill at the Majestic that week, but found time to attend Dockstader's matinee.

According to a story Al told several ghost writers, he presented his card to Charles D. Wilson, Dockstader's company manager, at the box office. In those days, shows let actors in for free.

"Can I see the show?" asked Jolson.

"No."

"Don't you recognize the profession?"

"We do, but who are you?"

A three-sheet poster, advertising Jolson, could be seen across the street. Al proudly pointed to it and said, "That's me," with all the assurance of his twenty-two years.

"Maybe," replied Wilson, "but that doesn't help me. I never heard of you."

Jolson paid his way in, saw the show, and went back to the Majestic Theatre for his own performance. While onstage, he noticed Wilson in a box seat. "I took several encores," Al remembered, "and as I went off from the last, I hissed at Wilson: 'I hope *you* paid to get in.' "

Al now figured out the gag and realized that Wilson had been sent to "look me over . . . I told my wife to wait for me while I hung around the stage entrance. I stayed there an hour, and I had about decided that I wasn't a discovery, after all, when Wilson hove up. 'Say,' he said, 'do you know where I can find a kid named Jolson?' "

Al did not sign with Lew Dockstader's Minstrels until Thursday, April 16th, when the show—and Jolson—was in Fort Worth. That was when Al finally met Lew Dockstader—a portly man of fifty-two with a handle-bar mustache, nineteenth-century manners, and a heavy taste for liquor.

Salaries in minstrelsy were far lower than in West Coast vaudeville owing to the heavy overhead; there were seventy performers in Dockstader's show. Dockstader offered Jolson a salary of seventy-five dollars a week for the first season, $100 for the second, and $125 (the same salary Lew claimed to be paying himself) for the remaining three.

Jolson signed because he saw it as a way around the blacklist that had kept him out of big-time vaudeville for two years. He would receive a featured spot in the olio—the only single "spot" in the show save for Lew Dockstader's own. Al believed that his appearance in this spot would sell him to the big-time bookers—blacklist or no blacklist.

It was a tremendous gamble.

Big-Time

"Al Jolson is coming to your town, wherever he is, if he hasn't
been there yet—Jolson and all his kind."
—"The Decay of Vaudeville."
American Magazine, April 1910.

With two months free before rehearsals started, Jolson took his
bride for a late honeymoon at the Moores' home in Pleasantville, New Jersey. These were the good times: Al pushing Henrietta
on the swing in the backyard, the two of them sharing the fun of a
young married couple. Fred, now managing the Savoy Theatre in
Atlantic City, thought that Al was crazy to have signed with Lew
Dockstader. The salary was too low, and no wife would tolerate
having to cross the country, spending every night in a different
hotel room. Fred offered to make Al his assistant manager at the
Savoy, but young Jolson turned him down. He was a performer.
Period.

The Moores were good hosts, but Al soon grew restless. He went
into New York to get vaudeville bookings, only to find the blacklist
still in effect. Al wound up more than one trip into New York at an
all-night crap game.

Rehearsals for the coming season with Dockstader's Minstrels
started in July at the Majestic Theatre in Brooklyn. Lew Dockstader
was proud of the traditions of minstrelsy, and was even something
of a historian on the subject. But he was also an innovator who
introduced satirical sketches in place of the old travesties and fla-
vored each performance with topical, up-to-the-minute local references. The hit of the 1907–08 tour had been "A Dull Day at the
White House," in which Lew "took off" on President Theodore
Roosevelt, complete with pince-nez and Rough Rider hat, in blackface.
Dockstader was also known for his impersonations of Grover Cleveland, Benjamin Harrison, and William Jennings Bryan, impressions
of political figures popular more than sixty years before David Fry.

Most social humor done on the variety stages, and almost all the
topical jokes told in the minstrel shows, expressed the view of the
"man on the street." But Dockstader's scenes and songs, like

"Everybody Works But Father" (about child labor), offered sharp commentary on many social issues.

Dockstader decided to break more new ground in the 1908–09 season, presenting, not the traditional minstrel show, but a complete "musical comedy in blackface" that would run the length of the program. It was a travesty on the then current efforts to reach the North Pole, with Dockstader himself as "Prof. Hightower" and Jolson as "Acie," his assistant.

Lew Dockstader and his 'Seventy Real Minstrels" opened the season in Plainfield, New Jersey, on August 10, 1908. It was an elaborate production, but *Variety* publisher Sime Silverman's review spotlighted Jolson. "It does appear as though Mr. Dockstader has subordinated himself for the benefit of Jolson, a newcomer in the east, young, with a pleasing personality, good voice, some new 'stuff' and the hit of the show, not even excepting Neil O'Brien, that great 'end.' " Sime pointed out that Al's material, "rapidly delivered, contained much dried up matter. Jolson is a natural minstrel, however, and his stage magnetism can win out always."

The Minstrels played a week in Cincinnati in November. Al had breakfast in the Sinton Hotel dining room the morning after the last performance there and waited on line to pay the check. According to a story he told several years later, the man in front of him was making a play for the cashier.

"Say, mister," Al said, "would you hurry up. I've gotta catch a train."

The man, much larger than Al, turned. "I don't hurry up for kikes," he said.

Jolson hit him, hard, and knocked him down.

Al himself received a more surprising blow just two months later. He was entering the dining room of the Pelham Hotel in Boston when he saw his brother, Harry, at the other end of the room. "Come over here," said Harry. "I want you to meet my wife."

"Quit your kidding. You're not married."

"But I *am* married. Lillian, this is my brother Al, the one I've told you so much about."

Al was seldom diplomatic. "Harry!," he said, looking at the young girl in astonishment, "she's not Jewish. And this comes after you gave me hell for marrying Henrietta."

Harry had met eighteen-year-old Lillian Wilson in July, when she was working as a chorine in one of the massive Hippodrome extravaganzas. Al, Harry, and their wives—Lillian was Swedish; Henrietta, Danish—were almost inseparable for the remainder of the

Minstrels' three-week stay in Boston. "Conditions," Harry wrote, "were so harmonious that Al suggested we take an apartment together . . . We didn't find the ideal apartment, fortunately, for Al and I probably would have been in a hot argument about something unimportant before two days had passed."

Al got his big chance before a New York audience when Dockstader's Minstrels opened a week at Springer's Grand Opera House at Twenty-third Street and Eighth Avenue on Monday, February 22, 1909. Al *(Rush)* Greason reviewed Jolson's olio spot in the *Variety* "New Acts" department, and that great trade weekly opened a file on "Al Jolson" that would hold hundreds of clippings over the next forty years. Greason's review, perhaps the most important ever given Jolson, ran as follows:

> Al Jolson would be welcome to vaudeville in the specialty which he is using as a feature of Lew Dockstader's Minstrels. Dressing neatly in evening clothes of faultless cut and of the new color called "taupe," Jolson offers a quiet quarter of an hour of smooth entertainment. As a singer of "coon" songs, Jolson has a method of his own by which lyrics and melody are given their full value. His talk moves along nicely and is kept within proper proportion to the rest of the act. Throughout the talk, Jolson introduces little tricks of speech, and for a finish has an odd, eccentric vocal performance in which he sings with a peculiar buzzing note. Of course, it's flagrant trick work, but it brings him back for a sure fire encore. For this purpose, he has a whistling solo that brings another recall. . . . As it stands now, Jolson's offering is capable of holding down a place in any vaudeville show. He is now in the next to closing position in the olio of Dockstader's Minstrels, following Lew Dockstader and Neil O'Brien among others, and Jolson is making good a mile.

The biggest agents and producers in the country saw Jolson that week, but there were no immediate offers for him to go into vaudeville. Al had other problems, too. He was overdrawn on his salary.

The minstrel life was difficult, with long seasons that were made up in large measure of one-nighters in cities like Fitchburg, Massachusetts, and Columbia, South Carolina. There was also a social side to minstrelsy consisting of late evening poker sessions aboard trains, usually with whiskey and cigars. Jolson already smoked and gambled, but his first season with Dockstader's Minstrels marked the beginning of a five-year period in which he did some heavy drinking.

He was now called "Jolie" by his fellow minstrels—the name his colleagues in the show world would address him by for the rest of his life, and the name he would use in countless references to himself in the third person. Al still lived the same way he had when making $150 a week in San Francisco. He left big tips, was a comparatively soft touch for down-and-out actors, and never passed up a night out with "the boys." Henrietta begged him to save money, but his only reply was a confident smile and lines like, "Why should I save money? I'm the greatest entertainer in the world. Some day I'll be a millionaire. Watch and see if I'm not right."

Al was broke within a few weeks of his New York triumph. (On March 9th, he wrote his older brother from the Selwyn Hotel in Charlotte, North Carolina, asking Harry to return ten dollars he had lent him.) Unable to obtain additional advances, he accepted an offer from I. P. Wilkerson: lead position in a minstrel show at the American Theatre in San Francisco at more money than Lew Dockstader had ever dreamed of paying any one performer.

Jolson knew Dockstader would not let him go, so he borrowed fifty dollars from a friend and made plans to run out on the show. Al and Harry had done the same thing to the Dixon-Bernstein Turkey Burlesque Show in 1904, and Al would do it again, many times, throughout his stage career.

Dockstader's Minstrels opened a week's engagement at the Crescent Theatre in New Orleans on Sunday, March 28, 1909. That night, after the performance, Al returned to the theatre and bribed the stage gang into letting him have his trunk. He and Henrietta were soon headed west.

Jolson received an ovation on his first appearance when Wilkerson's *Minstrels of Today* opened on Sunday, April 25th. Al and Johnny King were the chief endmen, but Waldemar Young of the San Francisco *Chronicle* said Jolson had "all the argument. He had one stunt which is worth the price of admission alone." Al continued making audiences laugh with his "mental telepathy" act during the second week of the show's run, but business was not up to expectations—chiefly due to *About Town,* a dull musical that made up the other half of the program. Wilkerson's backers deserted him, and he was unable to pay his actors on Friday, May 7th. Two days later, Al found that the company had struck.

According to the *Chronicle,* Jolson and King "buttonholed [house manager] Abe Cohn in the lobby and fired at him a volley which would have shaken the most resolute. Cohn, being diplomatic, argued with them. Very quietly, he convinced them that, as the show was playing the house on a percentage basis, the same as any traveling organization, he really had nothing to do with it. And that

being so, he couldn't very well turn over to them the night's receipts—not very well.

"Finally, they saw it as he saw it and doggedly put on the burnt
cork. The show went on to its finish. But when the curtain de-
scended, it came down for a week." A week for the American Theatre, but forever for Wilkerson's Minstrels. It made little difference.
I. P. Wilkerson had already received a wire from Hollis E. Cooley of
the Association of Theatrical Producing Managers; Lew Dockstader
was demanding Jolson's return.

Wilkerson sent Cooley the following note:

> Your favor at hand, and in reply I closed Jolson, as per my wire to
> you, and he left to join Dockstader in Kansas City, Mo. (our old
> town, by the way). He claimed he had no contract, so I believed him
> until I received your wire. Then I closed him and induced him to
> return to Dockstader, as all the vaudeville managers here were after
> him.
>
> With best wishes, I remain, yours truly,
> Pearl Wilkerson

Al Jolson rejoined Dockstader's Minstrels like a penitent child.
Herman Weaver, a member of the minstrel orchestra, described Lew
as "upstage," and Dockstader was especially cool to Al for the remainder of the season. Not that it really mattered. On Thursday,
July 1st, a man named Arthur Klein approached Jolson after a performance at the Warburton Theatre in Yonkers.

Klein, the twenty-four-year-old "Vesta Tilley of Managers" (so
called because his dapper dress resembled that of the famous male
impersonator), had been an actor in his teens, a member of the *Foxy
Grandpa* company starring Joseph Hart. In 1906, he had married
society girl Evelyn Kip and become a columnist for the *Morning
Telegraph*, New York's daily show-world/sporting paper, a position
he left two years later to become booking manager of vaudeville
theatre owner Percy G. Williams, a major cogwheel in the UBO.

Klein, whose position in the Williams office made him an important man in vaudeville, offered Jolson bookings in the biggest New
York theatres—if he could become his manager and collect 10 percent of Al's salary. It was a conflict of interest on Klein's part, but
Jolson soon agreed. He had been trying to crack "big time" vaudeville for years without success and, at this point, needed Klein more
than Klein needed him.

On Monday, July 12th, two days after Dockstader's show closed
its season, Jolson and Klein signed a seven-year exclusive artist-

manager contract in Pabst's Columbus Circle Cafe in New York. Klein immediately booked Jolson for four weeks in vaudeville, taking him, in essence, off the blacklist.

Al was scheduled to open at New York's Fifth Avenue Theatre on July 19, 1909. This was the big time he had dreamed of. Success at the Fifth Avenue could put him on the road to headline status, but a flop could mean a life in small-time vaudeville—or Dockstader's Minstrels.

Jolson was the fifth act on the bill at the Monday matinee, but scored such a hit that he was moved to "next to closing"—displacing Louise Dresser, the headliner—in the evening. Al Greason, who covered that performance for *Variety,* said: "The Fifth Avenue has not in a long time seen so flattering a demonstration for a single act, or any other sort of act for that matter." Jolie was on his way.

Jolson played the following two weeks at the New Brighton Theatre in Brooklyn, scoring what the New York *Dramatic Mirror* called "the big laughing hit of the bill" with songs like Shelton Brooks' "You Ain't Talking to Me." He played the week after that at Keith's in Philadelphia, and was a hit again. Then it all stopped. He had to go back to Dockstader's Minstrels.

Dockstader had Jolson under contract until mid-1913, and Klein's chief task, at this point, was to get his new client released. Klein went to the source: Dockstader's new booking agents, the Shuberts.

The commercial theatre of the early 1900s consisted of several hundred shows, most of which played only a few weeks in New York before going on the road, where, thanks to low overheads and the non-existence of competing forms of entertainment, huge profits were available. The road was ruled by two hostile camps: the Theatrical Syndicate, organized in 1896, and the Messrs. Shubert—dark and quiet Lee, and Jake (always referred to as "J. J." in programs), his frequently pugnacious younger brother.

In July, while Jolson was in vaudeville, Lew Dockstader decided to desert the Syndicate and begin booking through the Shuberts. "Lee 'n' Jake" had been extremely anxious to acquire the Dockstader show, and Klein knew one reason why: they were impressed with Jolson.

The Shuberts also produced their own shows, and although blackface comedians had never been used in musical comedy, Klein had little difficulty selling them on Jolson. The only trouble, Klein informed them, was his client's contract with Lew Dockstader.

The next few months saw Dockstader's Minstrels lose money on the road. The jumps between cities were awkward and too costly, and receipts in certain towns were minimal. Dockstader knew the

Shuberts did not have as many theatres as the Syndicate, but he also knew of their interest in Jolson.

Lew Dockstader gave Al Jolson his release in December. "I didn't want to stand in his way" was how he explained it to vaudeville headliner Rae Samuels. Dockstader did not want any more bad bookings either.

While the Shuberts were deciding where best to use Jolson, Art Klein booked his client into vaudeville. Al opened at New York's Colonial Theatre on December 27th (substituting for Ralph Herz) and was a hit, receiving great applause with his song, "Everybody." The real high point of Jolson's vaudeville career came three weeks later—his debut at Hammerstein's Victoria. The Monday matinees at Hammerstein's were torture for performers, since the audiences tended to be made up of fellow show people—actors, agents, managers, and producers. Jolson told John J. Iris of the New York *Review* that he was "so scared to death" that he could hardly hear the orchestra play his opening music, and that Mike Simon, the stage manager, had to tell him it was his turn to go on three times.

Jolson was so successful with a new song—Harry von Tilzer's "Hip, Hip, Hypnotize Me"—that it was impossible for the next act to go on until he had given a second encore and made a speech. A writer for the *American* Magazine thought the song was "frankly filthy . . . There is in every audience a certain percentage that may be counted on to greet evil suggestion with enthusiasm. On this occasion, that percentage laughed uproariously and applauded wildly. When Jolson came out to respond with an encore he frankly and proudly admitted in so many words that he had just sung a filthy song. The band, as he came out, again struck up the opening bars of the ballad about the hypnotist.

" 'No,' said Jolson, with mock severity, 'that's dirty. Don't play that.' More laughter from the audience. 'Ah-ha!' cried Jolson delightedly, 'that's what you want. I knew you wanted that. I ought to have opened with that.' "

Shortly after Jolson's reception at Hammerstein's, Lee Shubert summoned Art Klein to his office. Lee had decided to produce Al in a starring tour, and, according to a report in the anti-Shubert *Morning Telegraph,* the conversation went something like this:

"How much to you intend to pay Al?"

"The same money as he's now getting in vaudeville." [Al was then making about $300 a week.]

"Mr. Shubert," Klein replied, "you can have Al at his present vaudeville salary. For that money, he'll go back to Dockstader's Minstrels, and you at least *book* that show."

Klein then left Lee's office, pausing long enough to laugh outside the door. He had put one over on the Shuberts.

Al was worried when he heard about it, but Art said his time would come. He was about to get a raise in vaudeville, and the big shows would still be there in a year. Then, Klein told him, he would get the "real" money.

Jolson continued playing eastern vaudeville for the next five months, building his reputation and garnering top notices from Sime, Rush, and other respected critics of that genre. He was named on several "ideal bills" in *Variety*, and began frequenting the White Rats union office in New York. His closest crony at this time was Harry (Rolls) Wardell, an eccentric ex-burlesque comedian who originated such expressions as "Life Is Just a Bowl of Cherries" and "I'm the Matzoh Ball in the Soup of Life." Rolls had appeared in several productions at the Hippodrome and would understudy Jolson in three Winter Garden shows, but most of his time and talent were used in entertaining people *off* the stage. Confident his "pals" would take care of him, Wardell lacked ambition. But he "spoke Al's language," as contemporaries put it, and was the perfect complement to Jolie's tense and fast-paced style. Predictably, Al was the "pal" who wound up taking care of Rolls.

Jolson finished his eastern vaudeville engagements on May 28th and, with Rolls and Henrietta, left for California the following Friday. Henrietta had a close relationship with her mother, but had not seen either of her parents in two years. She had never met Al's father and stepmother.

Sime Silverman had made Al the *Variety* correspondent for the upcoming Jack Johnson–James J. Jeffries bout in San Francisco, and Jolson even spent a day at Jeffries' training quarters (Camp Rowardenen) with Wardell. While Al and Rolls were there, word came that Gov. James N. Gillett had barred the fight from California. Reno, Nevada, was chosen as the new site, and former champion Jim Corbett hired a special train to take the actors there from San Francisco.

The background of the Johnson–Jeffries bout has been discussed in several biographies of Johnson, the first black world heavyweight champion, and even served as the basis for a Broadway play and movie, *The Great White Hope*. Jolson's account of the fight, written in San Francisco two days after the event and published in the July 9, 1910, issue of *Variety*, is remarkably objective, considering, not only the racial climate of the time, but the fact that most of the actors were decidedly pro-Jeffries. (Jeff was managed by theatrical producer William A. Brady.)

"Johnson" Jolson wrote, "just played with him [Jeffries] as a cat does with a mouse. It's all right to say that, if Jeff were in his prime, what he would have done to Johnson, but believe me, it would have been just the same.

"The majority at the ringside must say that Johnson is the greatest fighter that ever lived. Jeffries did not hit him one good punch.

"George Little, Johnson's ex-manager, bet me $400 to $200, after the first round, that Jeffries would win. After the fifth round, I bet (another) $200 that Johnson would win. That made me break even, as I had bet $600 (on Jeffries) before the fight."

Jolson was one of the few writers willing to give Johnson credit for his victory. What effect this had on black people is hard to gauge, but the fact remains that Jolson was the only white man ever admitted to Leroy's, the black cabaret in Harlem, during the five years of its existence (1910–15).

Jolson opened a tour of the Orpheum Circuit in Seattle on July 24th. The high point of this tour came in December in Chicago, where Al shared top billing with the more established Bessie Wynn. "Mr. Al Jolson," said *The Billboard*, "although not a headliner, was without doubt the hit of the bill. He stopped the show at the opening performance and was a riot from start to finish."

Jolson felt he was entitled to a raise, and Art Klein, also in Chicago, called the UBO in New York and secured it. "They were only too glad to raise him every time he asked for it," Klein told Joe Franklin a few years before his death. "I went out and bought him a fur coat. I mean a fur collar. I think the fur was otter.

"He was living at the Grant Hotel there (in Chicago) . . . I brought him this coat, and he just clowned around there, showing the coat to all the performers."

Two weeks later, Jolson's tour of the Orpheum Circuit was halted by sinus trouble in Louisville. Al had taken out an insurance policy the year before, but filing a claim was hardly worth the effort. "I'll never forget the agile interne who was sent to examine me," he told *Variety* in 1912, "and make sure that I actually was sick so as to get the $12.50 per week they were good enough to allow. From the way the young doctor-to-be went about his work, I felt that he was afraid that I was shamming illness for the $12.50."

Jolson canceled the remaining three weeks of his Orpheum bookings, returned to New York, and underwent an operation on his nose. "Talking," as he recalled was "impossible," so he stayed in his hotel room and gave up shaving. His brother Harry came to see him, took one look at his week's growth of beard, and exclaimed, "Hello, papa."

Art Klein had stayed busy on Jolson's behalf. The agent, still not on good terms with Lee, had opened negotiations with Jake, the "other Shubert," about Al appearing in a big show that would open a new Broadway theatre.

In May 1910, Lew Fields (of Weber and Fields fame) had filed plans for the erection of a theatre on the site of the old American Horse Exchange at Seventh Avenue and Fiftieth Street; the Shuberts, his partners, took over the entire venture when Fields had a physical breakdown and went to Cuba to recover. The opening of the new theatre, called the Winter Garden, was set for March 1911.

Rumors traveled quickly along Broadway, and there seemed to be enough principals in the new show to stock five road companies of *Ben Hur*. Casting was still being done on February 7th, when Klein showed up in Jolson's hotel room with a Shubert contract. The salary was $325—more than Jolson had been getting a year earlier but below his present vaudeville salary. But Al had taken a cut upon joining Dockstader's Minstrels, and Klein felt the time had come to get his client into a Broadway show.

Al Jolson was about to make his first appearance in the theatre that would always be identified with him. The greatest career in Broadway history was about to begin.

La Belle Paree

"The Winter Garden is on the site of the old horse exchange. Judging from the smell of last night's show, things haven't changed much."

Unidentified Broadway "wag"
March 21, 1911

There were thirty principals in the cast of *La Belle Paree*, the musical extravaganza that opened the Winter Garden in March, 1911, with Jolson about tenth in importance. Among those who outranked him were internationally known *danseuse* Mlle. Dazie, opera diva Dorothy Jardon, clothes horse Kitty Gordon (known for her beautiful back), and comedienne Stella Mayhew. With close to a hundred performers in the cast, including chorus personnel and supernumeraries, *La Belle Paree* was a production that theatre economics would have made impossible to mount in the 1980s.

No rehearsal pay was given, so Art Klein had Jolson play another week at Hammerstein's Victoria shortly before he started work on *Belle Paree*. "Al Jolson sang, talked, and whistled the audience into a frenzy of enthusiastic approval," Robert Spears wrote in *The Morning Telegraph*.

He began with "Piano Man." As Gene Greene gave this song only last week, it will be seen that the blackface comedian had a pace cut out for him. But Al was decidedly "there."

Al talked about the girls he had loved and the way he had loved them. When the girls had nearly laughed themselves into hysterics, Al struck a sort of Romeo pose and pleaded soulfully:

"Girls, look me in the face."

While the girls were responding to his command, Al turned his attention to the men, assuring them that women are not necessary to their happiness. "You know they're not. Tell the truth. Speak up and admit it. Can't you get along without women? Be bold and answer."

Several Jolson enthusiasts shouted affirmatively, whereat Al started the girls off again by exclaiming: "You liars!"

He announced his intention of trying a new song. It was about "Missouri Joe," a fellow you had to show. The audience boisterously brought Al back for an encore. He took off his gloves, not to show his color, but to whistle through his fingers, at which he is melodiously adept. At another encore, Al tried to make himself heard above the applause. As the applause continued, he was seen to be talking. When it quieted sufficiently for him to be heard, Al dashed away, after saying: "Thank you."

Jolson reported for rehearsals of the Winter Garden show the following Monday. The production, officially titled *The Musical Review of 1911,* was actually made up of two main parts: *Bow Sing,* a one-act Chinese Fantasy Opera in which Al did not appear, and *La Belle Paree,* a two-act "Cook's Tour Through Vaudeville with a Parisian Landscape." The plot of *Belle Paree* revolved around the character Bridgeeta McShane, "a wealthy Irish-American widow sojourning in Paris for her health and other people's profit," played by Arthur Cunningham in drag. Buxom comedienne Stella Mayhew played Eczema Johnson, the widow's mulatto maid, and Jolson was Erastus Sparkler, "a colored aristocrat from San Juan Hill, cutting a wide swath in Paris."

La Belle Paree was simply a hinge for vaudeville routines by (Miss) Ray Cox, Yiddish dialect comedian Barney Bernard, young Hungarian beauty Mitzi Hajos, Jolson, Mayhew, and several other well-known performers—each portraying one of the eccentrics encountered by the Widow McShane in Paris. As Sparkler, Al perfected the tongue-in-cheek Continental effeminacy he would handle with such aplomb for the remainder of his Broadway career. Confidence, however, waned as the rehearsal time continued. *Belle Paree* was a monstrosity, with too many acts and no firm hand to give direction. Jesse Huffman and Bill Wilson, who were staging the production, pleaded for more time, and Jake Shubert, who was "supervising," finally agreed. Jake postponed the opening from March 11th to Tuesday, March 14th, and a delay in getting the license for the theatre forced a second postponement, to Thursday, evening, March 16th.

After a disastrous dress rehearsal, in which several principals were suffering from colds, Jake ordered another run through for noon of the following day. He finally postponed the opening again, to Monday night, March 20th.

Traffic along Broadway was completely jammed that evening. The new Winter Garden—there had been another in the 1800s—was beautiful, with a "flowered" ceiling centerpiece that gave the house a garden affect. The entire auditorium was latticed and carpeted, and roomy, comfortable chairs had been installed in every section.

There was a blue Dutch Cafe on the mezzanine level, and a Wine Room.

Backstage, however, it was bedlam, and Al Jolson was the most nervous of all. These were not his usual pre-performance jitters. This was dread—a sickening, self-conscious coldness. Jolson wanted to be home in bed that night, not onstage at the Winter Garden.

Al had a duet with Stella Mayhew in the first act titled "Paris Is a Paradise for Coons."

JOLSON   Never going back again to Yankee land.
MAYHEW   Got a lot of customs there that I can't stand.
JOLSON   Like hanging a coon.
MAYHEW   Working in June.
BOTH   Hunting chicken thieves night and noon.
JOLSON   Don't know how to treat us colored gentlemen.
MAYHEW   Call us colored ladies "wenches" now and then.
BOTH   There's one place, for the race—"

And on into the chorus. Tunesmiths of the period had found a way to wed the black American musical heritage with popular music by uniting the word "coon" with "June," "moon," and other Tin Pan Alley sundries. The men who wrote these "coon" songs were not bigots; the word "racism" had not yet been invented. It was an era that lacked social awareness and commitment. The Great Depression had not yet arrived to throw doubt upon the American dream, and Hitler had not showed what racism could do. The author of the surprisingly bouncy music for this "Paris" number was Jerome Kern, then at the beginning of a career that would include the scores for *Sally, Show Boat,* and many other great works of the American musical theatre.

The comedy went over well, but Al was not any more confident in the second act. The evening dragged on, and it was almost midnight when Jolson came on for his specialty.

An act called "Tortajada and Her Sixteen Moorish Dancing Girls" had preceded *Belle Paree* on the Winter Garden program. Al now opened with a travesty on Tortajada's kiss-throwing, but the effect was lost due to the time that had elapsed since her appearance. Al got through his monologue and sang "That Lovin' Traumerei" to moderate applause. "Jolson's ten-minute turn passed in good shape—but no more" was the way Joshua Lowe put it in *Variety.*

For the first time since he had put on blackface, Al Jolson had "laid an egg."

It was almost one o'clock before the final curtain fell. Jolson was disconsolate. He went to a bar, got drunk, and in his own words, "walked to Ninety-fifth Street instead of Fifty-third Street, where I was living, before I realized what I was doing."

The despondent Jolson told his wife that he expected to be fired. Klein had tentative bookings for him in Europe, and Al now said it was their only hope.

Her parents' hardy Danish background had made Henrietta Keller a strong person—stronger, in some ways, then Jolson. She told him she did not care about the show—or his career, if things came down to that. He could work on the back of a delivery wagon, as far as she was concerned, and she could always teach school. Her words failed to make Al feel any better.

A few hours later, after Al had slept away his whiskey, the reviews came out. The daily newspaper critics had not stayed long enough to see his less than memorable specialty, but two morning papers singled out his comic turn with Stella Mayhew.

Adolph Klauber in the *New York Times:*

> Among the very best features were those provided by the two unc-tuous ragtime comedians, Miss Stella Mayhew and Mr. Al Jolson, both of whom had good songs and the dialects and the acting ability to deliver every bit of good that was in them.

The New York Herald:

> Equally amusing was Al Jolson—whether he is Alfred or Albert, this modest seceder from vaudeville will not divulge—who possesses gen-uine Negro unction in his speech and manner. Yet by race, he might be thought capable of succeeding better with other types.

Jolson, however, was concerned about his "specialty." When Jake Shubert asked what could be done to "beef it up," Jolson de-manded an earlier spot on the program. There was a matinee that day, but the program was still long, and Al did not do much better than he had the night before.

The evening papers came out prior to that night's performance, and Al had a chance to see the review in the New York *World.*

> The trip was a long one and it was marked by rough places. Though a good natured, rollicking semi-vaudeville show, it proved to be half an hour too long. Surgical operations might be performed on almost any part of it to its great improvement.
>
> But Miss Stella Mayhew, as a Seventh Avenue colored queen, and Al Johnson *(sic),* as her fickle sweetheart, who meet unexpectedly on

the Paris boulevard, cannot be spared. They were the hits of the show—
the former with her song, "De Develin' Tune"—and they eclipsed even
Kitty Gordon, who, however, held a monopoly in harem skirts.

That night, March 21, 1911, the third performance of *La Belle
Paree,* marked the beginning of the Jolson Broadway legend. Exactly
what Al did that night was never written down, but Pearl Goldberg
Sieben, who knew Jolson in the 1940s, described his breaking through
the noise of the cafe society audience with a loud shrill whistle.
Whatever the details, Al's performance seems to have been strangely
reminiscent of the one he had given at the National Theatre in San
Francisco four and a half years earlier. The magic Jolson had when
he was "right" had reappeared.

Just as audiences had at the Fifth Avenue and Hammerstein's, the
Winter Garden audience now laughed, applauded, rose, and cheered.
And they stood again when Al came on for the finale.

Jolson had arrived.

That is not to say that he became an overnight star; things simply
did not happen that fast in 1911. During the following two months,
however, Jolson became the favorite of Winter Garden audiences.
The plot of *Belle Paree* was flimsy enough to allow for the additions
and subtractions of many acts, songs, and specialties, and it is doubtful
if any two performances were ever really the same. The Winter Garden audiences came to be made up largely of "repeaters" who came
to drink and view the "continental novelties" at leisure. Within a
few short weeks, the performer that they came to see was Jolson.
There was no slipping out to the Wine Room or the concession stand
for seventy-five-cent "Winter Garden Ice Cream" when Al was onstage. As Jolson's confidence grew, his performance opened up, and
he became known as "the Winter Garden comedian"—the hit of
Belle Paree.

Jolson also became a fixture of the Winter Garden Sunday Night
Concerts. Theatrical performances were illegal on Sundays in the
eastern part of the country, but producers got around the law by
staging so-called sacred concerts—programs of vaudeville acts, performed in evening clothes *sans* make-up, a religious hymn sometimes
closing the show.

The first Winter Garden Sunday Night Concert was given on March
26, 1911—the first Sunday the theatre was open. Al appeared, in
whiteface, singing and ad-libbing for about a half an hour. Audiences at these concerts were made up of actors on their night off,
managers, and agents, in addition to the general public. They were

a tough audience, but Jolson won them completely. He was the "entertainer's entertainer," and, as such, became established.

Jolson was only twenty-five, but he had found success. The Shuberts happily picked up the weekly options on his contract after May 13th, and made plans to star him in a new show the following season. The only thing Al seemed to be unhappy with, at this point, was his marriage. Henrietta and he had been having serious trouble for more than two years.

Al had started acting strangely towards his wife a few months after they were married. In January 1908 he had left San Francisco for a week's engagement in Los Angeles, leaving Henrietta at her parents' house in Oakland. It was only after the bewildered Kellers gave their daughter enough money that she joined Al in Chicago two weeks later. Al said he was trying to save money. He seemed to have enough to play cards, but not enough to pay for his wife's train fare.

Al did something even stranger after he clicked in *La Belle Paree*. According to Jean Carlson, he returned to the hotel after a performance, threw a sum of money on the bed, and told his wife to "take it and go back to Oakland."

Henrietta went. She missed her parents and had been receiving less and less attention from her husband. Jolson, it seemed, was a "man's man" who enjoyed the company of his own sex and disliked his wife's cross-examinations. Henrietta demanded that Al account for every moment he was not with her.

Some people thought there was a different explanation. Rumors about Jolson being a bisexual began when he was seen, quite frequently, with Melville Ellis, the Shuberts' noted pianist-designer and one of the most notorious homosexuals on Broadway. Al's association with Melville may have been entirely for business reasons. Shortly after he became successful in *La Belle Paree,* the Shuberts supposedly placed Jolson under Ellis' wing in order to give him additional polish. (Ellis did, in fact, spend time rehearsing Jolson on ballads like "The Rosary" by Ethelbert Nevin.) Adding more fuel to the fire was that Al now had a dresser—Frank (Pansy) Holmes.

"I was in the chorus [of *La Belle Paree*]," Holmes told journalist Acton Davies twelve years later, "and dressing Melville Ellis. And Ellis says, 'Don't bother about me tonight; I've only got a dress suit to put on. Go and see what you can do for Jolson.' And I went and never came back." "Pansy," as Al called him, dressed Jolson for the remainder of his stage career, sometimes playing a bit part in order to remain on the Shuberts' payroll.

Homosexuality is and always has been an accepted part of the theatre, and it is safe to say that if one-quarter of all adult males are homosexual (as Gay Liberation claims), three-quarters of all males in the theatrical profession are of similar persuasion. The percentage was somewhat less prior to about 1957, when live theatre was part of the cultural mainstream, and before *West Side Story* made acrobatic ballet an important part of the American musical. The theatre even dealt differently with homosexuality. Most casting was done by producers—hard-nosed money men like the Shuberts whose attitudes toward homosexuality were cynical at best. Blatant homosexuals were relegated to the chorus line and rarely given parts. ("Can you imagine watching that nance play up to that girl?" a producer would ask his incredulous assistant. "Nobody would believe it.") Today, of course, shows are cast by directors, choreographers, and casting agents, many of whom are homosexual themselves.

The Shuberts, although heterosexual and often openly hostile to homosexuals (Jake called them "goddamn pansies"), were well known for employing more homosexual designers and chorus boys than any other producers on Broadway. (They also produced the most shows.) One of Jolson's own gags of the twenties went like this:

FIRST SHUBERT CHORUS BOY   "Do you know Nance O'Neil?"
SECOND SHUBERT CHORUS BOY   "No. Who is he?"

Jolson often touched his listeners while speaking. He also pinched cheeks and occasionally kissed other men. Onstage, his work was filled with sly references to homosexuality, suggestive moistening of the lips, risqué use of the behind and hips, and what was then known as a "nance walk." Audiences thought that it was daring humor; people in the business sometimes wondered.

On Sunday, June 4, 1911, less than two weeks after signing a new two-year contract with the Shuberts, Jolson left New York and went to California. *La Belle Paree* still had another week to run, and the Shuberts were understandably angry. Al had intended to rejoin his wife in Oakland when the show closed, but there seemed to be no excuse for his leaving the cast. (Jolson later claimed to have been sick.)

Jolson played engagements at the Orpheum theatres in San Francisco and Los Angeles that summer, and the Los Angeles *Examiner* said one had to "be rather sophisticated to catch all of his rambling dope. But even though one be but a 'rube,' one cannot help enjoying the major portion of it, whether it be songs or talk. Mr. Jolson is funny—extremely funny."

Henrietta did not think her husband extremely funny when Al returned to New York without her. Traveling with Jolson's com-

pany were Johnny Peters and Mary Dewson, a black dance team Al
had met in San Francisco. Jolson introduced them as the originators
of the "Grizzly" and "Frisco Glide" and said they would be with
him in "his" new show.

The Shuberts now had other plans. Outraged by Al's runout, they
had resolved not to star him in a show that season. Jolson had no
legal leg to stand on. The Shubert contract merely said he would
perform as directed by the management, and Jake Shubert now wanted
him to tour the eastern cities in a revival of *La Belle Paree*. Jolson
would either do as he was told or be held in violation of his contract. At the same time, Al learned the Shuberts had signed up his
brother Harry.

Harry Jolson's career had been in serious trouble for some time.
In 1909, he had signed with the American Music Hall Circuit, William Morris' second attempt to break the UBO strangle-hold on
vaudeville. Harry found himself in serious trouble when that circuit
failed.

The UBO used Harry as a fill-in act when there was an infrequent
cancellation. He was appearing at Hammerstein's Venetian Terrace
when he got an offer from the Shuberts.

Harry was signed to an optional contract and put into rehearsals
for *The Revue of Revues* at the Winter Garden. The star of the show
was Mlle. Gaby Deslys, a blonde Frenchwoman who had risen to
fame in Europe with the help of a fictitious romance with Portugal's
King Manuel II.

The implication was clear: either Al behaved himself, or the Shuberts would push him into the background and promote Harry as
the "Winter Garden comedian." Al may not have taken this seriously, but he did agree to tour in *Belle Paree*.

With Al in line, the Shuberts began pruning Harry's part in *The
Revue of Revues*. "My 'bits' were taken away," he told his ghostwriter, Alban Emley. "Instead of letting me present a real specialty,
I was given only one short number before the close. I became so
discouraged that I was on the point of quitting, which is exactly
what they wanted."

The Revue of Revues proved to be a disaster when it opened on
September 27, 1911. Mlle. Deslys's English was barely intelligible,
and Harry, in one scene with Maud Raymond, failed to make anywhere near the impression Al had made with Stella Mayhew in *La
Belle Paree*.

The Shuberts had no further use for Harry Jolson. On Saturday
night, September 30th, he and several other members of the cast
were refused admission at the Winter Garden stage door, the door-

man acting "under orders from the Shuberts." Harry's attorney, Gus Dreyer, had a conference with Lee Shubert on October 10th, Lee saying he would "talk to [UBO General Manager Edward] Albee" and get Harry back his vaudeville bookings. Harry, of course, had no bookings to get back.

The Shuberts closed *The Revue of Revues* on November 4th and brought the company of *Belle Paree* in from its tour. The idea was to have key members of the *Belle Paree* cast support the $4,000-a-week Gaby Deslys in a new show, *Vera Violetta.*

Vera Violetta was set at a skating rink, with Al as Claude, a waiter, Gaby as Mme. de St. Cloche, and Jose (pronounced Jo-sie) Collins as Mme. Olga von Gruenberg. Among the other principals was nineteen-year-old Mae West, who left the cast during the out-of-town tryouts probably due to a clash with Gaby.

Since the show would run too long for several opening-night critics to meet their deadlines, Jake Shubert invited them to review the final dress rehearsal on Sunday, November 19th. This was a mistake, as there had been only one week of rehearsals and one week of tryouts. Jose Collins sang her mother Lottie's famous song, "Ta-Ra-Ra-BOOM-Dee-Aye," and lost the words completely. Al, however, was a hit with two songs—"That Haunting Melody" by George M. Cohan and "Rum Tum Tiddle," which he sang while racing up and down the center aisle.

"Jolson," Adolph Klauber wrote in the *New York Times,* "in the role of a colored waiter . . . succeeded in rousing the audience into its first enthusiasm of the evening, and kept them enthusiastic much of the time afterwards." Jolson's part in *Vera Violetta* was comparatively small, and yet he stole the show from Gaby.

Vera Violetta was the real start of Jolson's Broadway career. The show established Al in a way *Belle Paree* had not, and the Victor Talking Machine Co. had him record both "Rum Tum Tiddle" and "That Haunting Melody." The Shuberts became sold on Jolson all over again, and Melville Ellis, who was also in the cast, sent Al to the New York Public Library in an effort to provide him with some culture.

Al was not a very willing pupil. The son of a rabbi, his self-image was that of a race track tout, not a scholar. Learning was part of the "old ways" he had long ago rejected in favor of the fast, tough, sharp existence that led to success and admiration in America.

Jolson was a tough guy—with his mouth and, on various occasions, with his fists. His bad temper was only one reason for this behavior; there was also the desire to show the world he was a "man's man." In one respect, Jolson was a very sensitive human being who kept people at arm's length—or afraid—simply because he could not stand being hurt. The "tough guy" image was an effective—and so-cially sanctioned—way of doing it.

And it showed the world that you were not a "pansy," in the parlance of the day.

Outside of his relationships with Ellis and Frank Holmes, the only breath of scandal that touched Jolson involved drinking. Although not the boozer that Bing Crosby would be in the latter 1920s, Al was not above coming home drunk in the early hours of the morn-ing at this stage of his career. On New Year's Eve, 1911–12, he went out with some friends after the show and became so intoxi-cated that a policeman caught him trying to force his way into the Forty-second Street Library at two o'clock in the morning.

Vera Violetta ran through February 29, 1912. Five days later, a new show opened at the Winter Garden in which Jolson shared top billing with Stella Mayhew. This was another double presentation: a minstrel show in clown white make-up called *A Night with the Pierrots* and *The Whirl of Society,* a two-act satire of a then recent visit by the Duke and Duchess of Connaught.

Two important fixtures of the Jolson stage career made their first appearances in this show. One of them was the Winter Garden run-way, a long ramp that ran down the center aisle of the theatre. Broadway legend claims Jolson insisted on the runway as a means of getting closer to his audience, but it was actually put in for a burlesque of *Sumurun,* the Max Reinhardt mime then running at New York's Casino Theatre. Al played the Hunchback to Stella Mayhew's Sumurun, sang a song called "My Sumurun Girl," and was "the life of the party," according to the *New York Times.*

The other new fixture was a character named "Gus," a blackface version of the clever slave in Plautus' comedies. He was the under-dog who lived by his wits while enjoying his own private joke with the audience. Gus was "a man of many parts," and later shows would have him as a gondolier, Robinson Crusoe's Man Friday, Inbad the Porter in the age of Sinbad, and Bombo, Christopher Columbus' black navigator. Gilbert Seldes, who saw all of Jolson's shows, said Al created a "way of being" for Gus, whose "wit and bathos" were singularly creditable characteristics of Gus and "not Jolson." Re-proached by Columbus after a long absence, Bombo's "lips began to quiver, his chin to tremble. The tears are approaching, when his human independence softly asserts itself and he wails, 'We all have our *moments.'* " Gus proved the perfect character for Jolson, and Winter Garden shows the perfect vehicle for both.

Louis Sherwin of the New York *Globe* said *The Whirl of Society* "was about as lively as an afternoon tea given by the Browning Society of Kankakee," but all the critics praised Al Jolson. For the past year Al's name had been synonymous with "Winter Garden." Now that theatre was synonymous with "Jolson."

Song pluggers, publishers, and writers began pestering Jolson to introduce their songs. Al solved the problem by devoting two mornings a week to hearing new songs played by their composers. He would take the best songs, try them out with Melville, and decide which ones were suited to his talents. One that proved most successful was "Waiting for the Robert E. Lee," by Lewis F. Muir and L. Wolfe Gilbert. "Row, Row, Row" was another song that found its way into *The Whirl of Society*. "In 'Row, Row, Row,' " wrote Seldes, "[Jolson] would bounce up on the runway, propel himself by imaginary oars over the heads of the audience, draw equally imaginary slivers from the seat of his trousers, and infuse into the song something wild and roaring and insanely funny."

Al was a terrifically hard worker. Before 1924, many Broadway shows gave nine performances a week with an occasional tenth performance in the event of a holiday. Jolson also continued in the Sunday Night Concerts, giving more in fifteen minutes than any other four could give in a full hour.

"Jolson probably takes more chances at the Garden than anyone else would dare to," wrote Sime Silverman. "Sunday night [March 24], dressed in a tuxedo, he removed his collar and tie after the first few minutes, remaining neckless thereafter. As Jolson said, 'This is just like playing pinochle.' "

A Night with the Pierrots/The Whirl of Society closed for the summer on June 29, 1912. Henrietta was in Oakland, and Al, who loved to travel, bought a fashionable "touring car" to drive to California. The new car was a Packard, and that company's chief New York "demonstrator" was a short, fat, ugly, but entirely good-natured individual named Jimmy Donnelly. Al liked him so much that he refused to buy the car unless Jimmy came to work as his chauffeur. Donnelly wound up driving Jolson for the next thirty-three years.

Jimmy Donnelly was more than just Al's chauffeur; he was almost a paid friend. Whenever Al was nervous, he played cards with Jimmy to relax. Donnelly was not overly bright, but he proved an affable companion and reliable employee.

Al and Jimmy cruised around the country—resting for a week in Denver at an Elks' convention—and reached Oakland on July 28th. Henrietta was waiting, but Al spent most of the next two weeks with Senator Gus Hartman, an early Jolson fan. Al was bronzed and healthy looking from his trip, and showed that his wallet was in equally good shape by making three investments in California real estate at a total of thirty thousand dollars.

The summer over, *"The Whirl of Society* with Al Jolson" opened at the Lyric Theatre in Chicago on Sunday night, September 1, 1912. Stella Mayhew was no longer in the cast, but Melville Ellis, Ada Lewis, Lawrence D'Orsay (known for his "haw haw" Earl of Pawtucket characterization), and twenty-one-year-old Fanny Brice made up the difference.

James O'Donnell Bennett of Chicago's *Record Herald*, a tough critic, described Jolson as "a trim, compact young fellow with a breezy sense of blackface comedy, who easily dominates things from the rise to the fall of the curtain. He sings ragtime with voice, shoulders, arms, and legs; he dances with no thought for the morrow; he tells stories such as the man who started to commit suicide by lying on the Erie railroad tracks and starved to death." Bennett, who did not normally like musicals, came to see *The Whirl of Society* again.

Nellie Revell, the Shuberts' press agent in Chicago—a heavyset whirlwind with a sign on her office door that read "Enter without knocking and remain the same way"—arranged to have Al interviewed by Katherine Synon, an early-day Dorothy Kilgallen. She found Jolson fidgety and nervous. He said very little, and a lot of what he did say was in dialect. "I don't," he finally declared, "remember one line about mah past."

Al soon got over his "interview fright," and the Jolson tongue eventually wagged "faster than any other tongue in show business." The following is from the St. Louis *Democrat* of February 16, 1932.

"Sure I like St. Louis. It has a great zoo. Now laugh that off, but do you know where Mrs. Jolson and I will be early in the morning. At the zoo, of course. We'll stay there until noon. I like zoos—and you have a great one here. They take my mind off my work. . . .

"And this is a great old town at that. I've been coming here—well, let's see, in the neighborhood of a thousand years, I guess. Years ago, anyhow. The old Standard, I believe, was where I first did my blackface stunt. Haven't been here for four years or so—last time was a week at Loew's and before that in *Big Boy*. Yes sir—a long time. Say, do you know I'm a Kentucky Colonel?"

Although still not billed above the title, Al was treated like a star while on tour in *The Whirl of Society*—until November. Gaby Deslys was the reason for his sudden loss of status.

On November 16th, in Trenton, New Jersey, Gaby opened in a tour of *Vera Violetta*—a production so disastrous that Jake Shubert closed it after one performance. Gaby and a few other principals were sent to Baltimore, where Jolson and company were due to open a three-night stand in *The Whirl of Society* the following evening. The two shows were then combined—hastily rewritten so that Gaby, as "Vera," could present *A Night with the Pierrots* to the *Society* guests. The new billing was as follows:

Gaby Deslys in *Vera Violetta*
and
The Whirl of Society with Al Jolson

Adding insult to injury was that Washington, D.C., Al's hometown, was next on the show's route. He had looked forward to coming home in triumph as the "star" of a big musical production. Now he was playing second fiddle to a modestly talented blonde Frenchwoman who seemed to spend most of her offstage time eating garlic.

There is a story about Jolson returning home on this trip and finding his father in the act of preparing a chicken for use as kosher food.

"Congratulations," Moshe is reputed to have told Al. "I hear you're a big manager."

"What? A manager??"

"Yes, I heard you . . ."

"Pop, I'm not the manager. I'm the star."

Moshe suddenly looked sad. "I'm sorry. It is very disappointing."

"No, it's not, pop. Look, the company manager gets seventy-five dollars a week. I get five hundred."

"But you are not the manager," sighed Moshe. Al was fit to be tied.

The story is probably true—not because Moshe was naive, but because the rabbi, with a twinkle in his eye, could never resist giving Al "the business." "He never missed a chance to take Al's ego down a peg," said Mel Hess, son of Moshe's brother Yakov.

The tour ended at the Majestic Theatre in Brooklyn on January 25, 1913. The next Winter Garden show, starring Gaby Deslys and featuring Al Jolson, had been in preparation for weeks; the principals had had their scripts since Christmas.

The new show was *The Honeymoon Express,* loosely based on a play called *The Turtle.* The plot concerned a divorce interrupted by a telegram stating that the husband has inherited four million francs from his Uncle Maurice—if he is married. It was the sort of fare that Irene Dunne would play so well in films.

Jolson's part in *The Honeymoon Express* was not much larger than the one he had had in *Vera Violetta,* but there was plenty of room to expand it. (This was tolerated in the days before the modern "integrated" musical, and was practically expected in the case of a comedian like Jolson.) Al overwhelmed the audience and critics when the show opened on February 6th.

"Al Jolson is the real star," wrote Acton Davies in the New York *Evening Sun.* "There wasn't half enough for him to do. . . . But just at the end, he had a Spanish song which aroused shrieks of laughter. The audience simply would not let go; even Gaby herself had to take a back seat on the piano stool—which she did with charming grace, by the way—while the audience made Mr. Jolson sing song after song. It's really a pleasure in these apathetic theatrical days to see an artist get such an ovation. And every bit of it was deserved." What made it all the more remarkable was that Al had a cold.

That, however, did not stop him from performing in the following Sunday's Winter Garden Concert. "He sang his head off," Sime wrote in *Variety,* "employing all the new numbers sung by him in the Gaby show. Thirty-eight minutes Mr. Jolson was on the stage without leaving it. Talk about [Harry] Lauder holding 'em off for fifty-five minutes; the Winter Garden crowd would remain listening to Al Jolson until he dropped dead from exhaustion."

The following item appeared on page five of the February 21, 1913, issue of *Variety:*

JOLSON PAYS KLEIN $700

The action started by Arthur Klein to recover a sum based upon an agreement to pay him $50 weekly by Al Jolson has been settled by the comedian paying his former representative $700 in liquidation of all claims.

Arthur Klein had been an extremely good agent for Al Jolson from 1909 to 1911. It was Klein who got Jolson his first solo bookings in big-time vaudeville, had pressure brought on Lew Dockstader to re-lease Al from a one-sided five-year contract, gotten him raises from the UBO, and arranged his first two contracts with the Shuberts. Klein had even placed his piloting of Jolson ahead of his job as booking manager for Percy G. Williams.

Al, however, was dissatisfied with Klein's work on his last con-tract, which called for him to receive $425 for the 1911–12 season and $500 for 1912–13. "You know I can get $1250 a week in vaudeville," Jolson wrote the Shuberts on May 27, 1912. "All I have to do is exept *(sic)* it . . . I will never forgive Arthur Klein for sign-ing me for this money, as I was sick at the time, and he had no right to do it." Al stopped paying Klein his commission the following September.

On February 28, 1913, one week after Jolson settled with Art Klein, the following lead was featured in *Variety:*

AL JOLSON RECEIVES $10,000 BONUS TO SIGN FOR 7 YEARS

It was actually for five years—Jolson's first "big money" contract with the Shuberts. He was guaranteed $1,000 a week for thirty-five weeks a year, plus the $10,000 bonus for signing and, most impor-tantly, *10 percent of profits on the shows that he appeared in.* Jolson would be rich before his thirty-fifth birthday in 1921.

The contract had been drawn up in 1912 and held in abeyance until Jolson severed his relationship with Klein. Lee Shubert, who had not forgotten the way Klein made a fool of him by keeping Jolson in vaudeville in 1910, had finally evened scores with the Vesta Tilley of Managers.

Arthur Klein, whose contract with Jolson would not have expired until 1916, had given up well over $10,000 by accepting $700 in liquidation of all claims. It would not have made any difference as far as Jolson's career was concerned, but the fact remains that he played Klein a very dirty trick.

Klein, who died in 1964, had nothing but good memories of Jol-son. Apparently, the two men made it up. Jolson, being Jolson, may have offered Klein a present of some kind to make amends. It is also possible that Al may have done favors for Art at a later date (Klein headed the Shuberts' vaudeville empire in the early '20s) that were worth more in the long run than the commissions he had cheated him of in the 1910s.

Al was the same Asa Joelson who had leaped for a playmate's throat in 1896—and then wanted to be friends again the next day.

"That was Jolson," Eddie Cantor would remember, "hot and cold."

"The World's Greatest Entertainer"

"The Shuberts may run the Winter Garden, but Al Jolson owns it. That dandy performer does as he wills with the audience, whether Sundays or on weekdays."

SIME SILVERMAN, *Variety*

Those people old enough to have seen Jolson at his peak remember him as a galvanic figure belting out a song while dancing on the Winter Garden runway, or joking, with his feet dangling into the orchestra pit. Those mental pictures describe Jolson in the spring of 1913. Al was twenty-seven at the time—the king of the Winter Garden, and practically the king of Broadway.

Al Jolson was in more than three-quarters of the Winter Garden Sunday Concerts held from February 6 to June 14, 1913, the Broadway run of *Honeymoon Express*. Audiences at those concerts never seemed to get enough of Jolson, although things did not go to Al's liking on one occasion.

Stella Mayhew and her husband, Billee Taylor, had not appeared at the Winter Garden in months. On March 30th, according to *Variety*, "the couple were unannounced on the board, and appeared just before the closing of the first half of the entertainment. When they had given sufficient for nearly two full acts and thought they would retire for the evening, the audience held up the performance until Miss Mayhew reappeared with Mr. Taylor. She sang 'Society Bear' and the hubbub kept up until 'That Develin' Tune' (some rag, too) and 'My Kentucky Girl' followed, Miss Mayhew and Mr. Taylor (who had a solo, but a poor song for it) were a regular riot."

Another act was waiting in the wings, but Al just told the audience to "Go on home. The show's over." The actors—in the wings and in the audience—took note. The Winter Garden's "blackfaced nightingale" could not stand competition.

Gaby Deslys left the cast on April 26th, and a "second edition" of *The Honeymoon Express* opened the following Monday night. Grace LaRue took over for Mlle. Deslys, and young Ina Claire, fresh

75

from her triumph in *The Quaker Girl,* replaced Fanny Brice. Jolson's part was enlarged, and the Winter Garden's big electric sign now read:

THE HONEYMOON EXPRESS
with
Al Jolson
Ina Claire   Grace LaRue

Jolson had already interpolated "You Made Me Love You" into the show. He did this song, one of the great hits of his career, in many different ways—in dialect, as comedy, with pathos, and with pulsating emphasis. On some occasions, he increased the beat on "Give me, give me, what I cry for" so that it became "Gimme, gimme, gimme, gimme, what I cry for" after he dropped to one knee.

One of the more popular—and ridiculous—stories about Jolson has him dropping to one knee as the result of an ingrown toenail and then covering up so effectively that he decided to keep the "bit" in as good business. Jolson himself was the source for the story, since it was one of the anecdotes he gave interviewers at the height of his stage career in the early 1920s. Most of the writers were glad to get the "copy," and few cared whether Jolson was being facetious.

The truth, however, is that Jolson stole the bit from Blossom Seeley. "Stole" may be too harsh a word. Miss Seeley had employed it when singing "Toddlin' the Todalo" in *A Night with the Pierrots* at the Winter Garden a year earlier—grinding to the floor and stretching her arms out to the ceiling. It was effective, but did not cause the sensation Al did with "You Made Me Love You." The difference was in the performers. Blossom Seeley had a marvelous stage presence. Jolson's stage persona was like God's.

Jolson usually wound up appearing in a Winter Garden concert if he was anywhere near the vicinity of the theatre on a Sunday night. If he was in an orchestra seat, word would spread to the audience, and the chant of "Jolson! Jolson! Jolson!" would force him onto the stage. "If I know the Shuberts," Al told Barry Gray in 1946, "they paid some guy to sit there and yell, 'We want Jolson.'"

Jolson pulled a stunt of his own on Sunday night, June 8th. Programmed to appear that evening, he instead decided to take his wife and Jean Carlson to dinner. "He was pretty tired, and he didn't want to work," said Jean. "He wanted to just disappear.

"The three of us had dinner, and went back to the Ansonia Hotel.

There were three or four entrances, so Al rushed up and told them to put guards at all the doors to say he wasn't in. They were looking all over town for him. I don't know whether they caught up with him or not. I don't think so. But I know he was hiding around.

"He was like a little boy when he'd do things like that. He'd hide, even though he'd been standing out in full view of everybody just a little before."

The Honeymoon Express closed six days later. The UBO offered Jolson $5,000 to play two weeks at the Brighton Beach Music Hall, but the Shuberts, who had Al under an exclusive contract, made him turn the offer down. Jolson stayed in New York through July 1st, when he became a third degree mason at St. Cecile Lodge, and then took another auto trip to California. This time, his companions included Jimmy and theatrical impresarios F. Ray Comstock and L. Lawrence Weber. Henrietta traveled by train, and spent the next few weeks at her parents' house in Oakland, while Al traveled around "Frisco" with "the boys."

Henrietta, like the rest of Jolson's four wives, was a very patient woman. Her marriage to Al would not have otherwise lasted as long as it did. She partially made up for Jolson's neglect through her family. Like Ruby Keeler's family years later, the Keller family—Henrietta had a sister and a brother—were a close-knit clan, and Henrietta, like Ruby, was especially devoted to her mother.

Her mother was another reason Henrietta stayed with Jolson. Danish-born Sefani Lanep Keller saw it as a woman's duty to be a good wife, devoted to her husband. Henrietta had been raised to think in the same way. It would take years of neglect, humiliation, and abuse to change her mind.

The third reason for Henrietta's failure to rebel was Al Jolson himself. He was a naturally magnetic individual, and there was of course, the thrill of being married to a famous entertainer. There was also something deeper, something that appealed to the maternal instinct women of Henrietta Keller's generation nurtured. Jolson was a child, and, like a child, he demanded care, devotion, and attention *at specific times*. If he failed to receive it, he would throw a tantrum or become morose—in the manner of a child.

There was also something queerly noble about Jolson's frequent apologies and promises to reform his bad behavior. He seemed both innocent of any wrongdoing and totally remorseful—like a child version of Hercules bemoaning his misdeeds and wailing for the chance to make amends. Al was often truly sorry for the times he had been mean or thoughtless, even though he inevitably would do the same cruel things again.

It was these qualities—in Jolson and the women that he married—that made Al's marriages last as long as they did.

Jolson was impressed with some youngsters he saw at San Francisco's Orpheum Theatre that summer in an act called "Kid Kabaret." Unknown to Al, the "youngsters," twenty-one-year-old Eddie Cantor and fifteen-year-old George Jessel, had been haunting his familiar hangouts in an effort to find the great Jolie.

Al finally met George and Eddie at the Orpheum stage door and took them to a kosher restaurant on Turk Street in San Francisco. "It was the craziest dinner you ever *heard*," Cantor told his ghostwriter, Jane Kesner Ardmore. "Georgie and I, the two bigmouths, couldn't think of a thing to say. Jolson did a monologue. When he went to the men's room, Georgie and I flipped a coin to see who'd follow him. I won. A few minutes later, I came running out to tell him, 'Georgie, that Jolson! He does it like *anybody!*'"

Jolson became known to the entire country when the Shuberts sent him on tour with *The Honeymoon Express* the following season. It was like old home week when the show opened at Nixon's Apollo Theatre in Atlantic City on September 18, 1913; Fred E. Moore was the house manager.

Henrietta traveled with Al on this tour, but Jolson's treatment of her failed to impress Rae Samuels, a tall woman who specialized in dialect and "rube" songs. Miss Samuels played Marcelle for the first four and a half months of the tour.

"He was a mean man. He would never let his wife use that car when he was working. She could never phone and have the man (Jimmy) take her shopping or anything—never. He didn't care where she went, but he wouldn't allow her to go in the car.

"I had no trouble with him, but how selfish and how mean he was with that wife.

"I heard them quarreling. Henrietta's mother had bought a Singer sewing machine out there in Oakland. She had signed to pay two dollars a month on it, and he raised H-E-double L over that.

"Now imagine! It's hard to believe, isn't it, that he would be like that? But to the races, to gamble, he would *go!*"

Al had substituted the less dangerous vice of horse race gambling for drinking—as if celebrating his new income.

Jolson would become the most familiar theatrical figure on the American turf. He gambled on the races almost every day, but seldom wagered anywhere near the sums many thought. One source claimed Al had a code with his bookie whereby "five thousand dollars" actually meant "fifty." The code was designed to make those nearby think "Jolie" was a real "plunger." Al tended to think of heavy gambling as a sign of masculinity.

Bessie Harris, one of the chorines on tour, remembered hearing that Jolson had given his winnings to a bellhop on one occasion. (Jolie seemed to give more money to bellhops than he gave to Henrietta.) Miss Harris' recollections of Al were far different from those of Rae Samuels. "He was a kind man," said Bessie. "I remember one personal incident where I was crying to myself with a felon on my finger. He took me into his dressing room, squeezed the infection out, and dressed it like a doctor."

Jolson was obsessed with medicine, and one small satchel in his luggage was always filled with bottles of pills, liquids, assorted home remedies, and first-aid materials. Harry Akst, the composer of "Baby Face," summed it up in a 1951 article for *Cosmopolitan*. "Al knew just enough medicine to get himself into trouble, but not enough to get himself out.

"He patronized a small army of doctors, but insisted they never knew what they were talking about. He liked to tell them not only what was wrong with him, but also how to cure it. He always opened *Time* magazine to the page headed Medicine. When a newfangled miracle drug emerged from the laboratories, Al would have it before the drugstores."

Jolson did not miss the opportunity of having his father see him on stage when *The Honeymoon Express* played the Belasco Theatre in Washington, D.C. Moshe, Hessi, and their four children all sat in the balcony, Rabbi Yoelson having refused Al's offer of orchestra seats.

When the show was over, Al had Frank Holmes send an usher up to bring Moshe backstage. The rabbi refused.

"Tell Asa," he said, "that a father does not go to a son. A son comes to a father."

Al was shaken when he got the message, but he hurried to see Moshe. "How was I?" he asked, still the child looking for approval.

"You must have been good," his father told him. "Every time you weren't on, the people read their programs."

Al had tears in his eyes at that point, and Rae Samuels said there was something the matter with him for the remainder of the week in Washington. "Something," she correctly surmised, "happened to him there."

This was made emphatic when she found Al backstage in the Belasco's service elevator. He was banging his head against the padded walls.

Rae Samuels left the cast at the end of January 1914, when she signed a long-term contract with the UBO. She was in the show, however, long enough to see that Jolson did not like competitors.

In December 1913, *The Honeymoon Express* played the Royal Alexandra Theatre in Toronto. The people of that city, like their British cousins, loved to watch good dancing, and they gave prolonged applause to Doyle & Dixon's "Moving Man" number in the first act—just before Jolson's entrance. The audience was still applauding when Al entered, forcing him to hold his lines till it subsided. When Jolson came off, he walked past the dance team and said, "Don't let that happen again."

Al may have been a twenty-seven-year-old father figure to the chorines, but he was certainly not popular with many of his fellow principals. Not that he had cause to worry. More and more, *The Honeymoon Express* became a Jolson vehicle. Al was acquiring even greater self-confidence, and the following reviews, from February 1914, indicate the way in which he dominated the show.

[Kansas City] It is principally Al Jolson's show. He is on the stage only a short time in the first act, but he makes up most of the entertainment in the second. He is repeating the popularity he achieved here last season. The audience simply couldn't get enough of his songs and banter. He was encored so extravagantly, and was so generous in his responses that he was almost exhausted when he exclaimed toward the end of the show: 'Haven't you folks got any homes to go to?'

[St. Louis (Ralph E. Mooney in the *Star*] The show would be hopeless without him. It is his tremendously popular rendition of various song hits that keeps the pace alive. The other members of the cast are fairly capable, but would be lost without him.

[Columbus (Lisle D. Bell)] ". . . Time and again he disclosed that he is a superb comedian of the first water. His singing of 'The Bells,' simulating Irving and Shea in the famous play, was enough to show that he is to the average blackface comedian as diamonds to brilliants.

[Toledo (G. M. W. in the *Blade*)] . . . [Jolson] was, of course, the hit of the evening. None of his songs were new, but he sang them after a fashion of his own, acting them out and putting odd kinks into them. And best of all, he has a good voice, which is more than can be said of most of the other principals in the show.

Jolson really opened up when *The Honeymoon Express* reached Seattle, stopping the show for almost half an hour in the second act and singing everything from "You Made Me Love You" to "The Rosary." The tour ended at the Metropolitan Opera House in Minneapolis on Saturday night, May 30, 1914, leaving Jolson free to attend the opening of another Shubert musical, *The Whirl of the World*, at the Grand Opera House in Chicago the following evening. Willie Howard, one of the theatre's truly great comedians, pointed him out to the audience. "There was excited hand clapping and there was insistent calling upon him by name," reported James O'Donnell Bennett, "till at last, to keep the peace, he had to leave his seat in the second row. . . . In Europe, such caressing of a stage favorite is not uncommon. In self-conscious America, it is, and the audience's release of its liking at the Grand was pleasant to see."

At the age of twenty-eight, Al Jolson was the most popular musical comedy performer in the country, and even the old-timers who remembered such nineteenth-century greats as minstrel Billy Emerson said no one had ever captivated audiences like Jolson.

Al was not a person who just happened to be in the right place at the right time; he was clearly a unique and wonderful performer. What was his secret, if there was one? "The moment Jolson walked on a stage," wrote John Crosby, "you got the impression that something important was going to happen. Frequently, nothing important did happen, but you kept feeling that, in a minute or two, it would." Samson Raphaelson said watching Jolson come on stage was like watching "a duck hitting water."

The onstage Jolson was a curious amalgamation of two very different qualities. In one respect, he was ethereal, the "black Peter Pan of the Winter Garden." On the other, he appeared to be a "man's man," sharing an unspoken camaraderie with every male member of the audience. Al never pleaded with an audience, and he never asked for sympathy. He teased, cajoled, and thrilled them, in the manner of a great violinist or lover.

The audience was a replacement for Naomi, and, if Jolson made love to them, it must be remembered that he had a decidedly huge Oedipus complex. His mother had died when he was a child, but the audience was deathless. It would never leave him.

Henrietta underwent an appendectomy in April, but was fully recovered by June 16th, when the Jolsons sailed for Europe on the *Mauretania* with Jake Shubert, Al's friend Lou Rosenberg, and Melville Ellis. Their first port of call was England, where Jolson and Ellis entertained at a reception given by Mrs. Claude Graham-White, wife of the famous aviator, in honor of Prince Christopher of Greece, nephew of Queen Alexandra. According to the Shuberts' own New York *Review:*

> Jolson proved a revelation to all those present. He has never appeared publicly in London, and Mrs. Graham-White's guests had no idea what was in store for them when the famous Winter Garden entertainer appeared. He soon had the assembly in a roar of laughter and kept them in that condition for a solid hour, holding the platform largely through impromptu humor, his American specialties hardly fitting the occasion.
>
> Next day, practically every manager and agent in London made Jolson offers of record salaries for appearances in the music halls of London and the continent, and in musical comedy. Being under contract with the Messrs. Shubert, however, it was impossible for the comedian to accept.

Jolson and his companions proceeded on to France, Venice, and the Swiss Alps before sailing for home from Hamburg in late July. It was Henrietta's first visit to Europe, and, as things turned out, her last.

Dancing Around, Jolson's next Winter Garden show, marked the first time he received top billing on opening night. Ironically, it was the only time he would get competition. Most of the show's plot revolved around Bernard Granville (father of Bonita, and a great performer in his own right), and, during rehearsals, it looked as though Granville, not Jolson, would walk off with first honors. Al appeared lethargic.

Dancing Around was scheduled to try out at the Hyperion Theatre in New Haven, and the cast left New York on a special train on Sunday, September 27th. The show was not yet up to Broadway standards, and the dress rehearsal went on through the night.

Jolson rehearsed without a break until three o'clock on Monday morning and then left the stage, locked himself into an electrician's booth, and slept until ten. Then he went back to the stage and rehearsed, off and on, for six additional hours.

That night, the "Jolson magic" worked again, and Bernard Granville was hardly noticed.

Despite a cast that also included Cecil Cunningham, Doyle & Dixon, Lawrence D'Orsay, Melville Ellis, Frank Carter, and twenty-three-year-old Clifton Webb, *Dancing Around* was a poor show. The first act was weak, and Sigmund Romberg's score was hardly worth the effort with the notable exception of "Venetia," a ballad sung by Jolson in Act II. The reviewer for *The Strand* said there was "as much art in Jolson's rendition of 'Venetia' as there is in Caruso's singing of 'Canio's Lament,' and the human appeal is the same."

The main feature of the show's run at the Winter Garden was Jolson's repeated singing of an English novelty song called "Sister Susie's Sewing Shirts for Soldiers." Jolson first attempted to popularize this tongue twister by offering ten dollars to anyone in the audience who could sing the chorus through without a break. Later, he began a search for additional encore choruses, with Harold Atteridge, the show's librettist, and Melville Ellis as a two-man committee to select the winners.

Jolson sang those "winners" at a special "Sister Susie" matinee on Tuesday, December 15, 1914. One of them was called "Brother Bennie's Baking Buns for Belgians" by a youth named Irving Caesar. "I went down there and he pinched my cheek and so forth," recalled Caesar, "but I don't think he remembered me." Caesar would write "Swanee" five years later.

Al was still king of the Winter Garden Sunday Concerts. On January 24, 1915, he closed the show by holding the stage for forty minutes after seventeen other acts had gone ahead of him. "Jolson seemed to be trying out the house for endurance," remarked Sime, "although entertaining them every minute. About midway in his turn he told the orchestra to play a waltz, as he had to make a change. Al reappeared in a dress to travesty Olga Petrova, and his travesty was almost as funny as Petrova's act.

"Besides which Jolson sang songs, kissed Jose Collins on the mouth as she was seated in an orchestra chair, and shook hands with everybody he knew in the first row. In addition to the 'Susie' song, which closed his turn, Al sang 'All For the Ladies,' 'Fatima Brown,' and 'Tennessee, I Hear You Calling Me,' told some new stories, and got away with all of them. Jolson appeared to be having as good a time as the house. When you can do what Jolson can do at the Winter Garden, you are doing a lot. He does things no one else would think of, and if he is drawing as well during the week to *Dancing Around* as he does on Sunday night, he is the Shuberts' undefiled gold mine."

Dancing Around closed its Broadway run on February 13th and opened a three-week engagement at the Lyric Theatre in Philadelphia the following Monday. Al was slightly lame at this time—the result of a collision with a new angle in the Winter Garden runway—and "danced little," according to the Philadelphia *Inquirer*. Jolson's dancing—those impossible, quick little steps he did in the midst of up-tempo songs, was an amalgamation of the "eccentric" dancing he had seen teams like Fitzgerald & Gilday and Monroe & Chandler do in California vaudeville. The step (or steps) can best be seen between choruses of "Why Do They All Take the Night Boat to Albany?" in *Mammy*, one of Jolson's Warner Bros. movies. They were as much a part of the Jolson staple as the blackface, the two-fingered whistling, and the brown, nasal tones.

Dancing Around reached San Francisco on June 21st. Henrietta was living at her parents' house, Al having sent her home before the show began its tour. Jolson, though, spent little time in Oakland. The Panama-Pacific Exposition was in San Francisco, and Jolie was seen dancing on the fair grounds with a young lady other than his wife.

Jolson did not spend much more time with his wife when *Dancing Around* closed for four weeks during the summer. After a few days in Oakland, he went up to Santa Cruz, where a few young members of the cast had gone for a vacation. Al invited everybody to a mountain tourist camp, and one cast member remembered watching the "happy boy-man singing to the tops of those magnificent giant redwood trees."

The tour resumed in Portland, Oregon, on August 8, 1915, and things went well until October, when the bad spot on Al's lung became inflamed. Performances in Louisville, Lexington, and Dayton were cancelled, and Jolson checked into a sanitarium for a few days' rest. It proved insufficient, and one doctor told Al he would lose his voice completely if he did not quit for a long rest at once.

The critic for the Syracuse, N.Y. *Post-Standard,* unaware of Jolson's condition, said that he seemed "loath to work unless he sees the receipts in the box office. Possibly, if it had been a $3,000-house, instead of a house half that price, Syracuse theatre goers would have seen a better performance. That, however, is Al Jolson's own business." Jolson, anxious to become familiar with each audience before he stepped on stage, had started selling tickets in the box office before each performance. Mindful of the Shuberts' business reputation, he had also started counting the receipts at intermission.

Jolson, cranky and despondent, wired Henrietta to join him in Baltimore. He wanted sympathy, but Henrietta seemed more upset at Al's gambling at Bowie than she was by his poor health. Jolson told the press he had won five thousand dollars, but she knew the truth. And if he was so sick, why didn't he stay in his suite at the Hotel Belvedere instead of going to the races? Al, of course, said going to the races ("Dr. Outdoors," as he called it) was the best medicine in the world.

It may have been—for Al—but the Jolson voice did not show much improvement during the show's engagement at Baltimore's Academy of Music. And, just as Jolson made his audiences share his joy, he now included them in his misery.

> This Mr. Jolson is billed as the star of the production [wrote an angry patron to the Baltimore *Sun*.] But on Wednesday night he evidently thought Baltimore unworthy of so much as a twinkle.
>
> To say that the company was second rate is putting it mildly. The lengthy cast was made up entirely of unheard of persons, gathered together, if one may judge by appearances, for the provinces, owing to their cheapness. The scenery was on the verge of disintegration, the costumes were makeshift and dirty, and the entire performance reeked of bad burlesque.
>
> The audience was bored, as well it might be. This annoyed Mr. Jolson awfully. So he started in to punish it. In the first place, he cut out all of his songs. Mr. Jolson proceeded to "kid" the audience unmercifully, saying (in a scene) over the telephone that he sometimes sang, but wasn't going to sing tonight. Two of the scenes of the last act were cut out, and the entire performance given with an arrogant indifference that was insulting to the last degree.

Henrietta was appalled at Al's behavior. ("She said, 'Yes, you're a big star now, but you keep giving performances like that and you won't be for long,' " Jean Carlson remembered.) The Jolsons left for Washington on Saturday morning, leaving Harry Wardell to go on for Al as Gus in the last two performances in Baltimore.

By Monday night, in Washington, Jolson was mysteriously well, and the Belasco Theatre audience was treated to full-voiced renditions of "Tennessee, I Hear You Calling Me," "I'm Seeking for Siegfried," "When I Leave the World Behind," and "Bring Along Your Dancing Shoes." Al even agreed to play a benefit for a Methodist church in the southwestern quarter of the city.

Jolson had known J. Patrick Tumulty, secretary to President Woodrow Wilson, for several years, but when Tumulty arranged for Al to meet the president, on Friday, December 3, 1915, the immigrant from Seredzius was understandably excited.

Al was pushed through rows of senators, representatives, and military officers until he was in a room with a tall, raw-boned man.

"I'm Al Jolson," Al said, "and I want to see the president."

"I am the president," said Wilson, holding out his hand. So much for Jolson's knowledge of political affairs.

The president was scheduled to see *Dancing Around* with his fiancée, Mrs. Edith Bolling Galt, that evening. Here, at last, was Al's big chance to "show" his father. He sent half a dozen tickets to the Yoelson home.

When Jolson made his entrance, he found that those seats—those *front row* seats—were empty. Henrietta was there, looking her best, and President Wilson was there with Mrs. Galt. But Moshe, Hessi, and the children were conspicuously absent.

On Sunday, the tour over, Al went to the Yoelson home and saw his father.

"Why didn't you come? I sent you all those tickets."

"On *Shabbes* eve? I couldn't."

"I thought you'd make an exception. I was singing for the president."

"I was singing for God."

The old man had won again.

Al and Henrietta left for New York the following morning and checked into the same Biltmore Hotel suite that Henry Ford had occupied during preparations for the famous "peace expedition."

"Peace?" Al snorted later in the day. "Where do you get that stuff? There's a line of newspaper reporters outside my door a mile long shouting in queries as to how many passports I have and when am I going to sail. The peace chambers, they call these rooms, but I haven't the slightest idea why. My wife has persisted in quarreling with me ever since we got here. Peace, eh? Well, I'm against it."

The Jolsons spent the next two weeks vacationing in Florida. When they returned to New York, Al threw himself into rehearsals for *Robinson Crusoe, Jr.,* first of the great Jolson vehicles that would eventually include *Sinbad, Bombo,* and *Big Boy.*

Henrietta, as she always had, stayed up with Al the night before the opening with a pot of coffee—trying her best to keep him relatively calm while giving him last-minute notes she had taken during the last dress rehearsal. She was the perfect helpmate, but Jolson ignored her in every possible way once *Robinson Crusoe, Jr.* opened.

Robinson Crusoe, Jr. was a throw-back to the exotic "extravaganzas" popular on Broadway in the 1880s. The plot concerned a millionaire who falls asleep and dreams of being Robinson Crusoe when a movie company takes over his estate to make a picture. His chauffeur, Gus Jackson (Jolson) becomes his man Friday, but, unlike the characters in Daniel Defoe's novel, Crusoe and Friday are not confined to just one island. A pirate ship anchors off shore, captures them, and sentences Crusoe to walk the plank in the first act finale. The second act finds Gus and a revived Crusoe in Ragmachottschie, the Silver City. The millionaire finally wakes up, and finding it was all a dream, decides to throw a ball.

This ridiculous scenario provided Jolson with some of his greatest opportunities for comedy. There was the scene in which, hunted by cannibals, he popped out of a tree stump to ask, "Anybody got any aspirin?" and the burlesque on the famed meeting of "master and man," in which Al made his chin quiver as he vainly tried to find the words to thank his rescuer.

"I don't mind going on record as saying that he is one of the few instinctively funny men on our stage," wrote reviewer Charles Darnton in the New York *Evening World*. "Everything he touches turns to fun. To watch him is to marvel at his humorous vitality. He is the old-time minstrel man turned to modern account. With a song, a word, or even a suggestion he calls forth spontaneous laughter. And here you have the definition of a born comedian."

Jolson received no extra pay for his appearances in the early Winter Garden Sunday concerts. By 1916, however, he could tell the Shuberts whether he felt "strong" or "well" enough to do Sunday performing. Al was not billed to appear in most of the concerts during the run of *Robinson Crusoe, Jr.* at the Winter Garden, but he responded to the Shuberts' SOS sign to "save the show" on more than one occasion.

Halfway through the program of February 27th, for example, Jolie's name was unexpectedly flashed to the audience by placard. People exclaimed "Jolson" as they burst into applause.

One of Jolson's trademarks was the way he pointed to one person in the audience—or what seemed like one person—and cocked his head down as if acknowledging an earlier agreement. He would then ad lib a few lines, drawing laughs with the way he exaggerated the last word of the key sentence. Al had a tremendous sense of *living* on a stage, a joyous energy that enveloped the audience and made it one with him. "Every person has an aura about him, a kind of electricity he generates," said Samson Raphaelson, author of *The Jazz Singer*. "Someday, there will be a way to measure it. No one, though, had it like Jolson. That's what made him so great—so unique."

"Well, what do you want to hear?" Jolson would ask, his arms stretched out and downward in the manner of a host. The requests would come, and Al would sort them out like a man in charge of a gambling room in the back of a saloon. "Wait a minute, you want

'You Made Me Love You'? Professor, pass the mustard. 'You Made Me Love You.' "

Then he'd go into the number, interpolating ad lib lines and special bits as the atmosphere would move him. Then would come more clowning, Jolie telling stories, mugging, doing physical comedy, and getting very familiar with certain members of the audience. (Al once saw a man leaving his seat and asked, "Where are you goin'?" The man looked back and said, "I thought it was intermission." That, at least, is what Al later claimed.)

He'd sing another song, run up and down the runway and across the stage, whooping it up with dancing, whistling, and enough energy for two evenings' worth of musical comedy. The perspiration would be pouring from Al's face, the audience caught up in the ecstasy of his performance. "He's got 'em," one performer in the wings would whisper to another. And indeed he had. Al took up the time of several acts at this February 27th concert. Not until he sensed the time was right did he withdraw and allow the program to continue. It was eleven o'clock before the intermission came. After that, the audience was as tired as Jolson, and the rest of the performers came in for the dregs of its applause.

Things like that caused many actors to hate Jolson. At least a few, however, understood. "He didn't do it with malice aforethought," said one woman on that Sunday evening bill.

P.S.: The Shuberts soon agreed to pay Al an extra $300 for every Sunday concert he appeared in.

Jolson's biggest song successes in *Robinson Crusoe, Jr.* were "Yaaka Hula Hickey Dula' and "Where Did Robinson Crusoe Go with Friday on Saturday Night?" Al acquired "exclusive singing rights" to both songs from the publishers, Waterson, Berlin & Snyder, and was annoyed to learn that Belle Baker was using "Where Did Robinson Crusoe Go?" in her vaudeville act.

Al and Ted Snyder were in front row seats when Belle opened at the Palace on Monday afternoon, March 13, 1916. She did two choruses of "Crusoe," looked at Jolson, and said, "Come on, Al, join in." Jolson immediately jumped out of his seat, rushed up the aisle, and walked out of the theatre.

Jolson and Snyder asked Elmer Rogers, manager of the Palace, to have Baker cut the song out of her act. Belle, however, sang the song again that night, and said that she would sing it whenever she liked.

In an attempt to revive his failing marriage, Al told Henrietta he would take her to Hawaii when *Robinson Crusoe, Jr.* closed at the

Winter Garden on June 10, 1916. The Jolsons entrained for Oakland on June 14th, but Al changed his mind about going to Hawaii after reading a review of a show in Los Angeles called *Canary Cottage*, starring Trixie Friganza and featuring Eddie Cantor, the young man he had seen in "Kid Kabaret" three years before.

Jolson stuck his wife in a car, drove four hundred miles to Los Angeles, and saw *Canary Cottage* at the Mason Opera House that evening. Al did not go backstage after the performance. "He told me about it later," recalled Cantor. "It was tough for him to compliment any actor."

Al left Henrietta at her parents' house in Oakland when he went back east in August. His half-hearted attempt to save their marriage had ended.

Robinson Crusoe, Jr. opened a fifteen-month national tour at the Nixon Theatre in Atlantic City on August 28, 1916. To quote even a sampling of the reviews Jolson garnered on this tour would be superfluous, but the following testimonial to what was probably one of his greatest performances appeared in a letter published in the *Morning Telegraph*, an anti-Shubert paper.

> I happened to be in Boston last Saturday [November 11, 1916], and, in the evening, went to see Al Jolson in *Robinson Crusoe, Jr.*
>
> When this production was in New York, at the Winter Garden, I saw it several times, and always enjoyed it; but in all my experience as a theatre-goer, I had never seen a performer receive such an ovation as Mr. Jolson did last Saturday evening.
>
> Jolson has made his audiences laugh and applaud at the Winter Garden and other places, but at the Shubert Theatre in Boston the audience yelled. In fact, I have never heard such cheering and such genuine enthusiasm given to a performer or to a performance in all my experience as a theatregoer, which covers a period of more than twenty years.
>
> To be exact, Mr. Jolson stopped the show three times, and in each instance a scene was delayed and the audience simply wouldn't allow the performance to proceed. Mr. Jolson had to plead with his audience.
>
> Some of the people in the audience stood up, cheered, applauded, and threw hats in the air simultaneously during the second act.

Despite his obvious value to the Shuberts, Jolson was not yet a full "star" in the sense of having his name billed above the title. That honor came to him on Monday, January 1, 1917, after *Robinson Crusoe, Jr.* opened at the Garrick Theatre in Chicago. Ashton

Stevens' review in the Chicago *Herald Examiner* had listed the show's cast as follows:

Al Jolson .... AL JOLSON

The Shuberts finally gave Al star billing. "I'm sorry they did it," Jolson told a Chicago *Post* reporter, "and I'm going to write Mr. Shubert to restore the old order of things. I want something for a goal . . . to strive for. Years ago, I needed money, and needed it badly. I worked hard for it. Now I have all I need. Aside from recognition as a star, there's nothing much left to stir the ambition of a fellow in my walk of life. I'd like to have that star stuff ahead of me to be a sort of pacemaker to speed me up instead of having it in my pocket."

Jolson did not write "Mr. Shubert" to restore the old order of things, but the quote contains a *psychological* truth. For years to come, Al Jolson would tour more often, and more willingly, than any other star in the American musical theatre. The more one-night stands he played, the better Jolson liked it. He seemed to be on a great search for something "up ahead" at the next outpost.

Robinson Crusoe, Jr. played a total of eight weeks in Chicago before leaving to tour the smaller midwestern cities. Newspaper advertisements placed by Ben Atwell, the advance man, now referred to Jolson as "The World's Greatest Entertainer." It was the first time he received that billing.

Modern critics tend to think the billing was preposterous, especially since on surviving films and records Jolson does not appear to have been "The World's Greatest Entertainer."

It was readily conceded, in his day, that Jolson did not register in any medium except live theatre. On the stage, he was a truly great performer, perhaps the greatest of all time, although a flawed one. Jolson's colleagues considered his onstage references to money and receipts ("If those three-dollar seats are filled, we're out of trouble already") "unprofessional," and at least one critic took exception to the sometimes folksy way he took the audience into his personal confidence. Perhaps Al Jolson's greatest onstage fault, however, was his inconsistency. "On the great nights, when everything is right," wrote Gilbert Seldes, "Jolson is driven by a power beyond himself." On other nights, he was laconic or, on some occasions, forced.

James Barton was more skilled than Jolson, Danny Kaye more facile, and Sammy Davis, Jr. more versatile. Each of these extraordinarily talented men deserves a place among the truly great performers of all-time. No one, however, has come close to giving audiences the genuine experience that Jolson did. In that sense alone, he lived up to his billing.

Robinson Crusoe, Jr. toured through May 26, 1917 (Jolson's thirty-first birthday), broke for an eleven-day vacation, and reopened at the Metropolitan Opera House in St. Paul on June 7th. In July, the company played a two-week engagement at the Mason Opera House in Los Angeles, and Henry Christeen Warnack, who reviewed the opening-night performance for the Los Angeles *Times,* said Jolson was "the only man in the world who can imbue a nance part with anything except disgust."

Charles Chaplin and several other movie stars were in the audience that night, and many of the teen-aged chorines in the show were fascinated by the lure of Hollywood. Jolson, though, preferred the company of boxers, baseball players, and the people he found at Barron Long's Watts Tavern.

Al and a few cronies would go there after the night's show and hang around until 1:00 a.m., when the tavern closed and everybody headed for another place Long owned in nearby Vernon.

In Vernon, Jolson heard Mike Lyman and Blondie Clark do a song called " 'N' Everything." The number was the work of young George Gard (Buddy) DeSylva, a twenty-two year-old student who played ukulele in Long's six-piece "Hawaiian" band. Al took an immediate liking to young Buddy, told him he was "the greatest ukulele player" he had ever heard, and took him back to Oakland when *Robinson Crusoe, Jr.* closed for three weeks in mid-August. Given the rumors about Jolson's sexuality, it is tempting to speculate on the exact nature of their relationship. Al seems to have looked upon Buddy as a type of son—despite the fact that he was only nine years older.

Robinson Crusoe, Jr. began its third and final tour at the Orpheum Theatre in Ogden, Utah, on September 2, 1917, and played more than fifty different cities in the following two and a half months. Most of these engagements were one-nighters, and Jolson, with the consent of Jake Shubert, canceled two cities in order to attend World Series games in Chicago. Two other stands were cancelled due to wartime government appropriation of the railroads, a widespread situation with disastrous consequences for live theatre. Many of the country's local managers, unable to book live attractions, started showing movies—a venture that proved so profitable that they never went back to live shows. The "road" practically died as a result.

Talking pictures, radio, and the Depression dealt the final blow some twelve years later.

Thirty-one-year-old Louis Epstein owned and managed Scranton, Pennsylvania's Majestic Theatre in 1917. Epstein, who had been in the theatrical business since the age of twelve, was assistant advance man for a burlesque show called *Across the Pacific* in 1905, the year he met Al Jolson at the Academy Hotel in New York.

Since Epstein's salary was small, he "got a daytime job across the river in Hoboken, unloading peaches for four dollars a day—starting at 4:00 a.m. One day, a man whispered to me that I could make ten dollars a day if I had a helper to whom I could pass some of the peaches off the other side of the freight car." Lou recruited Jolson for the purpose.

They were soon caught, and Epstein lost his daytime job. Lou, however, did a valuable favor for young Jolson at the time. It was he who taught Al how to whistle.

"Al Jolson could whistle," said Lou's great-niece "Beanie" Hoffman Dworkin, "but not that sharp whistle with the two fingers. And Uncle Louie could do it. They would practice for hours and hours on end until Uncle Louie taught him how.

"It was a standing joke. We had records in our home of Jolson whistling, and my uncle would often say, 'I wonder if that was me doing the whistling or Jolson.' "

The next recorded meeting between Jolson and Epstein was in New Orleans in 1909, when Al was working for Lew Dockstader and Lou was managing *The Night Owls,* another burlesque show. It was Epstein who lent Jolson the fifty dollars he used to go to the west coast and work for I. P. Wilkerson.

"Eppy," as Al called him, prospered in the years that followed. He became the manager of *The Merry Whirl,* the best burlesque show in the business, and married one of the performers, Maudie Heath. He bought the Majestic Theatre in his native Scranton, but was facing an uncertain future when *Robinson Crusoe, Jr.* came to the nearby Academy of Music on November 5th.

Things had been mounting up on Jolson: sheet music, records, box office percentages, and the countless details that made up the life of a major star. Frank Holmes had been handling the correspondence, but there was an obvious limit to what even a valet could do. Jolson clearly needed an experienced manager he could trust.

Eppy accepted when Al offered him the job, put his nephew, Joe, in charge of the Majestic, and prepared to meet Al in New York at

Christmas time. With one sabbatical, from 1932 to 1940, Epstein would remain Al Jolson's manager until Al died.

"Uncle Louie was close to his own brother, [said his great-niece Beanie] "but his brother never amounted to too much—financially or otherwise. He was a night watchman—always an honest job, but never much of anything.

"He had a close feeling with Jolson—as though he were a brother. And then, I think, he idolized him, in a way. I think he had him on a pedestal, and though he saw all his faults, he idolized him. And I think it gave Uncle Louie a certain sense of accomplishment—of purpose. He was *Al Jolson's manager*.

"Al was very bossy. He could boss Uncle Louie around and Uncle Louie jumped. I saw it. And then, there were times when you would see them just sitting and talking as you and I would be sitting and talking."

Robinson Crusoe, Jr. closed in Springfield, Mass. on November 17, 1917. Jolson was now approaching the pinnacle of his stage career . . . and heading for his first divorce.

The First Divorce

"Outside of my liking for wine, women, and race horses, I'm a regular husband."

*S*inbad, Jolson's next show, opened at the Winter Garden on February 14, 1918. Al's name was now up in big lights—each letter four feet high—making him literally the brightest star on Broadway.

The first scene in *Sinbad* was an "Amateur Dog Show" at the "North Shore Country Club." Meehan's Leaping Hounds were featured, and the New York *Sun* reported that the "spectators held their breath while the long greyhounds gradually increased the height of their leaps one after the other."

Jolson, always a nervous wreck on opening nights, paced back and forth backstage and muttered about having to "follow a dog act." He had not objected to the hounds during the show's try-out in New Haven, and would not object to them again. Al's first appearance brought an ovation "such as a chief speaker at a political convention might" have gotten, and he forgot all about Meehan's Leaping Hounds.

Jolson was known primarily as a singing comedian, but his first song in *Sinbad* was a ballad. "Jolson," wrote Charles Darnton in the *World,* "whether he knows it or not, hits the singing mark of his career with 'Rock-a-Bye Your Baby with a Dixie Melody.' " Al sang the first chorus over the heads of the audience, as if he were alone in the vast theatre. On the second chorus, he seemed to reach out, yearning for them to embrace him. The power of that yearning, coupled with the snugly rhyming couplets of the lyric, made the song a standard.

Sinbad was another "extravaganza," similar to *Robinson Crusoe, Jr.,* and the remainder of Jolson's material was comic. His songs, outside of "Rock-a-Bye," included "Why Do They All Take the Night Boat to Albany?" "Cleopatra," "I Wonder Why She Kept On Saying, 'Si, Si, Si, Si, Señor,' " and " 'N' Everything." Al did not revive ' 'N' Everything" during his post-World War II comeback, but Gilbert Seldes singled it out for attention in "The Daemonic in the American Theatre," his great essay on Jolson.

> In the first weeks of *Sinbad,* he sang the words of " 'N' Everything" as they are printed. Gradually (I saw the show in many phases), he interpolated, improvised, always with his absolute sense of rhythmic effect; until at the end it was a series of amorous cries and shouts of triumph to Eros.

The Music Publishers' Protective Association having recently been formed, Louis Epstein made sure Jolson was listed as a co-writer on " 'N' Everything" and five other published songs in *Sinbad.* More songs would be added to the list as time went on, and a *Variety* columnist once referred to Jolson as "the best second chorus writer in the business." Al finally decided to donate his future royalties to the tubercular ward at Saranac Lake, New York.

Jolson now had all the trappings of a major star—a valet, a chauffeur, a manager, a wife he kept in California, and money. A new contract with the Shuberts, negotiated by Epstein, guaranteed Al $2,500 a week for the next five years, with 15 to 25 percent of gross receipts.

There were the usual hangers on: Harry Wardell and a teen-aged song plugger named Louis Schreiber. Jolson let Schreiber hang around his dressing room, took him along to parties, gave him his old ties, and allowed him to bask in what George Jessel described as "Al's reflected glory." In return, young Schreiber would run errands and make himself generally useful. Al eventually made Lou his "business manager" and got him a job with the William Morris Agency. Schreiber, whom chorine Dorothy Wegman described as "the biggest jerk I ever met," ended up as general manager of Twentieth Century–Fox.

Jolson's first entrance in *Sinbad* did not come until fifteen minutes after the start of the show, and one of Frank Holmes' duties was to turn on the dressing room water taps so Al would not hear the audience applaud the other actors in the cast. His colleagues called this the supreme manifestation of the Jolson ego. In truth, it was a clear clue to the man's self-doubts and insecurities. Red Skelton, who became acquainted with Jolson during the run of *The Wonder Bar* in 1931, said Al would have been too nervous to go on if he had heard that applause. Skelton pointed to the buckets that were in both wings as evidence of Jolson's extreme nervousness. The buckets were for Al to vomit in when he came off the stage.

Jolson had a certain paranoia about audiences, as if there were

only so much applause and that it might be given to other performers. Here again, Al was like a child, constantly afraid that he would
be supplanted.

He need not have worried in 1918.

Jolson's battles with conductors like Frank Tours and Oscar Ra-
din were well known along Broadway. Most pit musicians of the
1910s were classically trained, and tried to play musical comedy as
if it was opera. The results were often dull.

A new conductor named Al Goodman replaced Tours a few weeks
after *Sinbad* opened. Jolson and Buddy DeSylva had discovered him
conducting the orchestra for Blanche Ring in *What Next?* at the
Cort Theatre in San Francisco the previous August.

"Al Goodman," wrote Dan Wheeler, "was *different*. He liked Jolson in the first place, and sympathized with what he was trying to
do. He was young, eager, anxious to experiment with new ideas.
When Jolson would suddenly decide to change songs in the middle
of a performance, Goodman was always ready with the music at a
moment's notice. Jolson could follow his whims and know that
Goodman would follow them too, and that there would be no confusion in the orchestra, only an added spontaneity and excitement.
Under Goodman's direction, *Sinbad* took on a new sparkle and color.
Every performance was an adventure instead of a routine."

Sometimes, the two Als would argue bitterly, call each other names,
and wind up by not speaking. Goodman would then try to punish
Jolson by standing in the pit and giving him the deadpan. It was the
perfect way to get his goat.

"Laugh, damn you, laugh," Jolson would mutter through clenched
teeth so only Goodman could hear. "Laugh," he'd agonize. "If you
don't laugh, I'll kick you right in the face."

On Tuesday night, May 21st, Jolson cut the show a little to allow
for a Red Cross drive and a personal appeal. Jake Shubert dropped
in that night, found out what had happened, and asked house manager Stanley Sharpe why he had not been consulted.

Sharpe defended Jolson, and Shubert lost his temper. He berated
Sharpe, who walked out in disgust, leaving the Winter Garden without a manager. When Al found out, he told Jake he had been on the
verge of leaving the Shuberts until Sharpe had "talked him into"
signing a new contract. Three nights later, Sharpe was back.

Stanley Sharpe was one of Jolson's racetrack buddies. (Al won a
reported $80,000 by the time *Sinbad* closed on July 6th.) Going to

the races, or anyplace else, with Jolson was an experience, but at least one companion was upset by Al's peculiar borrowing habits. Jolson would generally take a few hundred dollars with him to the races. If he lost it all before the last race, he would elbow his companion: "Gimme fifty" or "Gimme a hunnert." Usually, the friend would give him the money, confident that Al would pay it back. When, however, he asked Jolson for the money, Al would look at him and ask, "What fifty?" He could not remember.

Al became his brother Harry's personal manager that season. Harry, now thirty-six, had been finding things in vaudeville extremely rough. Agnes Behler's husband, Dave Marion, had hired Harry as principal comedian for his Dreamland Burlesquers in 1915, but fired him after seven weeks. It was the low point of Harry's career.

Harry's wretchedness was doubled by Al's great success. Harry was still stuck in "middle time" vaudeville by 1918, telling everyone on the Pantages Circuit how Al had "pressured the Shuberts" into dropping him from *The Revue of Revues* in 1911. Harry, at the time, believed this to be true.

Harry had returned to New York following a tour of the small-time midwestern Miles Circuit when Al offered to become his manager. Al immediately went to the United Booking Office and told them there was no point in continuing the blacklist. He even offered to let Harry have his orchestrations if they would give him bookings.

The UBO agreed. Harry opened at the Bushwick Theatre in Brooklyn, played the following (1918–19) season on the Orpheum Circuit, and was never out of big-time vaudeville again during the next decade—even if he was occasionally billed as "Al Jolson's Brother."

A reviewer for *The Billboard* summed up Harry very well after seeing him perform at Chicago's Palace Music Hall in November 1919; "Harry sings well, burlesques 'Lucia' well, tells stories with good style, and is a capital entertainer without the genius of his famous brother."

That was about it. Samson Raphaelson described Harry as "a somewhat taller, thinner version of Al with a higher voice—but without the power."

The United States had been in World War I for more than a year by the time *Sinbad* closed for the summer. Jolson had been apathetic at the start ("I know two guys who ain't goin'," he had cracked *en tour* in *Robinson Crusoe, Jr.,* "me and the guy they send to get

me"), an attitude he shared with most Americans. Jolson's feelings
changed, however, after he heard Col. J. S. Dennis speak at a special
banquet the Friars tendered him at the Astor Hotel on Sunday night,
March 31, 1918. Many American soldiers had recently been killed
in the Argonne Forest, but Colonel Dennis said that the United States
had "not begun to feel the war" and would "be called upon to suffer
to the same extent" as the other allies if the fighting continued for
another two years.

Affected by the colonel's speech, Jolson met at least a dozen ships
returning from France with wounded soldiers over the remaining ten
weeks of the show's run at the Winter Garden. In July, after *Sinbad*
closed, Al and pianist Cliff Hess drove across the country entertaining thousands of servicemen at numerous military installations—truly
an unselfish act. Jolson was tired from his months on Broadway
and received no publicity.

Jolson and Hess arrived in Los Angeles on Tuesday, July 23, 1918.
Al fished and relaxed at the Avalon Country Club on Catalina Island
until he returned east with Henrietta and her friend Fritzie G. An-
gelo in late August. They stopped off for a week at Tahoe on the
way to New York, and every night, at dinner Jolson would suggest
that he and his wife separate. He would, he said, give Henrietta
money, a home, and an automobile. Al spoke entirely without feeling, as if discussing the weather or the food at New York restaurants.

"Al Jolson in *Sinbad*" reopened at the mammoth Century Theatre
on Sixty-second Street with a special Labor Day matinee on September 2, 1918. The Century was known as a "jinx" house because no
show except *The Century Girl* had managed to play there success-
fully. *Sinbad,* however, played to S.R.O., and Jolson introduced a
new hit song, "I'll Say She Does," which found its way into the
repertoire of every dance band in the country.

On Sunday night, September 15th, the Century was host to a special program under the auspices of the U.S. Army Tank Corps Welfare League. Ed Wynn was master of ceremonies, and Anna Fitzin
opened the program by singing "The Star Spangled Banner."

World War I drives like these were the direct ancestors of the
monster benefit shows of the 1920s. (TV telethons are their descend-
ants.) George M. Cohan was on the bill at the Century, but the man
Al had to follow was Enrico Caruso, the greatest dramatic tenor in
the history of opera.

Caruso opened with two powerful Italian war songs, but he saved the best for last—a rousing rendition of Cohan's "Over There" that sent the audience, including a thousand soldiers, into a veritable frenzy.

Jolson walked out on the stage. Half tongue-in-cheek, and half serious, he faced the audience and gave his famous line.

"Folks, you aint' heard *nothin'* yet."

The audience broke up completely, and Jolson got almost as many cheers from that one line as Caruso had received for his entire performance. Al had proved again that he was what the Shuberts called him: "The World's Greatest Entertainer."

He was definitely not the world's greatest husband. The Jolsons seldom dined in New York restaurants together, although Al, like many actors, liked an after-theatre supper. After one performance, he returned to the Biltmore Hotel and found his wife talking to Fritzie. Al suggested that they all dine in the room and told Henrietta to ring for floor service.

"Say 'eleventh floor service,' " Jolson told her, but Henrietta had already asked for "floor service."

Al was testy. "You're a fool."

"Al, I've been ringing for 'floor service' for weeks without saying 'eleventh floor' and the service has been quick."

Jolson slapped his wife across the face, grabbed her arm, threatened to break it, and threw her across the room.

It was not the first time he had struck her. She had once gone to visit Jean in Yonkers, had a tire blowout, and did not get back until one o'clock in the morning. Jolson, as it happened, was home early.

Al demanded to know where his wife had been. When she told him, he got angry, and Henrietta, in an attempt to pacify him, offered to phone the garage that had fixed the tire. The more she talked, the angrier Al got. He wound up socking her on the jaw, punching her in the nose, and giving her a black eye. All the punches were half swings, delivered in what might best be described as childlike fury.

Henrietta agreed to a separation shortly after the eleventh floor episode at the Biltmore. She then returned to Oakland, Al having agreed to let her sell their Sunny Slope Avenue cottage and buy a house which would belong to her in name as well as fact.

Lee Shubert needed the Century Theatre for a new play titled *Freedom,* so *Sinbad* was shifted to the Casino Theatre on Thirty-ninth Street until the Winter Garden became available on November 11th—the same day the Armistice was signed.

No Broadway actors' union was in power, and the Shuberts had Jolson give twenty performances in *Sinbad* in two weeks during the Christmas–New Year's season. Added to that was Al's schedule of benefits and concerts.

On Thursday night, January 2, 1919, after having given six performances of *Sinbad* in three days, Jolson collapsed into the arms of a stagehand after finishing a solo singing spot. The applause, amazingly, revived him, and he insisted on responding with an encore.

The next day, Jolson left for a rest in Atlantic City, and Ernest Hare took over the role of Gus. (In an effort to avoid a rush for refunds, the Shuberts continued to bill Jolson as the star of the show. An announcement was made regarding Jolson's "indisposition" just before the curtain rose at each performance.) Al returned on January 9th, but broke down again after the January 17th performance and went to Lakewood, New Jersey, to recuperate. This time, he did not return for ten days, and the show's gross began to suffer. The Shuberts needed the Winter Garden for a new musical called *Monte Cristo, Jr.,* so *Sinbad* moved to the Forty-fourth Street Theatre on Monday, February 10th. This was the fourth Broadway house the show had played inside five months.

Jolson was still not in good health. His voice was giving him trouble, and he was overhearing remarks to the effect that he "just talked his songs." On top of that, one of his doctors told him that his voice was "gone forever."

The old self-doubts returned, and Jolson's need for a sympathetic ear along with them. He called Henrietta up long distance, and the conversation went something like this:

"Honey, listen. I'm in bad shape. Get a ticket and come out here fast."

"Oh, Al. You sound terrible."

"I know, honey. I been like this since you left. Grab a train tonight. Don't bother packing."

"But Al, I can't. I'm selling the cottage, and I have to put the furniture in storage. I don't even have a storage house picked out yet, and I—"

"Don't bother me about that crap right now. Ship the furniture and stuff to New York if you want to, and I'll have it put in storage here. And sell the car. I'll buy you a brand new one."

"All right, Al. All right. I'll leave the day after tomorrow."

"That's right, honey. Look, I'm going to Palm Beach for a few days' rest, but I'll be back before you get here. Wire Eppy when you have your ticket."

Jolson went to Palm Beach and worked with what *Variety* described as "unusual zest" when he returned to *Sinbad* on March 18th. Henrietta's train arrived a few days later.

Al looked like a far cry from the sick and lonely man who had telephoned Henrietta. He was smiling and vibrant, the picture of good health.

The first thing Jolson asked his wife was whether she had sold the car. Assured she had, he asked her for the money.

Jolson peeled a few twenties off the role. "Here," he said, "go back to Oakland." When Henrietta remonstrated, Al told her she was "just a dumb hick, and . . . *I love you better when you're three thousand miles away.*"

Angry and confused, the still young Mrs. Jolson did as she was told. Once she had gone, however, Al had second thoughts. He had Harry Wardell send a wire to the depot in Chicago, where Henrietta had a long wait between trains. The wire said Al was having "a terrible time" and needed her at once. Against her better judgment, Henrietta went back to New York.

Al seemed glad to see her, but spent most of their time together telling her how good things would be when she got her new house and they were separated. On March 29th, immediately after *Sinbad* gave its last New York performance, Henrietta again left for Oakland. "Al and I went to the train with her," Jean Carlson remembered. "She was going to get that house; that was the specific reason for her going. And you know how enthusiastic Al could get if things enthused him. He was all hot and bothered about [her] getting that house—tickled to death with the idea."

Sinbad opened a two-week engagement at Poli's Theatre in Washington, D.C., the following evening, having given a total of 425 Broadway performances—a record for musicals in that era of short New York runs, low overheads, lucrative road tours, and quick profits.

Sigmund Freud, an older contemporary of Jolson's, would not have found Al's behavior towards Henrietta hard to analyze. Psychologists today call it "displacement." Simply stated, Jolson transferred all the love, resentment, and hostility he felt towards his mother to his wife.

Whereas Naomi had "deserted" him by dying, Henrietta could be made to go away and reappear—be "resurrected"—on command. Jolson's penchant for ignoring his wife was equally Freudian; his mother had ignored him during his first year in America.

The need for his wife when he felt ill or downcast shows the strongest identification of all. Henrietta was Naomi—a Naomi that Al felt he had to punish.

Sinbad, with a top ticket price of three dollars, grossed almost $45,000 in Washington. Rain and wind kept the take down to a paltry $10,000 over six days in Atlantic City, but the advance sale in Boston was excellent, and *Sinbad,* aided by the usual rave reviews for Al Jolson, settled down to a profitable nine-week run at the Boston Opera House.

Playing at the Opera House made Al recall Naomi's dreams of Steinway Hall. Jolson would never play at Steinway, but the Boston Opera House seemed a valid substitution. Eppy made the necessary plans, and Al gave a one-man recital program on Sunday night, May 18, 1919.

This was probably the first pop music recital ever given in an opera house. Jolson, accompanied by Cliff Hess at the piano, sang six songs in sets of threes in the first part of the program. His songs included "The Rosary," "Mighty Lak' a Rose," and "Old Folks at Home." After intermission, he came back to sing eleven more songs. These were Jolie's Broadway numbers, like " 'N' Everything," "Night Boat to Albany," and "Rock-a-Bye," the favorite, which he used to close the show. Jolson was accompanied by the fifty-piece Boston Symphony Orchestra, conducted by Al Goodman.

"Although without the customary blackface, Mr. Jolson was his usual distinctive self on the stage and the runway," wrote the reviewer for the *Musical Chronicle,* "singing with his contagious bodily and tonal energy, punctuating songs with occasional hopping and skipping and dancing and cavorting, and now and then that intimate repartee with the orchestra conductor which the Jolson fans so hugely enjoy. The sincerity of feeling which always marks his interpretations was keenly felt and appreciated in his splendid rendition of an interesting Irish song, 'Her Danny.' Most of the songs which Mr. Jolson has done so much to popularize were either on his program or were called for—and his spirited singing made Boston's first jazz recital a brilliant success." The Boston Opera House was sold out for the concert, with more than 1,800 people turned away.

At this time, Al Goodman's infant son fell ill back in New York. The illness, not thought serious at first, worsened after a few days, and Goodman planned to take a late train to New York after the show.

There was a spot, in scene three of the second act, in which Jolson rubbed a lamp and made a wish. This was usually a set-up for a gag line—one of the biggest laughs in the show. This night, however, as he came onstage, Al's deep set, haunting eyes were sad. As he rubbed the lamp, he said, "I'm going to make a silent wish."

The audience sat silent for a moment, vaguely aware of some deep meaning in his words. Down in the pit, Al Goodman knew instinctively: his son was dead. He did not need to read the telegram that Jolson later handed to him.

Jolson proved his friendship in the next few weeks. He paid the expenses of the baby's illness and death, took care of the remainder of the west coast debts Goodman had been struggling to pay off during the past year, and showed his sympathy in many different unobtrusive ways.

There was great humanity in Jolson, and it came out in the way he felt for Goodman at this time. It was as if the baby's death had struck a chord Al usually kept hidden when offstage.

Several days after the concert, Al received a long distance telephone call from Henrietta.

"Al, I've been speaking to Billy—"

"Billy? Billy who?"

"Billy Berkowitz, the agent."

"What agent? What are you, goin' into show business?"

"No, Al. Billy is the real estate agent. The deal is all set. I need a down payment of—"

"Down payment? For what?"

"The house. It's got—"

"Oh, that. Look, I changed my mind. Forget it. Tell the guy the deal's off."

"What?"

"I said the deal's off. I'm not buyin' it."

"But Al, I've been working on this for weeks. I've gotten all my friends to help me."

"I don't give a damn about your friends. Just tell that Berkowitz guy or whatever his name is that the deal's off."

"Al, this is the most inconsiderate, stupid thing I ever heard of—"

"Look, don't open your mouth to me. There'll be no house. That's final."

Al had done it again. Henrietta did as she was told, but she had reached the next-to-the-last-straw with her mercurial and egocentric husband.

The very last straw came in June. The Boston correspondent for *Variety* had the following item in his column:

> When Jolson winds up his local engagement, about the end of June, he is scheduled to start on an automobile trip across the country to California, where he will get his first view of his new home, recently built.

Henrietta made numerous phone calls in an effort to find out exactly who the house was for. Only one thing appeared certain: if there was a new home, it was not for her.

Henrietta made one more long distance call to Al. She told him she was filing for divorce.

Jolson sent Frank Holmes to Oakland to affect a nominal reconciliation. If Henrietta agreed to a simple separation, she could have all the jewels, money, and cars she wanted; but she would get nothing if she filed for divorce.

Henrietta, however, had made up her mind. "I don't want his money and motors now," she told a reporter from the San Francisco *Chronicle*. "What I want is my freedom." Henrietta's eyes were flashing as she told the scribe about Al using the money from the sale of her car to buy another auto, "which he used to entertain a musical comedy queen whom I have named in my complaint as 'Jane Doe.' "

On June 25, 1919, Henrietta Keller Jolson filed for divorce in Alameda County Superior Court, charging Al Jolson with desertion and cruelty. "Jane Doe" was never identified, but the complaint said she and Al had exchanged such gifts as "a moleskin scarf, a gold watch, socks, neckties, and other articles of clothing."

"Jane Doe" was Kitty Doner, a male impersonator in Jolson's shows for the past five years. Only nineteen years old when the Shuberts cast her as "Pinky Roberts" in *Dancing Around*, Kitty became Al's constant companion during the run of *Robinson Crusoe, Jr.*

Young Kitty fell in love with "Mister," as she usually referred to Jolson. It was a dangerous infatuation, especially since Jolson could never make up his mind whether he regarded Kitty as a girlfriend or a kid sister. He made fun of her slightly protruding upper teeth, but also kissed her in the Tunnel of Love at Coney Island. In March 1917, when *Robinson Crusoe, Jr.* was in Pittsburgh, he entered Kitty's room in the William Penn Hotel after midnight. Al stared out of the window for several moments, patted her cheek, and left abruptly. Their relationship remained platonic thanks to Jolson's strange behavior, but the gossip spread.

Al ignored Kitty completely during the first run of *Sinbad,* and it was not until the following (1918–19) season that he turned to her again. Kitty had begun seeing a charming Oxford graduate, the son of a Japanese prince and an English gentlewoman, and that made Al feel threatened.

After one performance, Al drove Kitty to the end of Riverside Drive in his cream-colored Packard. He pulled the car to the edge of a high spot overlooking the Hudson River, stopped, and poured out his rage in a torrent of words that culminated with "I've got a good mind to drive off this cliff."

His anger spent, Al broke down into tears. In snatches, he told Kitty that he would get a divorce from Henrietta and marry her. "Wait," he pleaded. "It'll all turn out all right. . . . Wait."

Kitty waited until June 7, 1919—two weeks before the end of the season and eighteen days before Henrietta filed for divorce. She then left the cast of *Sinbad* and went into vaudeville.

Al and Henrietta agreed on a settlement before her divorce suit came before Judge A. F. St. Sure on Monday afternoon, July 7, 1919. The Oakland *Tribune* described Henrietta as "so nervous that her voice trembled haltingly" during the trial. When the judge heard the settlement—a ridiculous $16,000 in cash, the Sunny Slope Avenue cottage, $4,000 worth of furnishings, one automobile, some jewelry, and a few Liberty Bonds—he said it was not fair. Henrietta, Judge St. Sure felt, should have gotten a lot more. "*I* don't think it's fair," she agreed, "but it's all that I can have." Al had threatened to have the case transferred to New York if she did not comply.

Jolson, who had retained his usual jocular façade before the inter-locutory decree was granted, suddenly fell apart. He appealed to Grace LeBoy, lyricist Gus Kahn's wife and a friend of Henrietta's, to intercede. Grace wrote to Henrietta, but the only reply she got was a telegram:

DEAR GRACE STOP MIND YOUR OWN BUSINESS STOP HENRIETTA.

Al then called Jean Carlson Sidman in Yonkers.

"He was practically crying." Jean remembered. "He said, 'Who do you feel sorriest for of anybody in the world?' I said, 'Who is this?' I didn't even recognize his voice.

" 'It's me—Al. Henrietta's divorced me, and you've got to try and help me get her back.'

"He practically lived on the phone to our house. He wanted me to go out to Oakland with him. I talked it over with Sam, and he said it was all right.

"Al didn't want me to tell Henrietta he was coming. I had a sister-in-law who lived in San Diego, and he thought that I could invite Henrietta down to her place." The idea was for Al to meet them when they changed trains in Los Angeles en route from Oakland.

Jean, however, wired Henrietta, telling her about the scheme and asking her to go along. Henrietta agreed.

They left New York, Al and Buddy DeSylva in one drawing room and Jean in another. "I got off in Oakland," Jean recalled, "and Al—I can still remember him—he was sitting in the Pullman, and he had the curtain up just enough so he could see out. He was peeking at Henrietta, and she didn't know he was there. Then I went home with Henrietta, and he went down to Los Angeles [with Buddy].

"We were supposed to leave for San Diego in a day or so, but the Santa Fe railroad went on strike, and they were only running as far south as Santa Barbara. I called Al and told him.

"Now, see, he didn't always think very clearly. I called him right from Mrs. Keller's house, and he knew Henrietta and her mother were right there. But he didn't realize that they knew what I was talking about. He was all excited about Henrietta coming out; that's all he could think about.

"So he said, 'Well, if the trains don't start within a couple of days, come down as far as Santa Barbara and I'll meet you there.' Which is what we did. Al met us and we drove down to Los Angeles. He was quite disappointed. Henrietta looked very well; she looked so nice that evening. He thought she'd be piqued and swooning all over the place, I guess.

"We stayed in Los Angeles a few days, and then we went, the four of us, to Catalina Island. Henrietta had talked to her lawyer about being with Al, and the lawyer said it would be all right as long as they weren't alone together in a room somewhere.

"Al had wined and dined us in Los Angeles, and on Catalina we went sight seeing, took boat rides—you know, the glass bottom boats. We had a nice time."

They went back to Los Angeles and stayed there until Al had to return east with Buddy. He had someone drive the girls to Pasadena, where they got a train to Oakland.

"We actually met Al's train coming through," said Jean, "and he was so surprised to see us. We just had time enough to run over and say good-bye."

Jean stayed at the Keller home for a few days before she returned home to Yonkers, bringing Henrietta with her for "a couple of weeks." Al was then in Philadelphia with *Sinbad*, but went up to Yonkers almost "every day. He took Henrietta all over the place. It was like Henrietta said, 'He was a wonderful lover, but he was no good as a husband.' "

Theatre historians have been unable to agree on Jolson's role during the Actors' Strike of 1919. Some say he sided with George M. Cohan against Actors' Equity Association; others state that he supported the union. In truth, Jolson had nothing to do with the strike, which began in August and ended on September 6th. He was on his summer lay-off the entire time.

On Saturday night, August 16th, he phoned Equity headquarters, expressing sympathy for the strike. "Mr. Jolson," Equity stated, "explained his position, which was that he had a considerable interest in certain attractions (and) could not join the Association." Jolson promised to send a check in support of the strike, and said he would "not appear" in New York while the strike" was on. There was little chance of him doing so in any event; *Sinbad* was scheduled to tour until 1921.

Al, with Buddy DeSylva, arrived in New York on Monday, September 8, 1919. Three nights later, *Sinbad* opened its nine-week run at the Shubert Theatre in Philadelphia, grossing $28,000 a week and playing to capacity at almost every performance despite an outrageously high top ticket price of three dollars.

There were no performances from Saturday nights until Monday evenings, and Al spent most of those times courting Henrietta. On Monday afternoon, September 22nd, though, he was in Newark, where Kitty Doner was trying out her vaudeville act at Proctor's Theatre.

Jolson had one ace in the hole for getting Kitty back to *Sinbad*. He took her for an early dinner and told her that his divorce would soon be final. "Now all you have to do," he told her, "is keep your nose clean and we'll be married." It was as close as he would come to a proposal.

Two weeks later, Al took Henrietta to see Kitty at the Colonial Theatre in New York. During intermission, Jolson left his wife and went backstage to Kitty's dressing room.

Standing in the hallway, Al took out a diamond ring and told

Nellie Doner that he wanted to marry her daughter Kitty. All he said to Kitty was "Good luck" and "I'll catch your act."

Henrietta returned to Oakland a few days later, and Al turned his full attention towards getting Kitty back in *Sinbad*. Feigning illness, he let Ernest Hare go on for him in Philadelphia while he went to surprise her at the Palace in New York.

Al took Kitty to a cheap hotel in the East Twenties, signed the register "Al Jolson and wife" and took her upstairs.

"What's in the bag?" asked Kitty. Al was carrying a suitcase, which opened to reveal numerous bottles of bootleg whiskey.

"What's the idea?" Kitty asked. She was laughing. He laughed, too, and they embraced. As they kissed, Al whispered "Henrietta." To Kitty, it was "like a crash of thunder." She began to giggle nervously, and Al, confused and hurt, put her at arm's length.

Kitty finally returned to *Sinbad* on Monday night, October 27, 1919. She anticipated some fun in her scene with Al that night. Never, however, did she guess what was in store.

No one ever looked as much like the king of performers as Al Jolson did with the full lights on him. The corners of his lips went up, showing a mouth of clean, fresh-looking teeth, and his eyes gleamed against his blackface makeup. The faultless dark suit just enhanced the picture.

In that scene with Kitty, he was masterful. "You know, folks, this little boy"—he pinched her cheek—"is really a girl. And, oh man! Is she full of *umph!* Nothing blaah about Kitty!" The way he said it made the audience laugh. "She thought she could get away from me," he boasted, "but you ain't heard nothin' yet." Al stepped over the footlights onto the small platform that was built across the orchestra pit to the front row, replacing the old runway. "Come 'ere!" he whispered loudly, his white gloves seeming to beckon every part of the audience. "I don't want her to hear. . . ."

Everyone was grinning in anticipation. "You know, folks, Kitty thought she could get away from me. Left the show—" He shook his white-gloved finger now and chuckled. "Aaah, but I got her back again." Now, with a luscious grin, he rolled his eyes and let them have it. "Brother, what it takes, I got! Folks, she's *ka-razy* about me!"

"Ah, I'm not," pouted Kitty, shifting uncomfortably. The audience howled.

That led Jolson into a long line of talk on women, ending with

"Do right and fear no man. Don't write—and fear no woman!" On that line, he pranced over to Kitty.

"By the twinkle in his eye," she wrote in her unpublished memoirs, "I knew that he was up to something. Pinching my ear and pulling my nose was the usual bit of business, but when he began affectionately stroking my cheeks—why was the laugh so big? The louder the audience laughed, the more I laughed; the more I laughed, the louder the audience laughed." Jolson worked this scene up to a frenzy, and the more Kitty asked, "What's it all about?" the more *he* rolled with laughter. Members of the audience were pounding each other on the back by this time.

When, at last, Miss Doner made her exit, she looked into a mirror. Jolson had stroked the burt cork from his face and slyly rubbed it on her cheeks with every pinch, pat, and caress.

Kitty had deserted Al, and Jolie had taken his revenge. He proceeded to ignore her for the balance of the season, and he never again mentioned marriage to Kitty.

The most historically noteworthy aspect of Jolson's 1919–20 season was his popularization of "Swanee," George Gershwin's first and biggest commercial song hit.

Gershwin first met Jolson in Atlantic City in April 1919, when *Sinbad* was playing the Globe Theatre, and *La, La, Lucille,* the first Broadway musical with a Gershwin score, was being readied for its out-of-town tryout at Nixon's Apollo. Charles Previn, the conductor of *Lucille* (and uncle of André Previn), introduced them. It is interesting to note that Fred Moore was still manager of the Apollo.

Gershwin and lyricist Irving Caesar wrote "Swanee" five months later. "In those days," recalled Caesar, "you wrote a song and then you tried to place it. We wrote 'Swanee' and then took it to the Capitol Theatre, where George played it for the chorus girls on a piano in the theatre's mezzanine. You know how it is—young fellows and girls. Well, anyway, Ned Wayburn heard some of the girls raving about the song and told us he'd put it in the *Revue.*"

"Swanee" and another Gershwin piece, "Come to the Moon," were presented by the famous Arthur Pryor Band when the Capitol's *Demi-Tasse Revue* opened on October 24, 1919. Fifty chorines with electric lights in their shoes danced to the songs, but few copies of sheet music were sold.

In late December, when *Sinbad* was in the midst of a two-week engagement at the Shubert-Crescent Theatre in Brooklyn, Buddy

DeSylva brought George to a party Al was throwing at the Biltmore in Manhattan. Gershwin, true to form, was soon at the piano, playing every song that he had ever written. Al became intrigued by "Swanee" and made plans to record the song at his next session for the Columbia Graphophone Company. By the end of January, Jolson was belting "Swanee" to the rafters in performances of *Sinbad*. Al Goodman had his pit musicians play the number faster than it had been played by the Columbia orchestra, and "Swanee," aided by a heavy advertising campaign, became one of the biggest hits of the season.

Sinbad opened a six-week run at the Auditorium in Chicago on January 25, 1920. The "roaring twenties" had begun. Prohibition was in, and Chicago would be famous as the city of Capone, Bugs Moran, and a host of other bootleg era hoodlums. To Jolson, however, Chicago meant wind—and colds. On Thursday night, February 5th, the night before the twenty-fifth anniversary of Naomi's death, Ernest Hare played Gus in *Sinbad*. Al stayed in his Blackstone Hotel suite and took the "gargle guns" prepared for him by Pansy.

The next nine weeks read like a travesty. Jolson left for Palm Beach, Florida, on Sunday night, February 8th, having missed four consecutive performances. He returned to Chicago on the 17th, but immediately checked out of the Blackstone and disappeared for two days. Al reappeared for one performance on Sunday, February 22nd, and then disappeared again. The show was now being advertised as "Al Jolson's *Sinbad*" instead of "Al Jolson in *Sinbad*," weekly receipts dropping from $60,000 to $14,000.

It was eventually discovered that Jolson had gone to Atlantic City with Buddy DeSylva, ostensibly to soak up "Good ol' Mister Sol" and get his voice back. On Wednesday, March 3rd, he showed up in New York and told Lee Shubert he was set to reappear in *Sinbad* when the show opened a three-week engagement in Detroit the following Monday.

Al found out the show had other problems. Ten members of the chorus had filed complaints with the new Chorus Equity Association, alleging unpaid salaries for extra performances over the last twenty-five weeks. The matter was scheduled for arbitration on March 17th.

Jolson was aware of the Shuberts' many underhanded practices, but he bristled at the chorines' action. Al knew that several girls had exaggerated matters when they filed claims for extra performances and "sleepers," and resented them not going through him first. Jolson had always made sure the chorines were fairly treated, and he felt their action was a personal betrayal.

True to his word, Jolson was back as Gus when *Sinbad* opened in Detroit. Al did not miss a performance for the next two weeks, but he was miserable—clipping his scenes short and never giving encores. He was angry and impatient with everything—his voice, the chorines ("You are breaking up what had been a happy family and forcing me to become a 'star'"), and Henrietta. She still had not agreed to stop the divorce.

On Friday, March 26th, Jolson went to New York to consult one Dr. Miller, a throat specialist, who advised him to rest for a few days. Al also went to Equity headquarters to correct the "erroneous impression" that he was against A.E.A. That done, he left to rejoin *Sinbad*. The advance sale in Pittsburgh was over $45,000—despite an unprecedented top ticket price of $4.40.

Jolson, however, soon suffered a relapse. Ernest Hare went on for him one night, and rumors flew about Jolson being out of the cast. There was a resulting drop in ticket sales.

On Wednesday night, April 7th, having spoken to the Shuberts, Al addressed the company. Unless they agreed to lay off one week without salary, the show would be closed in three days. The actors agreed to take the payless lay-off, but the stagehands said their contracts called for payment in all cases. Jolson did not even bother to argue; he just closed the show on Saturday night.

Jolson took a two-week rest and finished out the season by appearing in two Sunday concerts in New York on April 25th. He performed at the Century and Winter Garden theatres, and the Shuberts paid him $2,000 for the evening's work.

Al seemed to have recovered completely. He recorded "In Sweet September" for Columbia on April 30th, and left for Oakland five days later. He seemed determined to win back his wife.

Jolson and Frank (Pansy) Holmes checked into the Hotel Oakland, and Al began visiting Henrietta at her mother's house on East Fourteenth Street. The divorce was due to become final on July 8th, something Al felt he could not allow to happen.

"He was pleading with her," said Jean Carlson. "And, if he hadn't pulled one of his stunts, she would have married him again. He was out every day, taking her places in Oakland. But he was so undependable.

"Finally, after she'd said no a dozen times or more, Henrietta wrote to me. She said that she was thinking about calling off the divorce, but thought it would be just the same thing over again, so what was the use?

"He kept after her, though, and one day, while they were out someplace, she said to Al, "I'll sleep on it tonight. Just let me think it over. You come out to the house for dinner tomorrow night, and I'll tell you (my decision) then.'

"She made up her mind not to let the divorce go (through). Mrs. Keller got up a nice dinner, and they waited and waited.

"At ten or eleven o'clock, the phone rang. It was Al.

" 'Henrietta?' he said. 'Yeah, the crowd was going over to Catalina Island, so I just went with 'em.'

"So that did it. She said, 'What would have been the use? I just would have been bounced around again.'

"After twelve years, she just got a little tired of it."

"Mammy"

"Jolson can take a song and make it do things its composers did not dream were in it."

HEYWOOD BROUN, New York *World*

Al looked great when he and Pansy arrived in New York's Grand Central Station on Tuesday morning, July 6, 1920. His skin was bronzed, he was fifteen pounds heavier than he had been two months before, and, most importantly, his voice was strong. Al's fourth and final season in *Sinbad* would not start until August 30th, leaving him time for his newest interest, politics.

It would be ridiculous to compare Jolson's efforts on behalf of Warren Harding with the kind of politicing Hollywood stars like Paul Newman, John Wayne, Shirley MacLaine, and others have attempted in the last two decades. Al supported Harding mainly because of personal friendships, and only partially because the Republican party had promised to keep America out of European affairs—a philosophy that Al supported even more than did the average American. Europe, to Al Jolson, was a distant, pain-filled memory he preferred to keep physically, as well as emotionally, distant.

On Tuesday, August 10th, Republican National Headquarters announced that Jolson had accepted the presidency of the Harding and Coolidge Theatrical League. Al was in his suite at the Biltmore Hotel at the time. "He liked the Biltmore baths," remembered Irving Caesar. "Down the hall were these headquarters for the Harding campaign, which Will Hays was directing [as chairman of the Republican National Committee]. We were all in a room at the time, six of us, around five o-clock in the evening, and Al said, 'You know, Will Hays is down the hall, and he wants a song for the campaign, for Harding.' So we wrote it in about five minutes. It was a terrible song.

"Now we had the song, and Jolson sent someone down the hall to tell Will Hays to come over to hear it. We sang it for Hays, and then he asked Jolson, 'What do we do now?'

"He said, 'Well, you oughta start with a hundred thousand copies.'

" 'How much will that be, Al?'

" 'Seven cents (apiece).'

"Hays came back with a check for seven thousand dollars at once—within ten minutes. We each got a thousand dollars, everybody in the room. It was one of Al's few great generous gestures. I mean, he couldn't get away from it. It was our song; he didn't write it, such as it was. There was Buddy (DeSylva), myself; Lou Silvers was in the room; George (Gershwin) was in the room; Paul Lannon was there. Al liked Paul; he was a pretty good musician. Anyway, we each got a thousand dollars."

The song was published as "Harding, You're the Man for Us" by Al Jolson. None of the real composers ever complained about not receiving proper credit. The lyric was worse than the music, and the only thing worse than the lyric was the candidate.

Jolson toured in *Sinbad* for the next four months. It was a successful tour, netting $10,000 for three performances in Wheeling, W. Va., and playing to generally sell-out audiences. "Avalon," its title taken from the Catalina resort area, proved to be Al's big song hit.

Al was briefly laid up with a cold while in Chicago in October. Ernest Hare played Gus again, but there were so many demands for refunds that the Shuberts announced no one would understudy Jolson in the future. From this point, no Jolson show went on without Al Jolson. The Shuberts had finally admitted he was indispensable.

Kitty Doner was no longer in the cast. Fed up with her treatment, and Al's breach of promise, she had finally left him for good and gone back into vaudeville. Her last words to Al had been "I hate you. I wish you all the bad luck in the world."

Al, uncomprehendingly, just looked at her and said, "That wasn't nice to say."

He did not seem to know what he had done.

Sinbad shut down for four weeks the evening after New Year's. Jolson headed for Palm Beach, briefly stopping off in New York to record "Ding-A-Ring A-Ring" for Columbia. While in New York, he dined with Saul Bornstein, general manager of Irving Berlin Music.

Bornstein (later known as Bourne) was a dapper dresser who greeted everyone he knew with "How's your mother?" Saul, who also had a predictable weakness for mother songs, showed Al one he was about to publish.

It was a number called "My Mammy," banal and outdated even

in the early twenties. Despite a pulsating rhythm in the chorus, it was vastly inferior to "Rock-a-Bye," then Al's best-known "mammy" song. Al, however, said he would perform "Mammy" in *Sinbad* and allowed Bornstein to use his picture on the sheet music.

Jolson first sang "Mammy" onstage when *Sinbad* reopened at the Shubert-Majestic Theatre in Providence, R.I., on Monday evening, January 31st, and for the remainder of the tour stopped the show with it. The "mammy singer" had been born.

Of greater interest than the published lyrics are the lines that Al inserted. In the second chorus, where the music gives sixteen bars to "Ma-am-my, ma-am-my," Al interpolated "Mammy, look at me. Don't you know me? I'm your little baby." The lines referred to the night in which eight-year-old Asa Yoelson had rushed in to find his mother dying in childbirth, only to have her look straight through him with no sign of recognition.

"I always have a picture in my mind of a black boy and his life story when I sing that song," Al said in a ghosted story. "A southern Negro boy who has found life a bitter and terrible tragedy, who has been broken, abused, and who is down and out without a ray of hope left. He can't think of one human being in all the world who has treated *him* like a human being, not one who has shown him sympathy or affection, and he is just about ready to give up the battle of life in despair, broken hearted over cruel fate, when he thinks of his 'Mammy' and the soul in him cries out for her.

"There was one who loved him, one whose arms are open to him, one who is ready to comfort him, and the thought gives him renewed faith in life and in the future." What Al could not admit, of course, was that the boy was *him*.

The "Swanee" Al immortalized in song was really the Niemen River of his childhood. "Mammy," there is no doubt, was Naomi. Ironically, her grave is now in a black neighborhood in Washington.

Sinbad closed for the last time in St. Paul on June 25, 1921. Jolson returned east, attended the Dempsey-Carpentier fight in Boyle's Thirty Acres, near Jersey City, on July 2nd, and spent the next few weeks in starting his own racing stable.

On Saturday, July 23rd, Al bought Snapdragon II, a six-year-old plater, six two-year-olds, and a three-year-old for a total of $48,000. He also tried to buy Morvich, a first-class horse, for $75,000. Fred Burlew was willing to sell, but his partner, Ben Block, turned down Jolson's offer.

William Shea, from whom Al bought Snapdragon, was supposed

to serve as trainer of the Jolson stable. He never did, however, and the stable never had a formal manager. Buddy Ensor, one of racing's greatest jockeys (who finally died a pauper due to whiskey), introduced Al to "Colonel" John Donovan. The Colonel trained Al's horses until the mid 1930s.

"Jolson was in a class by himself," Donovan said in 1965. "There never was an entertainer who could shine his shoes, nor was there ever a greater guy. I trained his horses, handled his bets, and acted as his sidekick. One day, I saw him bet forty grand on Man o' War. You guessed it. That was in the Sanford Stakes at Saratoga—the only time the colt ever lost."

Ensor rode four winners in four starts one day, and Al gave him a $90,000 cut out of his winnings. "That day," said Donovan, "he bet so much that the Jockey Club complained, and Shubert insisted he remain away from the races." Donovan and Mose Shapoff, Jolson's trainer in the late thirties, agreed Al would never bet if he thought that a race was crooked.

Race track figures thought much more of Jolson as a person than did Jolson's fellow actors. He was a "man's man," and his interest in sports like boxing, horse racing, and baseball were all genuine. With sportsmen, Al felt no great need to prove himself. With theatrical performers, whom he looked upon as mean and phony, he remained on guard. "I wouldn't say he was 'anti-social,'" comedienne Patsy Kelly said of Al's relationship with actors. "He was just un-social."

On July 27th, Al took Bud DeSylva, Harold Atteridge, Con Conrad, and Sigmund Romberg up to one of Paul Smith's cottages in the Adirondacks to finish writing a new show. All agreed they would not shave until the show was finished.

One of the advantages of working in the Adirondacks was the close proximity to Canada, where there was no prohibition. When inspiration needed "wetting," Jolson and his cohorts simply hopped into a car and went to Montreal. They got enough "inspiration" to finish the whole show inside of three weeks.

The new show, *Bombo*, was another "extravaganza" set in two different time periods. In the present (1920s), Al was Gus, a young explorer's cook. In 1492, Gus became Bombo, servant of Christopher Columbus, who beats King Ferdinand of Spain at craps and is made duke.

Columbus seeks to prove the earth is round, but tries to use an egg to do it and is jeered out of court. Queen Isabella becomes interested, however, and, following Bombo's suggestion, pawns her jewels to finance the proposed voyage. Bombo foils an attempt to rob Columbus of his funds, and the three ships set sail.

Bombo quells a mutiny, and land is finally reached. Bombo and Columbus eventually reach Manhattan, which the former buys from the Indians for twenty-four dollars worth of trinkets.

"And if you give us Brooklyn," Bombo adds, "we'll throw in a pair of rusty scissors."

One scene had a Moorish princess carried in a caravan. So great was her beauty and mystique that no one dared to look at her. Bombo, of course, pops up in the carriage alongside her. When the action returns to the twenties, the princess turns out to be the maid of Mrs. Moore, a friend of the explorer for whom Gus works as a cook.

Bombo was originally scheduled to open at the Winter Garden, but the Shuberts' plan to use that theatre as the flagship of their foray into vaudeville forced a change in plans. Remembering the success Jolson had enjoyed in *Sinbad* at the uptown Century Theatre three years earlier, the Shuberts moved the opening of *Bombo* to the newly built Imperial on Fifty-ninth Street, across from Central Park. When Jolie balked, Lee Shubert offered to rename the new house "Jolson's Fifty-ninth Street Theatre."

Al accepted. He was thirty-five years old—the youngest man to have a theatre named for him in American history. Despite his ego, the thought overwhelmed him. Al was always a madman at openings, but he outdid himself when *Bombo* opened the new theatre on Thursday night, October 6, 1921.

Accompanied by Schreiber, he walked up and down the streets for hours before curtain time. Arriving at the theatre, he developed a psychosomatic case of laryngitis by the time he got his make-up on. A quickly summoned doctor tried to tell him he was all right, but Al, his voice suddenly hoarse, refused to listen. Jolie swore he could not sing, and practically begged his brother, Harry, not to let the stagehands raise the curtain.

When the curtain did go up, Al stood in the wings trembling and sweating. "When his cue came," Harry wrote, "I gave him a hard push from the rear and out he went. The ovation he received is one that he never could forget. For several minutes, the applause continued while Al stood and bowed. Probably the time that elapsed helped him regain his nerve. Never did he sing better than he did that night."

Al was still so nervous that he left two stanzas out of "That Barber in Seville." Every time he came offstage, he swore that he could not go back on, and when the first act curtain fell, he said there would not be a second act. The audience just stamped its feet and chanted "Jolson, Jolson."

Harry and some others finally got him out to make a curtain speech. With sincere humility, Al thanked the audience, telling them how proud he was to have a theatre bear his name. He also said that *Bombo* would be his last show. The strain of openings, Al told them, had become too great.

"I'm a happy man tonight," Jolie concluded. He walked offstage to tumultuous applause.

Al took thirty-seven curtain calls that night.

Bombo ran at Jolson's Fifty-ninth Street Theatre for the next six months. Al would often arrive at the theatre from a round of golf at Van Cortlandt Park with a three-car entourage consisting of himself and Jimmy in the first car, Frank Holmes, Louis Schreiber, and a third man in the second, and Al Goodman (who soon replaced Louis Silvers as the show's conductor), with one or two songwriters, in the third. Other men would join them at the stage door, providing Jolie with what seemed like a "grand entrance."

Al took care of daily business in the dressing room with Frank. There would be accounts from Sunshine Music (a new Jolson-owned division of Harms, Inc. that Max Dreyfuss had set up to publish the songs in *Bombo*), checks to sign, and letters. After a brief conference, Holmes and a stenographer would retire to another room and get out the resulting correspondence.

Jolson then would poke his head through the door of his inner room and call Al Goodman.

"Al, I'll hear that song now."

A typewritten sheet of paper with the new song's lyrics would be handed Jolson, who would sit, unseen by the composer, while the song was played on a piano just outside the dressing room. If Jolson liked the number, he would hand the lyric sheet to Schreiber or whoever else was serving as his "musical secretary." The latter would then pencil in Al's comments and directions. If the song did not impress Al, he would mug and toss the sheet into a big wastepaper basket. Whatever the verdict, Al would then go out and meet the young composer. He gave honest but gentle criticism, and was kind and patient with newcomers.

Jolson did not maintain a "casting couch," but he was present when the chorus girls were chosen. Often, Al would walk over and tell groups of them a funny story. Then he would watch their faces closely. Those with a sense of humor were usually hired.

"Other things being equal," Jolson maintained, "a chorus which has a sense of humor will do far better work and give a far better performance than one which has not. Humor is simply super intelligence. It is the intelligence that enables one to see the real nature of a thing.

"There is absolutely no appeal that can be made to stupidity. You cannot get results with stupid people, you can't even keep them disciplined. But with humorous people—that is, the super intelligent people—you need only explain the reason for a thing or an order to find ready obedience."

One of the "super intelligent" chorines chosen for *Bombo* was Miss Dorothy Wegman, a fourteen-year-old Jewish brunette who had convinced dance director Allan K. Foster she was two years older.

"To Al," remembered Dorothy, "there were, basically, two kinds of girls—the 'nice ones' and the 'others.' I was one of the 'nice ones,' and he watched over me like a father. I remember once we went to a cabaret after the show and someone told a joke that was off color. Everyone who heard it laughed, including me, and Al came up and said, 'Dorothy, get your coat, you're going home.' He had Lou Schreiber drive me."

Audiences were especially enthusiastic during the last week of the run of *Bombo* at Jolson's Fifty-ninth Street Theatre. Al responded eagerly, singing up to fifteen songs on certain occasions and keeping the curtain up until after midnight. Some of the chorines complained that this was interfering with their social engagements.

"Honestly," he told them, "the people out front encourage me so much that I'm in danger of working myself to death. Now, if you girls will bear with me for the rest of the week, I'll give you all a big party on the stage Saturday night." Everyone agreed, and Jolie kept his word.

After playing one week in Atlantic City and four more in Philadelphia, the show closed for the season on May 13, 1922. Jolson left for California on June 2nd.

Al visited the movie studios for a few days, spent some time vacationing on Catalina Island, and finally went to visit Henrietta in Oakland. Jolson found his ex-wife in the company of one Jack Silvey, manager of the Campaign Bureau of the California Development Association.

"Al," said Henrietta, "Jack and I are going to be married." Jolson was shocked, and, for one of the few times in his life, practically speechless.

Al returned to New York and married show girl Ethel Delmar less than one month later. He seemed intent on beating Henrietta to the alter.

Alma Osborne was the second Mrs. Jolson's real name, but everyone on Broadway knew her as Ethel Delmar. Al met her on June 9, 1919, George White having asked him to take a look at his new show, the *Scandals*, at the Liberty Theatre in New York. Ethel was a minor principal and "knocked Al off his feet right off the reel," in the words of another show girl.

Ethel, or Alma, was born in Easton, Pennsylvania, in 1900. At the age of sixteen, she went to New York and made her debut in the chorus of *The Century Girl*, becoming a principal in *The Riviera Girl* the following year. George White hired Ethel and three other Broadway show girls for his vaudeville act, "George White & Co." The *Scandals* followed.

Ethel was a classic beauty—fine features, raven hair, a show-stopping figure, and beautiful hazel eyes. Unlike Henrietta, she loved parties. Ethel easily fit into Broadway's social whirl, and a big room filled with people and bootlegged liquor was her idea of a perfect evening. She belonged to the "roaring twenties"—from the gum she chewed down to the small dogs she took everywhere she went.

Al and Ethel became further acquainted in September 1919, when the *Scandals* played the Forrest Theatre in Philadelphia and *Sinbad* was at the Shubert. White used Ethel in a second edition of the *Scandals,* and when that show played Washington at the same time that *Sinbad* did in March, 1921, Al gave Ethel plenty of attention.

George White's *Scandals* closed in Boston on April 9, 1921, and Ethel began planning an elaborate vaudeville act for the following season. Ethel Delmar & Co. in "Jungle Jazz" made its New York debut at the Fifth Avenue Theatre on Thursday, March 16, 1922, and promptly "laid an egg." This is from Sime Silverman's *Variety* review:

> The juvenile had a prolog and pilog, about Kipling's story of the girl brought up in the jungle, learning the language of the wild animals. Four of the wild specie were immediately after disclosed in full stage: lion, tiger, panther, and bear. Miss Delmar entered and "held court" for them. The tiger accused the panther of having left his (tiger's) home at four the same morning. The lion testified for the tiger, but

the panther, denying the charge, whispered in the ear of the judge (Miss Delmar) it was the lion's home he left. All the animals and Miss Delmar laughed at that, but the audience did not join in.

"Jungle Jazz" included songs and dances and used special drops and sets. As Al recalled it, Ethel "was getting twelve hundred fifty for the act and paying out thirteen hundred fifty. She had high priced animal actors out of the *Follies* jumping around and listening to her say, 'Do you love meh?'" Jolie sneaked into the theatre once and saw the act. "She did a fall that day," said Al, "and lit on her head. And I laughed. And she heard about that laugh."

Despite their obviously close relationship, Ethel was surprised when Al suddenly proposed marriage in July, 1922—surprised but far too overjoyed to look a gift horse in the mouth. She loved Jolie, but it was probably fascination, rather than passion, that led her to say yes. The king of Broadway had proposed, and that was all that mattered.

Al Jolson and Ethel Delmar were married on July 22, 1922, and spent their wedding night at a resort in Maine. They got back to New York on Wednesday morning, July 26, saw a matinee (*Spice*, with George Price, at the Winter Garden), and moved into Al's apartment that evening. No one, except Jimmy, Pansy, Eppy, and a few close friends, knew they were married.

By August 4th, when Al recorded "I'll Stand Beneath Your Window Tonight and Whistle" (a song about eloping), rumors of an "impending" second Jolson marriage abounded on Broadway. A false report—that Al and his new bride had been married at the Little Church Around the Corner in New York—reached the press on August 15th, and reporters from all major New York dailies spent the next three days trying to get verification.

"It's a lie," said Al to a reporter from the *Daily News* on Friday, August 18th. "A nasty story that's uncalled for. I am not married, positively. It's undoubtedly the result of a little birthday joke." Al even said he still loved Henrietta.

That same morning, a reporter from the New York *American* telephoned the Jolson apartment on West Fifty-ninth Street.

"Hello. Is this Al Jolson's apartment?"

"Yes."

"May I speak to Mr. Jolson?"

"Mr. Jolson is not home right now." The voice was later described as "sweet" and "feminine."

"Then may I speak to Mrs. Jolson?"

"This is Mrs. Jolson speaking." It was Ethel. The reporter tried to press her for details, but she cut the conversation short.

"I do not want to say anything about our marriage until Mr. Jolson comes home. Good-bye."

It is hard to say exactly why Jolson tried to keep his marriage to Ethel Delmar a secret, but her conversation with the scribe from the *American* made further subterfuge impossible. Al now did the only thing he could do. He had Claude Greneker of the Shubert publicity department issue a statement saying he and Ethel Delmar had been married.

The next day, every paper in New York carried the news that Jolson was a married man again. Al's attitude about his marriage seemed completely different when a reporter from the Evening *World* called him up that morning.

"Yes, this is little Egbert talking. Yes, Claude Greneker gave you the right dope as usual. I'm married. She's right here beside me now. Yes, we're very, very happy. Doggone, but isn't this a hot day?"

As far as the reporters were concerned, the marriage had not taken place until August 18th. Ethel may have been confused by all this, but she soon learned it did not pay to question Jolie.

Al and Ethel had a second honeymoon at the Ambassador Resort in Atlantic City. When they got back to New York, Jolson went into rehearsals for the new season with *Bombo*.

Jolson and the company left New York on a special train on Wednesday, September 13th. John Schneckenberger, an exact, efficient diminutive man who had forsaken a career in journalism to work for the Shuberts, was the company manager. He had served in a similar capacity for *Sinbad* the previous season, marking the beginning of a lifelong association with Al Jolson. "Schneck" managed Jolson's business till the day Al died.

Bombo opened the new season at the Park Theatre in Youngstown, Ohio, on September 15, 1922. "YOUNGSTOWN THINKS I'M GREAT," Al wired Ethel.

"YOUNGSTOWN," Ethel wired back, "IS THE PLACE WHERE THEY THINK THE KENTUCKY DERBY IS A HAT."

That night, Al dreamed about adopting a baby found on his doorstep—not surprising, in view of his recent marriage, his longing for (and apparent inability to father) children, and the then current stories about actresses adopting infants. Al told John Schneckenberger about the dream, and Schneck, in turn, phoned Greneker in New York. The nation's press was quickly deluged with releases about

"Youngstown Jolson," a fictitious baby boy Al had supposedly found wrapped in a basket outside his hotel room and adopted. It was the only time a wild story was invented by a press agent to help Jolson's career. At the time, of course, no help was needed.

Ethel joined Al in Chicago a week later, shortly after *Bombo* opened a big sixteen-week engagement at the Apollo Theatre. After the performance, she went back to Jolson's dressing room and found him talking to critic Ashton Stevens and Moe "Colonel Gimp" Snyder, an eccentric, quasi-underworld character later immortalized by James Cagney in the film, *Love Me Or Leave Me*. "The Colonel" had appointed himself Jolson's bodyguard. (He later tried to collect money for his "services," and Jolson, according to pianist Ray O'Brien, "had him thrown out of the theatre.")

Stevens described Ethel as "a dark, sweet girl in a dark gown, and gloriously unpainted." She was learning, rather quickly, to be Jolie's kind of woman.

However, there was still the gum.

"Put it out," said Al.

"It's one of the few pleasures I have left," sighed Ethel.

"Well?"

"Yes, I'm quite well."

"Well, how was it? Did you like me?"

"Yes but you work awfully hard," she said without a comma. "I don't see how you're going to keep it up.'

"Is that all you got to say? It's a hot night; that's why I'm all perspiration."

"Baby, you work too hard! You'll kill yourself! You need a team or something in there toward the last, to rest you."

"Colonel, you know that girl we saw dance in the cabaret? See her tonight and tell her I'll give her a hundred a week to fill a spot in the last act. If the Shuberts won't stand for it I'll pay her out of my pocket. That settles that, Ethel. And now, apart from the hard work, how was I? Eh?"

"First, answer me one question."

"Shoot!"

"Where," she laughed, "did you get all the beautiful chorus girls?"

"You devil!"

"Apart from that, Albert, you were great."

Chicago thought, so, too, especially on Tuesday night, September 19th, when Jolson smelled smoke while in the middle of a song. He looked down, saw some wire blazing in the basin of the footlights, and noticed people in the audience becoming uneasy. Al dashed through his song and started clowning. ("I just threw away an old pair of rubber gloves and the odor is terrible.") In the meantime, he was stamping out the blaze and risking shock.

Jolson told the conductor to play "Mammy." As he sang, Al stamped out the remainder of the fire in time to the music—finishing to a tremendous round of applause that gave way to cheers.

Bombo ended its Chicago run on January 6, 1923, and began a four-month tour of eastern cities. Ethel, however, did not go along. Al had already given her some money and sent her back to New York.

Jolie was doing the same thing to Ethel he had done to Henrietta, but the second Mrs. Jolson did not bear up well under the treatment. When *Bombo* reached New York in May, Al found that Ethel had been drinking.

This was something Jolson had not counted on. Angry and embarrassed, Al took a sub-lease on Ben Bernie's modest walk up at 543 Madison Avenue in the East Fifties. Ethel stayed in the West Fifty-ninth Street apartment with a maid—and all the bootlegged whiskey her alleged friends could get to her.

Ralph Reader, later a respected British theatrical producer but then a young, aspiring performer, recently arrived in the United States from England, saw *Bombo* at this time. "I'd heard so much talking about [Jolson] that I was determined to go and see what this . . . ham, as I thought he was, could be like.

"And it so happened that I couldn't get to the theatre until the last Saturday that he was playing there (June 9, 1923). I went down to get a seat for the matinee, and to my amazement, there was a notice outside the theatre which said: "There will be no matinee this afternoon. Mr. Jolson is taking the entire company to *the races!*'

"Well, all I can tell you . . . I have never felt so disgusted with an alleged performer . . . that he could cancel the show to take his cast to the races. But I did get a ticket for that night's performance, which was to be the last he was doing with *Bombo*.

"I walked into that theatre absolutely hating the very name of Jolson. . . . I took my seat—the place was jammed—and the show started.

"After about twenty minutes of the show, the tempo seemed to . . . heat up. And within minutes after that, on the stage, came a . . . blackfaced personality.

"Well, being the favorite that he was, the whole house cracked with applause. He hadn't opened his mouth, but there was nobody in that theatre applauding . . . more than I was.

"I sat through that performance; I still regard it as the most moving night of my whole life. When the performance ended, I couldn't go home. All I could see was . . . a wonderful "magic man," who hadn't been singing and talking to anybody in the theatre but me. I didn't know there was another person sitting next to me. I didn't know that there was anybody else within miles of me. All I knew was that this man was singing, laughing, talking, dancing . . . just to me.

"So I went up to Central Park, and I must have walked miles, just seeing that face and, above all, those eyes looking at me as he sang in a way I had never heard anybody sing before.

"I eventually went home. But I got up the next morning, as early as I could, and went down to the Winter Garden. I stood on the pavement opposite the stage door. All I could think of was the fact that he walked through that door; the people who were bringing some scenery out of the theatre knew him; they touched him; they'd heard him sing from backstage; they'd watched this . . . man.

"I've never been so emotional about anything, anybody, in my life.

"That was the first time I saw him."

Black Magic

"I was a flop, and I won't flop for anybody."

*B*ombo marked the pinnacle of Jolson's stage career, but Al had been serious about quitting the musical theatre. He began to think about alternatives to the stage shortly after *Bombo* opened.

The concert field was one possibility. Jolie's one-man show at the Boston Opera House in 1919 had sparked talk of similar concerts in other cities, and the tremendous response that "April Showers" had received in *Bombo* was a further incentive. Concerts, however, involved touring, and Al, in his mid-thirties, thought the time had come to settle down. On October 21, 1921, two weeks after *Bombo* opened, Jolie took his first apartment, a set of rooms two blocks from the Jolson Theatre at 36 West 59th Street.

Al found a possible answer to his professional future when, with Louis Silvers, he dropped in at The Friars and met Anthony Paul Kelly, a modestly successful author who had written the scenario for *Way Down East*. The three men talked about the movie business, Jolson telling Kelly he was "the bird that's got to write the stuff for me" if he went into pictures.

The motion picture industry had been after Jolson for years (the Shuberts had forced him to decline a reported $10,000 offer in 1914), and, while he had never given films much thought, they now seemed a viable alternative to stage work. They involved no touring, far less physical exertion than Al gave onstage, and no traumatic opening nights.

A. P. Kelly, who thought a liaison with Jolson would put his writing career on firmer ground, visited Al backstage in his dressing room a short time later and asked if he was "serious about this motion picture stuff."

"Yes," Al replied, "if I get myself a story. I'm afraid of pictures. I don't want to be a bust.

"I do sell-out business where the others starve," Jolie continued.

Look, I'm the highest paid comedian in the country, but . . . well, what if I should die, and leave no record?"

Knowing Jolson's mood swings, his frequent pessimism, and his forgetfulness, the film idea would probably have died a natural death had it not been for Kelly's tenacity and a short story in the January 1922 issue of *Everybody's* Magazine titled "The Day of Atonement." The plot concerned a boy who runs away from home to seek a career on the stage, but returns to take his dying father's place as cantor on the evening of Yom Kippur, the sacred Day of Atonement. It was similar to Jolson's own life story, and Al saw it as the vehicle for his first motion picture.

Al was cautious about movies. Many stage comedians of the early 1900s, including Eddie Foy and Fred Stone, had gone into pictures with disastrous results. Al did not want to join the list, and thought the greatest safeguard lay in getting the illustrious D. W. Griffith to direct him. That Griffith did not direct comedies seemed a minor point to Jolson.

Al had A. P. Kelly take "The Day of Atonement" to Griffith, but the director of *Birth of a Nation* feared the story's "racial" (Jewish) theme. Kelly then made the rounds of the major studios, but no one felt the subject would appeal to a national, non-Jewish audience.

Al sent A. P. back to Griffith. "I would have liked to do that story," he said, "but I want that 'record,' too." Negotiations for Al Jolson's first picture were soon opened with the Griffith corporation. Griffith himself, Al was assured, would come up with the vehicle.

By June 1923, Anthony Paul Kelly had devoted eighteen months of time and trouble to bringing Al Jolson and D. W. Griffith together in a film venture. Early in that month, Al Grey, Griffith's brother, asked Charles Schwartz, one of Jolson's lawyers, to draw up a contract. The contract was drawn and given to A. H. T. Banzhaf, secretary of the Griffith corporation, who prepared a new draft, between Al Jolson and D. W. Griffith, *Inc.*—instead of Griffith as an individual. Schwartz advised Al not to sign this revised contract.

Plans for Al's first film proceeded quickly, despite the lack of any signed agreement. The picture would be shot during June and July, Al's summer vacation, but permission from the Shuberts was still needed. Their contract with Al stated he was not to work in any entertainment medium, without their consent, at any time.

The Shuberts gave their consent. Their five-year contract with Al would expire in September, and nothing could be gained by making

Jolson mad. Lee and Jake could only hope that Al would not like movies.

Al insisted on a screen test, so Jimmy drove him to the Griffith Studios in Mamaroneck, N. Y., on Monday, June 11th. A test was made of Jolson in whiteface, but Al was far from pleased when he came back to see it two days later. He claimed it made him "look like a zebra."

Griffith disagreed. He described Jolson's affect on the screen as "striking," and said many of the biggest movie stars had been horrified by their first screen tests. To prove his point, he showed Al less-than-stupifying screen tests of some of his biggest stars.

Al agreed to go on, but asked Griffith that the shooting be done outdoors. Griffith agreed, and said he would have an outdoor set built by the time production started on June 22nd.

The film Al was about to make was called *Black Magic (Mammy's Boy* in press releases). The source was a 1919 script by Arthur Caesar, titled *Black and White,* about a white lawyer who disguises himself as a black man in order to clear his black client of a murder charge. There were comedy sequences, and Kelly, who was doing the adaptation, planned to write a special cabaret scene wherein Al would entertain.

Jolson's tentative agreement—just *how* tentative would later be debated—with Griffith called for him to receive $15,000 cash and one-quarter of the profits, and there was an option for three more films if the first one proved successful. Al's plan at this time was to quit the stage and spend the future making pictures in Mamaroneck. He was even trying to stop Ethel's drinking with talk of the big "dream house" they would have in nearby Scarsdale.

Preliminary shooting was done in the upstairs room of Keen's Chop House in New York over the next week. The scene worked on had Jolson, in blackface, getting into bed and being "vamped" by shapely Irma Harrison. "I didn't like that so much" was the way Al described it in 1926. What Al disliked even more was that Griffith did not direct it. Jack Noble, an assistant, was the man in charge.

Griffith's reluctance to direct the film himself was two-fold. In the first place, he did not do comedies. In the second, he knew Jolson's reputation. "It's not so bad when (actors) don't have money," Griffith had told A. P. Kelly. "But when they're rich (like Jolson) they get hard to handle."

Griffith, however, did not know the real Jolson—the insecure little boy who wanted a strong hand to guide him in the terrifying world of motion pictures. Al was shaken when he found that Noble, and not Griffith, would direct most of the scenes. It was just what he had feared—and why Schwartz had told him not to sign a contract with D. W. Griffith, *Inc.*

On Thursday, June 21st, Griffith and Banzhaf found Al having lunch with Jake Shubert at the Hotel Astor. Attempting to join them, they were rebuffed by the boorish Shubert. Griffith, who had already had a costly outdoor set built in Mamaroneck, feared Jake would talk Al out of doing the picture—which is exactly what happened.

The astute Louis Epstein was also against the movie venture. The way that Eppy saw it, Jolson was successful on the stage. Why, he asked, risk everything on a film that could bomb and leave that stage career in ruins?

That afternoon, at a "costuming test" in Keen's Chop House, at which Ethel was present, Griffith tried to have Al sign another copy of the contract. Jolson took a look, saw that it still said "D. W. Griffith, Inc.," and then asked to see what had been shot thus far. Griffith reluctantly agreed.

When the film had been run, and the lights turned on, Griffith was smiling. Al, he said, "should be quite pleased." Jolson, however, had already gotten an opinion that dovetailed with his own. In the dark, he had asked Ethel what she thought.

"I think it's the worst thing I ever saw," she said.

Al refused to sign the contract.

Al left the Fifty-ninth Street apartment early the next morning, instructing Ethel to tell callers he was ill and could not come to work. That day's shooting was to take place in Mamaroneck.

Al, with Eppy, went downtown, booked passage on the *Majestic,* which was scheduled to leave for England the following morning, and spent the remainder of the day at Aqueduct Race Track. Griffith, in the meantime, worked around his star, choosing to believe that Al was ill. Late that night, however, a friend told him Al was sailing for Europe.

The next morning, Griffith called the offices of the White Star Line and learned that Jolson was "aboard the *Majestic,* in his state room, and was not to be disturbed." Earlier that morning, Jimmy had driven Al, Ethel, and Eppy to the dock in Jolie's new $13,000 Rolls Royce. The car was a present from the Shuberts.

Jake was also sailing on the *Majestic.*

Ethel, who was not going along, gave her husband a farewell kiss for the newsreel cameras. Al would make no statement.

Jolson was unusually silent on the crossing, and a couple of the stewards overheard him crying in his stateroom.

Griffith, the southern gentleman, was shocked, but Kelly stood the most to lose by Jolson's departure. Frantically, he radioed Al on the *Majestic*. "Don't give people ammunition to say that you are yellow or a quitter. And don't be guided by a lot of jackasses who don't know anything about the picture game."

Jolson radiogrammed back: "I am not yellow, nor am I a quitter. I sailed for a rest because I was on the verge of serious collapse. After I rest up in Europe, I'll come back to America and finish the picture."

Jolson, Epstein, and Jake Shubert spent two weeks in England and then went to France. Ethel, occupied with the new house in Scarsdale, wondered whether Al would keep his promise not to sign another contract with the Shuberts—a contract that would keep him touring. At this point she was hoping against hope.

Al and Eppy arrived back in New York on board the *Leviathan* on July 23rd. Jolson walked down the gangplank in full English regalia—gray derby, white spats, blue overcoat, gray flannel sack suit, and a monocle. His remarks, however, were pure "Yankee."

"They hate us over there and never lose an opportunity to show their ill will. I never want to go again, unless perhaps it is with Mrs. Jolson, and then I would go only for the sea voyage. I saw only one good show abroad and that was of American origin, *Little Nellie Kelly*. This musical comedy is having a big success in London. The Paris revues are all alike and none of them is to be compared with the American productions.

"I was homesick all the time I was abroad. I missed the races and the fights and the good automobile roads around New York. I would rather spend one week of idleness in New York than a year in Europe. In order to make my trip memorable at all, I had to buy a monocle, white spats, and a gray derby. I wanted to give my wife a good laugh. She's never seen me in anything but a cap, a dark blue suit, and a pair of black low shoes."

Jolson did not mention *Black Magic*.

D. W. Griffith, Inc. finally filmed *Black Magic* with Lloyd Hamilton in Al's part and released it as *His Darker Self* in 1924. In April of that year, Griffith filed suit against Jolson for $571,696.72—$500,000 damages and $71,696.72 for actual money spent. A. P. Kelly also filed suit—$250,000 "for services rendered" in bringing Jolson together with Griffith.

Both suits were decided in the fall of 1926. Griffith's lawyer, Arthur Driscoll, was unable to prove that Al had made a firm oral commitment to do the film, and the famed director received only $2,627.28. The Kelly suit resulted in a hung jury, and A. P., who would have won little more than Griffith had, withdrew the case.

Kelly, who had staked virtually his entire career on Jolson's entry into pictures, saw his life run downhill from then on. Unable to work as a result of tuberculosis, he began to feel hopeless and despondent. His wife, the former Grace Canary, had divorced him long before.

On September 26, 1932, A. P. Kelly was found dead in his apartment at 410 West 110th Street in New York. On the floor by the couch on which he had lain down to die were the manuscripts of *Three Faces East* and *The Battle Royal,* two of his plays.

Kelly had committed suicide by inhaling gas.

The new Jolson home in Scarsdale was a two-year-old brick mansion built at a reported cost of $70,000. Ethel, basically a city person, had mixed feelings about living in Scarsdale, but any dreams she might have had of an idyllic life with Al were soon shattered.

Jolson and Jake Shubert had signed another five-year contract, Al to receive a guarantee of $3,500 a week plus 25 percent of the gross receipts. It was one of the most lucrative contracts in theatrical history to that time.

Ethel was shocked; "Albert" had not even bothered to discuss it with her first. Al, however, felt that a wife's place was in the home. *He* would handle his own business. Besides, Al argued, what else could he do—make pictures? Even she could see that he was "rotten."

"Al Jolson in *Bombo*" opened its third season at the Capital Theatre in Albany on October 15, 1923. The show was better than ever, but it lacked a new hit song. Al was used to having at least one new hit each year.

The current tour was to the west coast, and Bud DeSylva had an idea for a song about California. Al thought it might work, and told Bud to have Joe Meyer, composer of "My Honey's Lovin' Arms," write the music.

"Buddy came up to me when I came out of the Harms offices on Forty-fifth Street," Joe recalled. " 'Joe,' he said, 'Al likes you. He wants you to write a song for him to do this season.' Well, I went to one of the composing rooms at Clarke & Leslie, and I just sat

down and wrote 'California, Here I Come.' It was the greatest inspiration I ever had. Buddy got the song to Jolson, who was nuts
about it.

"He did it at a matinee, and it flopped for him. Al Goodman, the
conductor, got ahold of Jolson and said, 'Please, Al, let me reorches-
trate this song, because I know that it's a hit.' Jolson acceded, and
the song became a smash. Al sent me a congratulatory telegram."

Jolie came into New York in mid-December and took Bud and
Joe to Remick Music. "Jolson wanted five thousand, in cash, up
front, with the royalties, of course, to follow," Joe remembered. "Joe
Keit, of Remick, said he didn't have that much on hand, and offered
to give Al one thousand in cash with two notes for two thousand
each. Al said 'fuck you' to him and took us to Witmark & Sons at
1650 Broadway." Julius Witmark gave them five thousand dollars
in cash and published "California, Here I Come" with Jolson listed
as a co-writer.

Al recorded "California" and five other songs in January, when
Bombo played a three-week return engagement in Chicago. These
recordings were made for the Brunswick-Balke Collender Company,
which had offered Al $7,500 a side when his contract with Colum-
bia expired at the end of 1923. Brunswick also offered Al the backing of well-known dance bands, like Isham Jones', Abe Lyman's,
and Bill Wirges'. The results, heard today, sound forced, with Jolson's voice often reproduced less faithfully than on his 1911–13 disks
for Victor.

Bombo broke the house record at the Mason Opera House in Los
Angeles, grossing $75,200 over two weeks there that spring. But the
advance for a one-night stand at the Loring in Riverside was only
$1,800, and Al canceled the engagement.

The Loring Theatre management did not believe Al's wire stating
he had laryngitis. Money was refunded, with the house manager telling the audience that Mr. Jolson had seen fit "to cancel the engagement due to the small advance sale." The patrons were indignant,
and Jolson did not help matters by going to the fights in Vernon,
Calif., that same evening. He canceled another one-night stand, in
San Bernardino, the following night.

Al was well enough, however, to appear when *Bombo* was sold
out in Long Beach one night later, and West Coast Theatres, Inc.,
owners of the Loring, got the sheriff to tie up $4,200 in receipts
when the show played Santa Barbara. There was no doubt that Jolson had been feigning illness.

Bombo opened for another two-week engagement, this one at the

Curran Theatre in San Francisco, on May 18, 1924. The San Francisco *Chronicle* reported that "the audience refused to let the play end, and Jolson came before the curtain and sung and sung and sung until 11:35."

With Ethel three thousand miles away in Scarsdale, Al's thoughts became focused on another woman—a woman close at hand whom he had lost: Henrietta Keller Jolson Silvey.

"Al called her up," Jean Carlson remembered, "and he was so disappointed that she didn't recognize his voice right away. Well, she did recognize it, but she didn't admit it.

"He wanted to know if he could come out and see her, and Jack [Silvey, Henrietta's husband] said, 'Sure, bring him out.'

"So, he went out, and later sent them tickets for the show. Al sang the 'One I Love Belongs to Somebody Else' the night they came. He sang it so hard, he couldn't talk for two days after."

Jolson began to have real trouble with his voice when the show's run in San Francisco ended on May 31st. Al canceled a one-night stand in San Jose, but his doctors gave him an ultimatum the next morning: Either he took "an immediate and protracted rest" or he would "lose his voice completely and for good." Al acquiesced, and cancelled a sold-out performance at the Municipal Auditorium in Oakland that evening, losing thousands of dollars for the Shuberts and himself.

Rumors flew, and the newspapers carried various stories about Jolson's reasons for "suddenly quitting the show." One paper hinted at a row among the company; another said Jolson was eager to break away from the Shuberts and was using "these so-called fits of temperament" to inspire them to break his contract.

The remaining four weeks of the tour were canceled, and the company was sent back to New York. Al stayed behind in San Francisco for a few days with Frank Holmes and Schneck, finally leaving for New York with Frank on June 9th. Their train stopped in Ogden, Utah, and Jolson sent a telegram to the San Francisco *Chronicle* in answer to the various rumors.

COULD NOT SPEAK ABOVE A WHISPER. DR. HOUSTON TOLD ME TO REST, ALSO DR. GIBSON. WOULD RATHER CUT OUT ANY TOWN THAN OAKLAND AND SACRAMENTO, AS THAT IS WHERE I STARTED. JUST LARA—I DON'T KNOW HOW TO SPELL IT—BUT LARYNGITIS IS WHAT I'VE GOT, WHICH ONLY REST WILL CURE. WILL BE OUT THIS SUMMER WITH MY FAMILY FOR VACATION.
YOURS FOR CALIFORNIA, ALWAYS—
AL JOLSON

Jolson was like the boy who cried wolf. He had faked voice trouble in Riverside and San Bernardino. Now that he was really sick, nobody would believe him.

Al returned to Scarsdale to find Ethel had been drinking. Being cooped up in boring, suburban Westchester County had driven the former show girl right back to the bottle.

Ethel's drinking was already playing havoc with her beauty. She had gained weight, and her once fine face had flattened out and coarsened. Al went back to New York in disgust.

Jolson's voice was back to normal by the end of June, and there were five recording sessions for Brunswick between July 2 and August 6, 1924. The Shuberts had been looking for a new vehicle for Jolson, but without success.

1924 was a key year in the development of the American musical theatre. The modern musical comedy finally got off the ground, as composers, backed by ASCAP, won the right to control scores. The old practice of interpolating numbers, often without rhyme or reason, was practically abandoned, and "extravaganzas," like the ones Jolson had starred in, began to look old-fashioned in the new world of George Gershwin and Vincent Youmans.

The Shuberts were determined to present Al Jolson in a musical comedy—with a tighter plot than the extravaganzas and with a complete score by one set of composers. The only difficulty lay in finding a story that could easily be wrapped around Jolson's character, Gus.

Al and his brother, Harry, discussed the situation on the way home from the races. Harry suggested Al do a musical version of one of the old racing stories, like *Wild Fire* or *In Old Kentucky*. Al, at first enthusiastic, suddenly turned doubtful. The required horses would make playing one-night stands all but impossible.

Al forgot about the idea until a few days later, when he mentioned it in a talk with Jake Shubert. Jake was interested, figuring that horses would give the show added spectacle.

Rehearsals for "Al Jolson in *Big Boy*," a musical comedy based on Charles T. Dazey's play, *In Old Kentucky*, started early in October. Ralph Reader, the young Englishman who had admired Al so much in *Bombo*, was in the chorus, understudying a part:

"There was a kind of affection that grew up between Jolson and me. I had one scene with him, at the end of the first act, when just the two of us were on the stage alone. I'd been around and had experience, but I was frightened. He wasn't an ordinary person at all. . . .

"He *worked* at rehearsals. He'd clown a bit, but he'd 'go for' a scene. He was playing a jockey in the show, and the last scene had me saying, 'Well, what are you gonna do, Gus?' And that set up the line where he went into 'Keep Smiling at Trouble' This was, frankly, an overpowering situation for me because he *gave* so much. I felt like there was a dynamo pushing me away. He said, 'English, you're scared, aren't you?' I admitted that I was. He put his hand on my shoulder and said, 'All you have to do is keep your eyes on me. And whatever I do, whether I stand on my head or turn cartwheels, people will look at you.'

"It was the most wonderful piece of advice any man ever gave me. I made it pay off with some of the very biggest stars I worked with."

Jolson brought Reader with him when he was invited to have breakfast with President Calvin Coolidge at the White House on October 17th. Al, who had been appointed president of the Coolidge-Dawes Theatrical league, introduced a new campaign song, "Keep Cool with Coolidge," on the White House lawn.

Al made Coolidge laugh—no mean feat—by whispering in his ear. "If you don't laugh," he said, "I'll tell you a story that'll *really* make you laugh." The most memorable comment of the day, however, came from the First Lady, Grace Coolidge.

"Your dog must like me," Al told her at breakfast. "He hasn't stopped licking my hands since we sat down."

"Maybe he wouldn't do it," Grace said, "if you used your napkin."

Big Boy toured for six weeks before opening in New York. In Detroit, Al fell asleep in his hotel room and awakened to a radio message by Sophie Van Sheis, head of the Michigan State Charity Aid's Child Placing Bureau.

Miss Van Sheis' speech led Al to believe that a child could save his marriage to Ethel. "My wife and I have a lovely country home in Scarsdale," he said just a few weeks later. "On it, we have horses, dogs, cats, canaries, and all sorts of other pets. But in spite of that, there's always been something missing." It certainly was not liquor.

Jolson had Frank Holmes write a letter to the Placing Bureau, but any ideas Al might have had about adopting a child were abandoned in the next few months. Ethel had become far too dependent on alcohol to be a mother.

The Student Prince was enjoying a successful run at Jolson's Fifty-ninth Street Theatre, so *Big Boy* opened at the Winter Garden on Wednesday night, January 7, 1925.

The show's plot was predictable: Gamblers conspire to have Gus fired from the Bedford Stables so that their own jockey can ride Big Boy and throw the Kentucky Derby; the plot is eventually discovered and Gus rides the horse to victory. The race, in Act II, Scene Four, was staged on a treadmill with four live horses. Ray O'Brien, the pit pianist, confirmed the story about Al's horse littering the stage on opening night. "It's a good thing he's not an elephant," was what Jolie ad libbed.

Al Jolson, in *Big Boy*, garnered what are still the greatest critical accolades ever given a musical comedy star. The great humorist Robert Benchley crystalized the general impression in his review for *Life* Magazine:

> A while ago we intimated that some one (we forget who just now) might take Al Jolson's place. We were just crazy, that's all. We doubt whether anyone could ever take his place. Certainly no human being. We can't imagine what we were thinking of to have said such a thing.
>
> To sit and feel the lift of Jolson's personality is to know what the coiners of the word "personality" meant. The word isn't quite strong enough for the thing that Jolson has. Unimpressive as the comparison may be to Mr. Jolson, we should say that John the Baptist was the last man to possess such a power. There is something supernatural back of it, or we miss our guess.
>
> When Jolson enters, it is as if an electric current had been run along the wires under the seats where the hats are stuck. The house comes to tumultuous attention. He speaks, rolls his eyes, compresses his lips, and it is all over. You are a life member of the Al Jolson Association. He trembles his under lip, and your heart breaks with a loud snap. He sings, and you totter out to send a night letter to your mother. Such a giving-off of vitality, personality, charm, and whatever all those words are.

Even the acerbic George Jean Nathan was completely floored:

> The power of Jolson over an audience I have seldom seen equalled. There are actors who, backed up by great dramatists, can clutch an audience in the hollow of their hands and squeeze out its emotions as they choose. There are singers who, backed up by great composers, can do the same. And there are performers of divers sorts who, aided by external means of one kind or another, can do the same. But I know of none like this Jolson—or, at best, very few—who, with lines

of pre-war vintage and melodies of the cheapest tin-piano variety, can lay hold of an audience the moment he comes on the stage and never let go for a second thereafter. Possessed of an immensely electrical personality, a rare sense of comedy, considerable histrionic ability, a most unusual musical show versatility in the way of song and dance, and, above all, a gift for delivering lines to the full of their effect, he so far outdistances his rivals that they seem like the wrong ends of so many opera glasses.

Despite the settings (which included a flashback to 1870, where Gus's grandfather, also played by Jolson, rescues "Caroline Purdy" from the clutches of " 'Bully' John Bagby"), the audience saw a more sophisticated, urbane Jolson than ever before. Perched atop a platform that extended over the orchestra pit, Al slipped the second-night audience a little "inside information" on the show. "That opening night audience was a little hard boiled, but they had a right to be. They paid eleven dollars to come in. I personally had a row with the Shuberts—there are two of them, you know, Lee and J. J. (Jake-Jake)—over the price. I figured that five-fifty was enough, but they held out for the eleven dollar top so they'd have the cost of the production right back out of the opening night's receipts if it flopped." Jolson followed that up with some gags about screen actress Pola Negri, claiming to have given her two seats after learning she had tried to get them everywhere "for love or money."

Jolson's songs included "Keep Smiling at Trouble," "Hello, 'Tucky," "Who Was Chasing Paul Revere?," a by now obligatory mammy number, and "Who Wants a Bad Little Boy?" A few other songs were used and then tossed out by a dissatisfied Jolson, including "If You Knew Susie." The last named number became one of Eddie Cantor's biggest hits.

Big Boy grossed $5,000 a performance (as compared with $3,000 for the Ziegfeld *Follies*), and it should have been among the season's biggest money makers. Al, however, soon developed a severe case of bronchitis, forcing the show to shut down for two weeks. Dr. C. W. Cobly ordered him to take a complete rest, and Jolie went to Palm Beach, Florida—with Frank (Pansy) Holmes and Jimmy, but without his wife.

Ethel was highly visible backstage, however, when *Big Boy* re-opened on February 9th. "She'd come in all liquored up," remembered Ray O'Brien, "and Jolson would wind up smacking her. I knew what was going on. I said to Jolson, 'You met my aunt. She's quite a person, very smart. Would you like her to kind of help Ethel around a little bit?' He said, 'Let her alone! I'll take care of her.' And that was that."

Jolson had a relapse after four more weeks, and the March 10th matinee was cancelled. Al got through the next six performances, and was brooding over his condition when he learned, between performances on Saturday, that his friend Walter Camp (selector of the All-American football teams since 1889) had died.

That night, Al went out and gave what Lee Shubert called "a perfect performance, with no indication of his illness," for a sold-out house. It was Jolson's tribute to a friend. Al had a consultation with another of his doctors, Cornelius Coakley of 83 West Fifty-sixth Street, after the performance and was told to stop working "instantly." A midnight meeting with Lee followed, and *Big Boy* was closed.

Three weeks later, on Saturday morning, April 4th, Al and Ethel sailed for Bermuda on the *Araguaya*. This was Al's attempt to kill three birds with one stone: (1) regain his health, (2) stop Ethel's drinking, and (3) save their marriage.

The trip was almost totally successful on the first count, and the *New York Times* reported that Al "stopped the show" when he performed in the Lambs Gambol at the Metropolitan Opera House on April 26th, a few days after their return to New York. "Mr. Jolson," the review said, "sang two songs and told several stories in his familiar manner, all in a way to convince his audience that he was fully restored to health. He announced that he would leave for California on an extensive vacation late this week."

Al thought—or hoped—this second vacation would get Ethel permanently on the wagon. They sailed on an eighteen-day voyage on the Dellas liner, *President Adams,* on Thursday, April 30th, and stayed at the Biltmore Hotel in Los Angeles for a few days before proceeding to the Avalon resort on Catalina Island.

Once on Catalina, Jolson ignored his wife completely. Every morning, he rose early and went out to play a round or two of golf. His afternoons were usually spent with admirers or friends.

Ethel, who knew no one on the west coast, soon found ways of getting "bootleg hooch." While Al played golf, she drank . . . and drank.

What Ethel really needed was some genuine affection, but Al could only give that kind of love to an audience. He thought, of course, that he was doing all he could to save their marriage. And he probably was. Taking Ethel on long trips and being "strong" about her drinking was the best that he could do.

A second edition of "Al Jolson in *Big Boy*" opened at the Forty-fourth Street Theatre in New York on August 24, 1925. During the show's run, Jolson was summoned as a witness in the famous Rhinelander divorce case.

Alice Jones had been a maid in one of the Paul Smith cottages in the Adirondacks in August, 1921, when Jolson, DeSylva, Atteridge, Conrad, and Romberg were there working on *Bombo*. Alice wrote a letter to her future husband, Leonard K. Rhinelander, at the time.

> I was talking to Al Jolson today. He was in swimming, but he is some flirt with the girls. There is four fellows with him. His cottage is next to ours and they have their instruments. And we had some orchestra here today.

Alice eventually married Rhinelander, who subsequently sued her for divorce on the grounds that her father was a Negro.

Al facetiously dusted off the witness seat with his handkerchief, denied having known Alice Jones Rhinelander, and was told the newspaper headlines would be different as the result of his testimony.

"My God," said Al, "I hope so. My wife won't speak to me anymore. She won't even have breakfast with me."

It really was the other way around.

Big Boy played fifteen weeks in New York before moving to Chicago in December. The show broke all house records, grossing more than $60,000 a week at the Apollo, but the wind played havoc with Al's voice.

Eddie Cantor, who had emerged as a Jolson "rival" a few years before, was appearing in *Kid Boots* at the Woods Theatre in Chicago. Cantor was suffering from pleurisy, but did not dare close his show for fear *Variety* would headline, "JOLSON DRIVES CANTOR OUT OF CHICAGO."

Cantor claimed that Jolson "talked to me like a big brother. 'Eddie, show business ain't worth it. You need sun, kid. Go to Miami, close the show, get some rest and heat and get well.' . . . Finally, one night between the first and second acts, I quietly collapsed. The doctor stepped in, the show was closed, and I was trundled to the train for New York. . . . I arrived, picked up the *New York Times*,

and read: 'JOLSON ILL, CLOSES SHOW.' What I hadn't known—
all the time I was suffering with pleurisy, Al was sicker than I was,
with a throat infection. But Jolie wouldn't close the show, because
in his mind's eye he could see a headline in *Variety:* "CANTOR
DRIVES JOLSON FROM CHICAGO."

According to Ray O'Brien, Cantor *knew* Jolson was sick. "They'd
be having a late supper together, and Cantor would tell him, 'I'll
make a bet I'll be down in Florida before you are.' " The fact remains, however, that Al would not close his show till after Eddie
closed *Kid Boots.*

Big Boy was scheduled to reopen on Monday night, February 15th,
but a wire from West Palm Beach on February 9th said Al was

"VERY SICK AND ON ADVICE FROM DOCTORS MUST CLOSE THE
SEASON."

Rumors quickly spread that Al was dying or was dead, and the Associated Press reporter in Palm Beach went to Jolson's hotel to in-
vestigate. Al denied that he was dead.

"I'll be on the beach getting a sun in a few minutes and any doubters
can see for themselves. Fact is, I was just thinking of Mark Twain's
immortal wise crack."

Jolson did more than get a little sun on the beach. A photograph
of Al carrying Mary Eaton, the beautiful blonde ingenue of *Kid Boots,*
out of the water found its way into *The Billboard.* "Mr. Jolson,"
read the caption, "is seen rescuing Miss Eaton . . . from getting
wet."

This Chicago story has a postscript. Ralph Reader and eight of
the chorus girls had been doing an act in a Chicago speakeasy after
performances in *Big Boy* every evening. When Al closed *Big Boy,*
and the cast returned to New York, Reader and the chorines lost
their floor show jobs as well. Jolie heard about it, and he spoke to
Reader.

"What did you lose on that, English?"

The following Friday, Al sent Ralph and the girls every cent they
would have made in the club had *Big Boy* stayed in Chicago for the
rest of its scheduled run.

Jolson's throat condition seemed to worsen. The week following
the death report, he left Palm Beach for New York to be "under the
care of specialists," and was confined to his suite at the Ritz Carlton
Hotel. Jake Shubert accused Al of shamming illness, but Jolie, backed
up by his growing coterie of doctors, swore that he was sick. A

compromise was worked out whereby *Big Boy* would remain closed for the season with Al doing a minimum four-week guest appearance in *Artists and Models* at the Winter Garden.

Al's first night in the show, March 20, 1926, marked the fifteenth anniversary of the Winter Garden's opening. According to the *New York Times,* the theatre "was crowded to capacity, with the promenades jammed with the unfortunates who had been unable to obtain tickets and with even anxious enthusiasts in the lobby, receiving tidings of the doings from voluntary dispatch runners." Al was scheduled to do fifteen minutes at each performance, but wound up doing forty-three that evening. He sang seven songs, including Irving Berlin's "Always," "Keep Smiling at Trouble," "I'm Sitting on Top of the World," and "Who Wants a Bad Little Boy?" "In between times," said *Variety,* "he told a raft of stories, all except one or two being great. One that did a sad flop he blamed on J. J. Shubert, saying J. J. had given him that so that he would flop and then work for less next season.

"At his first appearance, Jolson made a short speech about his physical condition, which necessitated the closing of *Big Boy.* Then he began kidding the newspapermen who had said that he was naturally 'delicate.'

" 'Delicate?' shot Jolson, 'after working fifteen years for the Shuberts?'

"Jolson was spotted three numbers from the finale and worked in blackface, though he declared that on Monday night he'd abandon the cork.

"People who spoke with him before he went on claimed that he was nervous." They were right.

Eppy had worked out a deal with Jake Shubert whereby Jolson received $10,000 weekly for *Artists and Models,* with a percentage sharing agreement if the gross exceeded a specific figure. The Shuberts certainly did not lose money on the deal, as Al pushed the weekly gross up $15,000. Jake even talked Al into staying on a fifth week, little dreaming that April 24, 1926, Jolson's last night in *Artists and Models,* would also mark his final performance at the Winter Garden.

The 1920s saw the greatest parade of single male entertainers in history. Jolson, Eddie Cantor, Georgie Price, Jack Osterman, James Barton, and Harry Richman were the leaders.

Jolson first met Harry Richman at Oakland's Watts Tavern in 1917. Nine months later, when *Sinbad* was running at the Winter Garden,

Richman and his partner, Cliff Friend, showed up in Al's dressing room. Jolson subsequently spoke to Florenz Ziegfeld and got them a berth in the *Midnight Frolic*. They were fired after the first night.

At this time Richman was primarily a pianist. During the next few years, he served as accompanist to Mae West and the Dolly Sisters. In 1925, Al saw the big-voiced, lisping Richman, now a singer, perform in Atlantic City and predicted great things for him. Jolie began tutoring Richman in song stylism and got him a lucrative recording contract with Brunswick in April 1926.

The two men spent a lot of time together that spring. Al, who had been one of the first members of the Westchester-Biltmore Country Club in Rye, N. Y., brought Richman to play golf there twice. Following the second visit, Al received a letter from the secretary of the club informing him that Richman was considered "undesirable."

Al soon pressured Roy Jackson, vice president of the club, for the reason behind Richman's "undesirability." "If you want it straight," said Jackson, "and you asked for it—we don't want any Jews here."

Al went straight to the club's board of directors and handed in his resignation, hotly telling everything he knew about some of the club's other members and their general standing. A subsequent campaign was launched against the Biltmore.

Everyone knew Jolson was Jewish, but it was believed the club, having come into a better economic situation, was trying to discourage further Jewish membership. It is entirely possible, however, that Richman's ethnic background was not the only reason for his "undesirability." Harry had a reputation as a lothario, and was known to be bisexual as well.

Richman's autobiography, *A Hell of a Life*, includes comparatively little on Al Jolson. Richman claimed the publisher "cut out all the true stuff about Jolson because I could write another book on what a real bad person he was. Words can't describe the meanness of this man."

Richman's bitterness seemed to stem from Al's apparent coolness towards him after Harry scored his first major success with "The Birth of the Blues" in the 1926 edition of George White's *Scandals*. "I suppose I should have expected it," said Richman. "Jolson made a habit of discovering talent and then, when an individual became successful, dropping him." Richman claimed that Jolson treated him "in a kind of offhand way for several years."

A few years after Jolie died, Richman met Pearl Goldberg Sieben, who had known and worshipped Jolson in the 1940s. "*I lived* with your boyfriend," Harry whispered in her ear. The remark startled

Pearl, who had already heard rumors of Jolson's possible bisexuality.

Al's marriage to Ethel was dissolved that summer in one of those quick and painless divorces for which the 1920s became famous.

Al and Ethel sailed for Cherbourg on the *Leviathan,* July 3, 1926. Jolie, needing male company always, brought along Con Conrad and John Schneckenberger in addition to his lawyer, Nathan Burkan. Al cut up monkeyshines for the newsreels as they got on board.

"Stop acting so foolish before the cameras," Ethel chided. She was only twenty-six, but she looked middle-aged.

It took three weeks in Paris before the papers were set. Ethel then sailed home on the *Berengaria.* Al remained in Paris with his friends to accept service in the case.

The charge, delivered on July 5th, was desertion—supported by a letter written by Asa Yoelson stating his refusal to resume marital relations with his wife, the former Alma Osborne. Burkan and the French had made the whole thing very simple.

Just as he had first denied his marriage to Ethel in 1922, Al now denied the reports that appeared in American newspapers about the divorce. "I just paid five thousand dollars for new clothes for my wife at Poiret's," he told reporters. "That doesn't sound like divorce, does it?

"My wife sailed home on Saturday, and I intended to remain here. But after this shock, I'm leaving tomorrow morning, if I can get a boat."

Ethel was surrounded by reporters when her ship arrived in New York several days later. She was well prepared, however, and even intimated that the reported divorce was a mere press stunt.

"You know," she pined, "it's awfully hard to get things into the papers in Europe. How did the story go in the United States?"

Ethel very merrily deemed the divorce reports "a lot of blah. I'm Al's wife, and will continue to be his wife, time without end. I did not sign any application for a divorce." She claimed she would be there to meet him when Al returned the following week. "You can come and see for yourself," she said, "and if I'm not you need never write another line about me as long as I live."

Al and his entourage arrived in New York harbor on August 10th. Ethel was not there, and the divorce decree was granted two months later.

Even then, Al said that it was just "a little quarrel that meant nothing." He admitted there had been a divorce, but said he would remarry Ethel just "as soon as she will have me. I call her on the phone every night to propose, and she's promised me an answer when I'm in New York on Sunday. (Jolson was in Boston at the time.) In fact, we might remarry then and there, if she's willing.

"If I don't remarry her, I won't remarry anybody else. No one is as nice as she is."

There was no remarriage. Al let Ethel keep the Scarsdale home until the early 1930s. By then, she was a truly helpless alcoholic, and Jolson had her put in the psychiatric ward of the Brunswick Hospital Center and Nursing Home in Amityville, N. Y.

Ethel stayed there, under the name "Claire Osborne," until the early 1960s. Sometimes, she remembered Jolson, "in a childlike way," according to Pearl Goldberg Sieben, who visited her there. Al's will left a $100,000 trust fund to keep her in Amityville, but rising costs finally forced the Jolson estate to transfer her to Central Hospital in nearby Islip.

Ethel died there in 1976. She was seventy-six years old, with no money, no friends, hardly any memory—which may have been a blessing—and no vestige of the beauty that had captivated Jolson, and so many others, in the early 1920s.

The Jazz Singer

"It was his first picture, and he was like a little boy. He was
frightened to death. He was really frightened."

MAY MCAVOY

Rehearsals for the 1926–27 tour of *Big Boy* began in August and
continued, with one interruption, until the company left New
York for Wilmington, Delaware, on Friday morning, September 10th.
While hurrying to catch the train, Al ran into Karl Kitchen, columnist ("Up and Down Broadway") for the New York *Evening World*.

"I don't know why I'm going back to work," said Al, "but this
season is my last. The Vitaphone has given me the biggest thrill I've
ever had and after this year I'm going to play with it."

"Vitaphone" was a sound-on-disk process developed by Western
Electric to produce sound motion pictures.

Movies that "talked."

Attempts at making "talking pictures" had begun as soon as
Thomas Edison developed the first motion picture camera in 1889.
They had never gotten far, however, due to technical problems (mainly
the lack of a clear sound system that would fill a theatre) and the
fact that films had become popular, in part, due to their silence.
Immigrants unable to understand the dialogue in stage plays could
easily follow the action of short motion pictures, most of which contained few titles.

All that changed after World War I. Middle America had discovered the motion picture, immigration had declined, and the technical
problems were being ironed out as the result of the development of
electrically recorded sound. On April 20, 1926, the Vitaphone Corporation was formed on the basis of an agreement between Warner
Bros. and Western Electric, and the new Vitaphone process was used
to make sound films of leading vaudeville and concert artists and
provide synchronized scores for feature-length silent movies like *Don
Juan*.

On Thursday, August 26th, Jolson, George Jessel, Elsie Janis, Willie and Eugene Howard, Reinald Werrenrath, and the Four Aristocrats signed contracts to appear in Vitaphone shorts. Al reported to the Manhattan Opera House on West Thirty-fourth Street on Monday morning, September 6th and filmed "Al Jolson in a Plantation Act," in which he emerged from a cabin in blackface, wearing rural clothing and a big straw hat. The action consisted of Al tossing away the hat, doing a brief monologue, and singing three songs—"April Showers," "Rock-a-Bye," and "When the Red, Red Robin Comes Bob, Bob, Bobbin' Along."

That might have ended Al's association with the Warners, had Al not known the family from years of playing Youngstown and had he not mentioned his interest in "The Day of Atonement" to Sam Warner. The story had been made into a play called *The Jazz Singer*, and the Warners had acquired the screen rights earlier that year.

Jolson had met Samson Raphaelson, author of the story, at the Palais Royal in New York in 1922. The slim, bespectacled, young writer was unaware of Jolson's efforts to star in a film version of his story, but was honored when Al expressed interest in doing it as a play. "He told me what kind of entrance he wanted, and then proceeded to describe a Shubert musical," Raphaelson recalled in 1974. "Hell, I loved to see those shows, but I wouldn't have been caught dead writing one."

"Raphe" told Al that seeing him in *Robinson Crusoe, Jr.* had given him the inspiration for the story. ("His voice reminded me of the *chazans* I'd heard as a boy.") But he respectfully informed Al that the play he had in mind was a straight drama.

Raphaelson struck Jolson as a sincere scholar—a type of man, similar to his own father, whom Al could respect. "Son," he told him, "you go ahead and write that play. And if you have any trouble getting it produced, you come to me."

Jolson followed Raphaelson's efforts to have "The Day of Atonement" produced as a play with considerable interest. Early in 1925, Albert Lewis and Max Gordon, two producers in the Sam H. Harris office, took an option on *The Jazz Singer* as a vehicle for George Jessel, then a featured revue and vaudeville monologuist. The play had its world premiere in Stamford, Conn., on Thursday night, July 9, 1925.

"I was getting a shave in the Taft Hotel barber shop a couple of hours before curtain," Raphaelson remembered almost half a century later, "when the barber said, 'Hey, look who's here.' I put my glasses on, sat up, and there was Jolson. He said, 'You didn't think I'd miss this, did you?'

"We sat together that night, and the play was well received. Jessel came out to make a curtain speech. 'Thank you, thank you, every-body. I'm glad you enjoyed *my little play.*'

"All of a sudden," Raphe continued, "Jolson yelled out, 'author, author.' The whole place reacted; they knew Jolson anywhere. Fi-nally, Jessel said the author could not be located, and they lowered the curtain."

The Jazz Singer enjoyed a full season's run on Broadway before touring the country in 1926–27. Jolson spent that season on the road in *Big Boy,* playing Nixon's Apollo Theatre in Atlantic City in November 1926. Al's sister, Rose, was there with her two daughters, Ethel and Teresa, at the time.

Al rarely saw his sisters. In 1907, Rose, aged twenty-eight and working in a bicycle shop, married Nathan Flax, a salesman, and started raising a family that would include five children. Unlike her brothers, Rose did not stray from the orthodox Jewish fold. The Flax home was always kosher, and Rose, a *rebitzzen* in everything but name, became a leader in the Washington Ladies' Auxiliary of the Jewish Consumptives' Relief Society of Denver, the Hebrew Home for the Aged, and her local synagogue, Beth Sholom of Washing-ton, D.C.

Rose, now forty-seven, suffered abdominal pains while in Atlantic City and became too weak to leave her hotel room. Ethel and Teresa tried in vain to get a doctor.

Al did not waste a second once he found out Rose was ill. Two physicians were in her hotel room within an hour, and the eventual diagnosis was early cancer.

The medical science of 1926, aided, in large measure, by Rose Yoelson's will, soon had the disease under control. Al's eldest sister lived until 1939.

Al still visited Moshe and Hessi when he was in Washington. He was greeted warmly, but not with the great fervor he so desperately craved. Moshe never seemed to say what his son wanted: "Oh, Asa, I was wrong in everything I did, and everything that I believed in. Only you were right, and *I apologize.*" Al would never get that sat-isfaction.

Jolson had long spoken of doing something for "the old folks," but had never done much until now. Two weeks after rescuing his sister in Atlantic City, Al bought his father and stepmother a beautiful house at 1787 Lanier Plaza, in the posh northwestern section of Washington. Moshe and Hesse graciously accepted the new home, but they had a lot of memories after twenty years at 713 4 1/2 Street. Moving was not easy.

"I guess they got kind of used to the smells and felt as if they'd miss 'em" was the way Al put it in an interview with Francis Gilmore a year later. "Finally, though, I yanked them out by main force and set them up in a swell dump, four doors from the White House. Got a music room and everything. I told them, 'There's just one thing. You can't keep the coal in the music room.'"

Big Boy continued on tour for the next six months, playing a return engagement in Chicago in the spring of 1927—where Fred Becker swore he saw Al do the same caroms off the proscenium James Cagney did in *Yankee Doodle Dandy* fifteen years later. Al's songs included "(Take in the Sun) Hang Out the Moon," "Looking for Roses," "Dinah Might (Dynamite!)," "Ev'ry Rose Must Have a Thorn," and "One O'Clock Baby," as well as more enduring hits like "Red, Red Robin," "It All Depends On You," "Me and My Shadow," "Ain't She Sweet?" and the revived favorite, "Rock-a-Bye."

After four weeks in Chicago, *Big Boy* went to Denver, where Morris Safier approached Al about starring in *The Jazz Singer* for Warners.

In the spring of 1926, when George Jessel was starring in *The Jazz Singer* on Broadway, Warner Bros. signed him to do a silent comedy called *Private Izzy Murphy*. Jessel was to get $30,000, with an option on his services for two more pictures—at the same price—if *Murphy* proved successful. Jessel made the picture at the Warner studio in Hollywood that summer, and went on tour with *The Jazz Singer* in the fall. By New Year's time, *Private Izzy Murphy* had made money, and Warner Bros. decided to star Jessel in a film version of *The Jazz Singer*.

In the months that followed, the Warners made the decision to use Vitaphone in the song sequences. Jessel, whose contract had been conceived in terms of silent pictures, demanded a voucher for $10,000 additional money before he would leave New York, and Jack Warner used his "difficult" attitude as an excuse to approach Jolson. He already knew Al wanted the role.

Despite myths that Jolson took all or part of his salary in Warner stock, Al was paid $75,000 for *The Jazz Singer*—one-third down in cash and the remainder in installments of $6,250 a week. The Warners did not offer him any stock, and Jolson certainly did not put up any money, as Jessel often claimed, to finance the picture.

Warner Bros. has been portrayed as a "poverty row" studio by many film scholars. Such was not the case. Rin Tin Tin, one of the biggest money-makers in Hollywood, was a Warners' star, and the company was well financed by the investment banking firm of Goldman Sachs. Warners had already invested a lot of money in sound films, but Goldman Sachs still made sure they were never short on cash. It proved to be a wise investment.

Big Boy opened a two-week stand at the Biltmore Theatre in Los Angeles on Monday, May 23rd. Jolson had already come to terms with Morris Safier in Denver, and the only thing that remained was to sign the Warner contract.

Jessel, who still had two (silent) films to make for Warners, arrived in Los Angeles and supped with Jolson at the Biltmore Rendezvous on Wednesday night, May 25th. Al said nothing about *The Jazz Singer,* but invited George to spend the night in his hotel suite.

"When I got up, early the next morning," Jessel recalled, "Al was dressing. 'Go back to sleep, Georgie,' he told me. 'I'm going to play golf.'

"The next day, I read in the L. A. *Times* that Al had signed to do *The Jazz Singer."* Jessel was bitter for the rest of his life.

Shooting on *The Jazz Singer* was begun on Monday, July 11th, after *Big Boy* closed in San Francisco. The contract Jolson signed in 1923 gave the Shuberts exclusive rights only to his work in *musical comedy.* Lee and Jake, as a result, could not stop Al from doing *The Jazz Singer.*

Warner Bros. had assembled a good cast: Warner Oland, the Swedish-born actor later identified with the role of Charlie Chan, as Cantor Rabinowitz, Eugene Besserer as his wife, Sara, Otto Lederer as Yudelson ("the *kibbitzer"*), and May McAvoy as Mary Dale, the young, non-Jewish dancer who falls in love with Jack Robin and gets him his big chance on Broadway.

May told this author. "We got to be really good friends." Al knew that I could help him, and I certainly wanted to in every way I could.

"The techniques of stage and screen are so different. He was used to broad gestures and broad facial expressions to get across to an audience in the theatre. Pictures, of course, are entirely different. Things have to be treated more delicately.

"And then, when we got to him about the gestures being too broad, he stiffened up, and you could hardly see any expression then. He went from one extreme to the other.

"Many times, Al would insist something be done again. And after every scene, he'd come to me and say, 'How did I do?' and I'd say, 'Well, you know, I think maybe you could make a little bit more of this or that.' And he'd say, 'All right, boys, we'll take it again.'" May thought Alan Crosland was a very weak director.

"That's the way it went, and we did an awful lot over. As time went on, he got more accustomed to film making, but . . . act like he knew it all? Oh, no. Never! He was the most cooperative person, and just darling. I heard later he was hard to get along with—very temperamental, and very . . . bossy, in a way. You know—wanted to run the show, which I couldn't believe because [in *The Jazz Singer*] he was just like a newcomer. You wouldn't believe he had a big name in the theatre.

"Al seemed to be a very lonely man. My mother got to like him a lot, and she would say, 'May, why don't you ask Jolie to come up for dinner?' He came up quite often.

"We went out on several occasions—weekends—to nice quiet restaurants. He didn't like to go anyplace where there were crowds or people who might know him. He was a very shy man.

"Jolie was always so sweet and charming to my mother. He was a nice, nice man. That's all I can say—in spite of the mean and ugly things that I heard later. I just can't believe them.

"He did the most beautiful thing that I've ever had done. Just before the picture was finished, we went out to dinner—to a lovely little restaurant over toward Pasadena that was quiet and sort of up in the hills. You could see the city lights and everything like that. It was well known, but it was small and kind of private, with good food.

"We were having dinner, and he said, 'I have something for you. . . . I'd like you to have it because you've been so helpful to me all through this picture.'

"He pulled out a little package, a beautifully wrapped box, and handed it to me. I opened it, and my eyes popped.

"It was a cigarette case, and the whole top of it was diamonds, rubies, emeralds, and sapphires—in rows. It was just *beautiful.*

"But, needless to say, I didn't accept it. I couldn't. It was much too valuable a thing. I never had taken anything like that from anybody in my life, and . . . I guess it hurt his feelings a little. . . . If it had been something smaller, less expensive, I'd have taken it, but . . .

"Believe me, there was no romance there at all. It was just in appreciation. . . . No, I don't know of him having gone out with anybody else while we were making the picture.

"And after that, I never saw him."

The first sound scene was filmed/recorded at a refurbished studio in downtown Los Angeles on August 16, 1927. As Jack Robin, Al sang "Dirty Hands, Dirty Face" to a crowd at Coffee Dan's in San Francisco.

The audience applauded, and Al, as if onstage, said, "Wait a minute. Wait a minute. You ain't heard nothin' yet. You ain't heard nothin' yet. You wanna hear 'Toot, Toot, Tootsie'? All right, hold on, hold on. Lou, listen. Play 'Toot, Toot, Tootsie!' Three choruses, ya understand, and on the third chorus, I whistle. Now give it to 'em hot and heavy."

Al proceeded to sing "Toot, Toot, Tootsie," whistling on the second chorus, not the third. No dialogue was to have been included in the picture, but Al's ad libbing in the Coffee Dan's scene persuaded Sam Warner to include a sequence in which Jack Robin talks to his mother.

The scene chosen was the one in which Jack returns to his parents' house on Orchard Street and accompanies himself on the piano in the parlor. This scene had already been shot—on August 17th, with Al singing "It All Depends On You"—by the time that Sam made his decision, so it had to be remade.

In the remade scene, Al sings a chorus of "Blue Skies" and then turns to his mother. Eugenie Besserer's startled reactions leave no doubt but that Al's words were, once again, ad libbed.

Did you like that, mama? *(She giggles "Yes" off mike)* I'm glad of it. I'd rather please you than anybody I know of. Oh, darlin', will you give me something? *(She asks "What?")* You'll never guess. Shut your eyes, mama. Shut 'em for little Jakie. I'm gonna steal something. *(He kisses her)* I'll give it back to you some day, too. You see if I don't.

Mama, darling, if I'm a success in this show, well, we're gonna move from here. *(She says, "oh, no")* Oh, yes, we're gonna move up in the Bronx. A lotta nice green grass up there and a whole lotta people you know. There's the Ginsbergs and the Goldbergs. Oh, a whole lot of Bergs. I don't know 'em all.

And I'm gonna buy you a nice black silk dress, mama. You'll see. Mrs. Friedman, the butcher's wife, she'll be jealous of you. *("Oh, no")* Yes, she will. You'll see if she isn't. And I'm gonna get you a nice pink dress that'll go with your brown eyes. *("No, Jakie. No, I-*

I") What d'ya mean, no? Who's . . . who's telling you? What d'ya mean, no? Yes, you'll wear pink or else. Or else you'll wear pink. *(She giggles)*

And, darlin', oh, I'm gonna take you to Coney Island. Yes, we're gonna ride on the shoot-the-chutes, and, you know, in the Dark Mill. Ever been to Dark Mill? *(She answers, "No, I wouldn't—")* Well, with me it's all right. I'll kiss ya and hug ya; you'll see if I don't. *(They laugh)* Now, mama. Mama, stop now. You're gettin' . . . kittenish.

Mama, listen, I'm gonna sing this like I will if I go on the stage. You know, with this show. I'm gonna sing it jazzy. Now get this.

He launches into another chorus of "Blue Skies." This sound sequence ends when Warner Oland, as Cantor Rabinowitz, comes into the room and cries out "Stop!"

The "talkies" had begun.

Instead of reopening in *Big Boy* after finishing his screen work, Al did a week of personal appearances at the Metropolitan in Los Angeles for West Coast Theatres, Inc. The deal, handled by the William Morris Agency, called for Jolson to give five performances a day for a guaranteed fee of $17,500.

This engagement broke every box-office record west of Chicago, grossing $57,286.10. It was the beginning of "picture house" vaudeville, in which stars and, later, mini-musical productions, were offered with a feature film. Regular vaudeville found that it could not compete, and soon collapsed.

Jolson went up to Arrowhead Springs for a few days of fishing after his engagement at the Metropolitan. From there, he went to Chicago for the Tunney-Dempsey rematch, and, finally, to New York for the premiere of *The Jazz Singer* on October 6, 1927.

A mob—"one of those milling, battling mobs that used to blockade cinema premieres to watch the stars pass by in the days before they moved all the studios to Hollywood" was the way that Richard Watts, Jr., described it in the New York *Herald Tribune*—flooded the sidewalk and street in front of the Warner Theatre that night. All the Warner players in New York were there, along with Jolson cronies like Wardell and Eppy.

The film ended (with Al singing "Mammy") to applause that reached a climax with the audience demanding "Jolson, Jolson, Jolson." Al ran down the center aisle to the stage.

"God," he said. "I think you're really on the level about it. I feel good."

Roughly seven out of ten printed references to Al Jolson concern *The Jazz Singer*, the world's first commercially successful full-length talking movie. The film is a museum piece, at best, with tinny sound and make-up that makes Al look like an actor in *The Rocky Horror Show*. It is, nonetheless, historically important. Silent movies were a thing of the past a year and a half after the release of *The Jazz Singer*, but live theatre suffered most of all. The triple hammer blow of talkies, radio, and the Depression reduced the legitimate theatre to a life as "the fabulous invalid," its very existence a precarious affair.

When Jolson broke into show business, the theatre might have been called a profession—almost, but not quite, a sensible way to earn a livelihood. Since the thirties, it has been a "culture," its members sustained largely by work as cab drivers, waiters, and office workers. As bad as things had been for Al and Harry Jolson during 1903–04, they were never out of work for more than eight weeks at a time. Talented actors of the seventies and eighties have been known to go for years without theatrical employment.

The reviews for *The Jazz Singer* were not spectacular, but almost everyone thought Jolson had come through with flying colors, and word of mouth soon made it one of 1927–28's highest grossing films in major cities.

"Jolson wants to loaf" was the way *Variety* reported Al's plans for the remainder of the season. Jolson's contract with the Shuberts, however, had another year to run, and, when Jake demanded he reopen in *Big Boy*, Al reluctantly agreed.

The show opened a new tour at the Wieting Opera House in Syracuse (the Shuberts' own home town) on Thursday evening, December 1, 1927. Three nights earlier, Al had caught cold walking home from a rehearsal. Jake immediately took him to a specialist, but Al claimed that he felt no better.

He was able to sing at the opening, however—songs like "Mammy" and a new one called "Four Walls." Al seemed to be in fine health after the first act, but suffered a relapse on Saturday, and, abruptly, closed the show.

Al rested up at a resort in Asheville, North Carolina, and the Shuberts finally closed the show when Actors' Equity demanded that the cast be paid full salary for any lay-off time beyond two weeks. Two days after that, Al finally returned from Asheville. Jake fumed, but Jolie just shrugged and talked to representatives of the Dodge Motor Company about appearing on a coast-to-coast radio show.

On January 4, 1928—one week after attending the west coast premiere of *The Jazz Singer*—Jolson made his commercial radio debut on the "Dodge Victory Hour," a special one-hour program that included Will Rogers, Paul Whiteman, and Fred Stone in "pick ups" from Beverly Hills, New York, and Chicago. Al, broadcasting from the Roosevelt Hotel in New Orleans, sang two sets of songs accompanied by Dave Dreyer on the piano. In between the numbers, Al told stories, including one racy gem about Clara Bow sleeping "cater-cornered" in bed. The infant National Broadcasting Company promised to police itself more thoroughly thereafter, and *Variety* reported that stricter censorship would "be the order from within the radio broadcasting ranks as a result of Al Jolson's *bon mot*."

Four nights later, Al attended a testimonial dinner for William Morris at the Hotel Commodore in New York. Jessel, then at the beginning of his career as a "toastmaster," made a brilliant speech that evening, and Al called attention to it when he came out for his turn. The two men had not been speaking since *The Jazz Singer*.

Jessel walked onstage and took Al in a false embrace. While hugging Jolie, to the acclaim of all present, Georgie whispered in Al's ear. "Listen, you remember this doesn't go."

"Okay with me," replied Jolson, "but didn't I pick a great spot?"

Jolson vacationed at the Royal Poinciana Hotel in Palm Beach, Florida, prior to opening a week at Loew's State in St. Louis on February 13, 1928. Eppy worked out the deal, which gave Al a guarantee of $10,000 with a 50-50 split on any receipts over $25,000. Jolie worked in blackface, sang from a small stand built out from the stage, and wound up collecting $21,153.16—almost four thousand dollars more than he had gotten in Los Angeles.

Lee Shubert greeted Jolson on his return to Palm Beach. "Al feels fine," moaned Lee, "until it's time to go to work for me. Then he gets sick."

Al emceed the annual Kiwanis Club benefit at Palm Beach's Paramount Theatre on February 21st, and a special "Al Jolson Night" was held at the Venetian Gardens one week later at which Jolie sang and clowned for twenty minutes. Al left for New York the next day, traveling by steamer from Miami with Frank Holmes and Jimmy. He was in his suite at the Ritz Tower when Jake Shubert called him from Chicago.

Phil Baker, the popular accordianist and comedian, had fallen ill, and Jake wanted Al to step into *A Night in Spain* at Chicago's Four

Cohans Theatre. Jolson's contract with the Shuberts did not force him to accept, but he agreed to talk to Lee about a deal.

Eppy handled the negotiations by which Al received a total of $50,000 for a special four-week engagement in *A Night in Spain*. This figure—$12,500 a week—remained the record salary in the legitimate theatre for many years.

"I hope you know," said Lee, "that this makes you the highest paid actor in the world."

"I should be," answered Al. "I'm working for the world's richest producer."

"I won't stay rich if I have to keep paying actors like you."

Chicago brokers, confident of Jolson's drawing power, more than doubled their usual buy, and *A Night in Spain* grossed a profitable $40,900 during the first week of Al's engagement.

Jolson went to Hollywood when his stint in *A Night in Spain* was over. He was going to star in another film for Warners for $500,000—more than six times what he had been paid for *The Jazz Singer*.

The new picture was *The Singing Fool*, a story about a waiter and the blonde singer who spurns his affections. She marries him, however, when the songs he writes attract attention, and they have a son who becomes the apple of his father's eye. She runs away with a tall, handsome man and takes the child with her, but the boy get sick, and Al is summoned to his bedside. His son dies shortly after, but "the singing fool" picks up his life and vows to keep on singing.

Shortly before production started, Jolson, William Morris, Bill Perlberg, and a handful of Warner executives went to Union Station to meet Fanny Brice, coming to Los Angeles to make her first talking picture, *My Man*.

Al saw a wide-eyed girl deboard right after Fanny. She was small, like Josie, Henrietta, Kitty, and most of the other women Al had been attracted to since boyhood.

"Hello, kid," Al greeted her.

The startled girl looked up, seemingly surprised that the great Jolson knew her. Al had seen her as a specialty tap dancer in a show called *Sidewalks of New York* at the Woods Theatre in Chicago several weeks earlier.

The girl was eighteen-year-old Ruby Keeler.

Ruby

> Where Ruby had it over the rest of the line was she was beautiful in an unusually quiet way, like a young matron who would look more at home in a Junior League musical than in a Broadway leg-show. On stage, so the boys tell me, even in the scantiest, she carried herself with an air of aloof respectability which had the actual effect of an intense aphrodisiac. The other girls could dance half naked in front of you, and if you thought of anything you'd wonder how much it would cost. But seeing Ruby with her black lace stockings forming a sleek and silken path to her crotch was like opening the wrong bedroom door by mistake and catching your best friend's sister.
>
> —BUDD SCHULBERG, *The Harder They Fall*

Ethel Hilda "Ruby" Keeler was born in Dartmouth, Nova Scotia, Canada, on August 25, 1909, the oldest of six children born to Ralph and Nellie (Leahy) Keeler. When she was four years old, the family moved to the Yorkville section of Manhattan "on account of" it was the least expensive neighborhood, and her father got a job as a truck driver for the Knickerbocker Ice Company.

The family had rough times making ends meet, but managed to send Ruby to St. Catherine of Siena grammar school. St. Catherine's featured, among other things, a class in "rhythmic exercise," or "the drill," as it was usually called. Helen Guest, the teacher of this drill, soon noticed how young Ethel made the exercise a thing of beauty. She so informed Mrs. Keeler, and Nellie, who was the real head of the family, soon enrolled Ethel in Jack Blue's School of Rhythm and Tap, where she got the bulk of her dance training.

In the spring of 1923, Ethel, still only thirteen, answered a "call" and was hired as a chorine for *The Rise of Rosie O'Reilly*, a George M. Cohan musical. The show toured for more than six months before opening at the Liberty Theatre on Broadway on Christmas night. *The Rise of Rosie O'Reilly* was not a hit, but it ran long enough—eleven weeks—to entrench Ruby in show business.

Broadway chorus girls of the 1920s often supplemented their incomes by dancing in night-club floor shows after the legitimate the-atres let out around eleven o'clock at night. During *Rosie's* Broad-way run, Ethel, now called Ruby, won a beauty and dancing contest run by Nils T. Granland, a well-known night-club show producer then in the process of opening a new "speakeasy." Granlund did not hire Ruby—girls of fourteen rarely got jobs working for N. T. G.—but Earl Lindsay, one of the contest judges, offered her a two-year contract at seventy-five dollars a week to dance in his new club on the roof of the Strand Theatre.

Several weeks later, Granlund offered Ruby a featured spot as a dancer at the El Fey Club. The usual wire-pulling was attended to, and Ruby, released from her contract with Lindsay, became a prin-cipal attraction at the El Fey before she was fifteen. Larry Fay was the owner, but the club was soon identified with Texas Guinan, the legendary hostess whose raucous greeting, "Hello, sucker," made her the very symbol of the roaring twenties. "Give that little girl a great big hand" was another famous line of Tex's, often used after tap dance routines performed by Ruby Keeler.

Ruby never had the grace and ease of Eleanor Powell as a tap dancer. She was flat-footed, looked at her feet when she danced, and was stationary to the point of almost moribund. But she had appeal. She was only fourteen when she started dancing in clubs—an inno-cent amid a world of sophisticates, corrupt politicians, show people, and gangsters. It was to the gangsters that the teen-aged girl ap-pealed most. "She was so clean," wrote Henry Bentinck in the April 28, 1934, issue of *Radio Guide*, "so frankly unspoiled without being mincingly hoydenish, that she appealed to the decency of men who had any decency left."

Johnny "Irish" Costello was one of those men. A handsome, baby-faced Italian, he frequented the Broadway speakeasies to protect the interests of Owney Madden, a former killer who supplied most of the bootleg whiskey drunk in New York clubs throughout the twen-ties. Writers have tended to white-wash Ruby's relationship with Johnny, claiming he was just a friend protecting the young girl from nasty characters. The fact, however, is that Ruby was Costello's girl-friend from the time she was seventeen years old. Ruby was, by then, no longer innocent, but she recognized the value of her charm and could appear naive when the occasion demanded.

Under Johnny's patronage, Ruby's career in night clubs blos-somed. She starred in a big floor show at the Silver Slipper, of which Irish was part-owner, and headlined at Tex's 300 Club in September

1926. Ruby was now known as "Costello's girl" to the "in" Broadway crowd. Irish often brought her to the upstairs room at Nat Lewis' haberdashery, a hangout for many of the city's top bootleggers, and rumors flew about them being engaged. Ruby would never made a move without Johnny's approval, and Billy Grady, one of Costello's partners in the Silver Slipper, became her agent later that year.

Ruby returned to the Broadway theatre as a featured dancer in Lindsay's *Bye, Bye, Bonnie*. The show opened at the Ritz Theatre on January 13, 1927, and Ruby won a huge hand for her "Tampico Tap" number. Charles Dillingham, Ziegfeld's greatest rival, now wanted Ruby for the part of "Mazie Maxwell" in *Lucky,* his $313,000 vehicle for Mary Eaton. *Bye, Bye, Bonnie* was still running, but Lindsay was persuaded to give Ruby her release. It marked the second time she had deserted that producer.

Lucky was mistitled from the start, closing after seventy-one performances at the New Amsterdam Theatre. Dillingham, however, hired Ruby for his next production, *Sidewalks of New York,* starring comedienne Rae Dooley. *Sidewalks* opened in September 1927 with a cast including Dooley, Smith & Dale, twenty-four-year-old Bob Hope, and old-timers like James Thornton and Josephine Sabel. The show ran for 112 performances at Broadway's Knickerbocker Theatre before going on the road.

Jolson saw *Sidewalks of New York* at the Woods Theatre in Chicago on April 9, 1928. He already knew who Ruby was, but that night in Chicago was when he was smitten. Ruby was now eighteen, a five-foot-three, one hundred-pound beauty.

Ruby returned to New York after *Sidewalks of New York* closed in Chicago, and Grady booked her for a six-week tour of west coast picture houses at $1,250 a week. Ruby was accompanied by her sister Helen on the trip to California. Al was there when the train pulled into Los Angeles, and William Perlberg, later a producer but then a Hollywood agent, made the introductions.

Perlberg, who was handling the details of Ruby's picture-palace tour for Grady and the William Morris Agency, told her to drop by and sign the necessary contract the next day. When she got there, Ruby was amazed to find Al Jolson—greeting her like an old friend and insisting he could get her even more money than Grady had. Ruby protested, but Al spoke to Perlberg, made a few quick calls, and got her a slight increase.

Ruby was astonished, and a little frightened. "Johnny" might not have approved.

Ruby opened at Grauman's Egyptian Theatre in Los Angeles on June 15, 1928. After the first show, she received two-dozen long-stemmed roses and a card that read "Guess Who?"

After the second show, there was a cameo-like set of a brush, comb, and mirror.

And after the third performance, a lynx fur.

All, of course, were sent by Jolson. After the fourth show, he came backstage with Lou Schreiber. Lou asked Benny Rubin, who was on the bill, to tell Miss Keeler they were there.

"When I went to her dressing room to tell her who 'Guess who?' was," Rubin wrote L.A. *Herald Express* columnist James Bacon in 1971, "she was aghast and brought Al all of his gifts, wanting to return them. Naturally, he wouldn't accept them. He then asked that she and her sister go to coffee with them.

"Ruby begged off because she had a date. Al said: 'Is it that important you can't break the date?'

"A voice behind us said, 'Yes, it's that important.' We turned to see Jackie Fields, the famous boxer." Fields, who would win the world welterweight title, was looking after Ruby for Costello.

Al was at Grauman's Egyptian almost every day. Ruby and her sister were staying at the home of Mary Lucas, a chorus girl they had known in New York. One morning, the girls sunned themselves on the beach. When they got up to leave, they found Al, Jimmy, and the latest Jolson car. Jolie offered them a lift.

Ruby, horrified, began to count the days until the end of her engagement in Los Angeles. She was sure she would be rid of Jolson once she left for San Francisco.

She was wrong. Two dozen long-stemmed roses were in her dressing room at the Frisco Warfield after the first show. Again, there was the card, "Guess Who?"

Ruby called New York at once. "I was at my usual table at Dinty Moore's when I was called to the telephone," wrote Grady. "It was Miss Keeler."

" 'Where is Johnny?' she asked excitedly.

" 'I don't know, Ruby,' I replied, suspecting nothing. 'Want me to find him and have him call you?' She was now crying. 'What's the matter, Ruby, anything wrong?'

" 'Yes, that guy Al Jolson is out here and keeps sending me flowers and calling me to go to dinner with him. I don't want to go. I'm afraid. Get Johnny to wire me the money. I want to come home.'

"No use reasoning further. I knew from experience that young Miss Keeler had a mind of her own and once it was made up nothing could move her. It was her mind to come home so I went in search of Johnny Irish.

"Five days later, Ruby was home."

Work proceeded on *The Singing Fool*, which, like *The Jazz Singer*, was only a part-talkie. Al sang several of his old numbers—"It All Depends on You," "I'm Sitting on Top of the World," "The Spaniard That Blighted My Life," "Golden Gate," "Keep Smiling at Trouble," and a new one titled "There's a Rainbow 'Round My Shoulder." The only song that seemed to be a problem was "Little Fella," which Al was to sing to little Davey Lee. Al disliked the song and wanted to replace it.

He called Bobby Crawford, general manager of DeSylva, Brown & Henderson in New York, and asked where he could locate Buddy DeSylva. Buddy, Al was told, was in Atlantic City with Lew Brown and Ray Henderson, working on *Hold Everything* starring Bert Lahr. It was late in California, and three hours later in Atlantic City, but Al called Buddy.

What followed has become one of the most oft-told stories in show business. Buddy, Lew, and Ray were still up, but exhausted from hours of hard work. They tried to beg off when Jolson told them that he needed a new song, but Al reminded Bud of all he owed him, and the three tired songwriters reluctantly agreed to write the number.

When Al called back, an hour later, the new song was finished. The three tunesmiths had taken Al's suggestion of a first line ("Something like 'Climb upon my knee, Sonny Boy, 'though you're only three, Sonny Boy,'") and written other lyrics to complete it in the most banal and maudlin fashion imaginable. When Al heard it, he said it was just what he needed, and the three tired songwriters almost laughed themselves to sleep.

There is every reason to suspect that the story is true. Buddy reportedly titled the manuscript " 'Sonny Boy' by Elmer Colby," and the use of what was then considered a "hick name" would certainly indicate how DeSylva felt about the song.

DeSylva, Brown, and Henderson were probably the most dumbfounded men in the business when "Sonny Boy" became the most commercially successful song of Jolson's long career.

In July, Jack Warner said he wanted Ruby for a "gala presentation" at the new Warner Theatre in Hollywood. Grady set the price at $1,500 plus round trip transportation—after getting Warner's word that Jolson was in Florida and would not be near Ruby.

Al, of course, was still in California, and it was at his suggestion that Jack Warner asked for Ruby. By the second day of her engagement at the Warner Theatre, Ruby was back on the phone—crying about Al's attentions and asking Billy Grady to get "Johnny."

Ruby was brought home at once, and Grady remembered Irish meeting her at Grand Central Station "with a beautiful engagement ring, cementing their troth." That is interesting, in light of what *Variety* reported three weeks later.

On Friday, August 31, 1928, the last day of a week's engagement at the Fox Theatre in Washington, Ruby showed the ring around "backstage while in the company of her cousin, a local girl. Miss Keeler took the congratulations of the stage gathering becomingly. Whereupon the 'invisible master of ceremonies' (public address system) introduced her to the audience as a 'newlywed' and the orchestra played eight bars of the wedding march.

"Miss Keeler gave the lucky man's name as Costello and [his] place of residence as Manhattan, intimating that he had returned to Manhattan following the ceremony performed by the Rev. Father O'Grady of the Catholic University here.

"Miss Keeler said later it was 'all a joke,' the 'joke' part developing when the newspaper scribes wanted more details. She then said the wedding ring belonged to her cousin. Cousin, however, didn't play straight, denying the allegation and informing Miss Keeler that she had talked too much."

It seemed very strange to the reporters. But Miss Keeler's phone call to Grady that night was even stranger. "Jolson is here in Washington," she told him. "I was all wrong. I've fallen in love with him. Will you break the news to Johnny?"

Grady broke it to him, and the gangster took it. Costello's cohort, Tommy O'Neill, and Larry Fay found him standing outside of Dinty Moore's restaurant in tears.

The only time that Ruby ever talked about her courtship by Al Jolson, she said that a mutual friend invited them to dinner. "I was doing five shows a day," she said, "but I said yes, because you found time to have dinner. Al was at their home and that's how it went. He had a big ring he brought me and I said yes, I would marry him."

Parts of the true story are still missing. Miss Keeler's reluctance to discuss Al Jolson is familiar to most students of the subject. Less known is her refusal to discuss Johnny Costello. Was the ring that Ruby flashed in Washington the one that Irish gave her in New York, or the one she claims was given her by Al in Washington?

Writers have presented Ruby as a sweet and naive dancer chased and conquered by a "superstar," Al Jolson—a man more than double her own age. Al *was* more than twice as old as the nineteen-year-old Ruby, but Miss Keeler was by no means a wide-eyed innocent. She was a stubborn, somewhat sassy young woman who had been around and who knew all there was to know about speakeasies, Broadway night life, and gangsters.

At any rate, she was "Costello's girl" no longer. By the time that Ruby got back to New York to start a two-week engagement at Loew's Capitol on September 1, 1928, she was Al Jolson's fiancée. The engagement, however, was kept secret.

Costello's pals—fellow gangsters who thought they would be doing Owney Madden's lieutenant a favor by eliminating his arch "rival"—were the reason for the secrecy. Irish himself accepted Ruby's decision, but insisted on talking to Jolson. He had heard that Al had beaten his first wife "quite often" (it was only twice), and wanted his assurance he would never put a hand on Ruby.

Al gave his word, but Irish wanted more. He knew about the meager settlement that Henrietta had received and wanted to make sure Ruby would be properly taken care of if the marriage failed. The only guarantee of that was money, and Al agreed to give Ruby a wedding present of one million dollars—payable *before* the wedding.

The present did more than placate Costello; it put Ruby's mother solidly in favor of the marriage. "If that family had a desire in the world," wrote Grady, "it was to possess money, and lots of it."

Word of Jolson's promised "present" quickly spread through New York's underworld, and some gangsters wondered if Al was an "easy mark" for extortion. If Costello could do it, they figured, maybe someone else could. Jack (Legs) Diamond one of the era's more notorious criminals, called Al and demanded fifty thousand dollars— "or else."

Al called friends all through the city, asking for advice. It got him no place. Finally, that evening, he found columnist Mark Hellinger at Barney Gallant's place in Greenwich Village. Jolson explained the situation, and Hellinger said that he would see what he could do.

Hellinger called Owney Madden. The next morning, Al received another phone call from Legs Diamond. Legs claimed he had "only been kidding," and that "no one would hurt" Al.

Jolson was grateful to Hellinger, and he was to show it in a truly unique way.

Al got other threats, but of a different kind. He received a phone call warning him to "lay off Ruby Keeler."

"Listen, you sonuvabitch," Al snapped. "Get this: I'm leaving the Ritz Tower in exactly eight minutes. I'm walking down Park Avenue to Fifty-first Street. Then I'm turning west and walking on the north side of Fifty-first to Seventh Avenue, and then I'm going through the stage door of the Winter Garden. Take your best shot."

Was this bravado, or was Al just fed up? Anyway, nobody shot him.

Al planned to take Ruby to Europe for their honeymoon. Still nervous about gunmen, he had Eppy find out if they could be married at sea. Lou found that they could not, so Al resolved to marry Ruby quickly—out of town—and sail with no one the wiser.

Neither Jolson's name, nor Miss Keeler's, was entered on the passenger list of the *Olympic,* but the news that they were sailing on it managed to leak out. Costello knew about it, and he also knew someone had threatened Jolson. Irish had promised Ruby that no harm would come to Al, so he arranged a party for his friends in Atlantic City on the night of the sailing. He figured that would keep any of them from putting Al—and possibly Ruby—to sleep.

Harry Wardell, often described as Al's "human good luck charm," brought the films and records of *The Singing Fool* to New York for the world premiere. Wardell was still living off of Al, but, in this case, he seemed worth it. *The Singing Fool* was even more successful than *The Jazz Singer.*

On the stage, the critics had applauded Jolson the comedian. Now they praised him as a singer. "The chief interest in this production," Mordaunt Hall wrote in the *New York Times,* "is not in its transparent narrative, but in Mr. Jolson's inimitable singing. One waits after hearing a selection, hoping for another, and one is not in the least disappointed when he, as Al Stone, announces to the patrons of his night club that he is going to sing a thousand songs."

Few, indeed, took note of Jolson's hamming; fewer still seemed troubled by it. "There were," John Hutchens noted, "large spaces of celluloid when Mr. Jolson was not singing. But he was never very far from it, and you felt continually that he might be going into a song in just a moment. That was the kind of tragic, vocally quavering role he had, and for all its familiar hokum, he played it with all sincerity and genuine feeling, particularly in those scenes with his little son, played by a youngster named David Lee."

But the big hit of the picture was the new song, "Sonny Boy," sung—three times—by Jolson. "Sonny Boy" would lead *The Singing Fool* to a five-million-dollar gross within the space of eighteen months.

Large-sized silver tickets with a silhouette of Jolson sold for $11 top for the premiere of *The Singing Fool* at the Winter Garden on Wednesday evening, September 19th. Critics described the audience as "swanky," but there was not a dry eye in the house when the film ended. "JOLSON, JOLSON, JOLSON" brought Al up on stage.

Al looked at his audience. "What can I say?"

"Sing!" they shouted.

"Mr. Jolson," Mordaunt Hall wrote, "talked, however, and said he thought *The Singing Fool* was a better production than his first film, *The Jazz Singer*. He referred to the fact that he had been eighteen years with the Shuberts and that he was going back on the stage under their management, but would make several more pictures, possibly before doing so."

He did not refer to Ruby.

Ruby and her mother left the Keeler home at 80-13 Northern Boulevard, Woodside, Queens, early on Friday morning. Ruby was delivered to the Jolson suite in the Ritz Tower and subsequently left the hotel at two o'clock with Al, Mark Hellinger, and Tom Donohue, a photographer from the *Daily News*. Jimmy drove the party to the home of Surrogate George A. Slater in Westchester County.

Hellinger filed a complete report of the marriage ceremony. Ruby was apparently quite nervous.

Judge Slater murmured "Ahem" and adjusted his spectacles. "Do you, Ethel Ruby Keeler, take Mr. Jolson to be your lawful wedded husband?"

Ruby bit her finger. "I—I—do—do."

The judge turned to Al. "And do you, Mr. Jolson," he said softly, "take Miss Keeler to be your lawful wedded wife?"

Jolie nodded. "I do," he stated simply.

The judge cleared his throat again.

"Have you the ring, Mr. Jolson?"

Al dug into his vest pocket and brought out two gold rings in a little bag.

"I brought two of them, your honor," he said. "If one doesn't fit, the other ought to."

The judge smiled. Al slipped the ring on Ruby's finger and started to embrace her.

"Just a minute," cried the judge. "I haven't finished yet." Al and Ruby both stood at attention.

"And now," the judge said, "I pronounce you man and wife. And may God bless you." Al took Ruby in his arms and kissed her. Then everyone shook hands, including Jimmy, who was best man, Hellinger, and Donohue. It was 3:30 p.m., and, after a celebration at Ben Riley's Arrowhead Inn, Jimmy drove them all back to New York.

The marriage certificate is of some interest, and may even help explain why the marriage failed. When Al filled in the space calling for his mother's maiden name, he put down "Ethel Canton," not Naomi. Ethel was Ruby's real name.

Once again, Al was, in essence, marrying his mother.

Al and Ruby boarded the *Olympic* before midnight. Most of the "insiders" knew that they were sailing, so Al was not completely surprised when a small horde of reporters burst into their stateroom (C53). He was just angry, wearing what the New York *Herald Tribune* described as "an expression of mingled dignity." Ruby was wearing a brown dress and a red hat.

One of the reporters looked her over and asked, "Who's the dame?"

Al made a dive for him. The two men were locked in each other's arms when renowned gate-crasher Tammany Young intervened with, "Here, here, young fellers, what's this?" That broke it up.

Reporter after reporter asked Jolson if he was married. Al denied it to each one of them. Finally, a tired Jolson announced that the "housewarming" was over, and that any more reporters who crashed his gate were going to "get thrown out on their ears."

"Just tell us, Mr. Jolson, are you married?"

"I'll say nothing now," said Jolie, "but my public relations counsel will have something to say when the vessel sails, or, I should say, steams."

The baffled reporters returned to the pier. The "public relations counsel" was Eppy, also looking baffled. His face contorted when he saw that Al had failed to draw the curtains of his porthole and that the reporters were looking inside at him and Ruby.

"Draw the curtains," Eppy cried in Yiddish. Jolson drew the curtains.

"Is it okay?" Eppy asked, still speaking in Yiddish.

Al's head appeared between the curtains for an instant. "It's okay," he said. And he used Yiddish, too.

As he spoke, the ship pulled away from the pier. Eppy looked somewhat relieved as he turned to the reporters.

"It is true," he said, in English, "that Mr. Jolson and Miss Keeler were married this afternoon in Port Chester."

Shortly after the *Olympic* "steamed," someone phoned Johnny Costello at the Ritz Carlton Hotel in Atlantic City. As soon as Johnny heard the ship had pulled out, he put down the phone.

"All right, boys," he called out, "the party's over." Irish then went back to New York with his friends.

At this time, the New York *Daily News* was being rushed to newsstands with complete details of the wedding and the first photographs of the newlyweds. Al had given the entire scoop to Mark Hellinger.

Mark was now on board the *Olympic,* having sailed with Al and Ruby. This was his repayment for the way he had saved Al from Legs Diamond. Hellinger also had the right to send radio dispatches to the *News,* telling all about the Jolson-Keeler honeymoon.

Hellinger, however, was not "second man" on the honeymoon. He was third man. Louis Schreiber had also come along to keep Al company.

Jolson could feel awfully lonely on a honeymoon.

Personality of Jolson

More than anyone I know, Jolson needs praise and adulation. At heart he is a simple, generous, unassuming man. But praise he must have. When he gets it, the world seems a very, very good place to live in. When he doesn't, he is as blue as blue can be.

MARY JACOBS, *Radioland*, July 1934

That was it—the pinnacle of Al Jolson's career. Never again—until, perhaps, *The Jolson Story* was released in 1946—would he know anything approaching the popularity that had come his way with *The Singing Fool*. Jolie's professional decline would soon begin, but no one would have dreamed it in the fall of 1928. "Sonny Boy" had made Jolson the man of the hour—probably the biggest star in the world.

Not that he had changed—or would. Al remained Al Jolson—the comedian-singer with the leathery voice, rubbery face, shining eyes, and funny walk—bragging of his great success while feeling, at the same time, that no one liked him.

In the late twenties, Jolson told writer Ernest Haynes about an evening he had spent with a newspaper columnist. "It took me awhile to relax," Al told him, "to get over that nasty feeling that it wasn't *me* he wanted to be with—that it was Al Jolson, the big star. It's the hardest thing for me to believe that somebody doesn't want to try to show me off to his friends. I just can't believe that a person wants to be with me because he enjoys my company—or my friendship. I guess that's because I've never had any real friend.

"Well, I finally *did* believe it. After the show we went somewhere and had a few drinks. We talked about everything under the sun, and it was like medicine to me. I told him everything that was on my mind—things I'd stayed awake nights thinking about because I didn't have anyone to tell them to. Say, listen, I'd like to have you see the letter he sent me the next day."

Jolie went into the next room, brought out several typewritten sheets, and read them aloud. It was a long letter, the gist of which was the following:

Dear Al:

I want to tell you what last night meant to me. It showed what I believe to be the loneliest man in the world. Here was I, an insignificant newspaperman, talking to the greatest entertainer of our time or perhaps of any time. But when drink, the almighty leveler, had made us just two human beings talking to each other, I want you to know how much I was touched, how happy I was to be in the company of a swell guy, a fellow who's real from top to bottom. I want you to know that, newspaperman though I am, if I ever stoop so low as to sacrifice a friendship like ours, brief though it be, for some lousy piece of copy, I guess I'll just have to go and hang myself.

When Jolson finished reading, he looked up and said, "If he'd written another sentence, I would have cried, honest I would."

Jolson surrounded himself with "yes men" and cronies. He remained, however, an extremely lonely man who constantly sought motion in an effort to escape his feelings of aloneness. His off-stage life was therefore taken up with ball games, prizefights, horse races, and other action pastimes. He needed motion almost as much as he needed applause.

This might suggest an overwhelming sex drive, but women played a small part in his day-to-day existence. He had virtually no "love affairs"—just one-night stands with chorus girls or, more frequently, prostitutes. "I sometimes had to be in Al's hotel room in the morning," composer Joseph Meyer told this author. "There would be a woman coming out of his bedroom, a prostitute. Al would say to Eppy, 'Get her out of here.' Eppy would take care of the rest."

Ray O'Brien, pianist for *Bombo* and *Big Boy,* remembered Jolie on the road. "His [train] compartment was never empty at night. There was always a girl with him, and what do you *think* they were doing?"

Al liked women of all backgrounds—except Jewesses, whom he put on pedestals and left alone; they tended to remind him of his mother. Jolie seemed to be having an affair with a red-headed woman, a duPont heiress who sat in a box seat for virtually every performance of *Big Boy* at the Winter Garden. "One night," Dorothy Wegman recalled, "on his final exit, he looked up at her and told her 'Not tonight.' "

Al liked to have oral sex performed on him, and was fond of intercourse in various positions. Sidney Skolsky, who spend a fair amount of time with Al in 1943, usually found him with "a beautiful girl sitting next to him, always a different one at each of our meetings. 'She's a chandelier,' he'd whisper to me, meaning she was good at sex in the wildest positions, including hanging from the chandelier."

Jolson was not impotent, but there is good reason to suppose that he was sterile. "I'd give my right arm if I could have kids," he said one night to Dorothy Wegman, gripping her arm tightly as he spoke. The knowledge that he would die without fathering a child only increased his self-doubts.

He had an existential fear of death, and news of a death tended to affect him deeply. After George Gershwin's funeral in 1937, Al was seen to leave the temple and walk right across the street, oblivious to any traffic. He rarely said anything bad about a deceased person.

Charles Isaacs, one of Jolson's writers on the Kraft Music Hall of 1947–49, said that he was a "strange mixture of conceit and self-deprecation." Al's last wife was almost forty years his junior. Once, they stopped at a gas station. The attendant looked at the young Mrs. Jolson. "Sir, I really have to compliment you," he said to Al. "You have a lovely daughter."

Jolson blanched and grinned. "Son, I'm too old to have a daughter that young. She's my wife."

On the other side of the coin, he was a braggart. Jolie gloated over his successes (especially the financial ones), and frequently disparaged others in the entertainment field. Al could accept an unintentional insult with good humor, but he was inclined to make alibis over defeats in things like cards and golf.

He made living an adventure. One of the few real friends that Jolson ever had was Harry Akst, a diminutive man with a "sympathetic kisser" about eight years his junior. In 1923, Akst lost all of his money at the race track at Havre de Grace, Maryland. "I knew Jolson was playing in some show in Washington," Akst told writer Ernest Lehman, "so I hitched a ride to the capital and called him at his hotel.

" 'C'mon up.'

"In his room, I told how the nags had cleaned me.

" 'Whaddaya want me to do for you, Harry?'

"I had a manuscript with me, a little stinker I had written with Benny Davis. It was called 'Stella, You're Sweet as Vanilla.'

" 'Al,' I said, 'I want you to hear my latest song.'

"I told him the title, and he winced. I moved for the piano in his room, but he didn't even wait for me to start. He picked up the phone and called Waterson, Berlin & Snyder, the music publishers, in New York. He got old man (Henry) Waterson to the phone.

" 'This is Jolson. I just heard a great song, and I'm gonna sing it in the show.' Then he whispered to me, 'How much do you want for it?'

" 'Do you think maybe two-three . . . ?' I stammered.

" 'Five thousand dollars by tomorrow morning or some other publisher gets it,' Jolson said to Waterson, and hung up.

"Next morning, Walter Douglas, the professional manager of the company, arrived from New York with the loot and took the song, sight unseen and, fortunately, unheard. After all, when Jolson introduced a song, it *had* to be great."

Al introduced "Stella" after *Bombo* moved to Boston. When it failed to get the necessary response after three nights, Jolson had the orchestra conductor pass the parts up to him. Al proceeded to tear them in half in full view of the audience. That did not, however, stop him from recording "Stella" when the show got to New York.

"It was around this time," continued Akst, "that I got my first taste of the weird Jolson ego. Walking up Seventh Avenue one night, I met Jolie coming out of the Winter Garden stage door. He grabbed my arm.

" 'Ya like wild duck?'

" 'Love it. Happens that I never tasted it, though.'

" 'Come along, son.' "

Al took Harry to the place that he had sub-leased from Ben Bernie, "threw off his jacket, slipped on an apron, and disappeared into the kitchen. After about twenty minutes, the delicious aroma floating into the living room from the kitchen had me drooling. But every time I edged toward the kitchen, he shooed me away. 'Don't upset me now, Harry. I've gotta concentrate on this here recipe. You'll just have to have patience.'

"At long last, he emerged from the kitchen with a platter on which lay two beautiful golden-brown canvas-backs surrounded by wild rice. I couldn't get over it, particularly after tasting the dish.

" 'Gee, Al, I didn't know you went in for this sort of thing.'

" 'For years, son, for years. Ya gotta know everything.'

"The next day, his valet (Frank Holmes) told me about the duck—prepared and cooked by the chef over at Ben Riley's Arrowhead Inn and sent down to Al all ready to heat and eat."

Jolson was too cynical to be a crusader, but he did stand up for people who happened to cross his path. The great song-writing and performing team of Noble Sissle and Eubie Blake were in Hartford in December 1919—at the same time that Al played there in *Sinbad*. "After we did our first show," Sissle told writer Martin Abramson shortly after Al's death in 1950, "we went into a dirty little restaurant to get a bite, but the owner took one look at us and said, 'We don't serve colored people. Get the hell out of here.' Well, we were pretty sore about it, but there wasn't anything to do but get out. By accident, we bumped into a reporter from one of the local papers and told him about the incident. Sure enough, the next day the paper carried an item about it. And to our everlasting amazement, we promptly got a call from Al Jolson. He was in town with his show and even though we were two very unimportant guys whom he'd never heard of until that morning, he was so sore about that story he wanted to make it up to us.

"Well, that night he came over in a big car and said he was taking us to the swellest restaurant in town and he'd punch anybody in the nose who tried to kick us out. I can't tell you how grateful we were to him, but we told him we didn't like to go anywhere we weren't wanted. Then Jolson said, 'Wait a minute, I know where we can have a good time!' He turned the car around, drove us to a Jewish delicatessen and treated us to a wonderful meal. Then he bought up a load of pastrami sandwiches and took them out to the car. We sat in the car until the early hours of the morning eating our heads off and listening to the greatest star in America performing, just for us!"

Eubie Blake and Al were friends from that night on. They sometimes went to fights together and discussed the relative abilities of great black and Jewish fighters of the past: Jack Johnson, Joe Choynski, George Dixon, Abe Attell. And Sissle, president of the Negro Actors' Guild, represented that organization at Al's funeral.

He could be amazingly paternal. In 1924, Joe Meyer was his overnight guest up in Scarsdale. "I stayed in a room with (Louis) Schreiber. Just before he went to sleep, Al showed what a lonely person he was by coming in to tuck us in."

One of the strangest incidents concerning Al was that described by one scribe in the twenties. He was Jolie's overnight guest at his hotel in New York. "Just before I went to sleep, Al came into the outer room, where I was staying, and stuck newspaper in the cracks of the door. Then he took the lamp by my bed, smashed it to the floor, and said 'Good night.'"

He was a nervous, physical, impulsive man who often snapped his fingers and, when under great stress, cracked his knuckles. "Of all the actors I have ever met," Adela Rogers St. John wrote in 1930, "he has the most sensitive reactions. The man is like a tuning fork.

He is like some highly sensitized mirror that catches every gleam of light and throws it back, or some amazing sounding board that never misses the tiniest note sent against it."

He could be extremely nasty. Hal Kanter handled Tony Martin in the 1940s. Al, who knew Hal, saw the two at lunch and snarled, "Just remember, Martin, that you're nothing without Kanter." Al later told Hal he had just been "kidding." But there were other times. Mickey Rooney found himself making excuses for Al's rudeness.

Hal Kanter went to see Jolson about a possible appearance on *The Ed Wynn Show* in 1950, but Al did not think television was "ready for talent of my calibre." Arthur Godfrey just proved that "in order to be a success in show business today, all you have to do is show up." Al claimed to be able to "fart better" than Morton Downey could sing.

He was murder on successful younger people whom he thought did not have talent. Al admitted that Bing Crosby was a good singer, although he reserved judgment on whether Bing would have "made it" in the early days, before the use of microphones. He liked the way Buddy Clark sounded (which was, very faintly, like Al Jolson), although he called him "just a little punk" before Clark struck it big. Al appreciated Frank Sinatra's phrasing, but said Frankie could not "shine Buddy Clark's shoes."

Jolson *did* know and appreciate talent, however, and he could be extremely sensitive to the emotional needs of other performers. Miriam Franklin Nelson, who did the "Liza" dance for Evelyn Keyes in *The Jolson Story,* remembers the day "everybody came to see the routine for the first time. Afterward, when everyone got up to leave, Jolson came back to me and said, 'Everyone loved the number. I'm sorry no one told you.' So of course I have fond memories of Al Jolson."

Buddy DeSylva said that Jolson rarely laughed at any joke except to be polite. If a joke really amused him, he would say, "That's very funny" with a straight face. Eddie Cantor, whom he often pretended to take seriously as a "rival," was one of the few people who could make him laugh. He liked Cantor's "lamb being led to the slaughter" routine and often played jokes on Eddie just to see his reaction.

Al had a vocabulary all his own. Anything bad was "mogo on the gogo." If he took a liking to somebody, he or she was called a "mouse's ear." Someone extra-special was a "marmoset's niece." If someone walked up to him out of a crowd and started the inevitable "Al, you remember me . . . twenty-eight years ago . . . Duluth . . . ?" he'd shake his head and say, "I don't know you from a zozodont." Isodent was a popular toothpaste.

Younger men out of show business Al liked were addressed as "son." Those in show business he liked (e.g. Tony Martin) were called "kid." Martin once asked Jolie if it was because he could not remember his name. "Sure I remember your name, kid," Al said. "But let me explain. I only call the people I like 'kid.' When I don't call you kid, that's when you should complain. That means I don't like you." Martin remembered that conversation later, when Al was talking to Frank Sinatra. All through their conversation, Jolson called Sinatra "Frank." Not once did he say "kid."

As a boy, Al had looked younger than his years. After he reached thirty, the process reversed itself, and he tended to look older than he was, a fact the touched-up Hollywood photos of the 1930s tried to gloss. By 1927, when he was forty-one, Jolson looked middle-aged. His hair was virtually gray by 1930 and had to be darkened whenever he worked on a film. In between the pictures, Jolie let himself grow gray.

Al tended to age quickly at specific times—in 1937, 1943, and 1948. His hair was extremely thin in his later years, a malady which bothered him but little. Al wore a hair piece in his Warner films of the mid-thirties, but he lacked the patience to wear one in "real" life. Jolson never regarded his looks as very important, but he was usually a sharp, if not flashy dresser, and always looked well groomed.

In his later years, he started to affect a drawl—probably borrowed from his last wife, Erle—and often lapsed into minstrel show dialect. Al did not usually talk as fast as he had in the "old days," but he still demanded motion—from other human beings as well as himself. "He wanted everybody to jump when he was around," recalled a writer for *Variety*.

Some people said Al "mellowed" in his later years. In truth, he just got older. Charles Isaacs and Manny Mannheim, Al's writers on the Kraft Music Hall of 1947–49, went to his house in Encino for a story conference during the winter of 1948–49. It was bitter cold, and Jolie called up to his fourth and last wife, Erle, to bring down a glass of whiskey.

"Maybe the boys would like some, too," said Erle.

"Naw," said Jolie, "these guys don't drink." Mannheim could have killed him.

Jolson liked good coffee, and all sorts of food, including pastrami, gefilte fish, and various species of Chinese cuisine. He was even an adept at eating with chopsticks.

He had to read something in order to fall asleep—usually detective stories. Inner turmoil was responsible for most of his need for action, but Al may have been hyperkinetic as well.

Despite what he claimed, Jolson was usually an early riser. He might have breakfast, depending on his mood. Often, he would order breakfast and then change his mind. It was the same way on trips. Al might plan an auto trip, then change his mind and ship the car while he got on a train. Nor could he decide when—or whether—he wanted his wife. If there was a difference between a wife and an automobile, Jolson never learned it.

He was a "man's man," with a man's man's sense of humor. When the score of *Big Boy* was completed, he invited Georgie Jessel over to his apartment to hear the numbers. Joseph Meyer, who composed the score with James F. Hanley, was Al's accompanist for the occasion. "I was playing along, when I heard Jessel laugh at the top of his lungs. Then I felt a warmth on my sock. I turned around and there was Jolson with his fly open, pissing on me."

Al played golf at the Hillcrest Country Club in Los Angeles during the 1930s and 1940s. If he lost, he'd buy the winner a new suit or pay him an agreed on sum of money. If he won, the bet said he was allowed to urinate on the loser. Boxing great Joe Louis told sports journalist Art Rust, Jr., that he saw Jolson claim the bet on at least one occasion.

Al pissed on a lot of people.

He had a tough façade. ("Cantor could be rough; Jolson could be rougher" was a saying among the old-timers.) In March 1928, while in Chicago in *A Night in Spain,* Al appeared in a benefit for Joe E. Lewis, the comedian-singer whose throat had been slashed by gangsters several months earlier. The idea was to raise the money to pay Lewis' bills and set him up in business as a haberdasher. The show made sixteen thousand dollars, but Al knew that it would kill Joe if he had to quit performing.

"I'm leaving for the coast in a few days and you're goin' with me. You need rest, son. Then we'll see what we'll do about that store when you recover."

Lewis remonstrated, but Jolie insisted it was "friendship." For one year after that, young Joe E. Lewis was Al Jolson's personal guest. Finally, when his throat had sufficiently healed Al took him to the Plantation Club in Culver City. Fatty Arbuckle, the master of ceremonies, "spotted" Lewis in the audience. Within minutes, Lewis found himself performing. He did a take-off on Jolson's "Sonny Boy" and received an ovation.

Al had made sure that the columnists were there that night. A short time later, Lewis was offered a four-week booking at the Parody Club in New York on the same bill with Clayton, Jackson and Durante.

"It'd be suicide to follow those guys," Joe told Al, "even if I had my voice back."

"Take it," Jolson told him.

"No, Al. I'm scared."

Al's face hardened. "Then go back selling haberdashery."

Lewis took the booking—the beginning of a new career that lasted more than forty years.

He was a hypochondriac who exacerbated his physical ailments—including a very real "bad spot" on his left lung. Most of the shows closed due to Jolson's poor health would probably have remained open had his small army of doctors included a psychiatrist. His childhood ambition to be a doctor—the name "Asa," incidentally, means physician—coupled with his hypochondria, made medicine his hobby.

He was usually very sensitive to the physical ailments and/or disabilities of others. Al paid for an operation that gave a child back the use of his legs in 1929, the boy having been an extra in *Say It with Songs,* one of his films at Warners. A Mason, he gave generously to worthy causes, and even built a church for Indians in California in the 1930s. His total three-million-dollar bequest to charity was well publicized, but Al insisted that the many acts of kindness and unselfishness he performed for individuals be kept secret. He was strict about that point.

Jolson was never, of course, "disowned" by his father, who, incidentally, liked Bing Crosby as a singer. He was on good terms with just about all members of his family—when he saw them—and played the "older brother" to Gershon (George), his junior by twenty years.

"Nah, you don't wanna go to the Louis-Conn fight," he teased George before giving him a ticket. George was forty at the time.

He had a sly, fast sense of humor, which is apparent, along with his abundant cynicism, in the answers he gave to a N.B.C. questionaire in 1935.

Q   Name (professional)
A   Al Jolson.
Q   Real Name
A   Asa Yoelson.

Q   Manager, if any

A   The wife.

Q   Phone

A   Don't try anything.

Q   Personal press agent

A   Mahatma Gandhi.

Q   Phone

A   Sheet 1-0000.

Q   Talent (your specialty on radio—what do you do)

A   Get paid every week.

Q   Height

A   5 ft. 10 in.

Q   Weight

A   160.

Q   Complexion

A   Dark.

Q   Hair

A   Brown.

Q   Where and when born.

A   In bed and at night.

Q   Parents - who were they? Did their learnings or characteristics have any bearing on your radio success? Were they talented?

A   Rev. Morris Yoelson, formerly a cantor if that means anything.

Q   Any other members of your family musically or dramatically inclined?

A   Yes, musically. Brother is Harry Jolson, the vaudevillian.

Q   Marital status (husband or wife).

A   Ruby Keeler Jolson, status quo.

Q   Children (names and ages).

A   None

Q   Radio history, first audition.

A   October, 1932.

Q   First professional engagement, any special circumstances, anecdotes, humorous incidents.

A   Nice weather we're having.

Q   Chronological history—experience on the air including any prior to NBC with dates, comments, etc.

A   None and none and none.

Q Professional background—previous stage, opera, concert, and other experience.

A La Scala Opera Company
   Jitney Opera Company
   Heckscher Opera Comapny, Heckscher Theatre, New York
   Buenos Aires Opera Company, South America
   Metropolitan Opera Company
   Minsky's Burlesque

Q Educational background—schools, colleges, dramatic and musical training, names of instruments and teachers.

A Yale, Harvard, Princeton, Vassar, Ossining (twice).

Q What were your school and college activities (sports, singing, debating, etc.)?

A Catching butterflies.

Q Degrees

A 3rd degree fahrenheit.

Q Fraternities

A B'nai B'rith - they were also sore at me.

Q Lodges, clubs

A Ancient Order of Hibernians, Knights of Columbus, Knights of Gladness, Knights of the Road, Ancient Order of Hog Callers.

Q Do you live in the city or country and why?

A That's what I want to know.

Q What do you do to amuse yourself?

A See school and college activities and also Who's Who In Hackensack, Grove's Dictionary, Henderson's Seed Catalogue, and the World Almanac.

Q When and where do you write, sing, practice, or rehearse? Any stated hours or circumstances?

A Pay toilet at the Astor.

Q Have you any suggestions as to press stories regarding yourself? Like the movie public, the radio public is demanding intimate information about its favorites.

A Take the Aircaster, Ben Gross, and those of that type and throw in Louis Reid. Oh, hell, throw 'em all in.

Jolson skipped the remaining 250 questions.

Jolson was a businessman. This is not to say that he exploited others, but he was at home in the hard-nosed theatrical world of his times. He dealt with the Shuberts on their own terms, and he usually beat them. As childlike as he was in so many ways, as ethereal as he was on a stage, Al had no stomach for the Never-Never Land that ne'er-do-well performers like to live in.

Al's relationship with actors is best illustrated by an anecdote told by the "Street Singer," Arthur Tracy.

The story was about a vaudeville actor of the early 1930s. Out of work and needing money, he approached one of his cronies for a handout—one he knew was working and "in the money."

"Sam, I'm gonna level. I've been out of work some time now, and I'm running short. I need a little stake to tide me over."

"Frank, don't worry. With a talent like you've got, there's always work around. Keep you chin up. You'll be near the top again before you know it, and then laugh at how things seemed before."

"Well, Sam, you're a right guy. But listen, I still need a few bucks to keep me going. Can you do it?"

"Gee, I'd love to, Frank, but I'm tapped out. Some of the guys around can help you if you really need it, but I doubt you do. Listen, gotta run. Take care of yourself and give my regards to the missus."

Frank, a short time later, runs into Al Jolson:

"Al, look, I'm in a rough spot now. I've been out of work a bit, and I need a few bucks to tide me over. Can you do it?"

"Frank, listen to me. Vaudeville is dead, and it's not coming back. Times are getting rough, and people don't have money to invest in shows. Carol isn't getting any younger . . . and neither are you. I'll give you five hundred dollars, but I want you to take it and set yourself up in business."

Frank returns home.

"Well," his wife asks, "did you get the money?"

"Yeah, I got it all right," Frank bitterly replies. "It's times like these when you find out who your real friends are. . . . That son of a bitch Al Jolson!"

His reputation for being hard to work with was, in some respects, well earned. Al was polite to chorines and helped young performers, but he thought he knew a lot about how a show worked, and made sure that his directors knew it. Many thought he was a terror; others had tremendous respect for the hard way he worked during rehearsals. He knew what would work for him on stage.

He despised pretension. Charles Isaacs found that Al was not as hard to get along with as was rumored. Al agreed. "You know when I get rough?" he said. "When I meet a phoney. I can't stand phonies."

He knew every stage trick in the book, and wrote a few of them himself. On June 6, 1945, Al was a guest star on Milton Berle's CBS radio show, *Let Yourself Go,* and Berle tried to hog the mike by pushing Jolie's arm away. It was Berle's standard trick, but Jolson gave an unexpected push to Milton's chest that almost knocked him off the stage.

Berle's fiancée, Joyce Matthews, was a principal in *Hold On to Your Hats* in 1940. "Jolson used to steal gags from vaudeville actors," Berle claimed, "and then have his lawyer write them letters saying they had stolen the jokes from *him,* and that they had better cut the material from their acts."

He was a child in many ways, but not in the uncomplicated, simple, and unsentimental way that Babe Ruth was. Despite his cynicism, Al *was* sentimental. He never did grow up completely, since that part of him that was so sentimental was the eight-year-old boy who had lost his mother.

Jolson was a strange amalgamation of contradictions—a mixture of apparent toughness and vulnerability, supreme worldliness and childish simplicity, selfishness and selflessness, surface calculations and impulsiveness, extreme happiness and acute depression.

He bemoaned his faults and, like a child, tried to make amends to people he had wounded. Al often phoned his first wife, Henrietta, and her husband, Jack Silvey, with offers of money, gifts, and other assistance. He was constantly rebuffed.

"But I want to do things for you."

"The best thing you can do is leave us alone," his first wife would invariably tell him.

Despite his tough façade, he hated having people that he knew dislike him. In March 1909, just before deserting Lew Dockstader's Minstrels for I.P. Wilkerson's more lucrative offer, Al called on Josie Rooney.

"He came to our hotel and told the clerk he wanted to see Miss Rooney," recalled Josie's sister, Julia. "The clerk said she had left word not to be disturbed, and Al said, 'Oh?' He'd just had some beautiful eleven by fourteen pictures taken. That I remember very well.

"He'd found out the number of our room—we were on the first floor—and he rapped on the door. Josie said, 'Come in,' thinking it was me, and he came in with the pictures.

"He said, 'Oh, I just got some new pictures I wanted to show to you, Josie. It's very important; I wanna know whether you like any.'

She said, 'You get outta here. I don't want to talk to you. And he said, 'Now, you know you wanna talk to me.' He was being real sweet about it, but she had a temper. Finally, she took the picture that Al handed her and tore it up."

As a rule, however, it was Al who showed the "hard side" to his colleagues. He was frequently obnoxious. Once, he got into an argument with radio director Carlo DiAngelo. Jolson, the successful immigrant with the East Side mentality, pulled out an enormous roll of bills—something he did for effect on numerous occasions.

"Here," he said, "that's how much money I make in just a week. I've got over five million dollars from this business. What have you got?"

DiAngelo leaned forward. "I've got *friends*."

ACT TWO

Show Girl

"I put Ruby before my singing and singing is pretty sweet to me. Ruby is heaven's harmony. She simply has no faults."

The Jolson-Keeler marriage is usually pictured as running into trouble—and, eventually, the divorce court—when Ruby became a hit in movies and Al's own career declined. This scenario dovetails nicely with the usual depiction of Jolson as an egomaniac. But it simply is not true. Al's marriage to Ruby was on shaky grounds at the beginning, went through its *best* period when Ruby was a success in films, and ran into deep trouble after her career declined in 1936–37.

The Jolsons had their first recorded argument at dinner, aboard ship on their honeymoon on Sunday night, September 23, 1928. Ruby did not want to eat a fish that Al had ordered.

"Baby, that's already cause for a Paris divorce," Al told his teen-aged bride. "If you don't eat your fish, I become unhappy. Unhappiness gives a man the right to a French divorce. Eat your fish, baby, or I'll wireless my attorneys at once."

Ruby petulantly tapped her foot, but wound up eating the seafood to the accompaniment of an Al Jolson lullaby.

The ship pulled into Cherbourg on September 28th, and the Jolson party took a train to Paris. *The Jazz Singer* had been a big hit in the French capital, and the Jolsons were met by what Mark Hellinger described as a "cordon of reporters." Al piloted Ruby into a taxi while "scores of people craned their necks on the platform, trying for a look at him and the new Mrs. Jolson."

Al and Ruby took a suite in the Hotel George V and used a back elevator to get out to a Champs-Elysées restaurant for dinner. They went to a couple of night clubs and returned to the hotel at midnight. Overtaken at the door, the forty-two-year-old Jolson and his nineteen-year-old wife politely refused to divulge their plans—except to say that they "might" go to London.

"The only important thing is to have a honeymoon," said Ruby as the elevator closed. "When that's over, there'll be plenty of time to think about Broadway contracts."

Ruby was referring to a wire they had received from the legendary producer Florenz Ziegfeld. Before she had agreed to marry Al, Miss Keeler had been signed for *Whoopee*, Ziegfeld's new vehicle for Eddie Cantor. Ziegfeld wanted to hold Ruby to her contract. "Then we got to have more money," was Al's response, but Ruby agreed to join rehearsals for the show on October 22nd.

The Jolsons, with Mark Hellinger and Schreiber, attended a showing of *The Jazz Singer* at London's Piccadilly Theatre on October 12th. After the picture, Al got up to say a few words about London. He wound up speaking for twenty minutes, and the audience laughed at almost everything he said.

Al was thrilled by the reception. "It's better than New York," he said. "After this, I simply must appear on the London stage. I would like to appear in a revue. Anyway, I promise I'll be here sometime soon."

"Soon" turned out to be 1942.

The New York newspapers had been full of stories about Jolson and his teen-aged bride—especially the *News,* which had the benefit of Hellinger's dispatches. The *American,* however, published three scoops of its own, ostensibly based on telephone interviews with Ruby's mother, Nellie.

Ruby, according to her mother, had become "distraught" upon hearing a rumor that Al was going to remarry Ethel Delmar. There was a "dramatic scene" in which she told Al of her plans to kill herself, and he responded by proposing.

Nellie later claimed she had been "misconstrued," and that Ethel Delmar had sent Al and Ruby an "all the luck in the world" message just before they sailed.

"When they come back from Europe," Nellie added, "we're going to celebrate. Then we're all going out to California. Ruby and Mr. Jolson are buying us a home there." The *American* did not receive any more "exclusives" from Nellie until three weeks later, when the following story confirmed rumors that had circulated since the wedding.

JOLSON GAVE BRIDE MILLION

Al Jolson settled $1,000,000 on the pretty little tap dancer, Ruby Keeler, before he married her three weeks ago, the bride's mother, Mrs. Nellie Keeler, of No. 80–13 Northern Boulevard, Woodside, Queens, admitted last night.

She declined to say whether the million was in cash or in stocks and bonds, of which latter the mammy shouting comedian is understood to have amassed a considerable amount.

As to another report that Jolson had added to the million a $50,000 cash gift for his new mother-in-law, Mrs. Keeler said that "there was no such gift."

Al and Ruby were en route home on board the *Leviathan* when word came of the story. Al was livid, but seemed like the same old jovial-but-earthy Jolson when reporters crowded around him and Ruby after the ship docked in New York.

"How did you like London?"

"Very much," said Al, "even though it rained most of the time we were there."

"What are your plans?"

"I'll be goin' out to Hollywood to make another talking picture. I like makin' 'em, but don't get the idea I'm givin' up the stage."

"What about Mrs. Jolson? Is she going into that show with Eddie Cantor?"

"Yes, she'll be in *Whoopee*. And she'll have the best singing and speech lessons money can buy. Ain't that right, baby?"

Ruby pouted and nodded. She was holding a big doll Al had bought her in Europe.

"Would you describe yourselves as happy?"

"Happiest people on earth."

"Is that story about the million dollars true?"

Al flared up, drew the scribes away from Ruby's hearing, and delivered a scorching tirade against the New York *American*. "Bunk" and "baloney" were the only printable words he used.

"All I gave Ruby was myself," he hotly stated. "That's enough, isn't it?"

The subject was dropped.

Ruby reported for rehearsals the next day, and Al made plans to go to the west coast and sign another contract with Warner Bros. He arrived in Los Angeles on Monday morning, November 5th. Harry and Jack Warner, Darryl Zanuck, William Koenig, and several reporters met him at the station, and a few days later Jolie signed a three-film contract with the Warners for a reported $500,000 per picture.

Whoopee opened in Pittsburgh that week, and Al almost wore out the long distance wire with phone calls to Ruby.

"Oh, Al, it's wonderful. It's really a great show."

"Oh, that's fine, baby, just great. I don't know, I haven't been too well."

"I'm sorry, Al. What's wrong?"

"I don't know. These doctors tell me that I'm just run down. They want me to sit in the sun, but how do I do that with all these Warner brothers running around loose?"

"You ought to lie down."

"Lie down? That's a laugh. Listen, baby, I need ya. Need ya awful bad. Why don't you take the next train out to Hollywood."

"Al, I'd love to, but you know I can't leave the show."

"Can't leave the show? What do you mean you *can't* leave the show? Listen, I'm your husband. Nobody *has* to go on."

The gist of the above conversation was repeated several times that week, until the young, still impressionable, and not overly bright Miss Keeler finally agreed to leave the cast of *Whoopee*. Ruby, doubtless following Al's instructions, did not ask Flo Ziegfeld for a release from her contract. She simply left the company after the Saturday night performance and took a train to the west coast with nobody the wiser. (In Chicago, Ruby's conscience overtook her and she telephoned Flo Ziegfeld, saying that she "hoped he wasn't angry.")

She arrived in Los Angeles on Wednesday, November 14th. It was raining heavily, but Al was there to meet her—standing in the rain with Jimmy Donnelly, smiling and looking in radiantly good health. Just knowing she was coming had done wonders, Al told Ruby. The young Mrs. Jolson was too stunned to lose her temper.

Three nights later, Al, Ruby, Joe E. Lewis, Chicago radio manufacturer Stanley Hartman, and two young women went to the Cocoanut Grove in the Ambassador Hotel. The steward moved a table in between two others to accommodate them, and Al and a man described as "a big ginger ale and ice consumer" got their chairs tangled.

The man then made some remarks—ostensibly to the people at his own table but meant for Al to hear—about the Jews. "I didn't like the music," Al said later, "and the words were terrible.

"I got up and told him that my wife was present, and that his speech was obnoxious. He made a pass at me and I just knocked him down." The man rose slowly, and then Lewis hit him, too.

By this time, the managers were over, and the man was hustled out the door. "He got out of line and had it coming," Lewis said. "And he got a good smack on the nose."

Jolson's plans for the next eighteen months were set within the next few days. He would start his third picture, an all-talkie, in March, wrap up in four weeks, and then not work again until the fall. The remaining two films for the Warners would be shot during the 1929–30 season. After more than twenty-five years of almost continuous touring, Al felt he had reached the promised land. He had fame, wealth, leisure time, and a pretty nineteen-year-old *shiksa* bride. It was the American dream come true.

The Jolsons continued their honeymoon at a beautiful Spanish style villa in Palm Springs, but Al was soon spending more time with United Artists president Joseph M. Schenck than with Ruby. Al always needed male company, and Joe had been a friend of his for years.

Al and Joe were sunbathing together on the roof when Schenck said, "Al, I need ya." What Joe "needed" was for Al to star in pictures for United Artists, and the terms he offered sounded good to a man who had spent most of his adult life under contract to the Shuberts.

Jolson and Schenck used a brown paper lunch bag to draw up a "contract" whereby Al would star in four United Artists films for a total of two million dollars. This would later be termed the "banana bag" contract.

"Joe," Al is reported to have said, "promise me you won't say anything about this until I give you the word. I've got those three pictures to make for the Warners, and things might not be so pleasant if they know I've signed with you."

Schenck gave Jolson his word, and the two men later signed a formal contract.

Joe Schenck, unlike many people in the business, genuinely liked Al Jolson. Joe owned the Talmadge Apartments at 3278 Wilshire Boulevard, and offered to shoot Jolie dice, double or nothing, for a life lease on a flat. Jolson rolled and won.

Al took Ruby on a cruise to Honolulu in December and showed newsmen a beautiful lavalliere with a 24-carat diamond set in platinum. "It's for Ruby's Christmas present," Jolson stated proudly.

There was trouble, however, when the Lassco liner, *City of Honolulu*, returned to San Pedro, California, on January 4, 1929. Ship news photographers received word that Al and Ruby were having an argument in their stateroom. A moment later, though, the Jolsons appeared on deck—smiling and walking arm-in-arm. Al said he and

Ruby had "had a marvelous Christmas with a tree and ten cents worth of tinsel."

A few moments later, someone thought he overheard Al refuse to drop a lei around Ruby's neck. ("I'll drop something around her neck," said Jolson.) Once off ship, Al drove away with his lawyer, Nathan Burkan; Jimmy Donnelly drove Ruby back to Los Angeles in a separate car.

Rumors buzzed about a Jolson-Keeler breakup, but Al and Ruby denied them in a private breakfast interview with a reporter from the Los Angeles *Examiner* the following morning.

Al put his arm on Ruby's shoulders. "Separated? Look at us. We've just come back from a honeymoon in the Hawaiian Islands. When we got off the ship we spent all of yesterday together. Last night we went to see the fights at the Legion Stadium in Hollywood—and here we are. I've never been happier in my life.

"A lawyer from New York City who wanted to talk to me about some contracts and other business was waiting at the pier. I put Mrs. Jolson in my own car, then got into the second, which had been sent down for my use by my old pal Joe Schenck. The lawyer and I talked business all the way into the city. That's all there was to it."

Ten days after he dismissed the "separation" rumors, Al left for New York on business. Ruby stayed in California.

Jolson held court for reporters in his suite in the Ritz Tower. "Now," he said, "I want to correct, once and for all, these reports. Ruby and I are very happy. I expect an heir soon."

The line about the "heir" was quickly relayed back to Ruby. "I have nothing to say" was her astonished reaction. The young Mrs. Jolson said she had not gone east with her husband because she "preferred the California sunshine to the New York snow." It was a typical Al Jolson answer. He had called that morning, telling Ruby what to say.

Al was still assuring everybody of the success of his marriage when he arrived in San Francisco for a week's engagement at Loew's Warfield on January 31st. He had Ruby with him.

"Look," Al said to the reporters as he blew his wife a kiss, "the honeymoon isn't over yet."

"Will there be a Sonny Boy in the Jolson family?" asked a reporter.

Al appeared subdued. "No," he answered, "not at all." He looked at Ruby, and she shook her head.

"Isn't six performances a day a strain?"

"Strain? I told the management that I'd do ten shows a day if they wanted. Singing isn't work to me. It's a joy."

"You're making twenty thousand dollars for this week's engagement. Is it true about your income being more than half a million a year?"

"What of it?" replied Jolie. "I didn't always make it, but I got along just the same." He turned to Ruby. "Let's get back to the hotel and Java up."

The engagement at the Warfield was a typical Jolson triumph, drawing $57,400 and breaking the previous west coast record he had set at the L.A. Metropolitan seventeen months earlier. Al opened the first show with "There's a Rainbow Round My Shoulder" and followed up with "Sonny Boy" and "Mammy." "A name, a voice, and the Jolson exuberance are on sale at one theatre in San Francisco this week," Katherine Hill wrote in the *Chronicle*. "The verdict is unanimous—they're cheap at any price."

Al stayed in Los Angeles when Ruby went to New York five weeks later. No purpose for the trip was given—rumors again flew about a separation—but Ruby had already agreed to star in *Show Girl*, a Ziegfeld musical comedy based on J. P. McEvoy's short stories about "Dixie Dugan."

Billy Grady, still Miss Keeler's agent, had been working on the deal since December. Ziegfeld may have had some doubts left over from Ruby's quick departure from the cast of *Whoopee*, but Grady was quick to point out the value of his client's name—Ruby Keeler *Jolson*.

Al's next film for Warners, *Little Pal,* went into production on March 18, 1929. It was a bathetic emulation of *The Singing Fool*, with Davey Lee as "Little Pal," a celluloid twin brother of the late, lamented "Sonny Boy." And Jolson's acting could not have been worse.

Marian Nixon, Al's leading lady in *Little Pal*, remembered him as being "very happy" while the film was in production. Al continued to rave about Ruby and, in an interview with Cedric Belfrage, how much he loved talking pictures.

"The talkies are *not* spoiling the art of pantomime," said Jolson, pacing the floor of his dressing room at Warners. "If Charlie (Chaplin) wants to keep what he calls 'the great beauty of silence,' let him go lock himself in a room—become a nun's brother or something.

" 'The great beauty of silence.' Hah! I was at a party the other night, and from eight-thirty until around five a.m., Charlie never stopped talking.

"I think Chaplin is great. Why not become greater by doing something the public wants him to do?"

In order to show Belfrage what "the public really" wanted, Al let him see some of his new picture's rushes. "The lights went out," wrote Belfrage, "and the screen began doing its stuff. David Lee lay stiff and still on the ground—he had just been run over by a truck. A crowd of extras, gathered around the body, were repeating, over and over, 'He's hurt'—'Poor little chap'—'He's hurt!' Then Al burst through. 'My boy!' he literally screamed; 'my little boy! They've killed you! Oh, my little pal!' This continued for about ten minutes.

"When it was over, Mr. Jolson cheerfully admitted everything. 'I'll go quietly,' he might have been saying to some detective arresting him for obtaining money under false pretenses.

" 'Exaggerated?' he said. 'Yes—of course it's exaggerated. My God, I cried seventy-two times by actual count to make that scene. I got so hysterical the director couldn't stop me even after the scene was finished. But wait till you see that in the theatre. There won't be a dry eye for yards in every direction. That's the sort of stuff they like—and it's the sort of stuff we're giving them in the talkies. It's true that we have to broaden everything in talkies—that, in a sense, they're a step backward from a purely intellectual point of view. But they're giving the public entertainment—the kind of entertainment they want. There isn't any better justification than that.' "

Little Pal was shot in twenty-eight days, wrapping up a short time before Ruby returned from New York in mid-April. The Jolsons attended the first Academy Awards ceremony at the Roosevelt Hotel in Los Angeles on May 16th, and the Academy of Motion Picture Arts and Sciences gave Warner Bros. a special Award for producing *The Jazz Singer*, the picture that had revolutionized the industry.

Al accepted the Award for Warners with a memorable quip. "I don't know what Jack Warner's gonna do with this statue. It can't say 'yes.' "

Ruby, needed for rehearsals of *Show Girl*, left for New York again two days later. Jolie followed, with Frank Holmes and Jimmy, more than two weeks after that.

In New York, the fights between Al and his teen-aged wife continued. Al attended almost every rehearsal of *Show Girl*, giving Ruby more advice than she could possibly absorb and making her even more tense than she would otherwise have been. Ruby, who had never had more than a minor featured role in any show before, was shouldering a big Ziegfeld production. She was not yet twenty, and the knowledge of what was expected, plus the strain of the rehearsals, made her irritable and nervous. Miss Keeler had "a temper to begin with," according to Billy Grady, who was called in to make peace between the Jolsons whenever Al and Ruby had a fight.

"Knowing Ruby," Grady recalled, "I could only offer Al one bit of advice: 'Leave her alone. These rehearsals are tough. She'll come around in her own good time.' And she did.

"The show opened at the Colonial Theatre, Boston, after numerous rehearsals at all hours of the day and night. Miss Keeler was a tired young lady. Jolson, noted for his inexhaustible energy, demanded more attention from Ruby than he should have under the circumstances. There was a spat and I was again called in. Jolson, a soft-hearted guy with even more of a temper than his wife, was in tears. I suggested a ride in the country to break the tension. Jolson and I took off.

"To my surprise, instead of the ride in the country, the unpredictable Jolson ordered the chauffeur, Jimmy Donnelly, to drive to the nearest Catholic church. Jolson pleaded with me to go to the altar rail and pray that everything would be all right between Ruby and himself. I proceeded to pray while Jolson lit every candle he could find. The candle stands were ablaze with light, and Jolson stuffed bill after bill into the money slot. We went through the same proceedings in three churches, but at the third Jolie wanted to be really sure about the prayers so he had Jimmy Donnelly join me at the altar rail."

The first performance of *Show Girl* was on Tuesday night, June 25, 1929. Ruby was excellent as the sassy Dixie Dugan, receiving an especially big hand for her "Do What You Do" number in the first act. The best song in the score was easily "Liza," written for a second-act minstrel number with what one critic described as "one hundred beautiful girls seated on steps that covered the entire stage."

The high point of this number came when Frank McHugh sang the verse and Ruby stepped into a spotlight at the top of a magnificent series of platforms. Miss Keeler had barely gone into her dance when Jolson rose from his seat in the second row, scrambled into the aisle, picked up the refrain, and sang "Liza" at the top of his lungs.

The Jolson-Keeler "Liza" has become one of the most famous moments in musical comedy history. Why did Jolson do it? "I don't know" was Ruby's answer to that question on a 1971 Dick Cavett TV show. "I was just as surprised as anyone. I guess he just liked to sing. But I don't *know* why he did it. I'm not very bright, you know."

Jolson certainly *did* like to sing, but he rarely gave extemporaneous performances. The most likely explanation for what happened probably lies in what Matilda Golden, Ziegfeld's secretary, told author Charles Higham. According to Miss Golden, Ruby momentarily froze on the top platform in the dress rehearsal. Dance director Bobby Connolly yelled "Come *on*, Ruby!" and Jolson, who was out front, started singing the song back at her. It was apparently Ziegfeld's idea to have Jolie repeat the act during performances in order to boost ticket sales. Ruby was not told of the arrangement.

At least one Boston critic found the Jolson-Keeler "duet" an obvious and tasteless blight on what was otherwise a fine evening, and Ruby's friend, Patsy Kelly, was still indignant almost fifty years later. ("That was *her* show, not his.") Whether Al sang "Liza" as a p.r. stunt to help the show, to steal his wife's thunder, or simply because he "liked to sing" did not help his marriage. The Jolsons were quarreling—again—when Ruby arrived at the Ziegfeld theatre for the Broadway opening of *Show Girl* on Tuesday night, July 2nd.

The star dressing room had been done over in white organdy for Ruby, ruffles covering the walls. A magnificent 21-piece toilet set, containing brushes, mirrors, perfume bottles, and makeup boxes of solid gold inlaid with crystal and mother-of-pearl, was on the dressing table with a note, "To the greatest star I've ever had," from Ziegfeld.

Ruby was late, nervous and red-eyed, when she sat down to get ready. She used the toilet set, too upset to notice it was new or to appreciate the flowers that almost filled the room. Al ran in after her and saw the card. "Look," he exclaimed. "Look at what Flo gave you. Look at this." Ruby just went right on making up.

Al sang "Liza" to his bride again that night, just as he had done throughout the previous week in Boston. "This Ruby Keeler girl," Sime noted in *Variety*, "eased right into the role of Dixie Dugan. She looked and played it in a natural, pleasing manner without a strain at any time." Despite the fact that George and Ira Gershwin wrote the songs, the weakest part of *Show Girl*, said the critics, was its music. Al continued to sing "Liza" for a week after the opening; then he went to the west coast to see the Warners, and the *Show Girl* ticket sales plummeted.

On Monday, July 22nd, two days after Al's return from California, Ruby became ill. The nature of her illness was not disclosed, but Al told Ziegfeld she would have to leave the show and Ruby's understudy, seventeen-year-old Doris Carson, played Dixie Dugan for two performances. Ruby returned to the cast on Saturday night, but collapsed in her dressing room after the first act. Miss Carson finished the performance.

Miss Keeler entered Lenox Hill Hospital and underwent an operation at ten o'clock on Thursday morning, August 1st. Dorothy Stone took over Ruby's role in *Show Girl*, which, *sans* both the Jolsons, limped along and closed a few weeks later.

Dr. Alfred Hellman, who performed the operation, permitted Ruby to accompany Al to the premier of *Little Pal* (retitled *Say It with Songs*) at the Warner Theatre on August 6th. It was an exciting evening, with the usual crowds, and newsreel cameras immortalized the Jolsons as they stepped out of their car.

The reviews for the picture were not good. Critics who respected Jolson's talent tried to be kind, but even Mordaunt Hall admitted that *Say It with Songs* was "suitable as entertainment only to immature personalities." Talking films required more restraint than silents—not, as Al had claimed, exaggeration. And it became apparent that Jolson and Warner Bros. had erred greatly with respect to what "the public really" wanted when *Say It with Songs* was taken out of the Warner Theatre in Hollywood on forty-eight hours' notice. It marked the first flop of Al Jolson's long career.

Jolson was not troubled by the picture's failure. All Al really wanted to do was complete the two remaining pictures on his Warner contract as quickly as possible. Then the *real* pictures would be made at United Artists for his friend Joe Schenck. It seemed that simple.

The script for *Mammy*, Al's next film for Warners, was ready by the time the Jolsons left New York for Hollywood on August 20th. *Mammy* was Warner Bros.' title for *Mister Bones*, a stage show Al had toyed with doing in the spring of 1928. The plot concerned an end man in a minstrel show accused of attempted murder, and one scene had Al go home to his mother in a tearful scene vaguely reminiscent of *The Jazz Singer*. Louise Dresser, the same woman Al had displaced at New York's Fifth Avenue Theatre twenty years earlier, was borrowed from Fox to portray Jolie's "mammy." Warners claimed to be having trouble finding an ingenue for the role of Nora Meadows, Al's love interest, and Hollywood gossip columnist Louella Parsons asked Al if he had thought of Ruby for the part.

"Ruby isn't well enough," said Jolson. "And besides, I like her too much to have any possible disagreement about movies after we get home at night."

Clearly, Al did not want Ruby as his leading lady. Lois Moran was obtained on loan from Fox to play the role, and production started in September.

"Mammy," Jolson stated, "was my best picture, and Warner Bros. deserve full credit for its success, for not one of the brothers came on a set while we were making it." Seen today, the onstage minstrel sequences are brilliant—especially an early Technicolor reel in which Al sings his classic "Why Do They All Take the Night Boat to Albany?" and another scene in which he performs Irving Berlin's operatic parody version of "Yes, We Have No Bananas" at the head of an octette. Jolson shows himself a masterful comedian in these and other pieces, but his acting is embarrassing—almost as bad as in *Say It with Songs.*

Mammy finished shooting shortly before the stock market crash of October 29th. Al was in his broker's office that day when the market took another drop. Jolie suddenly collapsed, causing at least twenty other investors to gasp. A few seconds later, he looked up and weakly grinned; he had only been kidding to ease the general panic and tension.

Al was not hit as badly as many of his colleagues since he had most of his money tied up in utilities and real estate. (Eddie Cantor was wiped out almost completely.) Jolson lost about one and a half million dollars, close to half his total worth, but took his losses philosophically. A gambler by nature, Jolson saw the market as a sort of indoor race track. He looked on making money as a game.

On November 29th, while he was in New York, Al officially announced his retirement from the legitimate stage in order to devote his time to talking pictures and "limited engagements on the concert stage under the guidance of William Morris." This was for publicity, Al having signed to do a two-week concert tour under the Morris aegis.

Jolson's popularity was no longer at the fever pitch it had been at the time he married Ruby, due, primarily, to the failure of *Say It with Songs* and the simultaneous rise of other stars in talking pictures. But the concert tour for Morris more than proved his drawing power. The Depression was on, the top ticket price was an incredibly high five dollars, the advance work was not good, and the South was experiencing one of its most severe winters in years, but Al played to even better figures than expected. The tour opened in El Paso on January 18, 1930 with Jolson, accompanied by pianist Harry Akst and a string trio, giving a two-hour show. It closed in New Orleans on January 30th, where a crowd of 12,000 filled the New Auditorium.

There was talk of further concert tours in Europe, and one agent tried to bring Al to the Prosser Konzerthaussaal, home of classical music in Vienna. The man was in frequent cable touch with Eppy until he heard Jolson's price: $5,000 a performance.

A big minstrel parade, with Jolie in the lead, preceded the premiere of *Mammy* in New York in March. The film's reviews were only fair, however, and Al even offered to return the $50,000 Warners had advanced him on his next picture. The offer was declined, and production on Al's next film, *Big Boy,* started when he returned from New York.

Big Boy is the only record of Al Jolson playing Gus, the harlequin-like "man of many parts" character of his Winter Garden days. The film version of *Big Boy,* directed by Alan Crosland, is a clumsy effort that retains most of the plot but little of the magic of the stage show. Like *Mammy,* however, it reveals Jolson as a great comedian and an exciting singer. Gus, like Chaplin's tramp, is the underdog who baits his adversaries at every opportunity. Like Pseudolus in *A Funny Thing Happened on the Way to the Forum,* he uses guile. And, consistent with the Jolson image, he's a winner in the end.

But the film was not successful, and critics who had seen Al on the stage in *Big Boy* said that he was "totally ineffective" in the screen version. It was Jolson's third flop in a row.

The vehicle Joe Schenck selected for Al's first UA film was *Sons o' Guns,* a Broadway musical comedy about a playboy who finds himself in the army with his former valet, Hobson, as his sergeant.

Jolson finished shooting *Big Boy* on May 17, 1930, which left him free until September, when *Sons o' Guns* was scheduled to go into production. To fill in the time, he planned a concert tour of Europe.

Jolson intended to sail on July 5th, but agreed to postpone the trip when Schenck suddenly announced plans for a German-language version of *Sons o' Guns,* to be filmed in Berlin with Al and an all-German cast. Jolson's fluency in Yiddish, the immense popularity of *The Jazz Singer* in Europe, and the comparatively low cost of production in Germany were the reasons for the proposed venture.

Schenck's idea was to shoot the German version in August, but he changed his mind when told that *Sons o' Guns* would not be suitable for German tastes. A revised plan called for Jolson to make a different German-language film in Berlin in October and start *Sons o' Guns* in Hollywood about two months later. Finally, all plans to film in Germany were canceled owing to what *Variety* termed "the uncertainty of the new quota bill situation," and work on *Sons o' Guns* was rescheduled to begin in November. Much time had been lost, and Jolson was impatient.

The revised schedule left Al free to play a week at the Capitol Theatre in New York. Loew's, Inc. had offered him a guarantee of $20,000 plus half of the gross if receipts went over $80,000.

Jolson opened at the Capitol at 12:23 p.m. on Friday, September 26th, and did five shows a day. Publicity was almost non-existent due to the sudden nature of the booking, and the gross for the first day was only slightly above average for the Capitol. Saturday and Sunday, however, pushed the total take to almost $40,000. It seemed certain Al would break the $80,000 mark before the end of his engagement, but the grosses for Monday and Tuesday showed a dramatic drop—despite the theatre's always being filled. Word had gotten out about Al varying his repertoire at each performance. There were no reserved seats, and many people stayed all day, preventing new admissions.

Some of these same people would demand that Jolson sing encores. Once, called back for what seemed like the umpteenth time, Al spread his arms and asked, "What do you want for thirty-five cents?" They wanted plenty. And the gross did not reach $80,000.

Al returned to Hollywood to begin work on *Sons o' Guns* in mid-October. Ruby, who had signed to play a leading role in a new show, *The Gang's All Here,* stayed in New York.

Earlier, on Monday, September 29th, Ruby had walked out on rehearsals for another show, *The Vanderbilt Revue,* because of what the *New York Times* referred to as "differences with the producers as to how her part should be played." Broadway insiders knew the real story: Jolson had talked Ruby into leaving *The Vanderbilt Revue* the same way he had talked her into leaving *Whoopee* two years earlier. They also knew that Lewis Gensler, producer of *The Gang's All Here,* was a friend of Jolson's. (Gensler had written "Keep Smiling at Trouble," Al's big hit in *Big Boy*.)

Jolson arrived at United Artists only to find that Joe Schenck had changed his mind again. Schenck's executives were (accurately) predicting that 1931 would be a bad year for screen musicals, and Joe told Al he wanted to postpone *Sons o' Guns* until 1932.

Jolson panicked. He signed a contract with producer Max Gordon on November 18th and checked into Good Samaritan Hospital in Los Angeles with psychosomatic stomach cramps a week later. The contract with Gordon was canceled by mutual agreement.

Rehearsals for *The Gang's All Here* were postponed until January, and Ruby, convinced that Al was sick, returned to Los Angeles early in December. Two weeks later, she and a "recovered" Jolie went back to New York for a Keeler family Christmas reunion.

Shortly after New Year's, Al received a phone call from Lee Shubert. The Shuberts had filed suit against Jolson for running out on *Big Boy* in December 1927, but Lee said he would drop the suit if Al agreed to star in a new show the Shuberts were producing in association with Morris Gest.

The new show was *The Wonder Bar,* and it would mark Jolson's first appearance in a Broadway production in almost five years.

Hallelujah, I'm a Bum

"You don't understand, Al," they'd tell me. After thirty years
in show business, I don't understand."

*T*he *Wonder Bar* was based on *Der Wunderbar*, a Continental
musical about intrigue, murder, and suicide in a Parisian night
club. *Der Wunderbar* first opened at the Kammerspiele Theatre in
Vienna, producer Morris Gest purchasing the American rights in association with the Shuberts in 1930. The plan was to star Harry
Richman, but failure to agree on money caused the project to be
scrapped—until Lee Shubert approached Jolson. Al bought a half
interest in the show, which gave him 50 percent of the show's profits
in addition to a weekly salary of $5,000.

The book of the show required extensive rewriting, since the lead
role was originally Harry, a gigolo dancer (played by Carl Brisson
in André Charlot's production at the Savoy Theatre in London). Al
brought Irving Caesar in to do the job.

Caesar, who lived in Jolson's suite in the Ritz Tower during the
show's preparation, described Al as "a paradox . . . All his kindness and sweetness came out in his singing. Basically, he was very
hard. Al had no patience with the weak, only with those who stood
up to him as I did. He liked me very much; I used to fight with
him."

"Sam Wonder," the proprietor, was rechristened "Monsieur Al"
Wonder and became the starring role. Caesar also adapted several
songs in Dr. Robert Katscher's original score (the title song, "Der
Wunderbar," became "Good Evening, Friends") and added *"A Chazend'l Ohf Shabbes"* ("Cantor for the Sabbath"), an old Yiddish
folk number, for Jolson.

"He had no trouble with it," recalled Caesar. "He was a Litvak;
he talked Litvak Yiddish. But he couldn't read it. Neither could I. I
had to learn it by ear from a folk singer, a lady from abroad I helped
with some material. I taught it to Al, and it was one of the greatest
things he ever did." Anticipating Joel Grey's turn in *Cabaret* by more

than thirty-five years, Caesar also had Jolson sing "Oh, Donna Clara" in three languages—German, French, and English.

Ruby, who had left *The Gang's All Here* in Philadelphia *(Variety* said her tap dancing "fell flat"), was not in *The Wonder Bar,* but her friend, Patsy Kelly, was. Patsy clowned outrageously as "Elektra Pivonka" in "The Dance of the Dying Flamingo."

"In that scene," recalled Miss Kelly, "Jolson was supposed to shoot me with a shotgun loaded with blanks. One night, he put real buckshot in the gun, and I did leaps Nijinsky never saw. Jolson apologized and sent me flowers afterwards."

The Wonder Bar opened out-of-town at the Belasco Theatre in Washington, D.C., on Thursday night, March 5, 1931. Al displayed his usual enthusiasm when he visited his parents in Lanier Place.

"Pop, this is the greatest show ever done. I sing in Yiddish. I sing in French."

"Almost eight o'clock," replied the seventy-three-year-old rabbi.

"It takes place in a night club, and the scenes are all picked out in spots."

"Almost eight o'clock."

"Pop, I'm telling you about this show, but all you say is, 'It's almost eight o'clock.' What's at eight o'clock?"

"Amos 'n' Andy."

The Wonder Bar opened on Broadway at the Nora Bayes Theatre (done over in black, Chinese red, and silver) on Tuesday evening, March 17th. Ticket agencies, confident of Jolson's drawing power, bought up the theatre's lower floor for the first sixteen weeks in advance. But the reviews were not the usual Jolson raves, and several critics thought Al seemed uncomfortable in his new role of proprietor/c.m. Arthur Pollack of the Brooklyn *Eagle* said the part gave him "no springboard from which to leap to success. There were long stretches last night when he didn't click at all. That is unusual."

Al was extremely nervous during the show's run, and the buckets were again placed in both wings so he could retch right after finishing his scenes. On one occasion, he had someone grab a prostitute from off the street and bring her to his dressing room. Oral sex proceeded to ease some of Jolson's tension.

Caesar, like Joe Meyer, utterly denied that Jolson was bisexual. "Absolutely not," said Caesar. "He liked colored girls, though."

The Nora Bayes Roof Theatre (located on top of the Forty-fourth Street Theatre, now the site of the *New York Times* printing and publishing building) only had 860 seats, but high ticket prices, including a $6.60 top, coupled with the heavy advance sale, brought the show's receipts to $30,000 weekly until the end of April. That put *The Wonder Bar* among the Broadway leaders (like *Girl Crazy* and *The New Yorkers*), and Jolson was designated Honorary Collie of the Lambs Public Gambol, the first time a playing member had received that honor.

Business at the matinees, however, soon declined, and the gross fell to $29,000 for the week of April 27th. Brokers were beginning to get stuck with tickets.

Predictably, Al's throat began to hurt him, and the Shuberts began posting a weekly closing notice. Several of Jolson's songs were cut on May 11–12, and he was unable to appear at that week's Wednesday matinee. One of Jolie's doctors told Lee Shubert that, while Al was "not seriously ill," a four-day vacation would be necessary to "safeguard his health." The next five performances were cancelled.

All subsequent matinees were scratched, and the cast took a 25 percent salary cut, but *The Wonder Bar* was doomed. On Saturday, May 30th, Jolson sent word that he would not appear that evening, and the show was closed.

Al, who had a standing invitation to use Nick Schenck's private box at Aqueduct, spent the weeks that followed taking Ruby to the races. Painfully aware of how neglect had helped wreck his first two marriages, Al was determined to be different with Ruby. Where he never mentioned Henrietta's name in public, he now shouted about Ruby from the rooftops. And if horse racing was a part of his life, it was also going to be part of Ruby's. The only trouble was that racing bored Miss Keeler.

Al regarded his wife's lack of interest as a challenge. He and Johnny Donovan, who still trained Jolson's horses, presented Ruby with a two-year-old colt named Cimarron, a son of Hand Grenade, and Donovan registered a set of colors for her with the Jockey Club: "Green and gold halves, green sleeves and cap." Ruby, however, remained unenthralled by racing.

Jolson himself was an unusual turf follower in that he could attend the track for months and then lose interest for an equal length of time. Known as a "right guy" with the paddock mob, Al became ruffled when he felt he was not dealt with "squarely." On Saturday, July 4, 1931, Al thought someone had given him a "bad steer" and swore off horses for the season. Taking Ruby with him, Jolie left for the west coast and spent the balance of the summer fishing off Catalina Island.

Late in August, Al and Ruby returned to New York. Louis Epstein had made all the arrangements for Al to take *The Wonder Bar* on tour.

Eppy had outdone himself on the terms of Jolson's contract: a six-thousand-dollar weekly guarantee with a sliding scale on profits starting at 50 percent and going up to 75 percent for grosses at or over $10,000, 80 percent for $12,000, and 87.5 percent for anything over $15,000. That last figure was the top rate given anyone, including Sarah Bernhardt, and producers only granted it because they knew no one would ever do the necessary business. Jolson did.

Martin Fried, a former Broadway rehearsal pianist recommended by Caesar, replaced Louis Silvers as conductor. Fried, a talented musician, was an alcoholic. His father was also quite a lush, and Fried's own problems with the bottle started shortly after he scored his first success as the composer of the song "Broadway Rose" in 1920. He was separated from his wife by the time Jolson hired him for the tour of *The Wonder Bar*.

The show opened at the Shubert Theatre in Newark on September 18, 1931, and played close to forty cities in the following six months. "The man was a raving maniac on opening nights," remembered Patsy Kelly, "and every stand we played was like an opening to him. Once, I found him in a garbage can, saying 'I won't go on. They're persecuting me.' But we'd push him on, and then . . . you couldn't get him off. We called him 'Mr. Electricity.' He was a fantastic, unbelievable talent on a stage, but . . . I would say he was tormented."

Miss Kelly had some problems of her own on the tour. She had what *Variety* described as "some trouble" with other cast members, and "fainted in her dressing room" on Friday, November 20th. Patsy missed that night's performance and was fired.

Interviewed in 1978, Miss Kelly said the trouble started when she asked a stagehand for a cigarette and was handed a stick of marijuana. "I took about three puffs," said Patsy. "I thought it was like a Mexican cigarette or a what-do-you-call-it. Anyway, I went on the stage and I was in another world. Jolson said, 'Why you son of a bitch.' And I was fired. But the stagehand came up to Equity and told them what he'd done."

According to *Variety*, Miss Kelly was at the office of Actors' Eq-

uity in New York on Monday morning, November 23rd, with a
doctor's certificate. In any event, Patsy was back in the cast on Tuesday night in Pittsburgh. Vera Marsh had played Elektra Pivonka in
her absence.

Jolson had slipped by 1932, but was still a formidable live drawing card in what show business parlance termed "the sticks." In Des
Moines on February 23rd, *The Wonder Bar* grossed what Eppy later
claimed was the all-time high for a Broadway musical—$15,985 in
Depression money. That was in the spacious Shrine Auditorium,
where, according to Jolson, "the only way of putting the show over
seemed to be by long distance telephone."

"I put in all my spare time gargling. But the auditoriums weren't
the toughest spots. I'll never forget Nebraska. In Lincoln, we played
in the stadium of the state university, with a swimming contest and
a basketball game going on at the same time. But I didn't realize
what real competition was until we hit Omaha, where we were up
against a livestock show under the same roof. I put both lungs into
my songs, but the cows and their gentleman friends were in such
good voice that I had to hand it to them."

As always, Jolson's monologues and quips were spiced with topical allusions. At the Fox Theatre in Phoenix on March 18th, Al
incurred the wrath of Hattie L. Mosher, a wealthy eccentric well
known for her battles with the city. In one scene in *The Wonder
Bar,* an actress walked across the stage dressed as an old hag—ill
clad, slovenly, and dirty. When the actress came onstage in Phoenix,
Jolson exclaimed, "Here comes Hattie Mosher." Hattie sued Al Jolson and Fox–West Coast Theatres for $100,000 for humiliation and
an additional $50,000 for "harm done her credit and financial
standing." It was settled out of court.

Jolson invited the audience to smoke at the end of the first performance in Los Angeles. "And they did," reported the *Times'* Edwin
Schallert, "apparently with informal official sanction. He also passed
around the (soft) drinks. And then he told a sad tale about his wife's
shoes—wooden shoes perforce, and becoming very sobby about it,
finally rushed down the aisle to where Ruby Keeler was sitting and
kissed her."

The tour ended at the Curran Theatre in San Francisco twelve
nights later. It was time for Al to report to United Artists.

Joe Schenck and Lewis Milestone, the great director of *All Quiet
on the Western Front,* had visited Jolson in the dressing room when

The Wonder Bar was in Chicago three months earlier. Schenck had come to the conclusion that *Sons o' Guns* was dated, and was searching for another story for the first Al Jolson–UA vehicle.

By April, when Jolson showed up on the UA lot, Schenck thought he had the story—an original by Ben Hecht titled *The New Yorker.* The theme was the Depression and its effects, or lack of same, on the hobos in New York's Central Park.

Al was chagrined when Joe told him there was still no shooting script—*The Wonder Bar* could have toured a while longer—and he put his foot down when Schenck wanted to have William Anthony McGuire write the screenplay. Jolson knew McGuire, an alcoholic who had worked for Ziegfeld, as extremely unreliable, but he more than approved of Schenck's second choice, S. N. Behrman.

Jolie joked about the five dollars *per diem* living expenses United Artists automatically gave him as an "artiste," and remonstrated when Schenck told him he could attend conferences until the screenplay was completed. Al was restless—so anxious to work that he had William Perlberg book him for two weeks of picture house appearances.

"Al Jolson and his 'Wonder Bar' Revue' "—consisting of Jolson, Raquel Torres, a Fanchon & Marco chorus, and a few acrobats— opened at the Fox Theatre in San Francisco on Friday, May 13, 1932. Fine promotional work resulted in good business, and George C. Warren of the *Chronicle* reported that Al "was thunderously received, and kept the crowd laughing or applauding for the hour set apart for him and his revue." But the gross at the Fox in Oakland, where Jolson and company played the following week, was below expectations. Al reported to the UA lot, again, on Wednesday, June 1st. A script, of sorts, had been completed.

The plot revolved around Bumper, mayor of the hobos in Central Park, and his friend, John Hastings, mayor of New York. Bumper is carefree until he rescues a young woman with amnesia. Unaware she is the mayor's girl friend, Bumper falls in love with her and goes to work in a bank. He finally learns the truth, reunites the lovers, and returns to his existence in the park.

Judging by his later comments, Jolson must have been extremely puzzled. The story had a romance, but the hero did not get the girl— a rarity in 1930s dramas, let alone musicals. The script was vaguely reminiscent of Chaplin's *City Lights* of the year before, amnesia serving as a substitute for blindness.

What made the script even more unconventional was the character of "Egghead," a socialist who refers to the park's mounted police detail as "Hoover's Cossacks." Socialism gained many adherents during the Depression, but the idea of a secondary lead like Egghead in a movie musical was still light years away in 1932. *Pal Joey,* the Broadway musical with an unsympathetic hero, would not appear until 1940—and even an intelligent critic like Brooks Atkinson would find *Joey* hard to take.

Jolson had allowed his whole career to slide downhill for the last four years, banking all the while on a new career in films for Schenck. He now began to worry. Al called Irving Caesar, whom he had proposed to Joe Schenck as the man to write the score, and told him to come out to Hollywood.

"Al brought me to the suite that he was staying in at the time," Caesar remembered. "He had me lay on the bed and gave me the script to read while he went in the bathroom. He didn't know what to make of (the script), but I wasn't fooled. I found out later that the whole thing was actually based on a French story called *La Vie Est Belle*—'Life is Beautiful.' "

"A few days after I got out there, Jolson and I were riding down Sunset Boulevard. All of a sudden, Al leaned over and kissed me on the cheek. I was surprised; I said, 'What's that for?' He said, 'Nothing. I just like you and I want you to write the songs for my movie.'

"I told him, 'I don't know, Al. Something tells me I'm gonna be hurt by all this.' And I shook my head. He said, 'Cookie, you're always fighting with me.' Then he went to see his lawyer."

Lewis Milestone was busy cutting *Rain,* so Harry D'Arrast was assigned to direct the Jolson picture. It was hate at first sight. Al had no confidence in the script and even less in D'Arrast, whom he felt was a poor substitute for Milestone. D'Arrast returned the affection. He liked the story and said Fred Astaire, the Broadway dancer, would be better for the lead than Jolson.

Shooting started at ten o'clock on Thursday morning, July 7th, and ended at noon the same day. Jolson and D'Arrast had reached an impassse, and most of it revolved around the script.

"They had me playing almost a silent character," Al told Eileen Creelman of the New York *Sun.* "All I said for half the picture was 'yes' or 'no.' I had no dialogue. Now, that isn't what people expect from me. I know what kind of stuff I can do on the stage. That's the kind of dialogue I want now."

Schenck brought Chester Erskin in to replace D'Arrast, and production resumed two weeks later. Work continued through September, with Roland Young in the role of Mayor Hastings, beautiful Madge Evans as the mayor's girl friend, silent movie comedian Harry

Langdon as Egghead, and Edgar Connor as Acorn, Bumper's black sidekick.

On October 13th, Al flew to New York and signed a thirteen-week radio contract with General Motors at $5,000 a broadcast. Two days later, Joe Schenck called from Hollywood. The first preview of the new film, now titled *Happy Go Lucky*, had been disastrous. Extensive retakes were required, and Al would have to return to Hollywood at once.

Jolson arrived back at the studio to find that a remake of the entire film was needed. Schenck dismissed Chester Erskin and brought Milestone himself in to direct. Roland Young, who wanted no further part of the picture, became unavailable due to "illness," and Frank Morgan became the new Mayor Hastings.

By far the most sweeping change was the elimination of the Irving Caesar songs. In their place was a new score by the already legendary team of Richard Rodgers and Lorenz Hart, including half a dozen songs and "rhythmic dialogue"—dialogue in rhythm.

"A case in point," as Joseph Sullivan pointed out in *Motion Picture Herald*, "is the series of sequences that build up the refrain: 'Bumper's Found a Grand.' When one of the park bums spies Bumper and Acorn in the act of picking a thousand-dollar bill out of a garbage can, he immediately spreads the report to the various groups of the gang scattered throughout the park. These groups take up the refrain as they trek forth to find Bumper, keeping time to the rhythm of the song as they march along. This musical motivation reaches its climax when the groups foregather and surround Bumper, who then assumes the role of a musical soap box orator and renders a chanson, addressing his companions as 'Friends, Rummies, Countrymen, well, anyway, jes' friends; we find a thousand dollars, and friendship ends.' " Rodgers and Hart had used rhythmic dialogue to a lesser extent in two previous pictures, *Love Me Tonight* and *The Phantom President*.

Joe Schenck had promised Al the film would be completed by November 14th—four days prior to his first scheduled broadcast. This meant the script had to be rewritten, the songs and rhythmic dialogue learned, and the film entirely reshot—all within three weeks. A letter Richard Rodgers wrote to his wife Dorothy gives an account of a typical day in late October 1932.

> Today was one of those mad ones that made me satisfied that you were away. It started with writing, manuscripts to be done, conferences about rehearsals, orchestrations, and everything else. I had half an hour for dinner, alone, at the Derby, and then back to a rehearsal. Jolson wouldn't work because he wanted to go to the fights. I agreed

to go with him if he'd promise to work with me later. So to the fights we went (terrible ones) and then to his apartment where I rehearsed him for an hour. Then to meet the boys at Milestone's house to hear the final dialogue scenes, then home. It's two a.m., and I'm pooped.

Rodgers found Jolson "to be a sweet man who at the time was undergoing one of his frequent estrangements from his wife, Ruby Keeler." Ruby was no longer at Al's beck and call. In August, at, predictably, a prizefight, Darryl Zanuck had told Al and Ruby he was looking for a tap dancer to play the ingenue lead in *Forty-Second Street,* a "backstage" musical he was producing at Warner Bros. Al took that as a cue to brag about Ruby.

Within three weeks, a contract was signed giving Ruby $2,000 a week. *Forty-Second Street* went into production on September 26, 1932, and wrapped up less than six weeks later, on November 5th. Jolson, at the time, was in his fourth month of work on *Happy-Go-Lucky,* now retitled *Hallelujah, I'm a Bum.*

The film was still not finished by November 14th, so Jolson took a brief "vacation" from production to do his first broadcast for Chevrolet the following Friday evening.

Announcer Howard Claney introduced the program:

"Chevrolet, the world's greatest builder of cars, presents the world's greatest entertainer. Presenting Al Jolson . . ." "*Mammy, mammy, I'd walk a million miles for one of your smiles, my mammy.*"

The broadcast went downhill from that point on.

Performing in a hall before a women's club in San Francisco, Al Jolson experienced one of the worst cases of microphone jitters in the annals of commercial radio. "I heard him with a group of people who had all been Jolson fans," wrote Caroline Somers Hoyt in *Radio Stars.* "We were ready to give him a big welcome over the ether. And then, when he came on, our faces, which had been set for smiles, suddenly grew puzzled. We looked at each other and shook our heads."

"It seemed to me," wrote Jimmy Cannon, "that the microphone did not grasp the casual strength, the rich depth of his famous voice. The pickup was poor, and always there was a metallic humming as he sang. At times he sounded like a worn phonograph record. The jokes he told were mossy gibes—and he was as skittish as a race horse in traffic.

"Ken Strong, a weak straight man, didn't in any manner help the venerable material. Jolson's choice of songs was excellent. They were those he had sung when he was tops in our town. The radio didn't seem to befriend them as it should, but when he sang 'Rock-a-Bye

Your Baby with a Dixie Melody' there were flashes of his old, rough-and-ready genius."

Al knew that he had flopped, but he made alibis. The program was "too cut and dried." The straight man was no good. (Strong, a football player, was immediately fired.) The sponsor "wouldn't let me do what I wanted to do." (The bulk of the broadcast consisted of a routine based on Al's boyhood in Washington.)

And the more excuses he made, the more he kicked himself.

The second broadcast, from Los Angeles, was not much better than the first. ("Some of the gags he poured into the mike crumbled from old age and innocuous desuetude long before they got to the loudspeaker, while at least one must have set the rocking chair crew to rocking in more than one direction" was the way that *Odec* put it in *Variety.*) Al's last scene in *Hallelujah, I'm a Bum* was shot a few days later, and, after one more broadcast in Los Angeles, he left for New York on the Twentieth Century Limited with Pansy. Ruby was already in New York.

Jolson's next broadcast, from the National Broadcasting Company's Times Square Studio, was a marked improvement. Jimmy Cannon, who was in the studio, wrote:

> It seemed that time forgot which way it was traveling last night and hurried Al Jolson back to the halcyon days. It was the Jolson of the old Broadway, a red hot Jolson, whose fingers snapped like firecrackers as he made his New York appearance on the spotlight dappled stage of the NBC Times Square Studio. He thrilled the throng which crowded the steep aisles of the little theatre.

On Saturday, December 17th, Al returned to the Sherry-Netherland, his new Manhattan residence, feeling week and nauseous after playing a benefit on Staten Island. One of his doctors, Evan M. Evans, ordered him to bed, but Al went through with a particularly lengthy recording session three days later. Three nights after that, he left his rooms again, against Evans' orders, to do his radio show. Al was found to have the flu when he returned.

Jolson spent the next four days in bed, attended to by Ruby and Frank Holmes. His temperature down to normal by December 26th, Al left for Chicago two days later for a week's engagement at the Balaban & Katz Chicago Theatre.

That engagement proved a great balm for Al's battered ego. Over 100,000 people paid $54,500 to see Jolson give forty-one performances that week (Maurice Chevalier had grossed but $35,000 under similar conditions), and Jolie had enough energy left to make two broadcasts for Chevrolet, attend a press breakfast, and make several personal appearances.

Jolson said he liked Niles Trammel and the N.B.C. crew in Chicago so much that he wished he could do all his broadcasts there, but a costly line charge made that impossible. An irritable Al returned to New York and asked to be allowed to do *Presenting Al Jolson* without the "annoyance" of a studio audience. "It's added labor," Jolson claimed. "If the audience doesn't laugh, you think you're flopping. If they weren't there, you'd let the listeners at home make that decision. An audience only gives you seven hundred or so unnecessary faces in front to make smile or laugh. If you think about them, you can't think about your real work—pleasing the listener at the dials." The request was denied.

Chevrolet had succeeded in getting Al to memorize his lines. He now needed glasses when he read, and it was felt that this took the illusion of the "real Jolson" away from the studio audience. The idea was also to increase Al's spontaneity. He still came out with a script under his arm—more for security than anything else—but two mikes were used to give him more freedom of movement. The end result, however, was the same. Al Jolson, the man who "couldn't make a wrong move on a stage," felt and sounded forced, uncomfortable, and phony on the air.

Forty-Second Street had not yet been released, but the preliminary screening went so well that Warners decided to pick up Ruby Keeler's option. She would be featured in *Gold Diggers of 1933,* a Busby Berkeley version of Avery Hopwood's 1919 play, *The Gold Diggers,* with Joan Blondell in Ina Claire's original role. Ruby returned to the Warner Bros.–First National studio in Burbank in late January.

Al's own film career, if such it could be called, had taken another turn for the worse. Schenck was still not satisfied with *Hallelujah, I'm a Bum,* and Milestone insisted that Jolson return for still more retakes. Al refused, citing his ill health, and left for Florida as if to prove his point. The next two *Presenting Al Jolson* shows were broadcast from the Roney Plaza Hotel in Miami.

Al arrived back in New York on February 7th, the night before *Hallelujah, I'm a Bum* opened at the Rivoli Theatre to the worst reviews a Jolson vehicle had ever received. Mordaunt Hall of the *New York Times* said it was "Jolson's best film," and Regina Crewe of the *American* called it a "triumph," but the rest of New York's critics turned thumbs down on Jolson's only art film.

[William Boehnel, *World-Telegram*] . . . no hallelujahs shall be shouted here, for the production is a far from enthralling example of motion picture art . . .

[Richard Watts, Jr., *Herald Tribune*] . . . the result of so much activity of so many masterminds is not a happy one . . .

[John S. Cohen, Jr., *Sun*] . . . For the direction, the aim, and certain admirable bits, I have nothing but praise. Yet these musical satirists should finish something as well as they start it.

[Thornton Delehanty, *Post*] . . . Hecht must have gone berserk after seeing a preview of *A Nous la Liberté* . . .

Jolson, according to his contract, had three pictures left to make for Joseph Schenck. None was ever made. Al's personal salary— $500,000 per film—would have driven United Artists into bankruptcy had the pictures been as unsuccessful as *Hallelujah, I'm a Bum*.

It meant giving up one and a half million dollars—the equivalent of approximately $15,000,000 in 1988—but Jolson let Joe Schenck tear up the contract.

Schenck was one of the few real friends that Jolson ever had. It was a friendship Al truly valued.

On Sunday night, February 19th, Jolson told Jimmy Cannon that he was making his last broadcast the following Friday—eleven weeks ahead of schedule.

"I couldn't stand it," Al said "They wouldn't let me alone. I will never come back to radio unless I have a contract which absolutely forbids interference by sponsors.

"I was all set to fly to the coast this week. I wasn't going to say a word, but to just run out. I've done it before, and I was all fed up. But my friend, Lou Holtz, pleaded with me. He said it would look bad. We argued all night. Finally, I agreed to make this farewell broadcast.

"All they wanted was the name Jolson, and nothing else. I wanted to do great things on the radio. I wanted to dramatize *The Jazz Singer*. There's nothing more beautiful than that. But they wanted me to just sing songs.

"I wanted to dramatize incidents in my life—the early Winter Garden days, my courtship and other things. It would make good radio material. But they wouldn't let me. I offered them jokes. They edited them and said they weren't funny. I paid J. P. Medbury and Julius Tannen each a thousand dollars in advance. But they didn't like them. They had me so that every time I did come to a punch line, it went blah. I'm only a human being. What more could I do?"

The audience practically beat their palms red when Al did that farewell show five nights later. "What," wrote Cannon, "if his jokes were thin as his hair? And, of course, his voice isn't as mellowly strong as it used to be. Sure, he overacted, snivelling; tugging his coat collar around him; making his lip tremble too much when he intoned 'Brother, Can You Spare a Dime?' He was too jaunty for the love lyric, 'The Best Things in Life Are Free.'

"But he made up for all that, and more, when he shouted his Swanee swan song, 'Mammy.' The tune that made him famous was the last he sang. It is his trade mark, and his tradition. And he didn't let it down. He was the Jolson of the old Broadway that has gone on past him.

"His eyes flashed and he raised his wise, warning hand like a preacher chanting a sermon in jazz."

When Al finished, he was smiling. He knew he was through as a top line performer, but it did not seem to matter at that moment. Jolson had, to quote him, "more money than I'll ever spend," and he was in love, it seemed, with his wife, Ruby Keeler.

It is, however, doubtful whether Ruby or his millions mattered much to Al when he sang 'Mammy.' His mother, Naomi, had inspired him to go onstage, and it was to her that he now turned, in song, for comfort.

The "Has Been"

Ruby Keeler and her husband, Al Jolson, turn up at the Cocoanut Grove for the opening night of Eddy Duchin's orchestra.
　　　　　—Wirephoto caption, October 1935

Various explanations have been given for Al Jolson's professional
decline in the early 1930s. The theory most commonly ad-
vanced has his style of full-throated singing falling out of favor with
the rise of crooners like Bing Crosby.

The fact, however, is that low-keyed singing styles had been popular since the mid-twenties, when electric phonograph records were
first introduced. Cliff Edwards and Nick Lucas are much more typical of the pop singers of that day than Jolson. Al was as popular as
he had ever been in the mid-twenties, but that popularity rested on
his stage work. He was a musical comedy star, never a "pop singer"
in the full sense of the word.

The situation might have remained basically unchanged throughout the 1930s, had not Jolson left "Gus" and the theatre, and the
stage's own importance not declined. The sad fact was that Al Jolson did not—and does not today—register well in any mechanical
medium.

Jolson's talent, outside of his obvious gifts of comedy, song, eccentric dancing, and the like, was basically his genius for communi-
cating with an audience—establishing a unique "oneness" by which
every thought, joke, utterance, or lyric became a private moment
between Al and anyone who occupied a seat. This communication
was impossible in radio or movies.

Energy is one of the "X" factors in live theatre—the difference
between a competent performance and a great one. No one's onstage energy approached that of Al Jolson. Jolson in a theatre was
electricity personified—thrilling, immediate, memorable, and, unfor-
tunately, unrecordable. He was never captured on film.

Jolson felt uncomfortable behind a mike or in front of a camera,
and his acting, especially in love scenes, bordered on putrid. Had the
studio executives outfitted him in comedies, the Jolson film career

might have been different. But Jolson in films still would not have been Jolson onstage.

Part of Jolson's failure—in the 1930s and today—rested on his absolute refusal to become an intellectual. He was an instinctive artist, and his *conscious* approach to art and entertainment was essentially *bourgeois*. Where Chaplin thought in terms of *Modern Times*, Al Jolson thought in terms of syrupy dramatic scenes on radio. He wanted to do "great" things, but his stubborn refusal to develop his own intellect made that impossible. Jolson's thinking tended to be rather concrete and his mentality remained that of the average "man in the street" c. 1900—the sort of individual who thought that John L. Sullivan was a great American and saw little difference between an Andrew Carnegie and an Isaac Newton.

The greatest external factor in Jolson's decline was the deal with Joe Schenck—a deal that made Al much more complacent about his last three Warner Bros. vehicles than he might have otherwise been. *Hallelujah, I'm a Bum* was released in February 1933—almost two and a half years after *Big Boy*, Jolson's last film for the Warners. Had *Bum* succeeded, it would have been a Jolson comeback. Instead, it proved to be the biggest nail in his professional coffin. Hollywood producers no longer considered him a star of the first magnitude.

Al was out of show business for four months after his last broadcast for Chevrolet on February 24. 1933. Ruby was still working on *Gold Diggers*, and Al often met her at the Warner commissary for lunch—only to find out that retakes would prevent her playing golf with him that afternoon. This was strange to Al. For the first time since boyhood, he was an outsider, looking in.

Forty-Second Street opened in New York on March 9th, creating a new genre of film musical. Where Rodgers and Hart had tried to integrate the musical numbers with the story line in *Hallelujah, I'm a Bum*, dance director Busby Berkeley made each production number in *Forty-Second Street* a world unto itself. A song might start out as a routine in a Broadway show, but it would grow beyond the confines of the largest stage. Overhead shots and a kaleidoscope of arms and legs would give each number the distinctive Berkeley touch.

Ruby was established as the naive ingenue who taps her way to instant stardom by the end of the picture. Mordaunt Hall said that her "ingratiating personality, coupled with her dances," was a highlight of the film, and Richard Watts, Jr., of the New York *Herald*

Tribune dared to voice what everybody knew: Ruby Keeler was "rather more valuable as a cinema player than her celebrated husband, Mr. Jolson."

Gold Diggers of 1933 finished shooting on April 15th, and Al took Ruby to Hawaii for a vacation. This was the beginning of the "good years" of their marriage. Ruby, now in her mid-twenties, no longer bridled at Al's paternalism, his florid, often left-handed, compliments, and his habit of calling her "baby." It was "Baby, listen," "Com'ere, baby," "Baby," etc., ad infinitum.

Al was brown from the sun and Ruby broken out in freckles when the Jolsons returned from Hawaii. They immediately left for New York, where *Gold Diggers* was scheduled to open in early June, and Al took Ruby to the Baer-Schmeling fight at Yankee Stadium. Ruby said she didn't know what gave her the bigger thrill—Baer's victory or the opening of *Gold Diggers* at the Strand. The latter was another Warners-Berkeley-Keeler triumph.

The Jolsons went back to Los Angeles, and *Footlight Parade*, Ruby's next film, went into production on June 19th. James Cagney had the most important role, but Ruby and Dick Powell received almost equal billing. It was Ruby's third film, and the third time she played opposite Dick Powell.

Al was certainly not jealous of Powell, nor, apparently, of Ruby. He kiddingly called her "big shot" in private, but seemed to be genuinely proud of his young wife. Al even made plans to return to Warner Bros. as the star of a film version of *The Wonder Bar*. The deal was arranged in June—before Al returned to New York to guest star on the Kraft Music Hall, a new two-hour weekly radio show starring Paul Whiteman and his orchestra.

On the stage, Al (Gus) Jolson was seldom the protagonist of his own vehicles, leaving him free to bounce material off "straight" men like Bernard Granville, Forrest Huff, and Franklyn Batie. Al was always better as a "guest" than as a "star," a fact which was apparent on the air. His appearance on the Kraft show was considered a success—one of the few triumphs Jolie ever scored in radio. *Odec* did the review for *Variety*:

> Jolson gave them showmanship this night, entertainment of an emotional wallop and quality rarely heard on the air, and, what's more, impressive testimony to the fact that in radio, as in other entertainment fields, he remains in a class by himself. It was sterling stuff for the ether which he revealed in the productions he built around "A Cantor on the Sabbath," "Frivolous Sal" and "Sonny Boy" numbers. Through it all ran the good old hoke, but a hoke that dipped deep

into elements for the rocking chair mob, and the kind it revels in with tear ducts wide open. The Winter Garden reminiscences that led up to "I've Got To Sing a Torch Song" was strictly local in character, and the gag monolog was much too long for the purposes involved, but even there the emotional punch wasn't lacking.

Kraft-Phoenix immediately approached Al about becoming star of the Kraft Music Hall. Jolson's terms were rigid: complete control over his own material and $5,000 a broadcast, but Kraft agreed and signed him to do twenty-six weekly one-hour shows beginning Thursday night, August 3rd.

In the meantime, Al returned to California. Ruby was still working on *Footlight Parade,* and having trouble of two kinds. Warners wanted her to wear a tight and skimpy costume, but Ruby said that what she did was dance, not hand out "sex appeal," and claimed the costume was so tight she could not do the former. Warners backed down, but Ruby's second problem was not so easily solved. Walter Winchell, the ex-vaudeville dancer turned Broadway columnist, had written a scenario called *Broadway Thru a Keyhole* for Twentieth Century Pictures. Winchell described the story as about "a murdered gangster and a woman now happily married to another man."

Ruby, anxious to forget her past life as "Costello's girl," was horrified by rumors that the three main characters were based on Johnny, Jolie, and herself. Al became indignant when she told him. Jolson sometimes saw himself as womankind's protector, and he was in one of his best "How dare he make my wife feel terrible" moods when he saw Winchell at the Friday night fights at Hollywood Legion Stadium on July 21st.

Al walked over to where Walter was sitting, threw a right, which missed, and then a left which caught Winchell in the neck and knocked him down. "Write stories about my wife, will you?" Al said, his face set in grim determination. As he spoke, Al felt something hit him on the head. It was Mrs. Winchell, conking Jolie with a shoe.

Winchell took the whole thing very calmly: "The story of Mr. Jolson and his wife is a parallel to my story in a way, if they want to assume it was written about them. But it is a clean and great love story.

"Mr. Jolson took a sneak at me from behind in the stadium when I wasn't looking. I didn't even see him. I didn't say 'Hello' to him, as he says. I held my coat in my right hand and my hat in my left when he caught me on the neck."

Broadway Thru a Keyhole was released later that year with Texas

Guinan playing the part of "Tex Kaley," a Broadway hostess. Few reviewers—and far fewer picture-goers—connected it with Al or Ruby. nected it with Al or Ruby.

Jolson had been harboring a grudge against the columnist for almost three years prior to the *Broadway Thru a Keyhole* episode. In the fall of 1930, when Al was appearing at the Capitol Theatre in New York, Winchell had taken him to task for working on Yom Kippur. Al did not observe the High Holy Days, but he was extremely sensitive to allegations—however true—that he was a nonpracticing Jew. He was hurt by Winchell's jibes, and turned down offers to play the Publix picture houses in Chicago and Detroit as a result. Six months after that, however, Jolie interceded when the Shuberts tried to bar Winchell from the opening of *The Wonder Bar* at the Bayes Theatre.

This same willingness of Al's to help a friend is what finally put an end to the Jolson-Winchell feud. In December 1933—five months after the incident at Legion Stadium—Al was lying in the sun at Palm Springs with Irving Hoffman, a columnist for *The Hollywood Reporter* and a friend of Winchell's.

"Walter is in agony," said Hoffman.

"That's good."

"Going out of his mind."

"Great."

"An itch," said Hoffman. "He's got an unbearable itch."

Dr. Jolson sat up, stared off into space, and thought. "Irv," he said, "I'm going to give you something to send to Walter, but on one condition: he is never to know where it came from."

Al gave Hoffman a jar of ointment that cured Winchell's itch. Irv, however, could not resist the urge to tell Walter the identity of his benefactor. The feud ended, and the next time Winchell saw Al, he ran over and embraced him.

The eleven Kraft Music Hall shows Al did from August 3rd to October 12, 1933, did not live up to expectations. Al did not freeze up the way he had on the first Chevrolet show, but he certainly did not seem comfortable, and Abel Green of *Variety* found himself yearning for Jolson to "give out in the same thrillingly electric manner as he did at the old Winter Garden."

Ruby finished *Footlight Parade* in time to join Al in New York for their fifth wedding anniversary on September 21st, but quickly left to visit relatives in Nova Scotia. Al himself left for Los Angeles on October 14th, where his old friend from Oakland, Mervyn Leroy, had been doing advance work on the screen version of *The Wonder Bar*. Filming was scheduled to start on November 13th.

The film version of *The Wonder Bar* (entitled *Wonder Bar*) might best be described as a musical version of *Grand Hotel*. Jolson was no longer seen as a name big enough to "sell" a film alone, and so an all-star cast was used. Bette Davis, one of Warners' biggest stars, refused to play Liane, but dark-haired Kay Francis was talked into taking "the really charming part." Miss Francis was assured the role would be "rewritten"—and enlarged—for her.

"I didn't like the part the first time it was suggested to me," Francis told William French of *Photoplay*, "and after I got the script I liked it less. In the first place, there was no part for me at all. Just a bit—nothing more. It was a part any one of twenty girls on the set could play just as well as I. Naturally, I told them I didn't want to do it. They insisted—and I had to play it even though it was not "rewritten" into anything.

"If *Wonder Bar* were being made by an all-star cast from this studio, I wouldn't object to doing a minor part. Then I would feel that it was a matter of give-and-take between players on this lot. If I were asked to do a smart part in support of Jimmy Cagney or Warren William or Eddie Robinson or to fill in a cast for Stanwyck or Blondell, or any of our own women stars, I'd grin and do it.

"But this is different. Not only was I cast to a role in a picture I did not want any part of, but I was put in a picture in which the male lead (Jolson) *is not recognized as a screen star* and the girl with the only feminine part that can be called a part is borrowed from another studio." Kay was referring to Dolores Del Rio, Al's own choice to play Inez.

Dick Powell was almost as dissatisfied as Francis. "When they talked to me about *Wonder Bar*, I told them I didn't want to go into it. I knew Al Jolson would never let another singer do anything in it. But I didn't know how much he wouldn't until he took the good song that was assigned to me and gave me in exchange the eight bars he didn't like."

Almost everybody in the picture claimed that Al was "hogging scenes," and there was an immediate personality clash between Al and Ricardo Cortez, who played Harry the gigolo. Cortez had enough camera experience to block Al's little stage tricks, and he pulled a "dead pan" every time Jolson attempted any humor.

Al was as unhappy as everyone else in the cast, often singing lines like "Jolie doesn't work here anymore/I'm sure that I have told you this before" and "Headin' for the last round-up" as he strolled around the set. He meant what he was singing. On Sunday, November 19th, less than one week after filming started, he announced his retirement from motion picture acting.

"It's very strenuous, you know, to be a picture star," he said to a reporter. "I've had fame and glamour, and success, but after a man passes the forty mark, they don't seem to mean the same as when he was younger."

The film's rushes—including one scene in which Al did a routine in Russian dialect—were so good, however, that Jack Warner signed Al up for three more pictures only two days later.

Except for one musical segment, *Wonder Bar* was finished after four weeks' shooting. Al took Ruby for a week's vacation in Palm Springs, returning on December 20. Ricardo Cortez was getting married, and his friends threw him a bachelor party with gifts.

Al sent a ham, painted black.

The "Goin' to Heaven on a Mule" sequence in *Wonder Bar* was filmed in January. Seen today as racist, with a blackfaced Hal LeRoy gleefully dancing amidst watermelon sections, whites in blackface being "shot to hell" for drinking, and a collection of black characters who "landed up here" ranging from Old Black Joe to Uncle Tom and the Emperor Jones, the number is actually a Busby Berkeley travesty of *The Green Pastures,* Marc Connelly's play about heaven and the Bible as seen through the eyes of a nineteenth-century black child in the rural South.

Jolson had been interested in *The Green Pastures* ever since its Broadway opening in 1930. Wanting desperately to play "De Lawd," Al had tried to buy the film rights to the play from Laurence Rivers, Inc., the producer. Marc Connolly, the author, was convinced of Al's sincerity, but, like George Gershwin, who would declare *Porgy and Bess* "something more serious than (Jolson) could ever do," rejected Jolie's offer.

Al considered "Goin' to Heaven on a Mule" the "greatest" production number ever done, but *Wonder Bar* did not live up to Jack Warner's expectations, and did little towards resurrecting Jolson's career. Warners was now saddled with a middle-aged Al Jolson under contract for three picture. What kind of pictures was anyone's guess.

Al left for New York on Sunday, January 28, 1934, accompanied by his usual retinue—John Schenckenberger, Frank Holmes, Martin Freid, and one unusual guest . . . Al's brother Harry.

If Al's career was in bad shape, Harry's had ceased to exist. Vaudeville was dead, and thousands of performers were permanently out of work—including Harry. On June 21, 1933, Al's brother opened a cafe called "Harry Jolson's Rendezvous" in San Bernardino, California. When that failed, as it did within four months, he managed to get a few bookings in picture houses at low salary. Harry was in Los Angeles, with no immediate prospects, when Al asked him to accompany his party to New York.

Al offered to make Harry his New York agent, but Harry said he wanted to remain in California. "Suppose," he said, "I go back to Hollywood, open offices there as your agent, and book you for West Coast engagements?" Al agreed, and specified the terms.

Harry would work on commission, and also receive a guaranteed $150 a week for the rest of his life—providing he gave up performing. The brothers shook hands, and Harry returned to California. He opened offices, took out a license to run a theatrical agency, and sent Al a telegram. Jolie wired back:

> HOPE YOU ARE A BIG SUCCESS AS AN AGENT STOP YOU CAN'T
> MISS BECAUSE I'M YOUR FIRST CLIENT AND YOU'RE MY FIRST
> MANAGER STOP HURRAH FOR US STOP WITH THE SALARY I
> GET IF I WORK ONE WEEK YOU'LL LIVE A YEAR

Many performers never emotionally recover from having to give up "the business," and the telegram just rubbed the dirt in Harry Jolson's face. He was a failure; his younger brother was a success. Thirty years in the profession did not add up to a thing.

Al returned to the Kraft Music Hall on February 8th with songs, the usual banter, and a series of ten- to fifteen-minute "dramatic segments" with embarrassing attempts at acting.

"We should prefer," said the reviewer for the *New York Post*, "to have Mr. Jolson sing, and it is not because we are inordinately enamored of his singing. His voice is at its best when he has both knees in the footlight trough, but the microphone has no footlights. If there could only be an occasional light moment in his acting, or at least a moment that is not so highly overwrought. There is a tear in Mr. Jolson's every word. We find his broadcasts growing too humid for comfort long before he has worked himself up to sobbing into the microphone."

Ruby was still working on *Dames*, her fourth picture for Warners and her first on a new contract, when Al took another leave of absence from the Music Hall. He left for Los Angeles on April 13th, and, two weeks after his arrival, Warners announced that Al's next picture, *Go into Your Dance,* would go into production in the fall.

On June 1st, Al, Ruby, and Anna Mae Keeler, Ruby's youngest sister, sailed for New York on the *Santa Elena* through the Panama Canal. Anna Mae was seriously ill with what *Variety* reported as a "complication of diseases," and her doctors felt the voyage would do her some good. The ship arrived in New York on June 18, 1934, and Al, who had been scheduled to return to the Kraft Music Hall on June 28th, informed the J. Walter Thompson Agency that he wanted to "rest" for an additional three weeks.

The Jolsons and Anna Mae spent late June and early July at the house Al had bought for Ethel Delmar in Scarsdale. A good part of that time was spent in playing golf.

Golfing was another Jolson passion Al had determined Ruby would enjoy. (He remembered how his golfing on that 1925 trip to California had helped destroy what remained of his marriage to Ethel Delmar.) Shortly after they were married, Al got four-time Canadian Open champion Leo Diegel to give Ruby lessons. Al himself was only a fair player, but Ruby was a natural athlete, and immediately took to the game. Within a few years, she was on a par with some of the top amateur women golfers in California.

Ruby was supposed to be back at Warners for her next film, *Flirtation Walk,* by July 10th, but Al persuaded Jack Warner to extend her leave of absence. "Ruby needs the rest," Al told him. "The poor kid is weak from all that dancing," No "weak" person, though, could hit a golf ball the way Ruby hit them over those Westchester lawns. She once played Al, and beat him. According to Harry Akst, Al never played with her again.

Ruby returned to Warners later that month, and Al returned to the Kraft Music Hall for five more broadcasts. Before leaving for the west coast in mid-August, Al conferred with Harry Warner, eldest of the Warner brothers and head of the all-important New York office.

It was Harry Warner who suggested that Ruby co-star with Al in *Go into Your Dance.* Warner was diplomatic, but his reasoning was clear: Ruby Keeler's name was needed to put the new Jolson picture over. It was as simple as that.

Al's shaken ego had recovered by the time Carlisle Jones interviewed the Jolsons at their home in Bel Air, California, in September.

"It's the first time we've ever been in a picture together, but it's the first time one of my pictures has had a role good enough for Ruby. . . .

"We decided, when we were married, not to work together in any picture, ever. But we're used to each other now. We won't quarrel, will we, Ruby?"

"No, we won't quarrel," agreed Ruby.

There were no quarrels, but Al almost drove director Archie Mayo to distraction by giving Ruby suggestions about when—and where—to move.

Go into Your Dance was about an egocentric Broadway stage star (Jolson as "Al Howard") who is reformed by a sweet young tap dancer (Ruby as "Dorothy Wayne"). Filming, started in November, was postponed for two weeks when Al and supporting actress Glenda Farrell were both laid up with the flu.

The picture boasted a strong cast, including Barton MacLane as a gangster called The Duke, Patsy Kelly as Irma (who, like Elektra Pivonka in the stage version *The Wonder Bar,* did "The Dance of the Dying Flamingo"), and Helen Morgan as Luana Bell, The Duke's wife and lead singer in Al Howard's show.

Morgan, who had made her reputation as a great "torch singer" in the 1920s, was an alcoholic who made few attempts to stay off the bottle during the filming of *Go into Your Dance.* Her only song in the picture was "The Little Things You Used To Do," sung, as was her custom, while sitting atop a piano. Martin Fried was her accompanist in the scene.

Al had been keeping Marty on retainer—and the wagon—ever since the end of *The Wonder Bar* tour in 1932. "But Helen Morgan got him started drinking all over again," recalled Fried's wife, Pearl. "Jolson called me—I was in New York, since Marty and I had separated—and said, 'Pearl, you better come out here right away, or else I'm gonna have to fire Marty.'

"Al told me that he'd give *me* Marty's salary, but that he wouldn't give it to him because he would just drink it up. It took me a little while, but I came out to the coast with our son, Stan, and Al gave Marty's salary to me to handle until he got him back on the wagon.

"You know, he (Al) wasn't a bad man. He took Stan to ball games, and did all he could to help us. I always felt I had a friend in Al."

Harry Warren, who wrote the songs for *Go into Your Dance* with Al Dubin, did not share most of Pearl's feelings. "Jolson knew 'About a Quarter to Nine,' one of the songs in the picture, was going to be a hit," remembered Warren. "He kept on pestering Dubin and myself to let him write an extra set of lyrics to the chorus. We knew what his game was—to cut himself in on the credit and the royalties. So we told him that the song did not need extra lyrics, which it didn't, and we let it go at that.

"One weekend, though, the four of us—Dubin, myself, Jolson, and a friend of ours—went up to Arrowhead to do some fishing. The friend had heard 'About a Quarter to Nine,' and kept on asking Al who wrote it. Al, who had been raving about everything in the picture, just said, 'Never mind.' He wouldn't tell him."

Shooting on *Go into Your Dance* was completed early in February 1935. Warners was already planning *Shipmates Forever,* the next Ruby Keeler–Dick Powell vehicle, Al having made it clear that he did not envision Jolson & Keeler as a permanent screen team. He was not jealous of his young wife's screen career per se, but it rankled him that Hollywood no longer trusted him to carry a film on his own. He—Al Jolson—who had put across some of the weakest shows in Broadway history.

In March, Jolson signed as star and master of ceremonies for *Shell Chateau,* a weekly variety show the J. Walter Thompson Agency was putting together for Shell Oil at N.B.C. Al was in New York, in the midst of preparations for the first broadcast, when he received word that Ruby's sister, Anna Mae, had died in Hollywood.

Months before, when Anna Mae was in the hospital, she had asked for Al to stay with her at night. Her death touched Jolson deeply, and he cancelled two rehearsals in order to fly west and attend the funeral. Poor weather, as it turned out, kept him in New York.

Shell Chateau went on the air on Saturday night, April 6, 1935, but critical response was only lukewarm. Jolson, who had seemed uncomfortable as the m.c. on Broadway in *The Wonder Bar,* sounded positively embarrassing on the radio in *Shell Chateau.* Even Aaron Stein of the *New York Post,* who had liked the premiere broadcast, took exception to a joke Al told on the second show about a man who asked for money because he was hungry and then spent the money on caviar. "We know," wrote Stein, "that it was meant in fun, but even if it had been funny, we could not have liked it."

Ruby, shaken by her sister's death, arrived in New York the following Monday to attend the premiere of *Go into Your Dance* at the Capitol Theatre on May 2nd. The reviews were good, but the last half of the film was overly melodramatic, and *Go into Your Dance* was not as commercially successful as any of the movies Ruby had made with Dick Powell.

The Jolsons had lived in a number of homes since permanently settling in Los Angeles in 1932. When Al was making *Hallelujah, I'm a Bum,* they lived at 569 North Rossmore; in 1933, at 7357 Franklin, and, during the filming of *Go into Your Dance,* in the exclusive Bel Air district near Beverly Hills. Now, as he neared fifty, Al thought that the time had come to build a permanent home and "settle down." He had gone through a similar mood in 1921, when he was thirty-five.

While *Go into Your Dance* was in production, Al bought a five-acre orange grove in Encino, in the San Fernando Valley. Plans were drawn for a big colonial-style house overlooking the surrounding countryside, and Ruby enlarged the estate by purchasing a nearby lemon grove.

The house and the estate were only part of the new life Al now thought he wanted. On Monday, May 6th, he and Ruby went to a foundling home known as "The Cradle" in Evanston, Illinois. Arrangements had been made for the Jolsons to adopt a seven-week-old, half-Jewish/half-Irish baby boy who was immediately renamed Al Jolson, Jr. Al, however, called the child "Sonny Boy," a nickname Ruby refined into "Sonny."

Jolie had to rush back to New York for the next *Shell Chateau* broadcast, leaving Ruby to take Sonny to Encino by herself. Reporters caught up to her as she boarded a train for Los Angeles. "The baby can't say 'mammy' yet," said Ruby, "but he cries beautifully."

Less than two weeks later, an infection in the baby's inner ear forced Dr. J. Edwin Scobes to put him in the Children's Hospital in Hollywood. On Sunday, May 19th, Al, Jr., received one hundred cubic centimeters of blood in a transfusion, after which the doctors said he was "in pretty good shape." Al called several times a day to ask about his "Sonny Boy," and Ruby did not leave the hospital until Al, Jr., had made a complete recovery.

The September 28, 1935, *Shell Chateau* was the twenty-sixth and last on Jolson's contract. Al, who had not seen Ruby in almost five months, stayed in New York for four additional weeks, finally entraining for Los Angeles on Thursday, October 24th. Shooting on *Shipmates Forever* had finished in July, and Ruby was hard at work on *Colleen,* her last movie with Dick Powell, by the time Al's film, *The Singing Kid,* went into production in November.

The Singing Kid was an obvious, tasteless attempt to present a "streamlined" Jolson. Swing, snappy patter songs, and "hot" dancing were used as a counterpoint to Jolie's obviously dated "mammy" shouting and full-throated singing. A budding child star named Sybil

Jason (publicized as "Sonny Boy in skirts") was thrown in for insurance.

It did not work out. The cast (including Cab Calloway, who lent the musical numbers needed lift and sparkle) was uniformly excellent, but the script, by Warren Duff and Pat C. Flick (one of Jolson's writers on *Shell Chateau*), was forced and labored.

Sybil Jason has fond memories of "Uncle Al," who threw her a birthday party and gave her a brand new bicycle while *The Singing Kid* was in production. But Sybil's days as a child star were numbered, and *The Singing Kid* would be Al Jolson's last starring role in a motion picture.

Al returned to *Shell Chateau* for the first of thirteen additional broadcasts beginning January 4, 1936. N.B.C. and Shell were now allowing Al to broadcast from Los Angeles, and a Jolson hit of eight years previous was taken out of mothballs and provided with new lyrics.

> Golden Gate, we're comin' through ya.
> Shell Chateau says welcome to ya.
> Each Saturday night, the stars you all know
> Will shine at Shell Chateau.
> We bring to all you folks, you sons and daughters,
> That good old oil for troubled waters.
> Goin' strong now, won't be long now.
> This is Al in Shell Chateau.

"Is It True What They Say About Dixie?" sung by Al on four consecutive broadcasts, was a minor hit, but Jolson's contract with Shell was not renewed at the end of the thirteen weeks. Nor was *The Singing Kid* successful when it opened at the Strand Theatre in New York on April 3rd. Frank Nugent of the *New York Times* said Al was "singing as exuberantly as ever and trying with might and mammy to give zest to an indifferent score and a lifeless script."

Al was thoroughly disgusted. He tried to make himself believe the "time had come" to withdraw from the performing end of show business—to settle down, produce a few pictures, and become a gentleman farmer on his estate in Encino. The life Al now envisioned was a wealthy version of the one suggested to him by Fred Moore in 1908.

"I'm not the sort of person who enjoys living in an apartment," Jolson told Chet Green of *Photoplay* at this time. "I've always hated it—elevators, doors with numbers, screeching brakes and trolley cars under your window. Some people get to like it, you know? They don't hear the noise, they don't see the crowds, they don't smell the gutters. But I didn't get to like it—ever." Al proceeded to tell Green about his plans to produce pictures and safeguard his future by growing citrus fruits on his estate. He did *not* tell Green he had insisted on a separate apartment being built inside the house for his own private use—so he could escape from being a father, a husband, and a country gentleman and return to the illusion of living in the city.

Aside from two appearances on the *Lux Radio Theatre* (co-starring in *Burlesque* with Ruby and starring in *The Jazz Singer* with Karen Morley as Mary Dale), Jolson was inactive for the following nine months. Warner Bros. toyed with the idea of making a new version of *The Jazz Singer*, titled *Bowery to Broadway* and starring Al, to celebrate the tenth anniversary of talking pictures. Jolson liked the idea, but hesitated when Warners suggested that Ruby play Mary Dale, Jack Robin's *shiksa* love interest.

Al could have had a Broadway show at almost any time. Lee Shubert wanted him to star in the revised edition of the *Ziegfeld Follies* at the Winter Garden, and other producers, Billy Rose among them, were equally anxious to have "Jolie" work his magic on a stage again. Al, however, refused to commit himself for more than four weeks, and plans for his return to Broadway in the middle and late thirties never got beyond the talking stage.

Al was middle-aged and rich, and anything less than what would today be termed "super stardom" held no interest for him. He wanted to recapture the great popularity he had enjoyed in the days of *The Singing Fool*, but that was no longer possible. And so, despite the frequent urge to "slap on the burnt cork and sing," Al spent most of his time sun-bathing alongside his pool and visiting the race track—trying to convince himself that he was happy.

The greatest thing Al Jolson did in 1936 had nothing to do with show business. That year marked Moshe and Hessi's fortieth wedding anniversary, and Al's youngest sister, Gertrude, made a special request.

Moshe, now seventy-eight, had always wanted to go to the Holy Land, and Gertrude, who knew Al had contacts in the State Department, asked if he and Hessi could be sent to Palestine.

Al was fond of Gertrude; she had taken care of Moshe and Hessi until her own recent marriage to Isadore Sollod. "Gertie," he said, "I'll do it. But on only one condition. I want you to go along with Mom and Dad."

Moshe, Hessi, and Gertrude went to Palestine—where they traveled with a machine-gun escort.

That summer, Al and Ruby went to Wrigley Field in Los Angeles for the ten-round fight between Henry Armstrong and Alberto (Baby) Arizmendi of Mexico. Eddie Mead, a friend of Ruby's who had managed world bantamweight champion Joe Lynch in the twenties, sat in back of the Jolsons.

As the fight progressed, Ruby turned to Mead and said, "That's the kind of fighter *you* ought to manage, Eddie—that boy Armstrong."

"There's just five thousand reasons why I ain't managing him," replied Mead. "I can buy him for five g's, and all I need is $4,995 more to make the deal." When the fight was over—with Armstrong the winner—Al gave Mead a card and told him to call the next day.

Al agreed to finance Mead's purchase of the Armstrong contract from Wirt Ross, Armstrong's manager since 1932. Mead, anxious for publicity, got Jolie's okay to tell Jack Singer of the *Los Angeles Times* that the sale price was ten instead of five thousand dollars. It proved to be a bad move; Ross raised the price to ten thousand dollars as soon as he saw Singer's story.

Al was furious, and absolutely refused to give Mead the additional $5,000. George Raft soon came in with the necessary money and became Al's silent partner.

Jolson, however, was the active owner. He brought Armstrong out to his home in Encino and induced world featherweight champion Petey Sarron to defend his title against Henry in Madison Square Garden. Armstrong knocked out Sarron in six rounds and went on to win the welterweight and lightweight titles within the next ten months.

Jolson, who never saw a quarter of the money he had lent Mead, finally washed his hands of the whole deal after an argument with Raft at Los Angeles' Roosevelt Hotel in February 1938. The experience, however, did not dampen Al's enthusiasm for boxing. Armstrong had been a winner—a sharp contrast to the nags that made up Jolson's racing stable. Miquelon, the stable's star horse, won only one race in his entire life.

Ruby went to work on *Ready, Willing, and Able* in September, Warner Bros. having given up the idea of teaming the Jolsons in *Bowery to Broadway*. Jolson was in New York, dickering with Ruthrauff & Ryan about starring in *Café Trocadero*, a new C.B.S. radio program for Lever Brothers.

Ruby made a "surprise" guest appearance when the new show premiered on December 22nd. The Lever Brothers show (the title *Cafe Trocadero* was dropped after the first two broadcasts) would run longer than any other Jolson radio series. Why remains a mystery. The overall quality was poor, and Sid Silvers, Al's "second banana" on the first few broadcasts, received what one historian called "the worst reviews in radio history." *Land* of *Variety* did not mince words:

> New Tuesday night half hour for Rinso bowed in with Jolson in fine vigor. But there were a number of things that kept the first broadcast from being 100%. Sid Silvers was one of them. Script kidded about his gags and his performance being bad. But the script wasn't kidding. He was pretty wishy-washy and tallied few bright or smacko giggles. And with the burden squarely on his shoulders. Proving anew that comedian-authors usually don't do right for themselves.

Land did not have kind words for female vocalist Martha Raye either. Miss Raye was called "a dubious asset. She wasn't any funnier than Silvers. Just louder."

Greek dialect comedian Harry (Parkyakarkus) Einstein replaced Silvers on March 2, 1937. *Land* reviewed the show again, and noted that "the program is now routined for a comedy splash, a sample of Martha Raye, and finally the dramatic one-two to the chin put over by Jolson himself." This modest format kept the show running for another two years.

According to his contract, Al had one film left to do for Warners. That contract, revised in 1935, now called for him to act, write, and produce—a "three way" contract that an increasingly bitter Jolson referred to as a "no way" deal. Warners did not want to make another money-losing film with Jolson, and had little interest in whatever abilities he might have had as a writer. Nor did they want a man with Jolson's temperament producing movies.

Al was also annoyed because the studio refused to allow Ruby to work for his friend Bud DeSylva. Buddy, now head of production at Paramount, wanted to pair her with Fred Astaire, whom he wanted to borrow from RKO. Jack Warner, however, remained adamant, and Al retaliated by having Ruby turn down two Warner scripts in a row.

The Warner–Jolson/Keeler crisis dragged on until May 1937, when Al had his lawyers negotiate settlements on both contracts. On May

20th, Al received $20,000 for *not* making his final Warner Bros. film. Ruby's release followed two days later.

Within the next few months, the William Morris Agency placed the following message in *Daily Variety:*

> We are proud to announce that Al Jolson has exclusively authorized us to represent him for the negotiation of radio and theatre engagements. Any other person or persons purporting to represent Al Jolson in this connection do so without authority.

Harry Jolson had joined the Morris Agency as an "associate" shortly after becoming Al's west coast agent in 1934. But Al, now that he was out of pictures, felt he needed the full power of the agency behind him. He stopped paying Harry his weekly retainer fee of $150 as soon as he signed with the Morris Agency. The outraged Harry sued, but New York Supreme Court Justice Samuel H. Hofstadter granted summary judgment when the case came up for trial on July 21, 1941. Judge Hofstadter ruled the agreement was "repugnant to the statute of frauds" and could not be enforced in the courts.

Al tried to make amends by buying Harry a new car, a gift Al's older brother was not too proud to refuse. Harry went back to work for Al in 1946, after the success of *The Jolson Story,* and the brothers were on fairly good terms when Al died.

Such, however, would not be the case between Jolie and Ruby. Their marriage, never the love fest Jolson had presented to the public, was in serious trouble.

Jolson vs. Keeler

"I went to confession every day I was married to Jolson."

In the beginning of their marriage, Jolie had liked Ruby's family. Despite Nellie's indiscretions *vis-à- · vis* the press, he sometimes wondered why the Yoelsons couldn't be as intimate and folksy as this Irish clan.

Beginning in 1936, when Al's professional activity was lessened and restricted almost entirely to radio, he spent more time with Ruby in Encino. Ruby also had more free time. *Colleen* was finished before the end of 1935, and *Ready, Willing and Able,* her last Warner film, was not shot until the following September.

The inactivity made Jolson tense and restless. Resentful of his middle age, and of the new generation of stars that had come up "the easy way" and stolen his thunder, he took out most of his frustrations on Ruby. If she ventured an opinion on anything, Al told her she was "all wet" or "immature."

Always short-tempered and cynical, Al became increasingly hostile in the middle and late thirties, saying he was glad he lived in Encino because he hated the Hollywood "phonies" who lived in Beverly Hills. Almost everything he said around his wife was negative about something—when he talked. Mostly, he just sat and brooded—sullen, angry, and withdrawn.

Ruby tried to talk to him, but there was no way she could understand Al Jolson. He had a way of shutting her out that was maddening. More and more, she found herself retreating to her family—spending as much time as possible with Helen and her other sisters, and talking to her mother on the phone. Al, resenting this, made cynical remarks about the Keelers. Jolson had particularly pointed things to say about Ralph Keeler, Ruby's father, and he referred to the whole family as "shanty Irish."

Al had also become disenchanted with Al Jolson, Jr. Sonny was a

Al Jolson was still spelling his name "Joelson" when he broke into show business with the Victoria Burlesquers in October 1900. "For Old Times Sake" marked his first appearance on the frontispiece of a published song. The fourteen-year-old "Master Joelson" is seen with Fred E. Moore, his singing partner. *(From the collection of Larry F. Kiner)*

Julia and Josie Rooney. Al was smitten with Josie when he and Joe Palmer were on the same bill with the Rooney Sisters at George Castle's Olympic Theatre in Chicago in December 1905. *(Photo courtesy of Julia Rooney)*

Jolson in 1906, the year he branched out as a "single turn" in vaudeville. The twenty-year-old entertainer was the sensation of the Sullivan & Considine circuit.

The only known photograph of Henrietta Keller, the young lady who became the first Mrs. Al Jolson on September 20, 1907. She divorced the great "Jolie" in 1919. *(Photo courtesy of Kitty Doner)*

A scene from Lew Dockstader's Minstrels, 1908–09. This "musical comedy in blackface" was a send-up of then current efforts to reach the North Pole. Act II opened in "Boo Hoo Land," the first stop on Professor Hightower's voyage to the Pole. That's Dockstader as "Prof. Hightower" in the pot, and Jolson as "Acie," the assistant, on his knees. Edw. Von Roy is the chef, with Pete Detzel as "King Swastica" at right.

Jolson and Kitty Doner dancing on the fair grounds of the Panama-Pacific International Exposition in San Francisco during the summer of 1915. Kitty was in three of Jolson's Winter Garden shows before becoming a vaudeville headliner in the 1920s. *(Photo courtesy of Kitty Doner)*

Al Jolson as "Bombo" in Atlantic City during out-of-town try-outs for the show of the same title. Bombo's servant in this photograph is Frank (Pansy) Holmes, Jolson's valet-secretary for more than thirty years. Holmes played "Jenkins" in the show, which enabled Jolson to take him off his personal payroll and temporarily put him on the Shuberts'. *(Photo courtesy of Marjorie Olsen)*

President Calvin Coolidge and Al Jolson on the White House lawn on October 11, 1924. Al and Bud DeSylva introduced their campaign song, "Keep Cool with Coolidge," at this meeting. (Jolson sang; DeSylva played the ukulele.) Irving Caesar, the lyricist of "Swanee," "Tea for Two," etc., is the man wearing glasses (partially hidden) to Al's right.

May McAvoy and Jolson in *The Jazz Singer* (Warner Bros., 1927).

Jolson in *The Singing Fool* (Warner Bros., 1928), the film in which he first sang "Sonny Boy."

Jolson and his father, Rabbi M. R. Yoelson, at a family reunion at Al's sister Etta's house in Yonkers, 1931.

Al Jolson as "Bumper" in the first version of *Hal-lelujah, I'm a Bum*, 1932. The film was scrapped and remade later in the year.

Al and Ruby Keeler, his third wife, in 1933, the year that Warner Bros. released *Forty-second Street*.

A publicity shot for the *Kraft Music Hall* of 1933–34. This was Jolson's second starring series on the air.

Al and Ruby in *Go into Your Dance* (Warner Bros., 1935).

September 14, 1935. The cast of that week's *Shell Chateau:* singer Jackie
Hughes, Henry Fonda, orchestra conductor Victor Young, Fanny Brice, Al
Jolson, and an unidentified actress who did a scene from *The Bride the Sun
Shines On* with Fonda. The comedy team of (Al) Stone and (Tish) Lee is in
the foreground. *(Photograph courtesy of Tish Lee)*

The Jolsons with Al's uncle, Benjamin Yoelson. Al was elected honorary
mayor of Encino in December 1935.

Sid Grauman looks on as Al prepares to immortalize his own kneeprints at Grauman's Chinese Theatre in 1936. Al had worked for Sid's father, David (Pop) Grauman, during 1906–07.

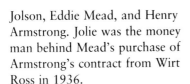

Jolson, Eddie Mead, and Henry Armstrong. Jolie was the money man behind Mead's purchase of Armstrong's contract from Wirt Ross in 1936.

A nicely retouched formal studio portrait, 1930s.

Tyrone Power, Alice Faye, and Al Jolson in a publicity still from *Rose of Washington Square* (Twentieth Century–Fox, 1939).

Jolson in *Hold On to Your Hats*, 1940, his last Broadway show.

Al and Al Jolson, Jr., 1943.

Jolson entertaining, World War II.

Larry Parks as Jolson. *(From collection of Greg Gormick)*

Al and his fourth wife, Erle Galbraith, at the races with Mr. and Mrs. Harry Cohn.

Jolie and his long-time manager, Louis "Eppy" Epstein, in Al's dressing room at N.B.C. during 1947–48. That season marked Al's return to the *Kraft Music Hall.*

Jolson, in his sixties, with young Eddy Arnold.

Lt. Col. Samuel Spitzer of Yonkers, a relative of Al, greets a tired Jolson and his accompanist, Harry Akst, on their arrival in Korea to entertain troops on September 17, 1950.

Norman Krasna, Jerry Wald, and Jolson at RKO. This photograph was taken just three days before Al died.

"momma's boy," not the "man's man" Jolie wanted. He was just a tot, but Al resented the way Sonny preferred Ruby and her family to him.

Al was twenty-three years older than Ruby. "It bothered him more than it bothered me," Miss Keeler told Denver *Post* movie editor Rena Andrews in 1981. "(Al) was a possessive man, which was difficult for me . . . He always felt I'd meet somebody. I guess that was it; I don't know. If I was gone for ten minutes—just shopping, mind you—I had to explain it. He didn't mind me working, but he also wanted me with him if he was doing something."

Sometimes he did, but sometimes he did not. When his radio show for Lever Brothers went off the air for the summer of 1937, Al took a trip to New York without Ruby. After a few weeks, he sent for her. And as soon as she arrived, he sent her back again.

It was the same stuff he had pulled with Henrietta—twenty years before.

Jolson remained in New York until it was time to resume his radio broadcasts early in September. George Jessel was his first guest star of the season, and Al Jolson, Jr., was on hand to greet them when the two men got off the airplane in Los Angeles.

Al raced down the stairway, ran to the two-and-a-half-year-old, and lifted him high off the ground. "Who am I, Sonny Boy?" he asked.

"You're the Jew," replied the child.

Jessel said it was the only time he had ever seen Jolson humiliated. The trouble in Al's marriage increased in the months that followed.

Ruby's chance to co-star with Astaire fell through, but RKO gave her one of the leads in *Mother Carey's Chickens,* a non-musical with Anne Shirley and Fay Bainter. Al spent most of his own afternoons at the Santa Anita Race Track. Anyone who wanted to find Jolson knew where they could find him between 1:30 and 5:30—every day except Tuesday, when his radio show was on the air. The Lever Brothers show did not begin its 1938 summer sabbatical until after July 12th, when Al's guest star was young Judy Garland.

Al stayed in Encino for the summer. If Ruby had guests over for dinner—young people, her own age instead of Al's—he would sit there and refuse to talk. He finished dinner hurriedly on those occasions and then went to his apartment, leaving Ruby to entertain her guests alone.

His sarcasm deepened, and his condescension. "Oh, so you're an expert on that, too," he said whenever Ruby had what seemed like an idea. "You're *too* smart."

Ruby's life became a living hell. "He'd fly into a rage at me for nothing," she would testify, "just because I didn't agree with him on something. He would keep me up all night, calling me 'stupid' and other names."

Al's third and final season for Lever Brothers began on September 20, 1938. The guest star on that show was flyer Douglas "Wrong Way" Corrigan, and *Variety* said the broadcast "was pretty much of a clambake."

> Jolson's show in the past was always a problem child so far as comedy is concerned. Situation is unchanged, the laughs still being few and far between. Script handed Corrigan for by-play with Martha Raye, Parkyakarkus and Jolson was only fair at best. One hearty juckle in the lesson to Corrigan on making love at the bow-off, when he "mistook" a window for the door. Actually, Corrigan had little to do and little to say for the $3,500 he received for the guest shot. A couple of gags anent his flight were okay.
>
> Comedy brunt still falls on Parkyakarkus, and the Greek dialectician is still giving out with those puns, anemic comedy at best.

Ruby was out of films. The Jolsons had a staff of servants, and Frank Holmes still took care of most of Al's personal needs, which left Ruby with little to do except play golf. Things that season fell into a pattern: Ruby leaving the house early in the morning for the golf course, and Al going to the races. It seemed more pleasant than being together.

Billy Rose had approached Al about doing a four-week stint in his next Casa Mañana frolic. Jolson had little intention of doing it, but the offer gave him an excuse to move the Lever Brothers show to New York on a temporary basis. Al arrived in New York on Saturday, October 22nd, and began negotiations with Rose.

Once again, Al suddenly began to miss his wife. He phoned her every night, and finally asked her to leave Sonny with the nurse and fly to New York.

Ruby did as he instructed, but, once she was in New York, Al quite predictably ignored her.

The William Morris Agency had been at work on Jolson's behalf. In December, after he returned to California, Al began preliminary work on *Rose of Washington Square* at Twentieth Century–Fox. It was his first film in three years, and the first time he had received less than top billing since 1913. Tyrone Power and Alice Faye (who remembered Al as an "obnoxious boor") were the stars.

Al played Ted Cotter, a second-rate vaudevillian who does all he can to shield Rose Sargent (Faye) from the charm and machinations of Power. Al sang some of his most famous songs, including "Mammy," "Rock-a-Bye," "April Showers," and "California, Here I Come." Rather than perform them "live," however, Al was forced to lip-synch to his own recordings. He looked uncomfortable and stiff as a result.

Gregory Ratoff, who replaced Roy Del Ruth as the director in late January, forced Al to re-record his songs. Advertisements for the film referred to Jolson as "the man who sings the past the way you want to remember it." At fifty-three, Al had become "nostalgia." Reviewers said he "stole" the picture from Power and Faye, but *Rose of Washington Square* did nothing to re-establish Jolson as a star.

It was a bad time for Jolie. His sister Rose died on February 10th—just as *Rose of Washington Square* was nearing completion. And his wife had found another, younger man.

He was John Homer Lowe, Jr., wealthy scion of a prominent California family and a successful dealer in real estate. Ruby had met John, a year her junior, at the home of golfing friends who had invited her to dinner, and they were more than good friends by the time Al's Lever Brothers radio show went off the air in March 1939.

In April, Al went to Mexico on a fishing trip—without Ruby. Six weeks later, he left for New York to see Lee Shubert about plans for a new show called *On the Line*, about a bandleader at the height of his career who leaves the business and seeks refuge in a foreign country.

In Chicago, en route back to California, Al spoke to reporters. "Mrs. Jolson and I," he told them, "have decided on a baby sister for Al, Jr., who is four years old now and getting pretty hard to handle." Al soon returned to Encino; the Jolsons never did adopt a baby girl.

In May, Ruby told Al she needed a vacation—from him. Al was shocked—neither of his first two wives had done anything like this—but he raised no serious objections when Ruby, her mother, and her sister Marjorie, sailed for Honolulu.

Karl Schullinger of the Lord and Thomas Agency had come up with an idea for a forty-five-minute radio show co-starring Al and

Judy Garland for Lucky Strike's Saturday night spot on C.B.S. When
Miss Garland was found to be unavailable, a new show built around
Al as m.c., was auditioned at Columbia's KNX studio in Hollywood
on Friday night, July 7, 1939. James Wright, a Lucky Strike executive, and writer Frank Wilson flew the audition disk to New York
for inspection by George Washington Hill, president of the American Tobacco Co.

Hill turned thumbs down on the disk and proposed show. Jolson—in his fifties—had now failed an audition. Pepsi-Cola was reportedly interested in him for a half-hour variety show on one of
the networks, but that idea was abandoned after Al made a trip to
New York in August.

In the meantime, Al was busy with more film work. In July, he
re-created the "Kol Nidre" scene from *The Jazz Singer* for *Hollywood Cavalcade,* Fox's "tribute" to the days of silent movies that
had gone forever with the coming of Al Jolson and the talkies.

In September, after Ruby had returned from Honolulu, Al went
into *Swanee River,* a romanticized biography of Stephen Foster starring Don Ameche. Al was cast as minstrel E.P. Christy and was effective as the vain performer-impresario.

The Jolsons celebrated their eleventh wedding anniversary with an
elaborate night-club party shortly after *Swanee River* went into production. Their marital problems, however, worsened in the next few
weeks, and reached a climax one night in Encino.

Nellie, Ruby's mother, came into the kitchen and made a remark
that sparked a fight between Al and his wife. It was the straw that
broke the camel's back, and Ruby told Al she was leaving him—
accompanying her mother back to her home in Toluca Lake with
Sonny.

"I hope everything will work out all right," a subdued Al told
Ruby as her luggage was put inside the car.

"Maybe," she replied.

That night—Thursday, October 19, 1939—Al invited Harry Akst
to Encino. Jolson was morose when Akst arrived. For hours he recalled the "good days" of his married life to Ruby. He had always
been a good provider—for the Keeler family as well as Ruby. What
had he done to deserve this?

Al was so despondent over the next few days that Don Ameche
thought he was on pills. When the cameras rolled, however, Al was
ready—a professional if not the same magician he had been on
Broadway in the 1910s and '20s. He called Ruby at her mother's

home every night and finally persuaded her to have dinner with him on Tuesday evening.

Jolie made a night of it, taking Ruby to the Al Smith–Henry Majcher fight at the Olympic Auditorium after dinner. He tried to talk her into returning to Encino, but Ruby had already made up her mind. She wanted a divorce.

Al had Jimmy drive her back to Toluca Lake.

Outwardly, Al started to accept the situation. He called Ruby the following night and offered her $400 a week with a lump settlement of $50,000 in the event of her remarriage. She refused, telling him her lawyers would negotiate the settlement.

The tabloid press soon broke the story: the Jolson-Keeler marriage was over. Al confirmed the rumors in a short telephone interview with the United Press on Thursday. "It just seems to happen to people out here," he said. "They called ours a perfect marriage and I never thought it would happen to us. But it did.

"There is no other man or woman involved. I love her and I'm still hoping she'll change her mind, but you can't argue with a woman. . . . Yes, I guess she's going to file for divorce. I don't know what it's all about. But it's sure awfully lonesome out here."

Ruby accepted the settlement when Al phoned her again that evening. The following day, she announced through her attorneys that she would sue Jolson for divorce.

In the meantime, Harry Akst stayed in Encino, telephoning his wife, Rose, repeatedly to tell her that he had to have dinner with Al, and probably spend the night with him as well. "You don't know how close I was to Reno," Rose later told Harry, "when you kept leaving me to cool off Al's torch."

The despondent Jolson agreed to a telephone interview with the New York *Journal American* on Friday. "She was more than my wife, y'know. She was my pal. And I was more than her husband. I was her friend. . . .

"I don't know what happened. I don't know why. But only yesterday she was crying and I couldn't help it. I put my arms around her and I said, 'Come on Ruby, kid, let's forget about this. Let's call the whole thing off and go back together again.' I couldn't bear seeing her cry like that. I love her."

Al, who left for New York the next day, was in an angry mood when a group of reporters met him on arrival in Penn Station.

"Mr. Jolson, why are you in New York?"

"To attend to a little business."

"Which business?"

"My own business."

"Won't you say a few words about Ruby's divorce suit?"

"What am I, a criminal? Do I have to talk?"

Ruby filed suit while Al was en route to New York. She charged extreme cruelty, and the complaint was entered in the Los Angeles Hall of Records as D-185771.

Hold On to Your Hats

"It's all right, folks. Jolson's back!"
—BROOKS ATKINSON, *The New York Times*

The theatre was the reason Al had come to New York. He was anxious to get back on Broadway, and Lee Shubert's *On the Line* was not the only vehicle he had in mind. Producer Vinton Freedley was planning a new musical about a radio western star. Al had shown some interest in the show a few months earlier and now, with Ruby gone, his interest perked.

Jolson spoke to Freedley, told him he would speak to him again in a few weeks, and left for Pimlico with Jimmy. They went to Washington from there, and Al called on his parents. Moshe and Hessi already knew of the impending divorce, but the rabbi, almost eighty-two, did not reproach his son. Moshe was not haughty, only sad because he knew that Al had never found true happiness with a woman.

Al left for Hollywood a few days later and checked into Cedars of Lebanon Hospital. The reason? "I'm tired." That, and a slight cold the New York winds had served to aggravate. The only tiredness Al felt was in his mind. He was losing Ruby, and he still could not accept it.

Al flew to New York with Martin Fried on Friday, December 1st, and confered with Freedley and his staff that weekend. The script concerned a singing cowboy of the airwaves who is sent out west and meets some real bandits. No *Show Boat* or *Of Thee I Sing,* but a good, solid professional script that would allow Al ample scope for clowning. There was an important part for a comedienne-singer (Martha Raye), and another good part for an ingenue. Al wanted Ruby for the latter.

Jolson and Fried flew back to Los Angeles on Monday, but Jolie returned to New York—his third trip inside of nine weeks—later that month to promote *Swanee River* with Don Ameche on the Kate Smith radio show. Three days before that, on December 26th, Ruby testified before Judge Thomas C. Gould in Los Angeles Superior Court.

Ruby, wringing a handkerchief, said Al's ridicule had made her "very nervous, and I think it has given me a slight inferiority complex." Newspaper accounts said she "glanced appealingly at the judge."

One of Ruby's complaints was that Al never seemed to like taking her anywhere. On occasions, when he went to "New York, Chicago, Palm Springs, or some other place, he would call me after a few days and ask me to come meet him.

"I would go to him, but after a few days, he would get tired of me and tell me to go home."

It was remarkably similar to Henrietta's testimony twenty years before.

An interlocutory decree of divorce was granted.

The news was relayed to New York. Al was getting a shave in the barber shop of the Sherry-Netherland when he was interviewed by a reporter from UPI.

Jolie smiled through the lather and said he was "sorry" he had given Ruby an inferiority complex, "but I couldn't help it." He laughed.

Al was in a totally different mood the following day. He was quiet, hoping "for the best," which was, to him, "forgiveness." He appeared to be in shock.

"I don't know what I can say," he told reporters. "An inferiority complex! Well, you could say an awful lot of funny things about that.

"What it's all about, I couldn't tell you. We both love each other. To me, she's still the most wonderful girl in the world. I love Ruby, and I want to give her everything in the world she wants. And if she wants a divorce, that's that.

"But you've seen men go to jail, haven't you? And they rant and rave and curse. But once they're in the prison cell and the key's turned in the lock, they have to quiet down and take it, don't they?

"Suppose I didn't have a very happy Christmas! Well, I'm going to have a swell New Year's. My little boy gets in here Friday morning to visit me." Ruby had been given legal custody of Sonny.

Al took Sonny to the premiere of *Swanee River* at the Roxy on Friday night, December 26th. Ten days later, they left for Miami Beach with Marty, Jimmy, and Frank Holmes. Jolson felt he needed two weeks' rest with "Mr. Sol" for the hard work to follow.

Al brought Sonny back to Ruby late in January. Ruby was friendlier to Al than she had been in months, but said she would "have to think about" appearing in the Freedley show. The lack of a definite "no" made Jolson happy. He flew back to New York, pinch hit for Ben Bernie over C.B.S. on January 21st, and went back to Miami Beach for an additional six weeks. For the first time since October, Al was not preoccupied with Ruby. He even thought about other girls, like Gloria Cook, a former Harry Richman paramour then being courted by a night-club owner.

Gloria dumped the night-club owner in a hurry when Jolson moved in. Jolie made no secret of the new show in the works, and Gloria was soon his most frequent companion—around town and by the Roney-Plaza pool.

Al had sent Charlie Washburn, who would be press director for the new show, to persuade Ruby to sign the contract. Washburn got back to New York within a few weeks, telephoned Miami, and told Al that Ruby was "wavering." Al then got on the phone, and asked her "like a friend."

Ruby finally consented to do the new show. She would later regret that decision.

Al returned to New York in March. Now that he had Ruby, Jolson wanted to obtain the show.

The rights to the production, now titled *Hold On to Your Hats*, were held by Alex Aarons, Freedley's long-time partner, and George Hale, the former dance director, a Wall Street broker-financier. When the Aarons-Hale option on the book expired on April 15th, Al was able to acquire approximately 80 percent of the show's ownership. Hale came back for the remaining 20 percent, and Aarons received $2,500 in payment for what *Variety* described as his "preliminary work on the show." Freedley walked away with nothing.

Ninety thousand dollars was needed for production money, and Al agreed to put up nearly all of it.

Ruby, with her sister Marjorie and Sonny, arrived in New York in May. She was disturbed to find that Al was now producer of the show, but Jolson soon convinced her there was nothing wrong. He had always "had a piece" of his shows. This time, he just had a bigger piece. What was wrong with that? Miss Keeler bought it.

Al took Ruby to the Stork Club with the Bobby Crawfords (Crawford was married to Mary Lucas, Ruby's old chorus chum), and the Jolson charm flowed freely. Ruby laughed and chatted with him, and, according to one observer, it looked as though she and Al were "courting all over again." Rumors flew about a reconciliation, but the Jolsons continued to live separately—Al at the Sherry-Netherland and Ruby, with Sonny and her sister, at 1 Sutton Place, where Al had supplied them with a comfortable suite.

The score for *Hold On to Your Hats,* by Burton Lane and E. Y. Harburg, was ready by May, and the production team was rapidly assembled: Raoul Pène du Bois to design the scenery and costumes, Edgar MacGregor to direct, Catherine Littlefield of the Philadelphia Ballet to stage the dances, and Hans Spialek and Don Walker to do the orchestrations.

Lou Epstein was back as Jolson's manager. Out of Al's life since *The Wonder Bar* in 1932, Eppy had stayed in show business as Mae West's personal manager. He had taken a group of Cotton Club performers to London in 1937, and had even discovered a new comedy team called Abbott & Costello.

There were other additions to the Jolson staff. Al, who felt that New York was no longer safe, hired two men from an agency as bodyguards. They were with him almost constantly.

The chorus call for *Hold On to Your Hats* was held on Tuesday, May 22, 1940. About a hundred girls applied, but most were tossed out on the first round. Those remaining were instructed to report for the first rehearsal on Monday, June 3rd, when the final choices would be made.

Al stayed behind with Eppy and Marty after everyone had left. Jolie tried one song, accompanied by Marty, and then quit. He picked up a microphone and threw it into the wings in a symbolic gesture.

Neither Eppy nor Fried went with Al when he left the theatre, but the two bodyguards covered him on both sides as he started walking east. They had gone a few blocks when a young girl stepped in front of them, asked Al if he was Mr. Jolson, and launched into a discourse about the Yoelson family and another family her father knew. Jolson was intrigued.

The girl, a seventeen-year-old brunette from New Rochelle, was Pearl Goldberg. Rejected along with other chorus hopefuls, she had remained in the theatre to watch Al rehearse.

Al brought her up to his suite in the Sherry-Netherland. She held no physical attraction for him—Al could never touch a Jewess—but there was an innate honesty and goodness about Pearl (or "Goldie," as Al called her) that he found compelling. No sooner were they in the suite, alone, then Al, for the first time, began to talk about his mother.

The words tumbled out of him . . . how cheerful she had been, how she had raised him in Seredzius, how she had kept their hopes up during the trip to America, her death, and her funeral.

It was the beginning of a long relationship with Pearl, a relationship that would survive Al's own death by more than three decades.

The *New York Times* account said Al looked "ready to explode" on the first day of rehearsals. He sat on the edge of the piano stool as George Hale helped make the final selections for the chorus.

"I'm nervous," Al said. "This show has got me so nervous I can't eat."

"Now, don't be nervous," Eppy said.

"I gotta be nervous," Al barked. "It's my makeup, ain't it?"

Al had on his horn-rimmed glasses. "In radio," he said, "you read everything off a paper, and in films you memorize a few lines at a time. There's going to be an exodus from Hollywood soon, what with $2,000 salaries being cut to $200, and you'll find that half the actors are going to have a tough time memorizing a whole show."

The *Times* reporter left as soon as the principals arrived: Martha Raye, Bert (The Mad Russian) Gordon, and Ruby. The final chorus picks having been made, the girls were given their instructions and dismissed. The rest of the day was spent reading the script.

Al became more edgy as the reading progressed, and hearing Ruby recite her lines in that Sunday School voice of hers only served to irritate him further. Al's pent-up hostility at her for leaving him began to hit the surface. He made nasty criticisms, and finally exploded.

His rage drove Ruby out through the stage door in tears. Al pursued her up Seventh Avenue with a fusillade of references to her relationship with John Lowe, her family, her morals, her attitude, and her lack of brains and talent. He hollered so loud and so forcefully that a truck driver slammed on his brakes as he drove by. Pearl, who was in Al's parked car with Jimmy—Jolson was taking her out that evening for her birthday—had a clear view of the proceedings.

There were the usual apologies from Jolie the next day, and Ruby agreed to remain in the cast. On one level, Al wanted to use the show as a vehicle to rekindle their marriage. On a more subconscious level, he wanted to use it to punish Ruby. On that second level, Jolson probably succeeded.

Al began by finding a new girl friend. Gloria Cook had gone into the hospital, forfeiting her chance of being in the show. Her place was taken by Jinx Falkenburg, a tall, dark-haired model who had been "Miss Rheingold."

Al spent his evenings squiring Jinx around to night clubs and his weekends taking her to the World's Fair or the races. She was a little better educated than the other girls in Jolson's life, and Al found himself engaging in fairly intelligent conversation with a woman for what may have been the first time in his life. Jinx was Ruby's opposite in many ways—the perfect girl for Al to spite her with. Miss Keeler might not have cared what Al did with his spare time, but she certainly did not like the knowing glances she was getting from the other members of the company.

After only three weeks of rehearsals—three weeks of what competent witnesses called "the greatest confusion in the history of the stage"—*Hold On to Your Hats* opened at the Cass Theatre in Detroit on Sunday night, June 30, 1940. Some of the minor players were ex-movie starlets who had never been on a stage in their lives, and the production team paced the alley outside the stage door dolefully wondering what was going to happen next. At one point, Lionel Stander missed his cue, leaving Ruby alone in the middle of the stage. She stood there, staring at the audience without the slightest idea of what to do, until Al Goodman, the conductor, saved the night by striking up the music for her dance routine.

The best part of the show was easily the comedy between Al and Martha—until Act II, Scene 5, when Jolson, as "The Lone Rider," sang over the airwaves for the "Nationwide Broadcasting Company." There was no script for that scene, but there was Jolson—electrifying the audience with one Al Jolson song after another . . . "Swanee," "Rock-a-Bye, "Sonny Boy" . . . and a few ad lib references to Ruby Keeler.

When the final curtain fell, Al thanked the audience and apologized for the show's understandable spottiness. He need not have bothered. The audience had seen the legendary Jolson do his stuff in person. It had been more than enough.

Scores of changes were made in the script during the following two weeks, but hard work was not Jolson's major worry. Ruby had suffered in silence at Al's "personal remarks" delivered to the audience, and his gallivanting with Jinx Falkenburg had caused her considerable embarrassment. She asked Al for a release from her contract. He refused to give it.

Ruby had signed a run-of-the-play contract, and she knew that

Actors' Equity would bar her from the stage—for life, Al warned her—if she broke it. Despite her later image as a homebody, Ruby loved the theatre. She agreed to stay in *Hold On to Your Hats*.

The company entrained for Chicago on Sunday morning, July 14th. Al stayed in Detroit for one more night, and flew out with Jinx the next day.

The rest of the company, and several reporters, were sitting in the auditorium of the Grand Opera House when Jolson arrived. He pushed open the lobby doors and stood there for a moment, "beating time while waving his soft brown straw hat." Al looked nervous. "I'm late at the doctor's," he said.

Jinx appeared in the lobby, spoke quietly with Al for a few moments, and left. Al then spun around and saw, as if for the first time, the people waiting for him. He started shadow boxing and did dance steps. He was "on."

Al clowned around for a few minutes, going into the box office, shaking hands with the reporters, and humming "Walkin' Along, Mindin' My Business," his own favorite number from the show.

"Look," he said, as he made sweeps into the carpet with his toe. "In Hollywood, they make chalk marks on the floor, and you've got to stay there. No, no more Hollywood for me, and . . ." He walked away and called over his shoulder. . . . "No more marriage either. You can put it in caps."

Before that night's performance, Al told Ruby that he did not want to have her in the show if she "wasn't happy being here," and that he "couldn't sleep from thinking about it." Ruby could have a release from her contract any time she wanted.

Ruby said she would leave after the Saturday night show.

A tremendous wave of applause greeted Al on his first entrance in the show that evening. Faltering, he said it was "too much" for him, and then climbed over the footlights to sit down on the edge of the stage. He began to talk, still faltering, about the "old days," then gave a sudden yell and sprang up, clutching his posterior as if the hot tin top of the footlights had singed him. It was the same stunt he had pulled at the Winter Garden almost forty years before; and it still worked.

From that point on, Al was all movement, bounding around the stage like a sure-footed demon. The reviewers were ecstatic, and *Hold On to Your Hats* was on its way to a profitable Chicago summer run.

The following night, however, Jolson tripped on stage and broke a small bone in his foot. He played the Wednesday matinee on crutches.

The Democratic National Convention in Chicago Stadium was still in progress. One scene in *Hold On to Your Hats* had Al enter from the wings with his guns drawn to apprehend the villains. Al now hobbled in—trying to cope with the two guns and crutches—turned to the audience and announced, "On the first ballot, it's Wallace 623, Bankhead 331 and McNutt 66." Then he faced the villains. "All right, you guys, stick 'em up."

Al, however, found the crutches cramped his style. Beginning that night, he used just a cane.

Jolson claimed to have trouble getting a replacement for Ruby on such short notice. This problem was supposedly solved when she agreed to stay an extra four weeks—the remainder of the show's run in Chicago. Miss Keeler later told Ann Marsters of the Chicago *Herald American* that she did so because she "felt sorry" for Al and his injured foot. She continued, however, to stay clear of Jolson.

It galled him. "She could have been more considerate and a little friendly," he complained. "I pay her $1,000 a week. I was married to her for eleven years. We have a little boy. She might have asked me, 'How's your foot?' or 'How do you feel?' " Al's onstage ad libs continued, only now they were more barbed.

At one point, during a scene between Al and Ruby, she went blank and totally forgot her lines. Al looked at the audience.

"You'll remember reading in the papers that I called somebody stupid. Well, I'm not saying a word!"

The humiliated Ruby wished that she had not agreed to stay the extra month. She kept even farther away from Jolson, spending her nights alone at the Ambassador Hotel while Al showed Jinx around Chicago night life.

The climax came the following Monday, July 22, 1940. The problem of Miss Keeler's replacement still had not been solved, Al continuing to hope that Ruby would change her mind and remain in the company until the show reached Broadway. Ruby, who had no such plans, went to Jolson's dressing room to talk the matter out before that evening's show. She was not prepared for what she saw when she opened the door. Jinx was there with Al.

Ruby slammed the door and ran to her own dressing room. She screamed for Eppy, and Al's alter ego came running.

Ruby's Irish blood was boiling. In a loud voice, she demanded

Jinx be dismissed from the cast. *She would not go on if Jinx was not immediately fired.* Eppy finally quieted her down and said the only solution was for Ruby to leave the cast at the end of the week—no matter what Al said. Ruby finally agreed to go on for that night's performance.

There was a song Al sang to Ruby in Act I, Scene 6. When the time came to sing it, Al gave the cue, ("I'm old enough to be your father, and I can give you lessons in carrying the torch") and added, in a voice that only Ruby could hear:

"I know he loves you and you love him," he said, referring to John Lowe, "so go on back to him and your golf."

Then he turned his glance away, and did not look at her again for the remainder of the song, "Don't Let It Get You Down."

When the final curtain fell, Miss Keeler went to Al with fire in her eyes. "All right," she told him, "put your understudy in!" This time, Ruby meant it. She was through.

Eppy, Hale, and the rest of the staff negotiated a peace settlement the following day. Al gave Ruby her release, with the stipulation that she finish out the week and give Eunice Healy, her replacement, time to take over the role. Ruby agreed, but she gave Ann Marsters an exclusive interview that afternoon.

"I realized that I made a mistake in joining the cast, and I am leaving it for more than one reason. I don't feel that I belong in the show, anyway. It is Al's and Martha's show, from beginning to end, and my part is merely incidental.

"The other reasons are longer and more complicated, and I do feel that I have been treated unfairly by people who couldn't possibly understand the situation.

"When I agreed to appear in Al's show, I thought we could work together as friends, and that he would have no more interest in my personal life or activities than I have in his.

"But—you see—it didn't work out that way. Perhaps I shouldn't say this, but I know now that Al hoped our working together would bring about a reconciliation between us.

"That is and always has been impossible, and I haven't been able to understand Al's strange attitude."

No one ever would.

Ruby gave her last performance in *Hold On to Your Hats* on Saturday night, July 27th, and returned to the west coast. Her plans were "to play a little golf and get a sun tan" and take care of Sonny.

Eunice Healy took over the role of Shirley with only two rehearsals and quickly became Jolie's new companion in Chicago night life, Jinx Falkenburg having fallen out of favor.

Philip Liebmann had wanted Jinx to go to California for a week to ten days in connection with a new Rheingold campaign. She was only making eighty-five dollars a week in *Hold On to Your Hats,* and the chance to take some time off and make hundreds seemed too good to pass up. She raced to Al and asked permission, but the psychological timing was bad; Jolson's reply was a loud, sharp "No!" Jinx was angry, and Al muttered "Run-of-the-play contract and she wants to go away" every time he passed her backstage for the rest of the Chicago run.

The show moved to Philadelphia, and Al, who felt more work was needed on the book, brought in his old friend, Joe K. Watson, as consultant. All the show needed was a little tightening; Al really called Joe in to have somebody to talk to from "the old days." Eppy had been driven to distraction by Al's nocturnal reflections. "I don't know, Eppy. All I ever tried to do for Ruby was be good to her. I set her brother up in business, gave her mother a new home, and . . . Eppy? You asleep yet?" Joe moved in with Al.

The only thing to mar the opening at the Forrest Theatre in Philadelphia was an accident Jinx suffered as she made an exit with a soft shoe routine. She caught her heel on a stone step, fell down a flight of stairs, and passed out. Al rushed offstage to make sure she had not been seriously injured. "He was so sweet and concerned," Jinx wrote. "It was the first time he had spoken to me since Chicago. He insisted that, even though I said I was all right, I was to go to a doctor immediately and have x-rays taken." Jinx was all right by the time *Hold On to Your Hats* opened in New York on September 11th, but her liaison with Al had ended. Jinx's place was soon taken by Betty Boyce, one of the showgirls in the company. Miss Boyce, another tall brunette, was with Al almost constantly during those last two weeks in Philadelphia.

Olsen and Johnson's *Hellzapoppin'* was still packing them in at the Winter Garden after a two-year run, so *Hold On to Your Hats* opened at the Shubert Theatre (where *A Chorus Line* was later to become a Broadway fixture).

After ten weeks on the road, *Hold On to Your Hats* was in smooth enough shape for Al to take great liberties with the script. His first appearance found him in an easy chair. "This is a gala night for me," he said, "because my kid is listening in on the coast. He's five years old. It's piped in and the kid will hear me sing." Al used a microphone for this scene, warbling snatches of standards like "My Blue Heaven."

The scene between Al and Martha at the end of the first act had the first-nighters screaming. Martha played the part of Mamie, an aggressive western woman. In the scene, she added to the script by tearing the buttons off Al's fly.

The best song in the score, from a purely musical standpoint, was "The World Is in My Arms," sung by Jack Whiting and Eunice Healy. Al's own numbers included "Walkin' Along, Mindin' My Business," "Don't Let It Get You Down," and "There's a Great Day Coming Mañana," which served as the first-act finale. But nothing in the score could match the way Al tore the roof down with his old songs in the broadcast scene.

Al pulled out all the stops in this scene at the opening. "You ain't heard nothin' yet," he told the audience, while throwing away the mike. "We don't need this gadget any more than we did before." It was getting late and "since all the critics" had gone, the house could "settle down and have a good time." He began with George Gershwin's "Swanee," and then went on to "April Showers," "You Made Me Love You," "Sonny Boy," and finally, "My Mammy."

Al, as "The Lone Rider," appeared in three disguises in the course of trying to capture Fernando (Arnold Moss) in the show—a Latin American female entertainer à la Carmen Miranda, a toreador, and a Mexican peon—a guise in which he sang "Old Timer" in the second act.

Hold On to Your Hats, while not a great show, was a hit in virtually every department. The songs, costumes, and dances were all favorably noted by the critics, the comedy was expertly delivered, specialists like dancer Gil Lamb provided extra touches, and even Russ Brown as "Dinky," Jolson's straight man, won some critical applause.

The real raves, however, went to Jolson:

[John Anderson (*Journal American*)] Al Jolson is back on the home grounds, back after ten years' absence from the stage . . . The old master is in a class by himself . . . the show is at its best when Mr. Jolson pushes it gently to one side and goes it alone . . .

[Sidney B. Whipple (*World-Telegram*)] Hollywood seems not to have changed Al Jolson. Certainly he has not become slothful or lazy. His feet travel as rapidly and as lightly as ever. He still throws his entire frame into every song he sings, shaking the words out of him in paroxysms of energy as in the old days, and he still projects his person-

ality to the top row of the galleries . . . It is good to have Al Jolson
back. Broadway is beginning to look like Broadway again."

[Richard Watts, Jr. *(Herald Tribune)*] For there is no getting around
it, Al Jolson remains, after all these seasons, a master showman and
a brilliant entertainer who can put over a song in incomparable fashion . . .

The only adverse criticism Al received was for leaving "Rock-a-
Bye" out of the broadcast scene.

Al was back, seemingly the king of Broadway once again. There
were parties (including a cocktail party in honor of Jolie at the Stork
Club on Sunday afternoon, September 22nd), newspaper interviews,
requests for special appearances, and fans ranging from the "I-saw-
you-at-Hammerstein's-in-1910" types to one married woman who,
having seen the show in Philadelphia, followed Jolson to New York.
Al wound up taking her husband to lunch.

There was still something sexual about Jolson onstage. He was
not handsome, he did not play romantic parts, and he was middle-
aged, but members of both sexes—including many heterosexual
males—often tried to mount the stage and touch Al at the end of
each performance. This was not a cult. Indeed, Al Jolson had been
passé for a decade. It was simply the same magnetism that had elic-
ited similar reactions from audiences in *Robinson Crusoe, Jr., Sinbad,* and other shows. On a stage, no one could touch Al Jolson.
No one.

Betty Boyce's place as Al's companion was soon taken by an eighteen-year-old chorine in the show named Joanne Marshall, and the
tabloid press soon called their relationship "the most torrid on
Broadway during the past season."

Al was friendly with Joanne's family, and there were rumors of a
possible wedding. Joanne neglected all her previous boy friends for
Al, including at least two chorus boys in *Hold On to Your Hats.* Al
and Joanne spent a good amount of time together in the first six
weeks of the show's run at the Shubert, but an argument at a posh
night club ended their relationship in late November.

Joanne Marshall went to Hollywood and became Joanne Dru. Her
brother, Peter, kept the Marshall stage name and wound up hosting
a popular N.B.C.-TV game show called *The Hollywood Squares.*
And Peter's son, Pete, became a major league baseball player under
the real family name, LaCock.

Al no longer limped, but he still used a cane in his first-act monologue. Late arrivals sometimes got a knuckle rapping. Al would pound

the floor and stop his monologue to greet them with exaggerated courtesy. "My name's Jolson, the owner of the show," he'd shoot down at them. "There are your seats. Now, are you comfortable?"

He would fling his compliments to the boxes. "Boy, if those seats are taken at two seventy-five—and I don't mean Wilkie buttons—everything's taken." In would come a woman with an oversized Scotch plaid hat.

"Where's your bagpipes, lady?" It was his manner that produced the laughs, and made the customers he ribbed among the laughers.

The most truly memorable Jolson "ad lib" during the run of *Hold On to Your Hats* came one night in the broadcast scene, as Al prepared to go into his numbers.

Jolson passed wind rather loudly.

Any other stage performer would have been abashed. Not Jolson. He simply said, in his third person style . . .

"Jolie made a fartsola."

The audience gave him an ovation. It was one of the great moments in the theatre.

Al hosted a Christmas party for the cast on Tuesday night, December 24th, assuring everyone the show would run until at least May 1st. There seemed little reason to think otherwise, even in that era of comparatively short runs for big hits. The gross of *Hold On to Your Hats* had declined somewhat since November, but it was still one of the hottest tickets on Broadway. Al figured that the decline was a temporary slump, and he was soon proved right. Within three weeks, the gross climbed back eight thousand dollars, and George Hale started looking forward to the profits that would roll in after New Year's.

They would never come.

The line made every major daily in the country.

Los Angeles, Dec. 28—(AP)—RUBY KEELER OBTAINED HER FINAL DECREE OF DIVORCE YESTERDAY FROM AL JOLSON.

Al went into another emotional tailspin. For nights, he stayed awake, talking to Eppy. More than ever now, he could not stand to be alone.

Three o'clock in the morning:

"I can't understand it, Eppy. I loved that girl, and I did everything I could to make her happy. Got her into *Show Girl* and the movies. The least that she could do is see me now and then. But she won't even talk to me. Hey, Eppy," Al clawed Epstein, "Ya awake?"

"Yeah, I'm awake," sighed Eppy.

"I don't know. I guess it's my fault. I was always yellin' at her. But next time it would be different, Eppy, honest. You know that."

"Yeah, Al, yeah. I know it. Go to sleep."

Eppy finally left the Sherry-Netherland and went to the Hotel Edison. "Uncle Lou had a suite there," recalled his grandniece, Mrs. Leon Dworkin. "He always went there when he couldn't take living with Jolson."

Mrs. Dworkin said the subject of Al's possible bisexuality was discussed in her family's dining room. "The family often wondered if the real reason Uncle Lou—who was completely masculine—would leave Al at those times had something to do with that," she said. Eppy often talked of quitting his job with Al, but always changed his mind and, invariably, moved back to the Sherry at Al's urging.

Frank Holmes still rose to make Al's breakfast in the morning— orange juice, a vitamin pill, toast, eggs and bacon, and coffee.

"I'm not hungry, Pansy," Al would say. "I couldn't seem to sleep last night. Just nerves, I guess."

"Yeah," said Eppy. "I was up last night myself. Al, look, about that busted flat. They want four hundred bucks to make it good. How do you want to list it?"

"I don't know, Eppy. I'm not in the mood. Can't you take care of it?"

"I took care of one in Detroit and you almost wrung my neck."

"All right. Put it under miscellaneous expenses."

"I can't. You and Hale said to cut that column out."

"Then put it under Act of God."

"For Chrissakes, Al. Let's just sit down and look the whole thing over."

"Look—damn it, Eppy. I don't feel well. Don't ya understand that? I don't feel well. Hey, Pansy, where's that breakfast?"

"You said you didn't want it, Mr. Jolson."

"That's cause Eppy's always spoilin' my appetite. Hey, Eppy, where ya goin'?"

"Out. I'll see you tonight at the theatre."

"I'll have your breakfast ready in a moment, Mr. Jolson."

"Yeah. Okay, Pansy. Brother, that guy can get on your nerves."

Epstein, however, was the man that Al still called on in emergencies. An "emergency" might consist of a young reporter or fan sneezing from a cold. "Eppy! Eppy!" Eppy would come running to Al's dressing room. "Get this kid out of here. Take him to a drugstore and then send him home with something for his cold, but get him away from me. This kid'll lay me up for six months with those germs of his."

And then, half an hour later, Al would leave the theatre and walk out into the rain without a coat.

Jolson came down with the grippe shortly after New Year's. He had microphones installed along the footlights in an effort to conserve his voice, but it was no use, and his doctors, Hertz and Leo Michel, said he would have to lay off for at least two weeks. Both physicians diagnosed pneumonia.

Al went into the hospital for a week. To pass the time, he learned the part of Jeeter Lester in *Tobacco Road*. This was one role Al could sink his teeth into. Nurses quickly spread the word about how good he was, and the producers of the play invited him to give a special Sunday performance for the benefit of war-torn England. Russ Brown came up to see Jolson, and read the part of Jeeter's son while an impromptu audience looked on. But Al never did play Jeeter at that benefit.

Jolson returned to *Hold On to Your Hats,* but his health was not much better. His chest was still congested, and a cyst had formed on the roof of his mouth. His teeth, usually strong, were also hurting, and his dentist, Samuel L. Lubalin, worked on him almost daily. Al had difficulty eating, and he claimed that he could barely talk. He spoke to his doctors one more time, and said he would close the show on February 1st.

George Hale flew into a rage. "I nursed this show along for a year before Jolson stepped in. Dammit, it's not fair." No swearing could convince Al's junior partner that Jolie was really sick, and even Eppy thought that he was shamming. Pearl Goldberg, however, thought that Al was really suffering. (Goldie claimed she knew when Al was lying; his lower lip trembled.)

Saturday night, February 1, 1941 marked the 158th and final performance of *Hold On to Your Hats* on Broadway. No sooner had Al taken his last curtain when a process server slapped him with a paper. George Hale was seeking damages for $100,000 if Al did not reopen *Hats* sometime that season.

Al simply shrugged his shoulders; he had been sued before. Three days later, he and Pansy left for Palm Beach, Fla.

The weather in Palm Beach was so bad that Al had a recurrence of pneumonia within a few days of his arrival. He even had to send to New York for a sun lamp.

At one point, Al called Ruby, inviting her to visit him in Florida. Ruby, however, made it clear that she and Al were through.

Ruby was out of Al's life. *Hold On to Your Hats* had been a hit, but its forced early closing had destroyed all hopes of a substantial profit. The show, moreover, had not brought Al back to the top pinnacle of show business. Talking pictures, the monster Al had helped establish, had diminished the importance of the legitimate theatre. The movies wanted *Hold On to Your Hats,* but without Jolson. Al was almost where he had been when Ruby had walked out more than a year before.

Al did what he usually did to get away from his troubles. He went to the track.

Jolson stayed in Florida until May. Hale, in the meantime, had withdrawn his lawsuit, Al saying he would take the show on tour in the early fall and make a profit "just as big as if we'd stayed on Broadway."

Al arrived in New York on May 15th, and then spent most of his time going to Belmont until June 4th, when he guest-starred on *It's Time To Smile,* Eddie Cantor's radio show. Plans for the tour of *Hold On to Your Hats* proceeded smoothly, and the new cast was assembled by July.

Al was in good spirits when the tour opened in Atlantic City's Garden Pier on August 27, 1941. He had even found a new girl friend in Bunny Waters, Jinx Falkenburg's replacement.

All of those good spirits vanished on Friday night, when Al learned that Ben Jacobson, lessee of the Pier, had absconded with approximately $1,400 in actors' salaries. Al dug into his own pocket in order to pay the seventy members of his company.

Al was further angered when he found that Jacobson's creditors had obtained an attachment against the Saturday night receipts. "To hell with 'em," he vowed. "I won't go on." The creditors, who knew he was not bluffing, "voluntarily relinquished" the attachment "in order not to give the resort unpleasant publicity on the eve of its biggest holiday weekend."

Hold On to Your Hats grossed only $9,000 for five performances in Atlantic City. Eppy blamed it on the "high top" of $3.30 and the low priced (75-cent) entertainment available at the other piers. The explanation did not placate Jolson, who was still fuming when *Hold On to Your Hats* opened a three-week engagement at the Shubert Theatre in Boston on Monday night, September 1st. Elliott Norton wrote the following in the *Boston Post:*

It is ten years since Al Jolson played here in a show called *Wonder Bar.*" Those ten years sit lightly on the shoulders of the star. His hair is thinning, a fact which he himself noted last night to the great delight of an audience which swooned with joy at his first appearance and was still swooning at 11 p.m. He is a little heavier about the middle and there is a touch of gray at his temples.

But the thundering vitality which has always been his trade mark is undiminished. He can still bellow a corny, sentimental lyric or a racy one with compelling gusto and relish and bring an audience to its feet with roars of approval. He can still make a second-rate song sound impressive and even downright exciting. He can, as he always could, take an audience so closely and intimately into his orbit that the show becomes a personal thing for pretty nearly every one of them.

. . . Discounting some lapses in taste, he gave them their money's worth. Whether you like his material or not, he is a really great clown, a forceful and skillful entertainer. Granted that last night's audience was on his side before he ever opened his mouth, there is no doubt that he would have won them over, at least ninety percent, if they had begun by sitting on their hands and staring.

Business was better in Boston. On Friday night, September 19th, Al, Eppy, and Bobby Crawford went out to a night club after the performance. Crawford, an ex-jockey who had made and lost two fortunes in the music business, had been flat broke when Al made him the show's company manager.

The next day, an employee of the Ritz-Carlton Hotel called Eppy and told him Bobby had died of a heart attack.

Al was silent when he heard the news. He kept to himself until the show left Boston.

Hold On to Your Hats grossed only $9,800 in four performances at the Shubert Theatre in New Haven. A disgusted Jolson replaced his advance man, Frank Cruickshank, with the veteran Ben Atwell.

Atwell had done a fine job with *Robinson Crusoe, Jr.* in 1916–17, but times had changed, and the people who had gone to see Al in *The Wonder Bar* ten years earlier had long since been weaned from live theatre. In Cleveland, Al watched crowds line up around the block to get into a movie while scores of his own tickets went begging at the Hanna Theatre box office. "Don't they want to see Jolie anymore?" he wondered aloud to a newsman. Apparently, they did not.

Business took an upturn in Toronto, and the following week— split between Rochester and Buffalo—saw the gross at a respectable

$20,000. Then the bubble burst completely. *Hold On to Your Hats* grossed only $10,000 in Cincinnati, and Al discovered that the rail and sleeper fares from Buffalo to Cincinnati alone had been more than $1,200 for seventy-eight people.

Al closed the show in Columbus a few nights later.

It was a wise move. Al might have drawn well in the smaller (one-night) cities, but the railway fares would have destroyed any chance of breaking even. The show's operating cost was ordinarily $2,500 a performance—$15,000 for six shows. "And no matter how you slice it," Al said, "I couldn't do more than six shows a week. Matinees are impossible when it's an expensive show like mine. By the time we get in, by noon, it (the scenery) just can't be hung in time for a 2:30 curtain."

Al's explanation for the closing certainly made sense. But many wondered if he had not been disheartened by a news report that he had read in Buffalo: Ruby Keeler had married John H. Lowe.

Al returned to Broadway with the company and managed to find jobs for many of the chorines.

Four weeks later, on Sunday, December 7th, Al was in his suite at the Sherry-Netherland, dressing to go out. Pansy was busy with the breakfast, and the radio was on.

WE REPEAT. THE JAPANESE AIR FORCE ATTACKED PEARL HARBOR THIS MORNING. PLEASE STAY TUNED FOR FURTHER DEVELOPMENTS.

Al let out a yell for Pansy. They stood, transfixed, as the announcer gave out the grim details. Half an hour later, Al put through a call to Steven Early, press secretary to President Roosevelt. "Must be somethin' I can do," he thought. Maybe he could sing 'em to death.

The Hell Holes

"I've worked in many a town before, many an audience in my long career in the theatre, from Lew Dockstader's Minstrels to Shubert musicals, but I've never had such a thrill as entertaining these boys."

Al Jolson's involvement with entertaining U.S. servicemen during World War II really began with a letter written to Early shortly after New Year's Day, 1941—a little over three months after passage of the Selective Training and Service Act. Jolson volunteered to head a committee for the entertainment of soldiers and said that he would work without pay. "Also," he wrote, "I would gladly assist in the organization to be set up (routing, booking, etc.) for this purpose. Naturally, this subject remains with you, but I want you to know that I will accept the assignment without hesitation. During the weeks before Christmas, we entertained as guests several hundred selective service men at our matinees [of *Hold On to Your Hats*] in New York. This brought many letters of thanks, not only from the soldiers, but from mothers and officers. Such letters were indeed gratifying and made me feel all the more the urge to serve my country in the only field I know—amusement. I am sure many noted actors would rally to this cause, bringing the stars directly to the camps."

Jolson did not go overseas at the beginning of the war, but his involvement with camp shows began only a few weeks after Pearl Harbor. After spending Christmas on the west coast and New Year's in Florida, Al flew back to New York and picked up a route from the United Services Organization, the new group his letter to Early had helped create. He was booked for two weeks of appearances at training camps in the deep South—his first appearances in that part of the country since 1908.

The tour opened at the Jacksonville Naval Air Station in Florida on January 21, 1942. Working in a modern camp theatre with a perfect public address system, Al, accompanied by Martin Fried at the piano, opened with "Swanee" and went through ten more songs interspersed with gags and clowning. The ovation was tremendous.

"Do you really mean it?" Al asked. "And if you do, may I come back? That's about the only thing we people in show business can do as our bit in the great war effort."

The U.S.O. had sought to charge admission to the shows, but Al insisted they be free. He and Fried left Jacksonville the next day and gave two shows at Savannah's Camp Stewart on Wednesday night. "We don't want to see any boy stand when we do our concerts, so we play to two houses nightly, and they average 4,500 boys per show," Al told *Variety*. "Each camp has its own fine military band for their concerts, playing the operatics as well as more familiar lighter pieces. They make for a nice break as one audience gives way to another.

"Sure I have to catch a two a.m. milk train, or thereabouts, to make my next one-night stand, but I'll do this as long as Uncle Sam will have me."

Booked for one show at Camp Croft in Spartanburg, South Carolina, Al was on stage for forty-five minutes—and then did a forty-five minute "encore" when an officer informed him that a lot of soldiers had missed the show because the theatre could not hold them all at one sitting.

The bond between Al Jolson and "the boys" in uniform is not hard to understand. Jolson was a figure from the "good old days" of peace, prosperity, and the simple virtues of the past he sang about in songs like "Mammy." The yearning in his voice recalled the feelings that so many of them had for their homes, families, and girls. At the same time, that ringing brass voice was inspiring—providing for the singing that men trained for battle could appreciate. This double-edged appeal of sentiment and inspiration made Jolson the perfect singer—and performer—for the U.S. serviceman.

The fifty-six-year-old Al was a father figure—a benign general who spoke in earthy terms and told the jokes that soldiers understood.

"Gypsy Rose Lee was gonna be here with us," Jolie would apologize. "But due to circumstances beyond our control, she couldn't make it. She'd already been signed to appear on the bare-asspirin program."

Al wound up his tour at Morris Field in West Palm Beach on February 7th. He had given a total of twenty-two performances in eleven different camps—entertaining some 60,000 soldiers, sailors, and marines.

After performing for the Navy Relief Show in downtown Miami's Bayfront Park on Saturday night, March 28th, Al went to Washington to see Brig. Gen. Frederick H. Osborn, chief of public relations for the U.S. Army. Osborn agreed to Al's request for a Specialist rating in the Dwight F. Davis army of the service, an over-age classification which would permit him to wear a uniform and have the same standing as an officer.

There was another reason for Al's trip to Washington. He wanted to go overseas to entertain the troops—as Elsie Janis had done in World War I—and figured Osborn was the man to see. The general was not immediately able to send Al to any battle zones, but he made plans for Al to go to Alaska in June.

On Wednesday, May 6, 1942, Jolson bought the first ticket to the premiere of *Yankee Doodle Dandy* on May 29th by purchasing a $25,000 war bond. Ironically, Al was not able to attend, since he had to leave New York to appear in the Navy Relief Show at the Municipal Auditorium in San Francisco on May 19th.

The trip to Alaska was begun without much fanfare: Al and Martin Fried got their shots at the Moore-White Clinic in Los Angeles and boarded a transport plane for Seattle a few mornings later. "It was still dark as we partook of a hearty breakfast," Al wrote in a dispatch to *Variety*. "Being a late sleeper all my life, it was the first time I had ever tasted oatmeal. I always thought it was used to put up wallpaper—which is still a good idea. Boarding the plane, we discovered that, although there were seats for eighteen, Martin and I were the only passengers. A plane to ourselves! We began to realize the importance of our mission. We were elated! The plane took off and stopped at Sacramento and other places and we still had the plane to ourselves. But at Red Bluff in came twenty-seven U.S. Army officers and out went our importance. Imagine having to sit on Fried's lap from Red Bluff to Seattle.

"We landed on a secret blacked out field forty miles north of Seattle. From this point on, Fried and I became military secrets."

Not quite. Jolson and Fried wound up performing at a war bond rally in Seattle and gave a show at Paine Field, an air base near Everett, Washington, before leaving for Alaska. In Fairbanks, they gave a performance in an open field at ten o'clock in the evening "with the sun almost blinding us." They left for Nome early the next morning, where the commanding officer told Al he expected him to do five shows. "This was necessary," according to Al, "because of the continual alert and the fact that there was no time when the entire personnel of the camp was allowed to congregate in a body—except at meal times. When I heard this, I suggested making a floor show out of dinner that evening. The mess hall wasn't exactly the Stork Club and the men in the audience were not dressed in tails, but it was by far the most appreciative audience I have ever played to. The dinner consisted of hash, dried apricots, and coffee. Martin, who has a delicate stomach, could only eat six orders.

"After breakfast the next morning, at a combination restaurant and filling station where you can get gas, we started for Anchorage under the guidance of J. W. Moore, a bush pilot. There are no greater fliers. Bush pilots fly by instinct, having no beacons or radio beams to guide them over the frozen wastes of the North country. . . .

"We arrived in Anchorage at 9:10 p.m., Anchorage time, and stayed at the Westward Hotel. When they told me to observe the blackout regulations and put my lights out I had to laugh, for in this part of Alaska at midnight it is so light that you can thread a needle on Main Street. We gave two performances in Anchorage, each for an audience of 1,500 soldiers. Each show lasted an hour and I almost wore the knees out of my pants singing 'Mammy.'

"But 'Mammy' really got a workout the next day, when Fried and I gave nine shows—each of an hour's duration.

"Until now, the transporting of our small piano had been an overture to an aspirin tablet, but from here on it became a major headache. In order to entertain all the boys detailed in the vicinity of Anchorage, it became necessary for us to give shows in foxholes, gun emplacements, dugouts, to construction groups on military roads; in fact, any place where two or more soldiers were gathered together, it automatically became a Winter Garden for me and I gave a show. Imagine carting the piano to these locations. Sometimes it was by truck, once on a side car and once on a mule pack."

It was now, in World War II, that Jolson proved himself "The World's Greatest Entertainer"—getting down and singing to two soldiers in a foxhole, giving extra shows in out-of-the way places near Juneau, and becoming closer to the men he entertained than anyone else could be.

During one rendition of "Swanee," Al heard a sob come from the rear of the small group of soldiers that made up his audience. When he finished singing, the young soldiers gathered around him, with the exception of a tall, lanky youth who stood by himself and wept.

"What's the matter, son?" Al asked. "Was my singing as bad as all that?"

"No, suh, Mista Jolson," said the boy in a rich southern drawl. "No suh."

"Don't you feel well?"

"Oh, yessuh, Mista Jolson," the youth said between his sobs. "It was on'y when you got to singin' about Dixie. Well, Mista Jolson, it jest kinda got me—thass all."

"Well, come and join us," Al suggested.

"Not yet. I could never let ma buddies see me this a'way. They'd swear I'm a sissy."

Al was touched, but he could not help smiling. Brightening, the soldier said he was "homesick. . . . You know, Mista Jolson, dis heah Arctic Ocean is an awful long way f'm thu-tty miles t'other side of Bummin'ham, Alabama."

Jolie detoured on his next trip down to Florida. "I made an important stop thirty miles the other side of Birmingham," said Al. "You see, I promised that kid."

Pearl Goldberg Sieben remembered seeing Jolson make one long-distance call after another from his suite in the Sherry-Netherland when he got back to New York. Soldiers who had given Al the numbers of their mothers and girlfriends were not disappointed. Al would introduce himself and tell the interested party that her son, boyfriend, or husband was in fine shape—sometimes adding that he felt a little homesick—in the Aleutians, Alaska, or wherever else he happened to be stationed. Jolson's memory on these occasions was phenomenal; he could remember obscure details about every soldier. One lieutenant asked Jolie to take his wife for a night on the town when he got to New York. Al agreed. He took the woman to dinner, a Broadway show (Star and Garter) and the Stork Club (with all the amenities, like wine, a gift of perfume, etc.) before taking her home to 212th Street in Washington Heights.

In late July, Al left for Trinidad, his second trip off the U.S. mainland to entertain the trooops. He and Marty were in Port of Spain on July 27th, did two shows in Willemstad, Curaçao on July 30, and went on to Aruba and Panama. The governor of Curaçao was in the audience in Willemstad, and Al used him as the target for most of his ad libs.

The entire trip took three weeks, Jolson and Fried playing to groups ranging from 125 in one spot to 2,500 in another. Mrs. Sally Osmon Rowe, Regimental Hostess at one camp, wrote to Jolson after he and Fried returned to the States. "Allow me to say on behalf of all the soldiers of the 33rd Infantry that you coming here is quite the most wonderful thing that has ever happened to us, and we think you're tops, not only as a performer, but as a person. We unanimously elect you Public Morale Lifter No. 1 of the U.S. Army."

Those sentiments about Al as a person were not shared by actress
Merle Oberon and singer Patricia Morison. They were in a unit with
Al, Frank McHugh, and Allen Jenkins that toured England several
weeks later.

At 5:00 a.m., Saturday, August 22, 1942—five nights after a successful guest appearance on Walter O'Keefe's *Star Spangled Vaudeville* N.B.C. radio show—Al and Martin climbed aboard an army
bomber headed for London with Miss Oberon, Miss Morison, Jenkins, and McHugh. Al was obnoxious from the very start of the trip,
according to what Morison told author Charles Higham.

Al, the last aboard the airplane, looked around him with con-
tempt. "Who the hell are you?" he snarled. "I don't need you. I've
just been to Alaska on my own and that was good enough for the
boys. Why the hell did they send you on this trip?"

They reached London early in the morning of the 24th, and while
everyone else rested Al dragged Martin off to do a show for a handful of American troops. Later that day, they met Oberon, Morison,
Jenkins, and McHugh at a railway station to begin the tour, and Al
got into the first of several loud and bitter arguments with Merle.
The contingent went to Ireland that night, and did shows in posts
near Dublin, Belfast, Limerick, Glasgow, London, and other spots
over the next three weeks. The tension between Al and Merle worsened in the meantime.

The troupe was scheduled to appear at the London Palladium on
Sunday, September 20th, with Ben Lyon and Bebe Daniels, but Merle
refused to appear, stating they were there to entertain the troops
"and not the general public." Al was furious, and announced he was
returning to the United States—alone.

"There's been no trouble whatsoever," Al told the London correspondent for the *New York Times*. "I just feel that I can do better
on my own than I could as a member of a troupe. If I want to crowd
in an extra show for defense workers in factories, I'd be able to do
it. No, there's been no row. I'm only going home to honor my contract. And as for Merle, she's returning to appear in a film. No, I
wouldn't know which one."

Al and Martin prepared to see a musical with Leslie Henson before leaving London. Al was depressed as he sat at the bar in the
vestibule of the Savoy Hotel. The squabbles with the troupe and the
aborted tour had gotten to him, and he had not "gone over" with
several audiences as well as he had hoped.

Suddenly, he heard somebody whistling "Keep Smiling at Trouble," the hit song of *Big Boy*. Al turned around and saw Ralph Reader. "English, English!" Al popped off his seat and greeted Ralph. They talked about the old times at the Winter Garden. "Those were great days, English, great days."

Finally, Al said good-bye and walked out of the lobby. "It was the last time that I ever saw him," Reader later said. "He looked so sad."

The contract Al mentioned in talking to the *Times* correspondent was for "The Colgate Show starring Al Jolson," a weekly twenty-five minute program on C.B.S. The Sherman & Marquette Agency had put the package together for Colgate-Palmolive, signing Harry (Parkyakarkus) Einstein, Elaine (Shakeyakarkus) Arden, and singer Carol Bruce as the supporting talent.

Carol remains one of Al's supporters. She had "heard a lot" of stories about Al being arrogant, mean, and self-centered, but found him to be comforting and kind—if rather high strung. (She can still hear him hollering for "Eppy!!")

"I had been discovered on Broadway (in *Louisiana Purchase)* prior to that, and now came this opportunity to work with 'the master.' Then, of course, to have gotten to know the master as a friend was something else." To a young Jewish girl like Carol, the idea of working with Al Jolson was "traumatic . . . at first, terrifying to be standing directly across with a microphone between us, and then, having watched his know how shortly before I was introduced, to have him say, 'All right, baby, sing for the people.' You know, the fear—my blood turned to ice water. But he certainly did everything to put me at my ease. I mean, this man—he indulged in all kinds of . . . *shtiks*—physical antics, grimaces, dancing, snapping his fingers, anything to make me comfortable. I saw a very human, and a very encouraging man."

Al's singing voice was far below what it had been twenty years earlier, and the comedy scripting by (as usual) Pat C. Flick was obvious and heavy. The program, however, was well paced. Al opened each show with an up-tempo number like "The Yankee Doodle Blues," "There's a Great Day Coming Mañana," "Where The Black-Eyed Susans Grow," "I'm Sitting on Top of the World," or "Yoo-Hoo"—many of the songs implying the promise of a better world to come after the war. His closing number would be either sentimental ("Sonny Boy," "When I Leave the World Behind," etc.) or something like Joe Meyer's "There'll Never Be Another War."

The show was moved from New York to Los Angeles after the

first twenty-five broadcasts. In March 1943, about a week before he
left for California, Al received a phone call from Jack Cohn of Columbia Pictures. The two men lunched at Lindy's the next day.

Cohn lost little time in getting to the point: Columbia wanted to
do a picture based on Al's life. Jolson had heard rumors for the last
six months, but seemed surprised to hear this offer from Columbia.
He promised to see Jack's brother, Columbia president Harry Cohn,
as soon as he arrived on the west coast.

The motion picture industry's interest in what would later be termed
"nostalgia" had been kindled by the success of *Yankee Doodle Dandy*,
Warners' biography of George M. Cohan starring James Cagney.
The studios, especially Warners, were on the lookout for similar biographical subjects. Al Jolson seemed a natural selection.

Sidney Skolsky, a Broadway columnist who had worked at Warners when *Yankee Doodle Dandy* was in production, tried to sell
the idea of a Jolson biofilm for nine months before Harry Cohn
hired him to produce it for Columbia in early 1943. The idea that
most of the studios turned the idea down because they considered
Jolson a "has been" is ridiculous; George M. Cohan was known to
far fewer people of the early '40s than Al Jolson. A lot, if not most
of the difficulty lie in the reluctance of studio heads to work with
Jolson. Buddy DeSylva, still production head of Paramount, was
candid with Skolsky. "Sid," he said, "I know I owe the guy a lot.
But . . . I just don't want the aggravation."

Jolson knew nothing of Skolsky's activities on his behalf—a detail
Sidney neglected to mention to Harry Cohn until after he was hired
to produce the picture at Columbia. Cohn, a no-nonsense businessman with almost absolute authority at Columbia, immediately phoned
his brother Jack in New York. The lunch with Al at Lindy's followed.

Jolson, Frank Holmes, and Monty Woolley (now a regular on the
Colgate program) left New York by train on Tuesday, March 24,
1943. Al ran into Jack Warner on the train and told him of the offer
he had received from Columbia. According to what Jolson claimed,
Jack immediately offered him $250,000 for the rights to do a Jolson
screen biography at Warners.

Harry Cohn made his own pitch when Al arrived at the Columbia
studio on Gower Street. Cohn said the Jolson film would be "just
another picture" at Warners. At Columbia, however, it would be a
special project—made with all the energy the studio could muster.

It took considerable haggling on the parts of Jolson, Cohn, Charley Schwartz, the Columbia legal department, Skolsky, and several agents from the William Morris Agency to iron out all the details, and it was not until May 26, 1943 (Jolson's fifty-seventh birthday), that a contract was signed giving Columbia film rights to the life story of Al Jolson for a five-year period. Al would get a percentage of the profits, plus $10,000 for recording the songs.

He would *not* star in the film himself.

In the meantime, Al continued with the Colgate show. Jo Stafford was now the show's female vocalist, and the program's new musical director was Gordon Jenkins.

Jenkins had initially balked at the idea of working with Al Jolson. ("I told my agent I was a *serious* musician.") Disturbed by Jolson's reputation as a hard man to work with, Jenkins spoke to Victor Young, Al's conductor for one season on *Shell Chateau* and two seasons of the Lever Brothers program.

"Young told me that the first day with Jolson was all-important. He said Jolson would be late—on purpose—for the first rehearsal, and would try to show me who was boss. But he said if I stood up to him, Al would respect me, and that we would get along from that time on.

"It all worked out the way Victor said. Al was scheduled to rehearse his songs first. But he was an hour late for that first rehearsal, and I was working with Jo Stafford by the time he got there. Jolson came up, virtually pushed her out of the way, and said, 'I'm ready now.'

" 'Well, I'm not,' I told him. 'I'm rehearsing Miss Stafford. I'll let you know when I'm ready for you.

"Jolson took a seat, totally abashed, and sulked. After a minute, he began to look around for sympathy, like a child. Finally, I finished working with Jo and politely told Al I was ready for him.

"And, as Victor had predicted, I never had trouble with Jolson from that point on." Neither did Jo Stafford; Jolie frequently had dinner with Jo and her husband.

Jenkins later worked with Judy Garland and Frank Sinatra. "Neither one, I have to tell you, had the electricity that Al did."

The last Colgate program of the season was on June 29, 1943. Al had already signed for one more thirteen-week cycle to begin on October 5th, which left him free to make a long trip overseas to entertain U.S. troops during the summer.

Martin Fried had been drafted at the age of forty-four a few months earlier. Al spoke to some friends he had in Washington, arguing, with considerable logic, that Marty would be of far greater value as Al Jolson's accompanist on morale tours than he could possibly be as a soldier. Fried was duly mustered out, but the first thing he did was to sue Jolson for back pay.

Al blew his stack, vowed that Fried would never work for him again, and asked his friend, Harry Akst, to accompany him overseas in July. Akst, four years older than the alcoholic Fried but not as much of a complainer about bad food, cold, etc., accepted.

Al and Harry flew down to Miami, got their shots, and boarded an army plane for British Guiana. Somehow, the trip took ten hours, and they arrived in Georgetown at four o'clock in the afternoon. They had mess with the soldiers, and then rehearsed for the performance that would follow.

Al had trouble with the high notes at the close of "Swanee." He turned to Akst in alarm.

"Is that an F?"

"Yep."

"Why can't I hit it? I could always hit it."

"Al, relax. It isn't necessary. We've got microphones and loud-speakers. Let's just take it down a couple of tones."

Al just panicked. He was ready to give up the whole tour.

"I went to work on him," Akst later would recall. "I had to sell Jolson on Jolson all over again. 'Look at Bing,' I pleaded. 'He doesn't rely on a high finish to get him over. It's the resonance in his low tones that has the beauty. You've got it, Al—and to spare. You don't have to cash in on the high finishes. That died with vaudeville.' I kept pounding away at him.

" 'Okay,' he muttered at last. 'Gimme a chorus of "April Show-ers" in D. We'll try one chorus.'

"I gave it to him. He tried it. And it was only great. Right then and there, in Georgetown, British Guiana, the new Jolson was born."

Al and Harry gave two shows in Georgetown, finished at 11:00 p.m., and left two hours later by plane for Belem, Brazil, where they had breakfast while refueling. "They called it breakfast," Al commented, "but we called it lots of other things. Powdered eggs, pow-dered milk, and if there's anything else that wasn't powdered, we'd like to know what."

They gave three shows in Natal—one for soldiers, one for sailors, and a third for the local population. Jolson and Akst were billeted with the soldiers that night, sleeping in cots covered with mosquito netting. A knock on the door wakened them at five, and they were treated to a breakfast of fried bread and coffee. Then it was on to Recife, "one of the best towns in South America. This trip gave us B.S.A. (bucket-seat-asthma). Gave two shows at Recife, at chapel, where they hold Catholic, Protestant, and Jewish services."

They flew back to Natal and did two more shows at the hospital. "I sang all the songs in my repertoire, then Harry played numbers requested by the sick kids—and how they liked it! Dinner again, with the men. Main dish was a thing called 'Spam'—oucha-ma-goucha! Awakened at 4:00 a.m., raining cats and dogs, ready to span the South Atlantic—but at last minute trip was cancelled out due to motor trouble. So gave another show at the hospital for shut-ins who missed yesterday's show—noticed lots of the same faces, however."

Al and Harry finally left South America at dawn the next day, arriving in Dakar at 6:00 p.m. (West Africa time) after a nine-hour flight across the Atlantic. "Dakar is the filthiest hole I have ever seen. Every known insect is there, breeding every known disease. At seven, we had dinner. Yes, you guessed it, 'Spam,' and for dessert a substitute for quinine called Atabrin—little yellow pills—which Akst mistook for soda mints. They gave him a bellyache, which, so far, is the only bellyaching he's done.

"Left by jeep for a twenty-mile ride to hospital. On arriving, I felt like asking one of the patients to move over. You know my trick back; well just imagine what twenty miles in a jeep on washboard roads did to it. However, I forgot all about my back when I saw the smiles of approval on the faces of the three hundred-odd kids. We gave the show outdoors—in pitch darkness—not due to a dimout but to lack of facilities. Luckily, an Army truck came along and spotted us with its headlight. Believe it or not, it started to rain as I was singing 'April Showers,' but (so help me!) it stopped when I segued into 'California, Here I Come.' "

Technical Sgt. Buell R. Snyder remembered that Al was kept busy after the show, "autographing everything from official passes and copies of Stars & Stripes to letters from home. A great many of the G.I.s held out wrinkled five-franc notes for Al to sign. Not having any French money on me, I handed him an American ten-dollar bill. Al crinkled the ten-spot a moment and hesitated. He handed it back to me unsigned. "Son," he said, 'my autograph isn't worth tying up this much dough. Invest it in war bonds.' Then he reached into his own pocket, pulled out a crisp new five-franc bill and autographed it. He thrust it into my hands and grinned, 'Here, sergeant, this is on the house.' "

In Marrakesh, French Morocco, Al and Harry were met by a staff car and taken to a beautiful villa where their sleeping quarters "resembled a Jake Shubert idea of a harem." They did a show at a converted gambling casino requisitioned by the Red Cross, and their "first real night's sleep" was followed by one show at a hospital and another for the Red Cross. They left for Casablanca early the following morning.

Akst began to call Al "Next Town Reilly" after a character they had known around the race tracks—a trainer who would bring a broken down nag to the track and, when it inevitably lost, go on to another track and try all over again. For Reilly, it was always "the next town."

It was the same way for Jolson. Al was never happy unless he was *going* someplace—as if the next town, or the next performance, held whatever answer he was searching for.

But the scenic beauty of Morocco was the only thing Al liked about North Africa. "He found Arab morals and mores offensive and unforgivable," according to Whitney Bolton, who knew Al a couple of years later. "He spoke of unprintable suggestions made to him by greedy Arab crones. His face would twist up with disgust as he recited them."

After Casablanca came Oran, Algeria, and then Algiers, where Al and Harry finally caught up with Gen. Dwight D. Eisenhower. Akst remembered them being "ushered into Ike's headquarters," where "Al handed him a letter from Mrs. Eisenhower. The general ripped it open and scanned it. Then he smiled and read part of it aloud. 'Al will give you a kiss for me, and a kick in the pants for not writing more often.' Eisenhower grinned at Al. 'About that kiss—you can cash that when you see my wife back in Washington. But the other . . .' The Supreme Commander turned and lifted up the skirt of his jacket. . . .

"Darned if Al didn't deliver the message."

From Algeria they went to Tunisia, and from Tunisia across to Sicily, where Al entertained the Seventh Army on September 11th. Jolson had already telegrammed Hal Hackett, canceling the thirteen Colgate shows he had been signed to do that fall.

Al started feeling weak in Sicily, however, and made an emergency trip home with Akst on Tuesday, September 21st. They arrived in Miami Beach by Clipper three days later and checked into the Roney-Plaza Hotel.

"I took up the phone in our suite and called my wife in Beverly Hills," recalled Akst. " 'I'm home, Rose! Tell the children!' I heard crying in the next room. When I hung up, I went inside. 'What's the matter, Al?' He was sitting there with his face in his hands.

'You've got someone to come back to,' he choked. 'Who've I got? Not a soul in the world cares whether I live or die.' "

Erle

"I was quite floored by that Southern drawl. But I had only to take one look at that kisser, that little face, and those big dark eyes. I knew with a dialect like that she would never stand a chance on the screen, though. So I thought I'd better marry the poor kid."

Less than two weeks later, on October 7, 1943, Jolson almost collapsed in the lobby of the Sherry-Netherland in New York City. Frank Holmes, who had rejoined Al in Florida, called Julius Hertz, Al's personal physician, who called in Dr. Evan Evans as consultant. Hertz thought that Jolson had malaria, complicated by pneumonia. "No," said Evans. "it's pneumonia alone."

Al's temperature was up to 103 by Saturday night. Rumors spread that he was dead or dying, and a nurse was moved into Al's suite to give him 'round the clock attention. Jolson's condition steadily improved, and he started talking about going back to Florida to recuperate.

Then he had a relapse, and his temperature rose to 105. "It's gotta be malaria," Al gasped to Hertz and Evans. He went on to describe a peculiar form he had heard about in North Africa. Hertz was used to "Dr. Jolson's" diagnoses, but agreed to make exhaustive tests.

The tests showed Al was right, and his doctors contacted a military hospital for the proper serum. A rigid, every-six-hour administration brought results, and Al was past the danger mark within a week.

After a vacation in Miami, Jolson returned to work on *Soldiers in Greasepaint,* a forty-five-minute show broadcast on a national hookup out of New York, on November 25, 1943. Al sang "People Will Say We're in Love" from *Oklahoma!* in the "new" voice he had used in Georgetown—deeper, far more mellow, and less strained than the Jolson voice heard on the Colgate show five months before.

Three days later, Jolson left for the west coast to play himself in *Rhapsody in Blue,* the film musical biography of Gershwin Jesse Lasky was producing at Warners. Sonny, now a nine-year-old sergeant at the Blackfox Military Academy, was there when Al's plane landed.

Al recorded "Swanee" on December 7th and lip-synched it for the cameras several days later. He still looked sick, and appeared much older than his fifty-seven years.

Al returned to Miami when he found that *Minstrel Boy,* Columbia's biography of his own life, would not be ready for production until March. Within several days, those seeing Al described him as the picture of good health. He had, it seemed, recovered fully.

Jolson went to New York five weeks later and then left for Hollywood on Monday, February 7, 1944. Casting for *The Jolson Story,* the film's new working title, would begin as soon as Al approved the script by Lawrence Hazard.

Al did not give that approval, and work on the picture was postponed until the fall. In the meantime, Harry Cohn made Jolson a producer.

No one knew why Cohn had done it except Sidney Skolsky. "I was a song plugger in my twenties," Cohn told him, "and I used to go backstage at the Winter Garden. Sometimes Jolson would see me and sometimes he would treat me like a jerk without even looking at the song. I vowed that one day I would have that son of a bitch working for me."

Jolson's first producing assignment was a new film-version of *Burlesque.* Al lined up Broadway stage star Alfred Drake to co-star opposite Rita Hayworth, but the tedium of waiting for Rita to finish her other commitments was more than Al could bear. He accepted an offer to headline the *Philco Radio Hall of Fame* show on May 28th in Philadelphia.

Al flew to Washington with Harry Akst, stopped off to see Moshe and Hessi, and then went to New York. On Sunday night, May 21st, Jolson and Akst saw the play, *Pick-up Girl.* During intermission, Al walked down the aisle and received a spontaneous ovation—what *Variety* described as "one of those electric salvos of applause that are accorded only to the greatest of theatrical celebrities." Any doubts Al had about his place in the show world should have been assuaged for a long time.

But, of course, they weren't. Jolson remained Jolson.

The Philco show was simultaneously broadcast over radio and telecast to those few homes with sets in 1944. After it was over, Al and Harry barnstormed their way west by station wagon, playing service hospitals out in the hinterlands, away from railroad connections. This was the "Purple Heart Circuit," and a lot of the boys Al was playing to had lost arms or legs. Audiences like these seemed to bring out the best in Jolson. He was the small child who, wanting to be a doctor, had told his mother he would "try harder" to make his patients smile if they were in too much pain. Now he did try, and succeeded.

Al and Harry had a general itinerary, but their means of transportation allowed them to make extra stops. At the end of their appearance in White Sulphur Springs, the chief surgeon of the hospital asked Akst if he thought they would have time before heading out to Texas. "Eastman Annex in Hot Springs is a little off the beaten path," the doctor said. "The boys there haven't had a live show in a long, long time. It would be wonderful if you could find the time to run down there."

Al had been signing autographs. "We'll *make* time," he shouted over.

Harry sighed and smiled. "Next Town Reilly" had won again.

This time, however, "Reilly" would find something up ahead.

Erle Chennault Galbraith Jolson Krasna remains firm: she did *not* ask Jolie for his autograph that day in Hot Springs, Arkansas. ("Are you kidding? In the *South?* With my upbringing!?") The fourth Mrs. Al Jolson's forebears on her mother's side were the de Chennaults of Kentucky—southern aristocrats upon whom Erle and her siblings were supposed to model their behavior.

Erle, born near Berea, Kentucky, on December 1, 1923, was an x-ray technician at the Eastman Annex when Jolson and Akst played there in June 1944. "I was standing all during the show, and my civilian dress must have been quite noticeable in that crowd."

After the performance, Jolson asked the colonel in charge to authorize a new batch of gasoline coupons. Erle was nearby, and Al asked to be introduced.

She remembered his first words as "characteristic . . . Al was not a man to waste time.

" 'I just wanted to see if you were as pretty up close as you were from the stage.' he explained, casual as anything. He asked me if I wanted to go into movies."

Erle did not give Al a definite answer, and the conversation ended seconds later. It would have been just another of those once-in-a-lifetime meetings between an old male star and a pretty young girl—had Jolson not been smitten.

But he was. A mental picture of the shy brunette haunted Al the next evening in Corpus Christi, Texas. He called a general he knew and got Erle's name and address.

Jolson was fifty-eight; Erle Galbraith was still twenty. Al, who still had trouble writing letters, asked Akst to help him write a short note to the girl. Harry refused: "You can make a damn fool of yourself if you want to, but I won't help you do it."

Jolson simply shrugged and summoned the hotel stenographer. He did not dictate a love note. The letter was, on face, a business proposition: Al was a producer at Columbia, and thought Miss Galbraith had screen possibilities. Would she come to Hollywood for a screen test?

Al and Harry were in Hollywood a few days later. They planed to Atlanta for a bond rally, went to New York for a couple of days, and left for Hollywood again on Tuesday, July 4th. Rita Hayworth, in the meantime, had been assigned to another film. *Burlesque* was canceled, and Al, who had not cared about being a producer in the first place, left for New York to appear on *Your All-Time Hit Parade*, an N.B.C. radio program with the Tommy Dorsey Orchestra.

Jolson received a visit from an elderly gentleman a few days after his return to Hollywood. The man introduced himself as a Los Angeles businessman who happened to be a friend of the Galbraith family in Hot Springs. "Mr. Jolson," he said, in what Al later described as "a real southern accent," "I just dropped by to talk to you about this offer you've made to Erle. As man-to-man, I can tell you that her parents are a little gun-shy of Hollywood. The Galbraiths are one of the oldest families in Arkansas. Naturally, a girl would be attracted by the glamour of the movies, but the family doesn't like it at all. I've come here, to explain these things to you, sir, because it would be *most* unfortunate if everything wasn't exactly as it has been represented."

Al assured him that he had, indeed, become a film producer, and that Erle would be placed under a contract. If anything, Al had outfoxed himself. Jolson was there to greet Erle with a bevy of Columbia executives when her train pulled into Union Station at six o'clock in the morning. She was as beautiful as he remembered, but her southern drawl, which had seemed so soft at the Eastman Annex, sounded like "the Arkansas twang of Bob Burns," as Jolson later put it, in Los Angeles.

Al did some fast talking and got her placed under a six-month contract at one hundred dollars a week. Columbia used Erle as an extra in *A Thousand and One Nights* and then ignored her. It never bothered Erle.

"I knew I'd never be an actress," she admitted. "For one thing, there's my very pronounced Arkansas drawl. And I haven't that kind

of ambition. But who could resist the chance for a wonderful vacation, and it was in that spirit I accepted it.''

Erle stayed at the apartment of another Galbraith family friend.
Since neither she nor Al were working, there was time to go to night
clubs, prize fights, and, of course, the races.

Jolson went to Palm Springs in October before leaving for a tour
of army hospitals with Akst. They wound up in Florida, where Al
told band leader Joe Candullo about Erle. ("Nothing much upstairs"
was the way Jolie described her, insisting there was "nothing serious" about their relationship.) Jolson and Akst drove up to New
York from there.

"Al loved to be spotted in a crowd," remembered Akst, "but he
hated to trade on the fame of his name. It was late at night, and we
were dog-tired, but in every town we came to, the hotel clerk would
say: 'Sorry. All filled up.' 'Al,' I kept saying, 'tell them who you are.'
But he wouldn't. Town after town—Asheville, Knoxville, Winston-
Salem—with me dying at the wheel. 'Sorry, no rooms.' 'Al, will you
please tell them?' 'No.' Finally, in the wee hours of the morning, we
pulled up to a little inn outside of Roanoke, Virginia. 'You wait
here, Al,' I said. I went inside.

"There was an old, old geezer behind the desk. He could hardly
see. 'All filled up.' 'Look,' I said, 'did you ever hear of Al Jolson?'
The old geezer's face lit up. 'Al Jolson! Say, you bet. I was in show
business myself. Stranded here in a minstrel show thirty years ago.'
'Well,' I said, sticking out the pouting lower lip and lowering my
voice. 'I'm Jolson.' A few minutes later, I went out to the car. 'C'mon,
Al,' I said, 'We got us a room.'

They spent the weekend in New York and hit the road again,
playing another string of service hospitals en route to California. It
was a rough trip, and Al complained of feeling run down by the
time they reached Los Angeles in late November. He made plans to
spend New Year's in Miami, but severe chest pains forced him into
bed on Saturday, December 23, 1944, and a doctor diagnosed a
recurrence of malaria.

A nurse, who described Al as "a pretty sick boy" when queried
by reporters, moved in the next day. Pills and shots soon had Jolson
in stable condition, and he was resting "fairly comfortably' by Monday. Al steadily improved until after New Year's, when he suffered
a bad relapse.

Dr. Ramon Spritzler rushed Al into Cedars of Lebanon Hospital, where he received special care. One week later, Jolson was released and sent back to his suite at the Beverly Hills Hotel.

Another relapse followed—far worse than the first. Al was gravely ill, and the Associated Press even compiled a biographical report for the use of newspapermen who might have to write obituaries.

The Warner brothers, Harry and Jack, saved Jolson's life. They requested Gen. Henry H. Arnold, head of the Army Air Forces, to supply a special plane to fly two physicians to Los Angeles. Largely because of Al's tremendous war work, the request was granted.

The two doctors flown to Al's side were his own physician, Julius Hertz, and Edgar Mayer, renowned specialist on lung afflictions. Mayer took one look at Jolson and ordered him moved back to the hospital. An operation had to be performed.

Parts of two of Al's ribs and a large section of his left lung were removed in a long operation at Cedars on January 16, 1945. The "bad spot" that had plagued Jolson since 1900 was finally gone.

After one week, Al was allowed visitors. Erle was the first.

In February, shortly after he was discharged from the hospital, Al wrote to Erle's father, asking for his daughter's hand in marriage.

The reply was a prototype of southern indignation. "You are old enough to be my daughter's father," E. F. Galbraith stormed. "I have never heard anything so insulting in all my born days."

Al was crushed. He would be fifty-nine in May, he wanted Erle desperately, and, being a singer, he was depressed over losing a good part of his left lung. Al was far from sure that he would ever sing again.

Erle told him not to worry about her father. "I can twirl dad around my finger." She left for Arkansas, returned to Hollywood the following Monday, and phoned Al in Palm Springs with the news that her father had consented.

For the first time, Al mentioned Erle to reporters. "I'm still waiting for her to say yes," he told them. "She's so pretty that I thought she should be in pictures and so she came to Hollywood, signed a contract with Columbia, and got a bit part in a fantasy film."

Her contract with Columbia having expired, Erle was now working at Twentieth Century–Fox courtesy of Al's old "gopher," Louis Schreiber. Brutally honest, when she spoke at all, Erle told reporters she was surprised that her relationship with Al had "not been known before."

On Friday, March 23rd, Al called Erle and—"officially"—proposed. She accepted and trained down to Palm Springs early the next morning. Al and Erle left at once for Blythe, only to find that, under California law, they would have to wait a few days before getting married. Not seeing any reason for delay, they went to Quartzite, Arizona, and were married by the Rev. E. B. Hart, justice of the peace.

Al had a commitment to appear as E. P. Christy in the *Lux Radio Theatre's* presentation of *Swanee River* in Hollywood on April 2nd. Shortly after that, Jolson and his young bride left for a honeymoon in New York. They went to the opening at Jamaica Race Track on the 21st (Al won $13,350 on "Easy Spell" in the first race), attended the world premiere of *Rhapsody in Blue* at the New York Hollywood Theatre on June 27th, and saw one Broadway show after another. The costumes for such musicals as *Carousel, Oklahoma!,* and *Bloomer Girl* were not lost on Jolson. "Seems to me we're in a day of crinoline and lace," he said. This was the style of dress "preferred" by all the women in the Galbraith family, but Al decided Erle was the "tweedy type." She eventually gave in and bought several tweed suits and dresses.

The fourth Mrs. Al Jolson, however, had a strong mind of her own. She put her foot down and demanded that Al fire his two longtime staffers, Donnelly and Holmes. The latter's blatant homosexuality and frequent nearness to Al doubtless rankled Erle, but the reasons for her attitude toward Donnelly remain unclear. "Mr. Jolson's whole life changed when he married Erle," Pearl Goldberg Sieben said in later years. "Before, there were a lot of doormen and other employees of the Shuberts that he would send money to at Christmas. All that stopped when he married her."

Erle claims nothing but pleasant memories of Jolie, but their married life was far from an ideal. Al was older now, but he still had the "Jolson temper." He also still made nasty cracks and got impatient at Erle for being "slow."

Erle, almost forty years Al's junior, did not resist her huband's efforts to play "Sugar Daddy." She also had enough maternal qualities to keep Al happy, and the native intelligence to deal with his temper. Whenever Al got angry, Erle would abruptly leave the room. Later, after he had calmed down, she would return and pretend nothing had happened.

Al and Erle returned to Hollywood in July 1945. Work on *The Jolson Story* was about to start.

Harry Cohn and two Columbia producers had visited Al while he was recuperating from surgery in February 1945. Cohn had walked in, looked at Al, and asked, "You gonna die?"

Al got out of bed and put on what was almost a performance. Harry Cohn appeared to be convinced. But when he left the room, he turned to his two underlings and said, "This guy's gonna die."

Unbeknownst to Cohn, Jolson had been fortified with shots to kill his pain. He collapsed just after the men left.

Cohn got hold of vocal arranger Saul Chaplin in March. "Take Jolson to the studio," Cohn told him, "and record everything he knows. I want to be insured in case the son of a bitch drops dead." Chaplin had Al record his entire repertoire. The recordings, done with only a piano (orchestral backing would have been dubbed in later), were only of fair quality. As things turned out, they were not needed. Al regained his full health by the time the Jolsons returned from their honeymoon in New York. Beginning in late August, the recordings for the soundtrack, with full orchestra, were made.

Al did at least a half a dozen takes of every song. For "Ma Blushin' Rosie," he reportedly did over twenty takes—the ten best of which were used to piece together the recording heard in the completed film.

Jolson still desperately wanted to play the part himself. In the weeks before production started, he asked Cohn, Skolsky, and assistant producer Sidney Buchman to reconsider their original decision. Cohn shrewdly asked Jolson to take a screen test. Al ostensibly agreed. But he never showed up to make the test at the appointed time.

Thirty-one-year-old Larry Parks had already been selected to play Jolson. A graduate of the Federal Theatre Project, Parks had appeared in a handful of Columbia B pictures in the last two years. Interviewed for the part of Jolson in August, 1944, he made a screen test (miming to a Jolson track of "Bye, Bye, Blackbird") three months later. Other actors had been interviewed, but Parks, according to one source, was the only man ever tested for the role.

Parks worked hard at miming to the songs. His lips were always perfectly synchronized with the recordings, and his flowing, stylized arm movements proved much more effective on the screen than Jolson's gestures had been in the thirties. (Al, of course, did not work well to playbacks.) According to Columbia's publicity department, Jolson worked with Parks for hours, until every nuance was perfected. In fact, Al did not coach Larry at all. Parks did not attempt to copy Jolson in delivering a song. Rather, he created his own version of the Jolson style—a version that worked well on film.

The fictional screenplay contained elements of Al's life story. As in real life, the celluloid Al Jolson is named Asa Yoelson as a boy. His entry into show business via singing from the balcony is also based on fact. The characters, however, are composites—fictional amalgamations of many people in Al's life from 1900 to 1939. In the film, a character called Steve Martin makes the teen-aged Asa Yoelson a part of his act and later becomes Jolson's manager. "Steve Martin" is a composite of at least ten real people: Al Reeves, Agnes Behler, Harry Jolson, Fred E. Moore, Arthur Klein, Frank Holmes, Jimmy Donnelly, Louis Epstein, John Schneckenberger, and Harry Wardell.

No mention is made of Jolson's mother having died when he was eight years old, and the only "real" characters in the entire screenplay are Jolson, "Papa" Yoelson, "Mama" Yoelson, Oscar Hammerstein I (who had nothing to do with Al's career), and Lew Dockstader. (A beautiful woman appears as Gaby Deslys in a Winter Garden production number.) Jolson's first two marriages are not referred to, and his third wife, the tap dancing star of *Show Girl, Forty-second Street,* and *Gold Diggers,* is called "Julie Benson" instead of Ruby Keeler.

Ruby had refused to allow her name to be used in the picture. Now a mother, she told Skolsky that she did not want her children "to grow up someday and maybe see the picture and know I was married to a man like that. Hear 'Ruby Keeler' from the screen and Jolson singing love songs to her. Making love speeches to her. Saying 'Baby, everything you want you'll have. This is Jolie talking to you.' I want none of that."

Ruby then demanded $25,000 for the "non-use" of her name. Only then would she allow the character of Al's wife in the film to be a tap dancer on Broadway and in movies.

At the time that shooting started, in October 1945, *The Jolson Story* was a black-and-white production budgeted at $1,150,000. After seeing the first rushes, Cohn decided to pull out the stops. Shooting was begun again—in color—and Jolson went back to the recording studio. Lusher, better, and more updated arrangements were provided by George Duning and the rest of the Columbia music department. (Jolson, who had taken Martin Fried back for the umpteenth time, managed to get him on the Columbia payroll. Fried was even listed as Vocal Arranger in *The Jolson Story* credits.) Al was kept recording until well into December. Harry Cohn was keeping his word. *The Jolson Story* had become *the* special project at Columbia.

Sidney Skolsky noticed that Al hummed a tune whenever he was waiting to hear a playback. Al was astonished when Sid told him.

"God, I didn't know I was doing that. That's an old song that my mother used to hum to me when I was a little child and she rocked me to sleep."

The tune was J. Ivanovici's "Danube Waves." A decision was soon made to write a lyric to the melody and use it in a scene late in the picture. Jolson contributed the first line and Saul Chaplin of the Columbia music department wrote the remainder of the lyric.

"Son," Al told him, "you're gonna make more money with this song than you ever made on anything before in your life."

"He was right," Chaplin remembered. "Mood Music, which was owned by Columbia Pictures, published it as the 'Anniversary Song' by Al Jolson and Saul Chaplin, and it eventually made a fortune. A few months after the song was released, I got a call from Jolson. Al said Mood Music wanted us to take a cut on the royalties, or else they would have to stop publication. He said we should both take a cut on royalties from four cents a copy to two and a half. I agreed. . . .

"Later, I found that Al hadn't taken *any* cut. Mood Music had asked him to, but Al got out of it by having *me* take a *big* cut."

Chaplin, to be fair, remembered Al's great generosity as well: "For instance, one hospital needed an iron lung. Someone mentioned it to Jolson, and he asked how much was needed. They said fifteen thousand dollars, and Al wrote them a check for the full amount.

"One last thing about Jolson: I've seen all the great performers, and he was the greatest. None of the other ones could touch him,"

On December 23, 1945, around the time of his eighty-eighth birthday, Rabbi Moshe Reuben Yoelson died in Washington, D.C. In accordance with Jewish law, the funeral was held within twelve hours. Al was unable to attend.

All his life, Al had been chagrined by what he felt was his father's stubborn refusal to give him wholehearted praise. Nonetheless, Al had admired the man he described as "a scholarly old gentleman"— an admiration that turned into reverence after Moshe's passing. In the years that followed, Al would subtly turn back to what he termed "the ways of our fathers." He recorded the "Kol Nidre," "Hatikvah" (the Israeli national anthem), and even adopted the melody from "Hindustan" into a new song titled "Israel." It was as if his father's death had brought Al to a peace with his religion—and his God. In the years that followed, he did not work on *Yom Kippur*.

Moshe Yoelson had been among the first rabbis to settle permanently in Washington, D.C. One of the founders of the Hebrew Relief Association, he had served Washington Jewry for over half a century. His good-humored wisdom and deep respect for the beliefs of others had won the Jewish community many friends.

Moshe was buried in Talmud Torah Cemetery, a couple of yards away from his first wife, Naomi. The family had the following line inscribed upon his tombstone:

THE CROWN HAS BEEN LIFTED FROM OUR HEADS

Such was the esteem in which the "scholarly old gentleman" was held.

There was one scene in *The Jolson Story* in which Jolson played Al Jolson. That was in the scene where Jolie does his famous dance steps in the midst of doing "Swanee" on the Winter Garden runway. Al rightfully insisted on performing this himself, so the entire sequence was shot from a distance. Al's great spontaneity—the scene was sung and performed live with a studio recording dubbed in later—makes this sequence a particular joy, and the overhead longshots add to the effect.

Harry Cohn was present when the sixty-year-old Jolson performed this sequence. Suddenly, while Al was singing, Joseph Walker, the cinematographer, yelled "cut." Cohn, who for all his hard exterior truly idolized Al Jolson, was incensed. "Nobody yells 'cut' when Jolson's singing," he roared. Harry calmed down after Walker had explained. A light had been flickering, which meant that the entire sequence would have had to be refilmed. Color film, Cohn was reminded, was expensive.

Except for that one day, Al was not needed during shooting. His presence only tended to disrupt production, and Sidney Buchman, the film's real producer, soon persuaded Al to show up only when his presence was essential. Shortly after New Year's, Al and Erle left for Florida, Jolson having promised Miami booker Buddy Allen that he would serve as m.c. for the March of Dimes benefit at the Lord Tarleton on January 30th. Work on *The Jolson Story* was almost finished by the time Al and Erle got back to Hollywood. March 24, 1946, was the last day of filming.

On July 20th, almost three months prior to the picture's world premiere, Jolson launched his "comeback." The occasion was a benefit at the Hillcrest Country Club in Los Angeles.

The show commemorated the twenty-fifth anniversary of the club's founding, and the program featured names like Danny Thomas, Danny Kaye, Jack Benny (who was m.c.), Frank Sinatra, Red Skelton, Gene Kelly, Xavier Cugat, Carmen Miranda, and George Burns, among others. Al did not go on till after midnight, but the magic flowed. It was the greatest "turn" he had done since the twenties.

Jolson told the eight hundred club members, who were jammed into the circus tent erected for the program, that his greatest thrill was stopping the show in front of his wife, Erle. "All she knew about me, as a performer," he said candidly, "was from my old scrapbooks or what Jack Benny and Groucho Marx told her. To-night I was showing off, to impress her."

The Jolson Story was previewed in Santa Barbara a few nights later. The regular feature at the theatre was *Ziegfeld Follies* with Judy Garland, Fred Astaire, and Lena Horne. Al's knees shook as *The Jolson Story* was shown publicly for the first time.

Jolson was so nervous that he could not remain in his seat for the entire screening. He made frequent trips to the back of the theatre, to the lobby, and back to his seat again. Cards were given to the audience at the conclusion of the picture, and the response was over-whelming. *The Jolson Story* was "immensely entertaining"—pre-ferred over the *Ziegfeld Follies* by an overwhelming majority of the audience.

As Al stood in the back of the theatre, near the exit, he heard two middle-aged women talk about the picture. "Isn't it a shame," said one, "that Jolson never lived to see this?"

The Comeback

"I know it sounds corny, but what I like to do is go home and play with my kids. Only I don't know how.

"I'm a bigger success than I ever was. So now that I want to sit down and play, I don't know how. It's what I want and don't want. I'm a ham, I guess.

"I have to keep on singing. Even if it's only in my bathroom."

T*he Jolson Story* was the subject of one of the biggest publicity campaigns in motion picture history. The film was tested and re-tested, with three different endings, and two songs, "Sonny Boy" and "Cantor on the Sabbath," were cut before the Santa Barbara preview. Press kits were sent to every movie theatre owner in the country, with suggestions on how to promote the film, ranging from the staging of Al Jolson imitation contests to radio interviews with local theatre managers who had played host to Jolson stage shows thirty years before. By the time the picture was trade-shown on September 12th, it was a tried and tested product—a guaranteed hit.

On Tuesday night, October 1, 1946—nine days before *The Jolson Story* opened at Radio City Music Hall—Al was given a testimonial dinner by the American Veterans Committee at the Hotel Astor in New York. The Friars' Bill Brandell and Phil Silvers made short speeches, Hildegarde sang "April Showers," and former New York Mayor James J. Walker presented Jolson with a scroll. The outline of Al's speech had been typed out the night before, but Jolson sounded genuine when he remarked that he was "at the age when . . . people quit. All I can say is 'thank you, thank you, thank you.' "

The dinner was broadcast over A.B.C. with "shuttle" pick-ups from Los Angeles (George Jessel, Frank Sinatra, Burns & Allen) and San Francisco (Eddie Cantor, Dinah Shore, Bob Hope). It was all part of the build-up for the picture.

The reviews for *The Jolson Story* were ecstatic—far and away the best notices any film associated with Al Jolson had ever received. The New York *Daily News* gave it four stars, and Howard Barnes of the New York *Herald Tribune* said that only the deaf could "fail to be enchanted by the musical numbers, from 'By the Light of the Silvery Moon' or 'Swanee' to 'Liza!' It may seem startling at first to hear Al Jolson's exhorting baritone coming from Larry Parks' lips, but the dubbing has been nicely effected . . . The film is essentially a testament to the excitement of show business and the appeal of popular melodies. As such, it is a captivating musical." No one seemed to notice that the final third of the film sagged, and only Dorothy Kilgallen was nasty enough to tell her readers that the real Al Jolson was nothing like the likable young fellow on the go portrayed so earnestly by Parks.

It was word of mouth, however, and not the critical response, that made *The Jolson Story* the hit of the 1946–47 season. Within four months, the country had gone "Jolson crazy." Al, who had been in what amounted to semi-retirement for three years, seemed like a new singer to the postwar "bobby soxers," most of whom thought Jolson looked like Larry Parks.

Al guested on Barry Gray's all-night New York radio show on October 26th. It was after three o'clock in the morning by the time he showed up at the studio, but Jolson had enough voice left to sing a half a dozen songs, clown, reminisce, and banter for at least eighty minutes. This show was entirely "no script," and Al seemed much more genuine than he had been—or ever would be—on any other radio program. The tape of this show is a "must" among collectors, and Gray still considers it the finest show he ever did.

The Jolsons returned to the west coast in November, Al having recently bought William Paley's Palm Springs mansion. With the aid of several agents, Jolson now made the final decisions on a slew of radio guest offers.

On December 27th, Jolson made the first of a long string of guest shots when he appeared on the *Amos 'n' Andy* show over C.B.S. from Hollywood. Less than three weeks later, he was on the Bing Crosby *Philco Radio Time,* and listeners clamored for his return. Al appeared on three additional Crosby-Philco shows that season—always on the first week of each month when the all important Hooper ratings were taken.

After that initial Crosby broadcast, Al and Harry Akst went to Florida for a March of Dimes benefit in Key West. Sammy Hamlin, probably the country's biggest Jolson fan, was in Miami at the time. "Sammy," Harry Akst told writer Ernest Lehman, "just happened to be in a lot of places Jolson was headed for.

"Sammy found out that Al and I were driving down to Key West the next morning at dawn. He came to me. 'Harry, if I could go along on that ride, in the same car with Al, it'd be the biggest thing that ever happened to me in my whole life.'

" 'All right,' I said, 'be on the front steps of the hotel at five o'clock tomorrow morning where Al can't help seeing you on the way to the car. But don't tell him I told you.'

"At dawn, Al and I emerged from the hotel. I looked around in the darkness. No Sammy. We went down the steps. Suddenly, I saw the inert form lying there, asleep. Hamlin had toured the Miami Beach bars all night and finally settled down on the steps, afraid he might miss Jolson if he went to bed.

"I kicked Sammy awake.

" 'Al,' I said, 'look. He sleeps on hard concrete not to miss you. What a sacrifice! What devotion.' "

"Al was touched. He took Sammy along."

Al returned to Hollywood, and the guest shots continued: *Maxwell House Coffee Time* with Burns and Allen on February 20th, another Crosby program on the 25th, and Eddie Cantor's *Pabst Blue Ribbon Show* on March 6th. Jolson and John Charles Thomas teamed with Crosby for a three-man minstrel show that made up the Philco program of April 2nd. Al had the last solo, singing "My Mammy." Not even Crosby, on his own show, dared to follow that.

On April 7th, Al appeared in the *Lux Radio Theatre*'s adaptation of Twentieth Century–Fox's *Alexander's Ragtime Band*. Six days later, he was on *The Bob Hope Show* for Pepsodent. The script contained the usual banter.

"Al, why don't you get your own show?"

"And be on the air only once a week?"

Jolson went to New York after transcribing a fourth Crosby show. He was slated to appear on the Jack Benny program on May 18th and record two songs in Decca's east coast studio. Al had also agreed to meet with leaders of the United Jewish Appeal concerning a possible radio broadcast on the life of the DP.

The motion picture division of the UJA's 1947 campaign to raise $170,000,000 for the relief of European refugees had launched a nationwide drive. Al's aid had been enlisted by former New York Governor Herbert H. Lehman, Henry Morgenthau, Jr., and Barney Balaban of the Chicago theatre-owning family. Within a week of his arrival, Al raised more than a million dollars via talks with show business executives and rank-and-file actors and technicians.

Al was in his element in New York on this trip, and his three-room suite in the Sherry-Netherland was usually crowded by ten o'clock in the morning. On Friday, May 16th, there was a woman reporter from *Time* magazine, a photographer, a man from *P.M.*, his photographer, and three men from the UJA—not to mention Martin Fried.

Al was smartly dressed in a youthful gray flannel suit, a blue shirt, and a dark blue tie. "A guy a thousand years ago invented this thing, time," he said. "If there wasn't such a thing, we wouldn't think about it. Look, I may not be here ten seconds from now, but I feel better than I did twenty years ago." The man from *P.M.* noticed that Al was subdued when he addressed himself to one person. In repose, he showed his age—the flabby underchin, the bifocals, and the thin film of hair with the sunburned scalp showing through. But when Al spoke to a group of three or four—small, but still an audience—he was young and vibrant.

Back in Hollywood on June 2nd, Jolson starred in a second Lux Radio Theatre adaptation of *The Jazz Singer* with Gail Patrick as Mary Dale and Ludwig Donath and Tamara Shayne (Cantor and Mrs. Yoelson in *The Jolson Story*) as Cantor and Mrs. Rabinowitz. Seven nights later, Jolson finished out the season by narrating *Operation Nightmare*, a dramatic show about the plight of Holocaust survivors.

Radio agent Hal Hackett had been trying to get Al his own radio program for the past six months. Elgin-American and Texaco had expressed interest in a weekly Jolson show, but Al himself was far from enthusiastic. He had had his own radio shows before, none of them entirely successful. Besides, he was now sixty-one years old, in an era in which most top stars were under forty. And he did not need the money.

Al changed his mind in June, when Kraft Cheese agreed to pay him $7,500 a broadcast. The final agreement was for four years, with an option at the end of every 39-week season.

"I didn't wanna do it," Al said later. "I was swindled into it by this tremendous ego of mine. I'm like a child, I tell ya! 'Al,' I said, 'Al, old fella, they wantcha again. They've finally seen the light.' I got 'em good, and I just couldn't resist rubbing their noses."

"The *Kraft Music Hall* with Al Jolson" premiered over N.B.C. at nine o'clock on Thursday, October 2, 1947. Included in the cast were pianist Oscar Levant, announcer Ken Carpenter, and female vocalist Milena Miller, who was dropped after the second broadcast.

"She was (Kraft producer) John U. Reber's girl friend," Music

Hall writer Manny Mannheim said in 1978. "Jolson didn't think much of her as a singer, and he got her fired. Later, Reber divorced his wife and married her. They had a son, but Milena was unhappy out of show business. After Reber died, she killed herself by setting fire to her body. Her little boy was nearby at the time, and died as a result."

The two writers, Mannheim and Charles Isaacs, had assured Jolson they were not "gag file" writers. ("I just don't want those bad jokes anymore," Al had said.) But though original, the jokes he now got bordered on the infantile. The gags fell into four categories: (1) Jolson is old. (2) Jolson is rich. (3) Jolson is an egomaniac. (4) Larry Parks.

Al did not work at the same high pressure he had worked on *Shell Chateau*. Now, if anything, he seemed too slow. And the meshing of his new, comparatively laid-back style with that of the acerbic Levant did not make for particularly enjoyable listening.

Jolson always wondered why his writers could not capture his personality in their scripts the way that Crosby's writers seemed to capture Bing's. Radio columnist John Crosby echoed Al's concern: "Just as Mr. Jolson isn't very well attuned to the new lyrics, neither are his writers very well equipped to handle his own special charm, of which he has almost more than any man alive. They know only that he's been around a long, long time and they keep harping on it. This curious impasse—young writers trying to cope with a vintage entertainer whose special essence eludes them entirely—has made the Kraft Music Hall a very crotchety and unsatisfying operation all year long—except when Jolson is singing."

During that first season, Jolson's singing was enough. Fans of *The Jolson Story* could not get enough of "Toot, Toot, Tootsie," "Swanee," and the other Jolson hits. Radio's official barometer, the Hooper Ratings, listed the *Kraft Music Hall* as the number one musical-variety program on the airwaves.

Al put his life in order—for the umpteenth time—that season. He gave his brother Harry a job with Al Jolson Enterprises, a corporation formed to handle his various business activities. With Erle, he adopted a six-month-old blond baby boy and named him Asa Albert Jolson, Jr.

They took him home to Palm Springs and installed him in the little house's one spare bedroom. Al plugged in his own desert-air lamp to make sure the atmosphere was "just right."

"Lookit him, honey, lookit him!" said Al. "What a kick, what a *sweetheart!* Makes you want to sing, or cry, or something."

The Jolsons hired a nurse approved by the adoption authorities, but Erle enjoyed taking care of the baby herself on the woman's day off. "She wished that the nurse could take *three* or *four* days off each week," said Al.

"We'll send him to a good school—and a hard one," he continued. "Want no spoiling of the boy." Al was thinking of Sonny, who changed his name to Albert Peter Lowe the following year.

"It was a hard decision for the (fourteen-year-old) boy to make," said Ruby, "but he had to make it himself. He chose to change his own name to Albert Peter Lowe, and we can only pray he will never regret it."

Erle had found what she considered "the perfect home." It was the estate Al had owned with Ruby Keeler.

Al repurchased it from Don Ameche—at a loss—and gave it to Erle as a third anniversary present in March 1948. Whatever feelings Jolson had about the place were lost in the whirl of his new career. Al moved the Kraft show to New York for two weeks during May.

Trouble had developed over the proposed sequel to *The Jolson Story.* "Al Jolson in Songs He Made Famous," an album of eight numbers designed to capitalize on *The Jolson Story,* had been a best seller, and Decca quickly signed Al to do more recordings. A strike by the American Federation of Musicians would rule out orchestra accompaniment on commercial records made in 1948, so Decca had Jolson record nine songs in three weeks in late 1947—some of them from *The Jolson Story* but at least one from its proposed sequel. Decca planned to straddle the releases through the coming year.

Things were fine until Jonie Taps, Cohn's executive in charge of music, insisted Decca withhold marketing the disks until the new film was ready in 1949—a particularly unwise stance, since the contract giving Columbia film rights to Jolson's life story was due to expire on May 28th. Al, outraged by Taps' insistence, started having lunch with Louis B. Mayer at the M-G-M commissary. Rumors quickly spread about the sequel being done at M-G-M, with Gene Kelly playing Jolson.

Harry Cohn agreed to Al's terms quickly, and work on *Jolson Sings Again,* starring Larry Parks, began that summer. Al started doing the recordings for the soundtrack on August 17th. If anything, they were superior to those he had done for *The Jolson Story—*

clearer, stronger, and more vibrant. "During the intervals between songs," wrote Henry Levin, "when the sound engineers were involved in their technical procedures—repositioning microphones, reloading tape—the orchestra members did not leave the room as they would have done ordinarily. No, not with Jolson there, enthralling them with anecdotes drawn from years of entertainment. . . . When the engineers were ready, another song was recorded, then played back. And after each playback, the orchestra applauded—loudly, and sincerely, because Jolson was in great voice, possibly better than he had been in the twenties and thirties."

Since *Jolson Sings Again* covered the years from 1939 to 1947, Al saw no reason why he could not play himself. Parks, however, had received an Academy Award nomination for his work in *The Jolson Story,* and neither Cohn nor Buchman, the film's producer, saw any reason not to use him again. They also knew that Jolson was no motion picture actor.

On September 27, 1948, Al made a screen test, miming to his own recordings of "Is It True What They Say About Dixie?" "It All Depends on You," "Baby Face," and "For Me and My Gal." The results were disappointing. Jolson still seemed uncomfortable working to playbacks—labored and completely out of synch. After each song, Jolie shrugged his shoulders, painfully aware of his own failure. He looked old and paunchy—nothing like the dynamic young minstrel of the 1910s.

Parks retained the role.

Larry Parks was great at miming Jolson's songs, but he was not much of an actor. He had trouble playing the more emotional scenes with Evelyn Keyes in *The Jolson Story,* and Jolson, wishing to be helpful, suggested that musicians be brought in to get Parks in the mood with background music.

Parks had similar trouble in *Jolson Sings Again,* and got into an argument with Jolson. Al's resentment of Parks surfaced, and with it his disdain for Larry's talent. Jolson could, indeed, be cruel at certain moments. There was a deep well of anger in him that released itself as arrogance when he felt threatened, and as hatred when he was provoked. "It don't take much to get me pissed," he once admitted. That day on the set, Parks did whatever it took.

The child who had lost his mother—that part of Al Jolson who actually hated the world for it—surfaced. A look of venom came into his eyes as he stuck his face into Parks'.

"You crippled cocksucker," Al said.

Parks turned white. Jolson turned and, like a madman, pulled his bankbook from his pocket. "Here. Here, that's what I've made in show business. Take a look." He shoved the bankbook under the eyes of a lighting technician. The account showed over two million dollars.

Al stormed around the set for several minutes as terrified actors, crew people, script girls, and producers either froze or ran for cover. They had never seen such anger.

Harry Cohn was informed. Normally a hard-nosed cynic, Cohn gave everybody on the picture two days off to recover from the incident.

Jolson was banned from the set.

Al opened his second season for Kraft with Judy Garland as his guest star, marking the second—and last—time that "Mr. and Miss Show Business" would ever work together. They dueted on "Pretty Baby" after Judy did a solo, "Johnny One Note."

Jolson looked much older than he had a few months earlier. He was also starting to lose his hearing. Often, he would let a remark go by unanswered because he did not want to ask the speaker to repeat it.

The quality of the Kraft shows declined. The jokes seemed even more banal, and budget cuts forced the elimination of the chorus. Added to this was a loss in Jolson's stamina. Where before, he might do one verse and a chorus, have the vocal group come in for a few bars, and then come back for the finish, his numbers were now limited to one quick verse and chorus. *The Jolson Story* mania had cooled, television had begun, and there was a predictable drop in the KMH ratings. In April, Kraft decided not to pick up the show's option for another season.

The last show was recorded (Al having followed Crosby's lead and gone to transcription) on May 18, 1949, and broadcast eight days later on, coincidentally, Jolson's sixty-third birthday. Al spent the last few minutes of the program thanking everyone connected with the show by name—right down to the "gopher" who ran out for coffee.

The cast gathered in Al's dressing room after the program. "The shows have been good," Jolson complained. "I don't know why they have to cancel us."

"I'm just as happy," said Levant. "I won't have to shave on Thursdays anymore."

"You're not worried about the future, are you, Al?" asked Isaacs.

Al grimaced. "When you get to be my age, you don't worry about little things like that. When my new picture *[Jolson Sings Again]* comes out, dey'll be swarming around me offering me shows," He lapsed into dialect. "Da older I get, da better I sing."

Groucho Marx, the guest star, stuck his head inside the door. "Well, Al, see you on television."

"Nuts to television," Al grunted. "When I was in New York, Milton Berle asked me to be on his show. He said I wouldn't have to do much. I told him that's what I was afraid of with him."

Jolson described television as "a bunch of amateurs knocking themselves out, all trying to do road company Berles, and all looking, acting, and sounding the same." In truth, he was afraid of the new medium—afraid he would fail in television the same way he had failed in radio in 1932. William Paley offered him a quarter of a million dollars to do six TV programs for C.B.S. the following (1949–50) season, but Al turned him down—ostensibly because the fine print on the contract called for him to do an additional thirty-nine shows if the network struck a deal with a sponsor. Another one of Al's excuses was the quality of kinescoping, the technology whereby TV shows were recorded. Television studios were then located in New York, and Al said he did not want to go to New York in order to do live TV. (No one thought of *filming* TV shows until Desilu came into being several years later.)

In August, Jolie made a tour of New York film theatres to plug *Jolson Sings Again*. "In playing six houses per night for three nights, starting at 8:00 p.m. and traveling with a police convoy to make timetable connections, Jolson literally proved himself the iron man of show business," Abel Green wrote in *Variety*. At each theatre, Al began by undoing his shirt, throwing off his tie, and telling the audience that, unlike the usual Hollywood stars who "do nothing" on personal appearance tours, he was "here to entertain you." (At one theatre, he came on the stage to great applause, undid his collar, and gave the audience the "up yours" gesture with his fist and elbow. This was the real Jolson—a masculine pixie with more than just a touch of impudence.)

Al's last line, before he sang his songs, was "I will now do an imitation of Larry Parks." This was Jolson—live, not lip synched. "After you see Jolson in action," wrote Abe Montague, "you first realize what a road company Larry Parks is in the picture, although, mind you, we all think he does a remarkable job."

Extra police were on duty as crowds jammed the streets and side-walks at each theatre Jolson played. It was a fine tribute.

But Al would never play New York again.

Jolson Sings Again opened at Loew's State Theatre in New York on Wednesday evening, August 17th. Seen today, the film seems labored, with laconic editing and a rather trivial story, but the critics of 1949 found little to criticize. "Mr. Jolson's name is up in lights again and Broadway is wreathed in smiles," wrote Thomas Pryor in the *New York Times*. "That's as it should be, for *Jolson Sings Again* is an occasion which warrants some lusty cheering. . . ." Otis Guernsey of the New York *Herald Tribune* said the music was "what Broadway used to describe as 'great,' and that raspy, pleading Jolson delivery still makes the pulse beat faster. . . ."

Abel Green was more perceptive in *Variety:*

> It is only natural that the durability of Jolson, as the all-time No. 1 performing personality in contemporaneous show business, would be matched by an equally rich real-life story. *Jolson Sings Again* proves that. Where *The Jolson Story* was Horatio Alger with an Equity card, *Jolson Sings Again* is perhaps more emotional because Jolson's come-back is played against a background of other young hopefuls suppos-edly having usurped him with the bobby-soxers. Producer-writer Sid-ney Buchman has done a skillful job in keeping on high pitch the not easy premise of an oldster making a comeback. You can't become emotionally excited about a guy who has money back-to-back—in real and reel life—and who sits around his Encino home moping be-cause he's relatively a has-been. Buchman, however, has made emo-tionally appealing the picture of a great star who finds he can't even play a benefit because the Community Chest thinks today's Hopes, Gene Kellys, Judy Garlands, et al., mean more than Jolson, who finds himself relegated to "many others" in the benefit billing.

Jolson continued making personal appearances to promote the picture over the next two and a half months. Friday, August 19th, was "Al Jolson Day" in Chicago. Several honorary titles were be-stowed on Al, who appeared on a raft of local d.j. shows and sang before 100,000 people at Soldiers Field during the Chicago Music Land Festival on Saturday evening. Later that night, 10,000 people were turned away from the Oriental Theatre, where Al was appear-ing with George Jessel.

In September, Al took Erle with him on a promotional tour that included stops in Philadelphia, Baltimore, and Washington, D.C. While in Baltimore, Al took his wife to see St. Mary's, where he had been confined more than fifty years before. "The gate's open," Jolie told her. "It was always shut when I was here. I remember bars all around."

Once again, Al met with Father Benjamin. Erle asked the priest, now in his seventies, if Asa had been a "bad boy."

"He was like other boys," replied the cleric. "Some boys run away from Harvard, too, you know."

That night, Al took over two hundred of the kids to see *Jolson Sings Again* at the Hippodrome.

On Wednesday, September 27th, the Jolsons were received by President Harry Truman at the White House. Al, who was about the same age as the president, greeted Truman with a snatch of "I'm Just Wild About Harry" and gagged about being friends with Wilson, Coolidge, Harding, and Roosevelt—"and no cracks about me being palsy-walsy with Abraham Lincoln."

Truman remembered seeing Al with Dockstader's Minstrels at the Grand Opera House in Kansas City "in 1908 or '09." Jolson asked him if he thought that he would run again:

"I don't know whether they'll want me. Maybe I can run on the slogan, 'I need the job.' "

"With show business going the way it is now, I think I'll use that slogan, too."

The president looked thoughtfully at Al. "Well," he said, "don't quit. It'll kill you."

The Jolsons flew back to Los Angeles, where Al appeared on several late night radio programs. One of these was the Steve Allen show of October 26th, and the tape of that show sounds as fresh and new today as it did thirty-nine years ago.

Five days later, on October 31st, Al signed a three-year contract with C.B.S. for television and radio. Al would limit himself to guest spots for the remainder of the 1949–50 season, but the fall would see him star in a new minstrel TV series. A big parade down Broadway would be planned to ballyhoo it.

Al was honored as the show business "Personality of the Year" by Variety Tent 11 at the Statler Hotel in Washington, D.C., on Saturday night, November 19th. Stephen Early, now Under Secretary of Defense, presented Al with a large bronze and mahogany plaque and described him as "year in and year out, one of our greatest personalities. Al Jolson is a perennial." Al then went to work: "California, Here I Come," "April Showers," "Mammy," "Sonny

Boy," and for an encore, "Brother, Can You Spare a Dime?" He also joked and kidded Vice President Alben W. Barkley.

Al began his work for C.B.S. by doing three Bing Crosby Chesterfield programs over the next month. In December, he took Erle to Hawaii and gave two performances for a total of 12,000 GIs with Martin Fried at the piano. They flew back to Los Angeles on January 3, 1950, and the guest shots continued.

In between the whirl of radio appearances, recording sessions, and awards, the Jolsons adopted a baby girl, named Alicia after Al.

Alicia was only two weeks old when Al and Erle brought her home. Several months later, hospital tests showed she was retarded, and Erle still remembers the way Jolie yelled at the physicians. But there was nothing anyone could do.

In April, Jolson went to New York for what proved to be the final time. Al, who had wanted to play the lead in a proposed light musical version of Dubose Heyward's *Porgy* in 1933, was trying to buy the screen rights to *Porgy and Bess*.

Jolson wanted to play Porgy in whiteface this time, with an all-black cast. He opened negotiations with Lawrence Langner of the Theatre Guild, but no one seemed interested. Al was as wrong for the part in whiteface in 1950 as he had been wrong for it in blackface seventeen years before.

Al returned to the west coast for yet another show with Crosby. He now talked of making a big trip to Israel in September. TV could "wait until the fall of '51."

Al and Erle moved back to Encino from Palm Springs in May. Later that same month, Jolson starred in a radio version of *Jolson Sings Again* on the Lux Radio Theatre.

William Keighley, the m.c., introduced Al to the audience. Jolson clowned around for several minutes and read out a few lines where it would be necessary for the audience to yell out either "Mammy," "Rock-a-Bye," or "Swanee." ("And I'll sing any damn thing you want me to.")

Then he introduced the cast. He brought out Barbara Hale (who played "Ellen Clark," a thinly disguised "smart as pigs" version of Erle), said a few words about her, and stopped. "Wait a minute! Folks, I want ya ta meet my wife—sittin' down there in the fifth row."

Erle was extremely shy. The audience applauded, but could not get her to stand up.

"First one I've had that was bashful," Jolie bawled out. He pointed

at her. "Be prepared for a good sock in the jaw later, f' not gettin'
up!"

Jolson ducked behind the curtain and came back a minute later
with his wife. "What are we havin' for dinner?" he asked. The audience applauded even louder, and Al finally got Erle to take a bow.
Laryngitis had kept Al out of the Friars Frolic a few weeks before,
but he looked healthy this night, wearing navy blue slacks and jacket,
a white sport shirt, and his glasses. ("Can't see a damn thing without 'em!")

Al was not in especially good voice for this broadcast, but he seemed
spontaneous enough—almost the Al Jolson of the Winter Garden
days. No one knew, of course, that this would be his last commercial broadcast—and performance.

His Last Performance

"Hey, don't look so sad. I'm gonna be around for a long
time. My father lived to be ninety-five years old."
—AL JOLSON TO PEARL GOLDBERG, late 1940s.

On June 30, 1950, U.S. ground forces entered the Korean conflict. Al Jolson immediately wired Secretary of Defense Louis
Johnson, volunteering to entertain the troops.

Two weeks later, Al received a wire back from Johnson. The Secretary said the USO had been deactivated, and there were no funds.
Al slapped the telegram. "Funds? I *got* funds! All I'm askin' for is
clearance."

It was September by the time that clearance came. Al had desperately wanted to be the first big name to perform for U.S. soldiers in
Korea. During World War II, an article in the *CBS Roundup* had
taken him and other stars to task for ostensibly avoiding the China-
Burma theatre of war because it was "too tough." Al was hurt. "Those
guys don't know what they're talkin' about," he had exclaimed. "I've
just never been booked in that area." Now he was determined to
remove all private doubts.

Harry Akst refused to go at first. "I didn't tell him," Akst said
later, "but my reason for not wanting to make the trip to Korea was
that I didn't want him to go. I felt he wouldn't go if I didn't. I didn't
think he could stand the trip. Not that he seemed ill, but he was too
old—sixty-four. I had been with him in '43 on the tour through
South America, Africa, and the Near East, and I had seen the price
he had paid—malaria, and later on, the loss of part of a lung.

"The next day, I got a call from Abe Lastfogel, head of the William Morris Agency. 'Harry, I wish you would go to Korea if you
can see your way clear. What I mean is, Jolson would like you to go
to Korea. He wants you to be with him."

Akst agreed to go—against his better judgment.

Jolson and Akst flew to Honolulu on Monday night, September
11, 1950. Al wore an old ski cap, a hunting jacket from Abercrom-

bie & Fitch given to him by Nathan Kramer, and a pair of high boots from the second act of *Hold On to Your Hats*. He joked about the clause in the army travel orders stipulating they were not to accept outside engagements. "Whadda they think we're gonna do?" he asked. "Play Loew's Pusan?"

They flew all night to Honolulu and spent the following day in a Boeing Stratocruiser that came down with engine trouble on Wake Island. Al and Harry had to spend the night on the island in a damp and drafty Quonset hut, lying, as Akst recalled, "in the upper berths of double decker beds because the place was still infested with rats from the old days of Japanese occupation. Jolson and I wrestled with sleeping pills. When morning came, we both had miserable colds and hacking coughs."

Al pretended to be in good shape when they finally arrived at Haneda Air Force Base in Japan on Thursday morning, September 14th. He made jokes about the long air trip and told reporters that he planned to "sing all the old songs" he had helped make famous or "anything asked" of him. Later, after he and Harry got to the Imperial Hotel, Al did not even take time to unpack. "Where's the nearest hospital?" he asked in a hoarse voice.

At the army dispensary, three blocks away, a young army medic peered down Jolson's throat, turned to the doctor beside him and whispered, "This man can't sing."

Jolson overheard him. "Listen, son," he said. "I *gotta* sing."

They shoved him in a cabinet, draped a Turkish towel around his head, and had him inhale mentholated steam for thirty minutes. Within the next few hours, Al and Harry gave their first show in Japan—a concert in the courtyard of an army hospital in Tokyo. Then it was back to the dispensary for more mentholated steam.

Akst remembered Al spending the next two days "shuttling back and forth between the Imperial Hotel and the Tokyo-Yokohama area and getting right back into bed—scribbling messages on a pad to save his voice." There was a performance in a mess hall in Iwokuni. "The Australian contingent had lost their wing commander that day. They were brokenhearted. Al had to go outside and coax them into the hall and work on them until he finally had them smiling through the tears."

Al and Harry arrived in Korea on Sunday morning, September 17th. Jolson was scheduled to do six shows a day in outposts like Chinghai, Miryang, Masan, and Kyongsong. There were no steam cabinets in those places, and the only thing Al had for relief was a little bit of Dobell's Solution, a gargle Akst had managed to wrangle from the Red Cross. They traveled by jeep and helicopter—always with the "Purple Cow"—a small piano painted a deep purple that Al called "a latrine on wheels."

During one performance, men were called away right in the middle of a song. A few minutes later, rifle fire interrupted Al. "Why can't those crazy guys stop all the rifle practice and come to the show?" he asked. "They're not our boys, they're snipers," an officer replied. "But don't worry, Al—they're lousy shots."

Al and Harry were guests at a luncheon held by Maj. Gen. W. B. Kean, commander of the Twenty-third Division. "Jolie was going on nothing but nerve by then," remembered Akst, "and even Kean could see it in his face. 'Al,' he said, 'don't you think you've done enough already for the boys?' 'How could anybody do enough for them?' Al replied. General Kean's son was lying in a hospital in Osaka, critically wounded by a personnel mine. On the way back to Tokyo, Al visited his bedside and then stayed up half the night to get a call through personally to General Kean in Korea."

They had lunch with General Douglas MacArthur the day after Inchon was secured. Jolson, the eternal immigrant who thought the U.S. was the greatest country in the world, felt honored.

Over lunch, the general asked Jolson what he thought of Japan and the Japanese people.

"I haven't seen much of the country," Al replied, "but what I have seen has certainly impressed me. I think within twenty years the Japanese will be ready for the kind of democracy we have in the United States."

Al was charmed by Mrs. MacArthur, a lady with a southern accent that reminded him of Erle. Back at the Imperial Hotel, he went looking for a certain newspaper correspondent. "If anybody ever tells me anything bad about MacArthur again," Al seethed, "I'll punch him in the nose."

Jolie left Japan with Harry the next morning. Al was tired, and the old familiar Jolson bounce was missing. He walked slowly now, and painfully—looking a lot older than the sixty-four he really was.

But novelist MacKinlay Kantor thought he was the same old Jolson on the flights from Wake to Honolulu and from there on to Los Angeles. "Conversationally, he bounded like an eager puppy from the Korean War back to Dockstader's Minstrels, from Dockstader's Minstrels to Georgie Jessel, from Jessel to New York, to girls, to Hollywood, to World War II in Italy, to Eddie Cantor, to girls, to

Broadway, to Korea again. People wanted to keep buying drinks, but we had an awful tussle with Jolson every time money was mentioned. He kept pressing crumpled dollar bills upon the stewardess. When he ran out of dollar bills he cashed a traveler's check."

They arrived in Los Angeles on Wednesday night, September 27, 1950, having listened to the Ezzard Charles-Joe Louis bout on the pilot's radio channel. Erle was at the airport with Asa, Jr., as Al ambled down the steps. He was honest with reporters this time. The trip *had* been rough.

Al and Harry had been gone sixteen days, only seven of which had been spent doing shows for U.S. servicemen in Japan and Korea. In those seven days, however, the sick Jolson had given an incredible forty-two shows. Al, with only one good lung, had pushed himself beyond the limit.

A few days after his return to California, Al granted an interview to George Fischer.

"Well," said Jolie, "it's a funny thing. The Morris office asked me would I do a television shot around Thanksgiving and then (another) one a month later. And I asked them, did they know anything where I could entertain, for nothing, that would be interesting. I'm not interested right now in television; I'm not interested in radio; I'm not interested in anything. I need a rest, because the day I got back from Korea, I started to leap around, people asking me questions, and right now I'm really two shakes ahead of a fit. My pulse is fast and I don't sleep good, so I think I'll go someplace up in, I don't know, maybe Arrowhead or Palm Springs or someplace and take, well, I think a week'll do it—if I sleep, anyway. If this little interview doesn't turn out good, it's because, as I said before, I'm two shakes ahead of a fit and I'm a little nervous. In fact, I've gotta go over to Columbia Pictures now and tell Harry Cohn I may not do a third one."

Al and Erle went down to Palm Springs. Jolson rested, soaked himself in sunlight, and felt better within days. The old restlessness returned, and he went back to Los Angeles. Plans for a third picture at Columbia were never more than tentative at best, but Jolson had a deal brewing for a film called *Stars and Stripes* for Jerry Wald and Norman Krasna at RKO. There would be a fictional plot involving a love interest, but Al would play himself—Al Jolson, performing for the soldiers overseas.

Harry Akst thought the deal sounded "wonderful. . . . But don't spend your time in the make-up department trying to look like Jolson the lover. Don't try to eradicate the creases or crow's feet. Just be the Jolson of today."

"How do I look, Harry?"

"A few days in Palm Springs does wonders for you, Al." Akst, however, then reached for his drink.

The Galbraith family had moved out to Beverly Hills, so Al and Erle had dinner at her mother's house on Tuesday night, October 17th. Later, Harry Akst drove by to pick up Jolie. They were going to the fights at the Olympic Auditorium—Enrique Bolanos vs. "Little Duke" Dukison, 10 rounds, lightweights.

Al complained of indigestion while the main event was on. "Spanish food," he muttered. "Spanish food."

"Why do you eat Spanish food?" asked Harry. "You know it always gives you indigestion."

"I *like* Spanish food," Al said, hitting his chest lightly. Akst drove him back to Mrs. Galbraith's house after the fight, but Al continued to complain about the feeling in his chest.

Al and Erle drove back to Encino. The feeling in Al's chest had worsened, and he now sensed the beginnings of a heart attack. It was after 2:00 a.m., but Jolson detoured to the home of Dr. Ramon Spritzler. The doctor, who had married into the Jolson family, was roused out of bed.

Spritzler took a cardiograph, looked at it, and told Al there was a distinct change for the worse. There was nothing to worry about, but . . . "don't go to any more Koreas."

Al had begun to feel better. "I have to go up to San Francisco next Monday for a radio guest shot for Bing Crosby. Then I've got a picture to make."

"Make the picture, and another picture, and do all the guest shots you want. Just don't go to any more Koreas."

Al, who always wanted more than one medical opinion, went to another doctor the next day and asked for a cardiograph—without mentioning the chest pains.

The physician looked at the cardiograph. "This is the same heart that was okayed for a million dollars' worth of insurance, isn't it?"

Al felt somewhat relieved. He had taken out the policy the year before.

As Al was leaving, the physician spoke again. "You say you're going to San Francisco?"

"That's right."

"Great heart specialist up there—Dr. William Kerr."
Al made a mental note of the name.

Jolson dropped in to see Jerry Wald and Norman Krasna at RKO
on Friday, October 20th. The script of *Stars and Stripes* was being
worked on, and Al wanted to discuss his role and songs. Wald recalled the visit.

"Al clowned around, kidded us about the huge sum of money he
was getting ('And Larry Parks won't get a nickel of it,' he cracked),
and even did a satire on Al Jolson.

"But the thing that impressed everyone here was the way everyone
on the lot, from the biggest stars to the errand girls, kids who weren't
even born when he made *The Jazz Singer,* made a rush for the win-
dows just to see him when the news flashed from office to office that
he was on the lot."

Wald, however, did not say what Jolson looked like. Surviving
photos show an obviously sick man putting on a show for him and
Krasna.

On Monday, Jolson, Harry Akst, and Martin Fried took a two
o'clock flight from Los Angeles and arrived in San Francisco at 3:45.
After registering at the St. Francis and sweating away an hour in the
hotel's Turkish bath, Al called Bill Morrow, Crosby's writer and
producer, to discuss the show. He invited Morrow to have dinner
with them, but Bill was too busy. The best he could do was give
Jolie an update on San Francisco's restaurants. Al decided on Amelio's.

Marty, who was off the wagon, went off to "have dinner" by
himself. Al and Harry left the hotel around seven and took a cab to
Amelio's, but there was a "Closed Monday" sign on the door. They
went to Tarantino's, the world-famous seafood restaurant on Fish-
erman's Wharf. It was crowded, but there always was a table for Al
Jolson.

They started with prawns and clam chowder, and, as Jolie told
the waiter, *"the speshiality de la maison"*—Rex Sole. Jolson was
immediately recognized, and people kept coming over to congratu-
late him on the work he had done for the GIs. When he and Harry
finished dinner and got up to leave, everybody in the place stood up
to applaud and cheer. At the door, Al turned and blew a kiss.

They got back to the St. Francis at 8:45 to find Martin at the
desk, finishing a note that said he would "see them in the morning."
Al grimaced; he knew what Marty would be up to. "Why don't you

come upstairs with us. We'll play gin rummy." Martin knew when he was beaten. Al went to the lobby newsstand for a deck of cards.

"Eighty-eight cents!"

"But these are Bicycle cards."

"I don't want to ride them. I want to play with them." He went back to the desk and bantered with Bill Berger, the room clerk. "Well, now I have to go upstairs and win these guys' money. Good night, kid."

Up in suite 1220–21, Al stripped down to shorts, shoes, and socks. "Why don't you finish the (Truman) parody on 'I'm Just Wild About Harry?'" he asked Akst. "I'll play rummy with Marty. He's a sucker, but I'll waste my time with him anyway."

"I went into the bedroom to wrestle with the parody," remembered Akst. "In a few minutes, Jolie called in, 'I blitzed him the first game.' A few minutes later, 'I blitzed him the second game.' Then, 'How're you coming along with the parody?' I went in and showed him what I'd written. 'Looks good,' he said. 'Here, you sit down and play with Martin. I'm gonna take a rest.' He went into the bedroom.

"I hadn't been playing more than a few minutes when Al called out, 'Marty, do me a favor, will ya? Go downstairs and get me some bicarbonate of soda.'

"When Fried left, I went into the bedroom. Jolie was lying on the bed, thumbing idly through a magazine.

" 'What's the matter, Al? Aren't you feeling well?'

" 'I shouldn't have gone off the lamb chop diet,' he said, beating on his chest with a stiff finger. 'I have a little indigestion.' "

Neither Al nor Harry mentioned "heart attack." After all, Al *had* just had a seafood dinner.

"The bicarb will relieve you," Harry said.

"Maybe," Al said, looking worried. "But you better call a doctor."

Harry called for the house doctor. There were two, but both were out on call. The operator offered to send up the hotel nurse.

'Look up Dr. Kerr," said Al, "and ask him to come over." He remembered the surname of the heart specialist—it was the same as that of Walter Kerr, the theatre critic—but could not remember his first name. The phone book was filled with Kerrs, but Akst finally located the right one.

"It's late," Kerr told Akst, "and I'm quite far from the city."

"But Doctor, I don't think you understand. It's Al Jolson, and it's an emergency."

Jolson waved his hands. "You crazy bastard! You want everybody to read in the papers tomorrow morning that Al Jolson had to get a doctor for indigestion?"

Kerr, however, said he would be there in half an hour. Harry looked relieved.

A few minutes later, Fried arrived with the bicarbonate of soda. Akst prepared it, and Al gulped it down. He belched.

"That's good," said Harry.

Al shook his head. "No, that ain't good." Still in pain, he tapped his finger on his chest. Suddenly, he looked at Akst. "Harry," he said quietly. "I'm not going to last."

"My heart jumped," Akst said later. "I looked down and saw he had been taking his pulse. 'Al, don't talk that way,' I said. 'It'll pass. It's nothing but indigestion.' "

The hotel nurse, Anne Murchison, arrived.

"Nurse," Al said, "I've got no pulse."

She took his wrist and felt it. "You've got a pulse like a baby," she said in a reassuring voice. With her other hand, she rubbed his back.

Akst followed her to the bathroom.

"Is this a heart attack?" he whispered.

"Definitely not," she said, as she prepared a glass of aromatic spirits of ammonia.

"But how do you know?"

"A heart attack is usually accompanied by an ashy pallor, which Mr. Jolson does not have." Al was still tanned from Palm Springs.

Kerr and Walter Beckh, one of the house physicians, both arrived a little after 10:00 p.m. "I'm a little embarrassed about this, gentlemen," said Al. Two doctors, "Dr." Jolson knew, should not be called in on a case—unless for a consultation.

They got ready to examine him, first asking him a few brief questions about what he had done that day and what he had been eating.

"Pull up a couple of chairs," said Jolie, "and let's talk."

Harry brought the chairs to Jolson's bedside, and the two physicians sat.

"Which of you is Dr. Kerr?" Al asked.

"I am," said Kerr.

"I must be an important guy," Al said.

"Of course you are, Mr. Jolson." Kerr thought that Al meant he was important enough to have two doctors come to his hotel room late at night.

"No, I'm a real important guy," Al said. He was smiling. "Hell,

Truman only had one hour with MacArthur. I had two." He glanced at Harry.

"Suddenly," Akst recalled, "without warning, Al reached for his pulse. I thought he was trying to raise himself up. We looked at him."

"Oh," he moaned. "Oh, I'm going," he said sadly.

Then he sank back on the pillow, his eyes closed.

A few minutes later, the hotel's assistant manager came to Bill Berger at the desk. "The press will be calling," he said. "Don't tell them anything. When the coroner comes, send him up to 1220–21. Mr. Jolson just died."

You Ain't Heard Nothing Yet

"After I go, I'll be forgotten."
—AL JOLSON in private conversation,
c. 1940

They tried to revive him. Stimulants were given, and Kerr frantically massaged Al's heart for half an hour, but it was no use.
Death had come at 10:35 p.m., from a massive coronary occlusion.

Erle, who received the news over the telephone, went into shock.
Family members stayed with her around the clock until the funeral
on Thursday—one of the biggest funerals in show business history.

Meanwhile, the obligatory tributes were paid to Jolson's memory.
Bob Hope, speaking from Korea via short wave, said the world had
lost "not only a great entertainer, but also a great citizen." Most of
the other tributes were along similar lines. Even Larry Parks said
that the world had "lost not only its greatest entertainer, but a great
American as well. He was a casualty of the [Korean] war."

Radio disk jockeys dedicated broadcasts to Al's memory. One d.j.
called up Fanny Brice for a "reaction" to his death. "I never liked
him," said Miss Brice, one of the frankest people in show business.

Others found nice things to say, whether they had liked Jolie or
not. Jimmy Durante said the world would "mourn this great and
colorful personality, both as an entertainer and as a kind, generous,
and unselfish person."

"To me," said Edgar Bergen, "the American stage reached its height
thirty years ago, and one by one we have been losing out great entertainers. Now we have lost the greatest of them all."

Bobby Clark simply said that "Jolson was one of the really great
entertainers of all time."

Danny Kaye, then only thirty-seven, probably summed up the general feeling best. "I can't believe that Jolson's dead," he said. "I
thought he would live for five thousand years."

Editorial cartoons eulogized Al on October 25th. Talburt of the

Scripps-Howard newspapers drew a pair of white gloves on a black background. The caption read, "The Song Is Ended." Bruce Russell of the Los Angeles *Times* showed a weeping globe-headed Whistler's Mother with the caption, "Al's Mammy."

Al's funeral was held at two o'clock on Thursday afternoon, October 26, 1950, at Temple Israel at 7300 Hollywood Blvd. Early in the morning, despite threatened rain, the crowds began to converge on the temple. Police estimated upwards of twenty thousand people.

At nine o'clock, a hearse brought Jolson's body to the temple, and a half hour later, the huge doors were opened to enable the public to file past his bier. A disabled veteran was first on line.

Al lay in state dressed in a blue suit, a decoration presented to him by the post-Mussolini Italian government in his lapel. He was draped in a white fringed *tallis*. Some thought this was hypocritical; Jolson was never a religious Jew. Others answered that the *tallis* was Al's way of reaffirming his religious beliefs.

By 11:30, when the doors were shut, 2,132 people had filed past Al's body. Thousands more could not get in.

At noon, the doors reopened to admit 1,500 mourners to the funeral. The service is remembered for the eulogy delivered by George Jessel. Jessel said, in part:

> And not only has the entertainment world lost its king, but we cannot cry, "The king is dead—long live the king!" For there is no one to hold his scepter. Those of us who tarry behind are but pale imitations, mere princelings. And American Jewry suffers as well—and I must psychologically inform you of the great inspiration that Al was to the Jewish people in the last forty years. For in 1910 the Jewish people who emigrated from Europe to come here were a sad lot. Their humor came out of their own troubles. Men of thirty-five seemed to take on the attitude of their fathers and grandfathers; they walked with stooped shoulders. When they sang, they sang with lament in their hearts and their voices, always as if they were pleading for help from above. And the older they got, the more they prayed for the return to Jerusalem. Or yearned for the simple little villages where they spent their childhood. And the actors, even the great ones, came on the stage also playing characters like their fathers. Vaudeville and the variety and the musical comedy stage had Ben Welch and Joe Welch, monologists with beards and shabby clothes telling humorous stories that had a tear behind them. Likewise did this happen in legitimate theatre. David Warfield in *The Auctioneer* and many others in plays bewailing the misfortunes that had happened to the Jew. And then there came on the scene a young man, vibrantly pulsing with life and courage, who marched on the stage, head held high with the authority

of a Roman emperor, with a gaiety that was militant, uninhibited and unafraid, and told the world that the Jew in America did not have to sing in sorrow but could shout happily about Dixie, about the Night Boat to Albany, about coming to California, about a girl in Avalon. And when he cried "Mammy," it was in appreciation, not in lament. Jolson is the happiest portrait that can be painted about an American of the Jewish faith. Jolson was synonymous with victory—at the race track, at the ball game, at anything that he participated in, he would say, "I had the winner, ha ha, why didn't you ask me?" This was not in bravado alone: this was the quintessence of optimism. Whatever you're in, whatever game you play, feel like you are the winner.

The irony is that Jolson had told Erle he did not want Jessel to do his eulogy. It had taken considerable talking on the parts of Johnny Hyde and Ben Holzman of the William Morris Agency to persuade her to let Jessel do it. More ironic still was the eulogy delivered by Rabbi Max Nussbaum: "Whatever he was came to him from his father. It is from him that he inherited the comedy and the smile. But more than that, it is from Rabbi Yoelson that he received the form and content of singing. When you listened to any of his songs, you noticed the half and quarter tones, the sigh and the sob, the sudden inflections of the voice and the unexpected twist—all these are elements that come out from the Cantorial singing of our people."

There was not one word about Naomi.

Al was buried at Beth Olam Cemetery in Los Angeles after an additional private ceremony later in the day. Erle, Asa, Jr., Harry Jolson, his second wife Sylvia (Lillian had died two years before), and the rabbi were the only people present.

Jolson's will was filed for probate in New York on the same day. The bequests to numerous charities made the public think of Al as a humanitarian. Those who knew Jolson were outraged. The estate came to more than four million dollars, but Jolson had left nothing to Louis Epstein, Harry Akst, Martin Fried, Jimmy Donnelly, or Frank Holmes. Al had left his brother Harry only ten thousand dollars— the same amount he left John Schneckenberger.

Holmes and Donnelly may have been left out to appease Erle, but it is doubtful whether Al would have provided for them in any event. Donnelly died the following year. He spent his last days in a home in Riverdale, New York, blind and broke but refusing to blame Jolson for his troubles. Holmes spent the remaining eight years of his life running a cigar stand in Jamestown, New York.

Akst, a friend of Jolson's, had only been in Al's employ during the times when they had entertained for servicemen. A well-known composer ("Dinah," "Baby Face," "Am I Blue?" etc.), he presumably did not need Jolson's money.

Martin Fried's alcoholism made him a poor risk as anybody's heir, but Al's refusal to remember Louis Epstein is a mystery. The only clues are these: Epstein was Jolson's "alter ego." As such, he suffered Al's abuse. It was Eppy who reminded Al to say *Yahrzeit* for his mother every winter. Al said the prayer, but he probably resented the reminder of Naomi's death. Al was frequently contemptuous of Lou, whom he regarded as a low-minded burlesque manager. (Eppy did not put Jewish women up on pedestals the way he did.) Another possible reason for Al's failure to include Lou in his will was voiced by Eppy's grandniece, Beanie Dworkin.

Eppy, it appears, was very close to Erle, and it may have been that Al was jealous. The charge appears ludicrous. Lou was just as old as Al, and far less charismatic. Jolson's mind, however, tended to work strangely. He remained, right to the end, a jealous man.

In any event, Jolson's failure to include Lou Epstein all but destroyed Eppy. For the remainder of his life, Lou's face would take on a sad and bewildered look whenever he mentioned "Mr. Jolson." He died at the age of sixty-eight in 1954, while serving as road manager for *An Evening with Beatrice Lillie.*

Jolson left $10,000 each to his half siblings—Emil, Mike, Gertrude, and George. The last named was concerned with keeping Al's death a secret from his mother, Hessi—eighty years old and in poor health since Moshe's death five years before.

The TV set was never turned on again in the Yoelson home. George never knew when Al's death might be mentioned by an entertainer or a newsman. For many years, the only letters that Al wrote had been to Hessi. George now told his mother that he had instructed John Schneckenberger to send the letters to him. "It will be easier," George said. "Your eyesight isn't as good as it used to be, and you worry too much."

From that time on, George "read" Al's letters to his mother.

Hessi suffered a stroke in December. She died on January 8, 1951, never knowing that her "Asikla" was dead.

Early in November, William Warford of Station WIL in St. Louis started a movement to have Al awarded the Congressional Medal of Honor. Representative Helen Gahagan Douglas (D-Calif.), a former actress, refused to sponsor the measure, but Louis B. Heller (D-N.Y.)

introduced it on November 27th. The bill said that Jolson, "without regard to his health, unselfishly and unstintingly gave his strength to entertain members of the armed services in and around Korea."

The bill was defeated, principally because Jolson had never been in the armed forces and had not died from a battle injury. President Truman, however, had already decided to award Jolson the Civilian Order of Merit for "extraordinary fidelity and exceptionally meritorious conduct." Secretary of Defense George C. Marshall presented the medal to Erle and three-year-old Asa, Jr., in Washington on December 6, 1950.

Erle was determined to erect a monument to Jolie that would also be his final resting place. On Wednesday, February 7, 1951, Los Angeles Superior Court Judge Newcomb Condee allowed $84,000 to be withdrawn from the estate—$9,000 for a plot of ground at Hillside Memorial Park and $75,000 for a monument. The latter would be a six-pillar marble structure topped by a mosaic dome. It was designed by Paul Williams, a prominent Los Angeles-based black architect. A 120-foot cascade of water dropping into a pool would be provided by the Hillside management, Al having told Erle that he wanted to be buried near a waterfall.

Judge Condee said the expenditure was justified because "it involved a man so well known." Not everyone shared that opinion. Paul V. Coates of the Los Angeles *Mirror* said that the monument was in bad taste—especially since Jolson had already made sure his name would be immortalized by leaving most of his money to charity.

Subsequent Coates pieces brought a deluge of letters of which Coates claimed 99 percent contained "distasteful sidelights about Jolson." The columnist cited Louis Epstein and Harry Akst as examples of Jolson's "neglect." Eppy could not be reached for comment, but Akst said, "Al doesn't merit these barbs."

Akst was suing the estate but not contesting the will—only making a claim for services rendered. Harry insisted Al had meant to pay him for his help in entertaining servicemen. "He died so suddenly," he said, "that many of his plans were not fulfilled." Akst sued for $100,000.

Jolson's body was reinterred at Hillside on September 23, 1951— exactly eleven months after his death. Jack Benny did the final eulogy.

"The Sweet Singer of Israel, The Man Raised on High" was engraved on the inside of the dome above the black-and-gold sarcophagus, and a three-quarter lifesize statue of Jolson, eternally resting on bended knee, served to complete the picture.

Al Jolson was finally at rest.

A little more than two months later, on December 7, 1951, Erle married Norman Krasna. Krasna, forty-two, and one of the country's most successful playwrights *(Dear Ruth, John Loves Mary)*, had met Erle through Jolie at RKO. "I couldn't have married anybody who didn't love him (Jolson)," Erle said in 1983. By then, however, Krasna had had thirty years of living in the shadow of Al's ghost. He cringed whenever someone said the name, "Al Jolson." Krasna died in 1984.

The estate in Encino was put up for auction in 1953. Four years later, Asa, Jr., having reached the age of ten, a vault that had been left to him by Al was opened. In it were transcriptions of the shows Jolson had done for Kraft from October 1947 through May 1949—recorded at the highest fidelity possible in the postwar period.

Decca, which had been repackaging their Jolson records, released several LPs of Al's Kraft material from 1958 through 1965. According to Al's contract with Decca, royalties on any new material released after his death had to be at a rate *as high or higher* than those of the company's biggest star. No new post-war Jolson material has been released since 1965 as a result.

Harry Jolson tried to emerge from obscurity in the year following Al's death. *Mistah Jolson,* Harry's autobiography, was published in late 1951, and Al's older brother appeared on the TV show, *You Asked For It,* singing "You Made Me Love You" in blackface. Harry's "comeback," if it could be called that, was short-lived. His health began to fail in 1952, and a leg had to be amputated. Harry lost the other leg in 1953 and died on April 26th of the same year. He was seventy-one.

Almost all the people who knew Jolson well are gone. John Schneckenberger died in 1952, Louis Schreiber in 1961, Harry Akst in 1963, Louis Silvers in 1971, and Al Goodman in 1972. One of the saddest fates was that of Henrietta. Her second husband, Jack Silvey, became an alcoholic and jumped off the Golden Gate Bridge in the late 1930s. Henrietta married again; her third spouse, Arthur Wristen, was a shady character who dealt in questionable stocks and made his aging wife's life hell in many ways. Henrietta died in San Luis Obispo, California, in 1967 at the age of seventy-nine.

Erle and Norman Krasna moved to Switzerland in the 1960s and did not permanently return to the United States until 1980. Ruby Keeler made few professional appearances until her second husband, John Lowe, died in 1969. At that time, a "nostalgia" boom had begun in response to the dramatic changes then occurring in American society, and Ruby was asked to play Eleanor Dawn's original role in a revival of the 1920s musical comedy, *No, No, Nanette*. The success of that show, coupled with the "discovery" of Busby Berkeley musicals by cinema students and nostalgia freaks, led to Keeler becoming even more popular than she had been in the 1930s. Ironically, she made her "comeback" at the age of sixty—the same age Al had been at the time *The Jolson Story* was released.

Al Jolson has not fared well since the mid-1960s. The use of burnt cork is now looked upon as an insulting caricature of black people rather than as a theatricalization with overtones of harlequins and ancient rites, and Jolie's performances in films range only from the adequate *(Go Into Your Dance)* to the embarrassing *(Say It with Songs)*.

A seemingly endless flow of books on film have tended to dismiss Al Jolson as a boorish ham who made it to the top on "drive" alone. Writers have consistently portrayed him as a two-dimensional egomaniac whose only motivation was self-love.

The genius of Al Jolson has been lost. Unlike Bert Lahr, who portrayed the tortured spirit straining helplessly against the confines of the body, Jolson gave the world a character of wit and magic. Al was an *inspiring* performer—the embodiment of optimism who made one think the human soul could never be defeated.

On a stage, Al Jolson, like his character, Gus Jackson, *was* invincible. It was only when he left the stage that he failed—in the movies, on the radio, as a husband, and, say many, as a person. He remained a child all his life—alternately boastful and self-deprecating, generous and cynical, sympathetic and insensitive, keeping people at arm's length and wondering, in turn, why he felt so alone.

Ralph Reader—"English" from the *Big Boy* days—never knew about Naomi or Al's childhood in Seredzius. He was, however, asked to say some words on Al a few years before his own death in 1982:

"It wasn't that he *wanted* to give so much," he said, struggling to explain Al to young people who had not been born when Jolie passed away.

"It's that . . . *he had to.*"

Notes

ACT ONE

Scene One

Moshe Reuben Yoelson was originally Moshe Reuben Hesselson, one of five sons born to Meyer Hesselson, a shoe and boot dealer in the duchy of Kurland, now part of Latvia. Moshe's name was changed in order to keep him out of the czar's army. (All males were liable for conscription into the czarist army at the age of twenty except one son, usually the eldest, in each family. Meyer Yoelson bribed czarist officials into listing two of his sons as the only sons of fictitious families named "Yoelson," saving them from army service. (His two other sons escaped to the United States in their teens.))

Sources for Al Jolson's early life in Europe include "Brothers Under the Cork," by Harry Jolson (ghosted by his wife, Lillian), which appeared in two installments in *The Saturday Evening Post* (December 1929); *Mistah Jolson*, by Harry Jolson and Alban Emley (House-Warven, 1951); *The Immortal Jolson*, by Pearl Sieben (Frederick Fell, 1962), plus an interview with Pearl. [See Act II, Scene 5 ("Hold On to Your Hats"), for details of Pearl Goldberg's relationship with Jolson in the 1940s.]

Sources for Al's early life in the U.S. (1894–97) include *Mistah Jolson*, interviews with Rose's daughters, Teresa and Ethel Flax, and interviews given by Jolson on a September, 1949 trip to Washington. These interviews were carried in the *Washington Post*. The date of the Yoelsons' arrival in the U.S. (April 9, 1894 on the *Umbria*) is from that ship's passenger list, a microfilmed copy of which is now available at the New York Public Library. Naomi's death is taken from *The Immortal Jolson*, the Pearl Goldberg Sieben interview, and the interview with Ethel Flax, who confirmed my belief that Naomi died in childbirth. The date of her death (the 12th day of *Shvat*, 5655, which translates to February 6, 1895) is from her tombstone.

No mention of Rich & Hoppe's Big Company of Fun Makers has been found in contemporary sources. The only first-hand references to it are in *Mistah Jolson* and a 1920s interview in which Al Jolson spoke of his first entry into show business. He did not refer to Rich & Hoppe's Big Company of Fun Makers by name.

The story of Al's forays with the Fifteenth Pennsylvania Volunteers, the Walter L. Main Circus, and St. Mary's Industrial School for Boys, was told by Al at least a dozen times in published interviews, with considerable variation re specifics. The sequence of events related in this chapter has been gleaned from careful studies of reports in the contemporary *New York Clipper* (a theatrical trade weekly that covered circuses), checked against dates for the Spanish-American War. All records of St. Mary's were destroyed in a fire (hence the lack of exact dates), but a letter from the Rev. Thomas J. Bauernfeind, Chancellor of the Archdiocese of Baltimore said that there was "every indication that Mr. Jolson was at one time a resident of St. Mary's Industrial School."

The Yoelson home life of the late '90s is drawn from the interviews with Teresa Flax, Ethel Flax, and Marvin Cantor (Etta's son). The *Children of the Ghetto* episode is from various interviews given by Al, checked against the records of the play's pre-New York tour schedule and contemporary criticism of the dramatic content. The Eddie Leonard story is from Harry, but the dates and context were obtained from contemporary trade paper reports.

Al Joelson's adventures in New York in 1900 were assembled from various sources, including a 1931 interview in which Al mentioned the first horse race he attended, an article called "Bellevue to Broadway," *Weber and Fields* by Felix Isman, and some reminiscing Al did on the Barry Gray Show of October 27, 1946.

The story of how Al joined the Victoria Burlesquers is from *Mistah Jolson*, but specifics as to dates and certain names were obtained form three trade papers—the *Clipper*, the *Billboard*, and the *Dramatic Mirror*. (*Variety* did not start until 1905.)

Scene Two

The story of the fourteen-year-old Al's "affair" with Grace Celeste is from *The Immortal Jolson*, plus the interview with Pearl. Mrs. Sieben knew Fred Moore's daughter Kitty, who proved an excellent source of information on her father's partnership with young Al, 1901–03. The professional side of their relationship was chronicled in the trade papers of the day.

Harry Jolson's reminiscences, as contained in "Under the Cork" and *Mistah Jolson* are quite detailed with regard to "The Hebrew and the Cadet," although I have relied on the trades for certain specifics. Al spoke of Henri Courte in interviews during the run of *Bombo* at Jolson's Fifty-ninth Street Theatre, 1921–22. The information on Joe Palmer's background is from Joe's 1916 obituary in *Variety*.

Scene Three

Julia Rooney proved an especially delightful three-hour interview at the age of ninety-one. I spoke to Josie Rooney very briefly, but she declined to go into many specifics.

The data on the various circuits Palmer and Jolson played on in the first few months of 1906 are from contemporary news and advertisements in *Variety*. The follow-up information on Joe Palmer is from various items culled from trade papers, 1906–10.

Information on Al's career in California vaudeville from September 1906 through February 1907 would be far more abundant had Pop Grauman not refused to advertise in newspapers. The National Theatre was totally ignored by the daily press as a result. I have relied on contemporary trade papers and the memory of William Walsh for most of my information.

Jean Carlson proved to be a goldmine of information on Henrietta Keller. The story of how Al met and courted Henrietta is from her. Conrad Keller's anti-Semitism is from Pearl Sieben, who got it from Al in the 1940s.

Harry Jolson ignored his 1908 trip to California in his autobiographical writings; the information in this chapter is from *Variety* and other trades. Harry did admit having resented Henrietta; I have simply put the Jolson's argument in its proper historical setting. The information re Al going to Chicago and signing with the Interstate Circuit is from *Variety*.

Al told how he joined Dockstader's Minstrels in a 1915 article in *Green Book*.

Scene Four

The Immortal Jolson places Al and Henrietta's "honeymoon" at the Moores' home in New Jersey in 1906. I have placed their stay in May–July 1908, when it occurred.

The information on Lew Dockstader, I. Pearl Wilkerson, et al., is from *Variety*, the *Clipper*, *Dramatic Mirror*, *Billboard*, an interview with Rae Samuels (who knew Lew in the 1910s), reports in daily newspapers, and a published interview with Herman Weaver, a violinist in Dockstader's orchestra.

The Arthur Klein biographical data are from Klein's obituaries. His doings re Al Jolson and Al's vaudeville career are fairly well documented in the trades. The story of the coat with the fur collar was told by Klein on the Joe Franklin Show about a year before Klein's death in 1964.

Al talked about his illness in Louisville in a 1912 article in *Variety*. The story of Harry's visit to the convalescing Al is from *The Player*, organ of the White Rats at the time. The first Jolson-Shubert contract (February 7, 1911) is in the Shubert archives.

Scene Five

Data on the preparations and rehearsals for *The Musical Revue of 1911*, the first Winter Garden show, is from *Variety*. The opening of the show was covered by virtually all of New York's 14-odd daily newspapers at the time. Jolson's single "turn" was covered in *Variety*. Al's behavior following his "flop" is from the 1912 article in *Variety* and *The Immortal Jolson*.

The Jimmy Donnelly material is from a contemporary article in *Vanity Fair* and comments by Pearl, who knew Jimmy at the same time she knew Jolson.

The Frank Holmes quote is from "Mr. Jolson Acts Up for His Bride," a 1922 interview/article by Ashton Stevens. The Melville Ellis information is from *Variety*, Kitty Gordon, and Rae Samuels.

The data on the Winter Garden shows and Sunday concerts are from contemporary trade and newspapers. The Cantor-Jessel anecdote is from Cantor's autobiographical *Take My Life*.

Scene Six

Rae Samuels and Bessie Harris were very helpful in providing contrasting looks at Al backstage during the tour of *The Honeymoon Express*. Information on Al's trip to Europe is from a report in the New York *Review* and a publicity article printed in various newspapers during the tour of *Dancing Around* in 1915.

Data on *Dancing Around* and its tour are from a scrapbook given me by Kitty Doner and reports in many different daily papers. *Robinson Crusoe, Jr.* info. is from various contemporary sources. The Louis Epstein material is from Beanie Dworkin.

Scene Seven

Most of the material on Al's mistreatment of his wife comes from Henrietta's testimony in the Jolson-Keller divorce trial in 1919. The story of Al's efforts to win his wife back is from Jean Carlson.

The material on Kitty Doner is from Kitty's unpublished memoirs. Information on Al's career, health problems, etc., is from contemporary trades.

Scene Eight

The background material on Ethel Delmar is from newspapers of the day, combined with information I assembled from old cast lists, etc. *Variety* and *Billboard* were fine sources of information on this period in Al's stage career, while the Ashton Stevens article ("Mr. Jolson Acts Up for His Bride") provided an interesting glimpse of the early days of the Jolson-Delmar marriage. The Ralph Reader material is from Barrie Anderton of the Int. Al Jolson Society.

Scene Nine

The material on *Black and White* is drawn from courtroom testimony in the Griffith-Jolson and Kelly-Jolson lawsuits of 1926. Information for the balance of the chapter is drawn largely from contemporary papers, but the interview with Ray O'Brien, cited in the text, was very helpful. Pearl Sieben and Melvin Felsinger (lawyer for the Jolson estate) were fine sources of information on Ethel's later life.

Scene Ten

The late May McAvoy proved to be a fine interview. The remainder of the material for this chapter is from contemporary papers, the interview with Jessel serving to confirm a good part of the material.

Scene Eleven

The information on Ruby Keeler's childhood is from various interviews given by Miss Keeler at the height of her film career in the 1930s. The material on her early years in show business is from similar sources checked against contemporary trade reports. Joe Candullo was a source of data on Miss Keeler's years as a hoofer in night clubs, as was Billy Grady's autobiography, *The Irish Peacock*.

A brief interview Miss Keeler gave in Denver has been checked against contemporary reports in *Variety,* and Grady's book, to piece together the true story of just when and where Ruby agreed to marry Al. The wedding scene is from Hellinger's report, and the New York *Herald Tribune* provided the scene in which a bevy of reporters crashed the Jolson-Keeler honeymoon suite on the *Olympic.*

The Mark Hellinger Story, by Jim Bishop, provided the material on Legs Diamond and gave me the inspiration to comb every issue of the New York *Daily News* printed from September through the end of October 1928. There was quite a bit of information.

ACT TWO

Scene One

Hellinger's reports and Nellie's statements in the New York *American* make up the basic material for the first part of this chapter. Several books, including *The Irish Peacock* and Charles Higham's *Ziegfeld,* proved good sources of data for *Show Girl.* The rest of the material is culled from trade papers and specific articles cited in the text.

Scene Two

The late Patsy Kelly proved great fun, as well as a fine source of information on *The Wonder Bar.* An interview Al gave in Los Angeles, at the end of the show's tour, was helpful, as were various reports in *Variety.* Data on the production of *Hallelujah, I'm a Bum* are scarce, due to Joe Schenck's apparent efforts to conceal the fact that the picture was made twice. The radio reviews by Jimmy Cannon, also a great writer on boxing—and whatever other subjects he tried his hand in—appeared in the New York *World-Telegram.*

Scene Three

The production schedules of Ruby Keeler's films were compiled from weekly listings printed in *Variety.* The rest of the material is from various articles, cited in the text, in addition to the Fried and Jessel interviews, newspapers, and editor Abel Green's superb coverage of Jolson's doings in *Variety.*

Scene Four

Newspaper reports, interviews, and Harry Akst's article, "The Jolson Nobody Knew" in *Cosmopolitan* are the basic sources for the Jolson-Keeler marriage breakup. *Growing Up with Chico,* by Maxine Marx, was of some help in confirming that Miss Keeler knew John Lowe, Jr., before she was divorced from

Jolson—a conclusion further borne out by reports in Chicago newspapers during the run of *Hold On to Your Hats*.

Scene Five

Pearl Sieben, newspapers, *Variety*, Jinx Falkenburg's autobiography, an article in the New York *Mirror* about Al's then recent girlfriends, and certain confidential information provided by a member of the show's technical crew made up the bulk of information for this chapter.

Scene Six

Al's dispatch to *Variety* provided most of the information on his June 1942 trip to Alaska. Charles Higham's *Princess Merle* was the source for some of the material regarding the trip to the British Isles; the rest is from Ralph Reader and trade/newspaper reports. Carol Bruce, a charming lady, proved to be a very refreshing interview.

Information regarding Sidney Skolsky and *The Jolson Story* is from Skolsky's book, *Don't Get Me Wrong, I Love Hollywood*, checked against reports in *Variety*. (I have given far more credence to the latter.)

The material on the late Gordon Jenkins was obtained by Greg Gormick, while "The Jolson Nobody Knew" proved to be the definitive source for data on the Jolson-Akst tour of July-September 1943.

Scene Seven

Details of Al's collapse and subsequent recovery were obtained from *Variety, The New York Times,* and several other newspapers. The Erle Galbraith information is from "The Jolson-Crosby Story," a 1947 interview/article by Ed Sullivan, as well as "My Husband, Al Jolson," a ghosted magazine piece done, ostensibly, by Erle, and an interview with Manny Mannheim.

Scene Eight

Information on the shooting of *The Jolson Story,* Parks' clinching of the role, and Jolson's lack of professional involvement are drawn, in the main, from reports in *Variety* and research done by Greg Gormick.

Variety continued to be a great source of data, with newspaper interviews given by Jolson in Washington, Baltimore, etc., fleshing out the balance of the chapter. Tapes of all of Jolson's 1947–49 Kraft shows are readily available, as is film of Al's rather pathetic 1948 screen test. "Swanee Song," by Charlie Isaacs, proved extremely valuable, as did the interview with Mannheim. The episode on the set of *Jolson Sings Again* is from a member of the crew.

Scene Nine

"The Jolson Nobody Knew" remains *the* source for information on the last two months of Jolson's life. Further sources include Fischer's interview with Jolie, c. October 1, 1950, a piece written on Al's visit to RKO a few days before his death, and an article in *Meet at the St. Francis,* a book about the famous hotel in which Jolson died.

Curtain Call

Newspaper coverage of Jolson's funeral—and will—was excellent. Follow-up articles on Jolson, his cronies, etc., appeared in various papers for months after Al's death, and did not really cease until his reburial in September 1951. Pearl Sieben contributed the information on Jimmy Donnelly, and Beanie Dworkin provided the final material on Louis Epstein.

Stageography

This stageography includes all vaudeville, minstrel, and legitimate stage show appearances made by Al Jolson from October 1900, when he joined the Victoria Burlesquers, through the Loew's New York area tour of August 1949. It does not include his five-week guest appearance in *Artists and Models* at the Winter Garden (March 20–April 24, 1926), his four-week guest appearance in *A Night in Spain* at the Four Cohans Theatre in Chicago (March 11–April 7, 1928); picture house engagements in Los Angeles (September 1927), St. Louis (February 1928), San Francisco (February 1929), San Francisco and Oakland (May 1932), and Chicago (December 1932–January 1933); performances for U.S. servicemen (1918, 1942–44, 1950); unbilled guest appearances in productions like *Show Girl* (June–July 1929); appearances at Soldier Field and the Oriental Theatre in Chicago (September 1949), nor benefit performances. No information is available on Rich and Hoppe's Big Company of Fun Makers, and no listing has been included for *The Children of the Ghetto*, in which the thirteen-year-old Joelson appeared as a supernumerary for three performances beginning September 18, 1899, at the National Theatre in Washington, D.C.

Cast listings and major cast changes in Broadway shows have been included, along with listings of original scores. (Many of the songs in early musicals were by composers other than those listed in the credits. These have been omitted.) An asterisk (*) denotes songs sung by Jolson. A few of the major Jolson interpolations of songs by other composers have also been included.

AL JOELSON (Unbilled)

Walter L. Main Circus

1898	Oct. 3	Harrisburg, Pa.	1898	Oct. 13	Annapolis, Md.
	4	Newport, Pa.		14	Rockville, Md.
	5	Middletown, Pa.		15	Martinsburg, W. Va.
	6	Shippensburg, Pa.		17	Cumberland, Md.
	7	Waynesboro, Pa.		18	Piedmont, W. Va.
	8	Westminster, Md.		19	Meyersdale, Pa.
	10	Hagerstown, Md.		20	Evans City, Pa.
	11	Frederick City, Md.		21	Ellwood City, Pa.
	12	Ellicott City, Md.		22	Burton, Ohio

Victoria Burlesquers

1900	Oct. 8–13	Bijou	Washington, D.C.
	15–20	Westminster	Providence, R.I.
	22–27	Court Street	Buffalo, N.Y.
	Oct. 29–Nov. 3	Empire	Rochester, N.Y.
	Nov. 5–10	Dunfee	Syracuse, N.Y.
	12–17		
	19–21		
	22–24	Empire	Fall River, Mass.
	Nov. 26–Dec. 1	Howard Athenaeum	Boston, Mass.
	Dec. 3–8		
	10–15	Unique	Brooklyn, N.Y.
	17–19	Wonderland	Easton, Pa.
	20–22	Gaiety	Scranton, Pa.
	24–26	Auditorium	Springfield, Mass.
	27	McDonough	Middletown, Conn.
	28–29		
	Dec. 31–Jan. 5, 1901	Bijou	Washington, D.C.
1901	Jan. 7–12	Dewey	New York, N.Y.
	14–16		
	17–19	Burt's	Toledo, Ohio
	20–26	Star	Milwaukee, Wisc.
	Jan. 27–Feb. 2	Dewey	Minneapolis, Minn.
	Feb. 3–9	Star	St. Paul, Minn.
	10–16	Miaco's Trocadero	Omaha, Nebr.
	18–20	Mirror	Des Moines, Iowa
	21–23		
	Feb. 25–March 2	Smith's Opera House	Grand Rapids, Mich.
	March 4–9	Capitol Square	Detroit, Mich.
	11–13	Grand Opera House	Columbus, Ohio
	14–16	Empire	Indianapolis, Ind.

MASTER JOELSON & FRED MOORE
Victoria Burlesquers

1901	March 17–23	Sam T. Jack's	Chicago, Ill.
	25–30	Smith's Opera House	Grand Rapids, Mich.
	March 31–April 6	Miaco's Trocadero	Chicago, Ill.
	7–13		
	14–20	People's	Cincinnati, Ohio
	21–27	Standard	St. Louis, Mo.
	April 28–May 4		
	May 5–11	Star	Milwaukee, Wisc.
	12–18	Dewey	Minneapolis, Minn.
	19–25	Star	St. Paul, Minn.
	May 26–June 1	Miaco's Trocadero	Chicago, Ill.

Vaudeville

| 1901 | June 17–22 | Ramona Pavilion | Grand Rapids, Mich. |
| | 24–29 | Lake Michigan Park | Muskegon, Mich. |

Victoria Burlesquers

1901	Aug. 12–17	Bijou	Paterson, N.J.
	19–24	Lyceum	Boston, Mass.
	26–31	Westminster	Providence, R.I.
	Sept. 2–7		
	9–14	Bon Ton	Jersey City, N.J.
	16–21	Dewey	New York, N.Y.
	23–28	Novelty	Brooklyn, N.Y.
	Sept. 30–Oct. 5		
	Oct. 7–12	London	New York, N.Y.
	14–19	Olympic	New York, N.Y.
	21–23	Gaiety	Albany, N.Y.
	24–26	Empire	Rochester, N.Y.
	28–30		
	Oct. 31–Nov. 2	Burt's	Toledo, Ohio
	Nov. 3–9	Miaco's Trocadero	Chicago, Ill.
	10–16	Star	Milwaukee, Wisc.
	17–23	Dewey	Minneapolis, Minn.
	24–30	Star	St. Paul, Minn.
	Dec. 1–7	Miaco's Trocadero	Omaha, Neb.
	8–14	People's	Cincinnati, Ohio
	15–21	Standard	St. Louis, Mo.
	22–28	Buckingham	Louisville, Ky.
	Dec. 30–Jan. 4, 1902	Empire	Indianapolis, Ind.
1902	Jan. 6–11	Empire	Rochester, N.Y.
	13–18	Empire	Detroit, Mich.
	20–25	Star	Toronto, Ont.
	Jan. 27–Feb. 1	Lyceum	Boston, Mass.
	Feb. 3–8	Westminster	Providence, R.I.
	10–15	Royal	Montreal, Que.
	17–19	Grand Opera House	Ottawa, Ont.
	20–22	Star	Hamilton, Ont.
	Feb. 24–Mar. 1	Isham's	Syracuse, N.Y.
	March 3–8	Dewey	New York, N.Y.

Al Reeves' Famous Big Company

1902	March 17–22	Waldmann's	Newark, N.J.
	24–26	Star	Troy, N.Y.
	27–29	Gaiety	Albany, N.Y.
	Mar. 31–Apr. 5	Star	Brooklyn, N.Y.
	April 7–12	Miner's Bowery	New York, N.Y.
	14–16	Star	Scranton, Pa.
	17–19	Bijou	Reading, Pa.
	21–26	Kensington	Philadelphia, Pa.

Keith Vaudeville

1902	June 2–7	Keith's Union Square	New York, N.Y.
	9–14	Keith's	Boston, Mass.
	16–21	Keith's	Philadelphia, Pa.

J. W. Gorman Specialty Company

1902	June 30–July 5		
	July 7–12	Ft. Wm. Henry Park	Lake George, N.Y.
	14–19	Summit Park	Utica, N.Y.
	21–26	Sacandaga Park	Gloversville, N.Y.
	July 28–Aug. 2		
	Aug. 4–9	Norumbega Park	Boston, Mass.

Vaudeville

1902	Sept. 22–27	Casto's	Fall River, Mass.

The Dainty Duchess

1902	Sept. 29–Oct. 4	Lyceum	Philadelphia, Pa.
	Oct. 6–11	Kernan's Monumental	Baltimore, Md.
	13–18	Kernan's Lyceum	Washington, D.C.
	20–25	Academy of Music	Pittsburgh, Pa.
	Oct. 26–Nov. 1	People's	Cincinnati, Ohio
	Nov. 2–8	Buckingham	Louisville, Ky.
	10–15	Empire	Indianapolis, Ind.
	16–22	Standard	St. Louis, Mo.
	23–29	Hopkins'	Chicago, Ill.
	Nov. 30–Dec. 6	Star	Milwaukee, Wisc.
	Dec. 7–13	Dewey	Minneapolis, Minn.
	14–20	Star	St. Paul, Minn.
	21–27	Sam T. Jack's	Chicago, Ill.
	Dec. 28–Jan. 3, 1903	Empire	Detroit, Mich.
1903	Jan. 5–10	Star	Cleveland, Ohio
	12–17	Lafayette	Buffalo, N.Y.
	19–24	Star	Toronto, Ont.
	26–31	Empire	Rochester, N.Y.
	Feb. 2–7	Palace	Boston, Mass.
	9–14	Dewey	New York, N.Y.
	16–18	Star	Troy, N.Y.
	19–21	Gaiety	Albany, N.Y.
	23–28	Star	Brooklyn, N.Y.
	March 2–7	Gayety	Brooklyn, N.Y.
	9–14	Dunn's Star	Philadelphia, Pa.
	16–21	Miner's Bowery	New York, N.Y.
	23–25	Bijou	Reading, Pa.
	26–28	Star	Scranton, Pa.
	March 30–April 1		
	April 2–4	Grand Opera House	Springfield, Mass.
	6–11	(Holy Week Lay-Off)	
	13–18	Westminster	Providence, R.I.

THE JOELSON BROTHERS
Vaudeville

1903	Aug. 10–12	Morrison's	Rockaway, N.Y.
	17–22	Henderson's	Coney Island, N.Y.

The Mayflowers

1903	Aug. 29	Eleventh Avenue O.H.	Altoona, Pa.
	31	Cambria	Johnstown, Pa.
	Sept. 1		
	2	Academy of Music	Tyrone, Pa.
	3		
	4		
	5		
	7	Garman's Opera House	Bellefonte, Pa.
	8		
	9	Kane's	Renovo, Pa.
	10		
	11		
	12		
	14		
	15		
	16		
	17	G.A.R. Opera House	Mt. Carmel, Pa.
	18		
	19	Shenandoah	Shenandoah, Pa.
	21	Minersville O.H.	Minersville, Pa.
	22		
	23		
	24		Conshohocken, Pa.
	25		Coatesville, Pa.
	26		Royersford, Pa.
	28		Long Beach, N.J.
	29		Asbury Park, N.J.
	30		Somerville, N.J.
	Oct. 1		Boonton, N.J.
	2		Freehold, N.J.
	3	Baker Opera House	Dover, N.J.

Vaudeville

1903	Oct. 26–31	Arch Street Museum	Philadelphia, Pa.
	Nov. 9–14	Casto's	Fall River, Mass.
	16–21	Casto's	Lawrence, Mass.
	23–28	Casto's	Lowell, Mass.

Little Egypt London Gaiety Girls

1904	Feb. 8–13	Unique	Brooklyn, N.Y.
	15–20	Olympic	New York, N.Y.
	22	Grand Opera House	Bethlehem, Pa.

23	Grand Opera House	Pottstown, Pa.
24	Academy of Music	Lebanon, Pa.
25	Columbia Opera House	Columbia, Pa.
26	Keaggy	Greensburg, Pa.
27	Grand Opera House	Uniontown, Pa.
29	Academy of Music	Cumberland, Md.
March 1	Connellsville	Connellsville, Pa.
2	Geyer's Opera House	Scottdale, Pa.
3	Waynesburg O.H.	Waynesburg, Pa.
4	Lyric	Washington, Pa.
5	Coyle	Charleroi, Pa.
7	Cambria	Johnstown, Pa.
8	Eleventh Avenue O.H.	Altoona, Pa.
9	Garman's Opera House	Bellefonte, Pa.
10	Temple Opera House	Lewistown, Pa.
11	Carlisle Opera House	Carlisle, Pa.
12	Grand Opera House	Harrisburg, Pa.
14	Fraternity	Shamokin, Pa.
15	Academy of Music	Pottsville, Pa.
16	Shenandoah	Shenandoah, Pa.
17	Minersville O.H.	Minersville, Pa.
18	Fulton Opera House	Lancaster, Pa.
19	Hanover Opera House	Hanover, Pa.
21	City Opera House	Frederick, Md.
22	Academy of Music	Hagerstown, Md.
23	Rosedale Opera House	Chambersburg, Pa.
24	York Opera House	York, Pa.
25		
26	Grand Opera House	Norristown, Pa.
March 28–April 2	(Holy Week Lay-Off)	
April 4		
5		
6	Red Bank Opera House	Red Bank, N.J.
7–9	Bijou	Reading, Pa.
11		
12	Mauch Chunk O.H.	Mauch Chunk, Pa.
13		
14		
15		
16		
18–23	Dunn's Star	Philadelphia, Pa.
25–30	Unique	Brooklyn, N.Y.
2	Taylor Opera House	Danbury, Conn.
3–4	McDonough	Middletown, Conn.
5	Loomer Opera House	Willimantic, Conn.
6–7	New London O.H.	New London, Conn.
9		
10	Bristol Opera House	Bristol, Conn.
11	Alhambra	Torrington, Conn.
12–14	Park	Worcester, Mass.
May 16–June 4	Theatre Royal	Montreal, Que.

Dixon and Bernstein's Turkey Burlesque Show
No Available Data

Vaudeville

1904	Aug. 8–13	Berkshire Park	Pittsfield, Mass.
	Sept. 1–3	Morrison's	Rockaway, N.Y.
	5–10	Henderson's	Coney Island, N.Y.

JOLSON, PALMER AND JOLSON
Vaudeville

1904	Oct. 31–Nov. 5	Keeney's	Brooklyn, N.Y.
	Nov. 7–12		
	14–19		
	21–26		
	Nov. 28–Dec. 3	Keith's	Philadelphia, Pa.
	Dec. 5–10		
	12–17		
	19–24		
	26–31	Poli's	Bridgeport, Conn.
1905	Jan. 2–7	Hathaway's	New Bedford, Mass.
	9–14		
	16–21	Orpheum	Utica, N.Y.
	23–28	Poli's	Hartford, Conn.
	Jan. 30–Feb. 4	Poli's	Springfield, Mass.
	Feb. 6–11	Colonial	Lawrence, Mass.
	13–18	Poli's	New Haven, Conn.
	20–25		
	Feb. 27–March 4		
	March 6–11		
	13–18		
	20–25		
	March 27–April 1		
	April 3–8	Trent	Trenton, N.J.
	10–15		
	17–22		
	24–29		
	May 1–6		
	8–13	Proctor's 58th St.	New York, N.Y.
	15–20		
	22–27	Proctor's 23rd St.	New York, N.Y.
	May 29–June 3		
	June 5–10	Proctor's 125th St.	New York, N.Y.
	12–17		
	19–24		
	June 26–July 1		
	July 3–8		
	10–15		
	17–22		
	24–29		

| July 31–Aug. 5 | Spring Grove Park | Springfield, Ohio |

General Western Vaudeville Circuit

1905	Aug. 14–19	Olympic	Chicago, Ill.
	21–26	(Travel)	
	Aug. 28–Sept. 2	Orpheum	Minneapolis, Minn.
	Sept. 4–9	Orpheum	Denver, Colo.
	11–16	(Travel)	
	17–30	Orpheum	San Francisco, Calif.
	Oct. 2–14	Orpheum	Los Angeles, Calif.
	16–21	(Travel)	
	23–28	Orpheum	Omaha, Neb.
	Oct. 30–Nov. 4	Orpheum	Kansas City, Mo.
	Nov. 5–11	Orpheum	New Orleans, La.
	13–18	(Travel)	
	20–25	Columbia	*Indianapolis, Ind.
	Nov. 27–Dec. 2	Columbia	*Cincinnati, Ohio
	Dec. 4–9	Hopkins' Temple	*Louisville, Ky.
	11–16	(Travel)	
	18–23	Olympic	*Chicago, Ill.
	25–30	Columbia	*St. Louis, Mo.

* Joe Palmer and Al Jolson only

PALMER AND JOLSON
Western Vaudeville Managers' Association

1906	Jan. 8–13	Sid J. Euson's	Chicago, Ill.
	15–20	Crystal	Milwaukee, Wisc.
	22–27		
	Jan. 29–Feb. 3		
	Feb. 5–10	Bijou	Dubuque, Iowa
	12–17	People's	Cedar Rapids, Iowa
	19–24	Garrick	Burlington, Iowa
	Feb. 26–March 3	Lyric	Terre Haute, Ind.
	March 5–10	Grand Opera House	Marion, Ind.
	12–17		
	19–24	Bijou	Evansville, Ind.
	26–31	Bijou	Decatur, Ill.
	April 2–7	Majestic	Chicago, Ill.
	9–14	Masonic Temple	Fort Wayne, Ind.
	16–21	Crystal	*Detroit, Mich.
	23–28	Haymarket	Chicago, Ill.
	April 30–May 5	Bijou	**Lansing, Mich.

* Independent house; performed as "Meyer and Johnson"
** Independent house; Al Jolson only

William Morris

| 1906 | May 6–12 | Arcade | Toledo, Ohio |
| | 13–19 | Chester Park | Cincinnati, Ohio |

20–26	Cook's Park	Evansville, Ind.
May 27–June 2	Mannion's Park	St. Louis, Mo.

AL JOLSON
Vaudeville

1906	June 4–9	Crystal	Detroit, Mich.
	11–16	Bijou	Lansing, Mich.

Sullivan & Considine Circuit

1906	June 23–29	Family	Butte, Mont.
	July 1–7	Washington	Spokane, Wash.
	9–15	Star	Seattle, Wash.
	16–21	Grand Opera House	Victoria, B.C.
	23–28	Orpheum	Vancouver, B.C.
	July 30–Aug. 4	Grand Opera House	Bellingham, Wash.
	Aug. 6–8	Everett	Everett, Wash.
	9	Alcazar Opera House	Snohomish, Wash.
	10–11	Everett	Everett, Wash.
	13–18	Orpheum	Seattle, Wash.
	20–25		
	Aug. 27–Sept. 1	Grand Opera House	Tacoma, Wash.
	Sept. 3–9	Grand Opera House	Portland, Ore.
	10–15		
	17–22		
	24–29	Novelty	Oakland, Calif.
	Oct. 1–6	National	San Francisco, Calif.
	8–27	Bell	Oakland, Calif.
	Oct. 29–Nov. 3		
	Nov. 5–10	National	San Francisco, Calif.
	12–17	Novelty	San Francisco, Calif.
	19–24	Unique	San Jose, Calif.
	Nov. 26–Dec. 1	Novelty	Stockton, Calif.
	Dec. 3–8	National	San Francisco, Calif.
	10–15		
	17–22	National	San Francisco, Calif.

Vaudeville

1907	Jan. 21–Feb. 3	Chutes	San Francisco, Calif.
	Feb. 4–16	Wigwam	San Francisco, Calif.
	Feb. 18–March 3	Franklin	El Paso, Texas

Sullivan & Considine Circuit

1907	April 1–6	Bijou	Lincoln, Neb.
	8–13	Empire	Des Moines, Iowa
	15–20	Elite	Davenport, Iowa
	22–27	Bijou	La Crosse, Wisc.
	April 29–May 4	Unique	Eau Claire, Wisc.
	May 6–11	Unique	Minneapolis, Minn.
	13–18	Grand Opera House	Fargo, N.D.

20–25	Bijou	Winnipeg, Man.
May 27–June 1	Bijou	Duluth, Minn.
June 3–8	Bijou	Superior, Wisc.
9–14	(Travel)	
15–21	Family	Butte, Mont.
23–29	Washington	Spokane, Wash.
July 1–7	Star	Seattle, Wash.
9–14	Grand Opera House	Bellingham, Wash.
15–20	Orpheum	Vancouver, B.C.
July 22–Aug. 10	(Lay-Off; illness)	
Aug. 12–17	Grand Opera House	Victoria, B.C.
19–24	Grand Opera House	Vancouver, B.C.
26–31	Grand Opera House	Tacoma, Wash.
Sept. 2–14	Grand Opera House	Portland, Ore.
16–21	(Travel)	
23–28	Acme	Sacramento, Calif.
Sept. 30–Oct. 5	National	San Francisco, Calif.
Oct. 7–12	Bell	Oakland, Calif.

Western States Vaudeville Association

1907 Oct. 14–19	Empire	San Francisco, Calif.
Oct. 21–Nov. 2	Wigwam	San Francisco, Calif.

Sullivan & Considine Circuit

1907 Nov. 4–9	National	San Francisco, Calif.

Walter Sanford's Players (Stock Co., Globe Theatre, San Francisco)

1907 Nov. 11–16	*Behind The Mask*
18–23	*His Terrible Secret*
25–30	*The Great Wall Street Mystery*
Dec. 2–7	*On The Bridge At Midnight*
9–14	*The Factory Girl*

Sullivan & Considine Circuit

1907 Dec. 16–21	Bell	Oakland, Calif.

Alpha Circuit

Dec. 23–Jan. 4, 1908	Victory	San Francisco, Calif.

Sullivan & Considine Circuit

1908 Jan. 14–20	People's	Los Angeles, Calif.
23–29	Majestic	Denver, Colo.

Interstate Circuit

1908 Feb. 24–29	Grand Opera House	Nashville, Tenn.
March 2–7	Staub's	Knoxville, Tenn.
9–14	Shubert	Chattanooga, Tenn.
16–21	Majestic	Montgomery, Ala.
23–28	Lyric	Mobile, Ala.
March 30–April 4	Majestic	Birmingham, Ala.

April 6–11	Majestic	Little Rock, Ark.
13–18	Majestic	Fort Worth, Texas
19–25	Majestic	Dallas, Texas
April 27–May 2	Majestic	Houston, Texas

LEW DOCKSTADER'S MINSTRELS

1908 Aug. 10	Plainfield	Plainfield, N.J.
11	Bijou	Perth Amboy, N.J.
12	Lyceum	Red Bank, N.J.
13–15	Casino	Asbury Park, N.J.
17–22	Savoy	Atlantic City, N.J.
24	Collingwood O.H.	Poughkeepsie, N.Y.
25	Rand's Opera House	Troy, N.Y.
26	Van Curler Opera House	Schenectady, N.Y.
27	Majestic	Utica, N.Y.
28–29	Wieting Opera House	Syracuse, N.Y.
31	Burtis Auditorium	Auburn, N.Y.
Sept. 1–2	Lyceum	Rochester, N.Y.
3–5	Star	Buffalo, N.Y.
6–12	Euclid Ave. Opera House	Cleveland, Ohio
14–19	Nixon	Pittsburgh, Pa.
21	Majestic	Erie, Pa.
22	Grand Opera House	Sharon, Pa.
23	Park	Youngstown, Ohio
24	New Castle Opera House	New Castle, Pa.
25	Elyria	Elyria, Ohio
26	Valentine	Toledo, Ohio
Sept. 28–Oct. 3	Lyceum	Detroit, Mich.
Oct. 4–10	McVicker's	Chicago, Ill.
11	Burtis Opera House	Davenport, Iowa
12	Grand Opera House	Burlington, Iowa
13	Greene Opera House	Cedar Rapids, Iowa
14	Grand Opera House	Sioux City, Iowa
15	Boyd	Omaha, Neb.
16	Oliver	Lincoln, Neb.
17	Tootle	St. Joseph, Mo.
18–24	Grand Opera House	Kansas City, Mo.
25–31	Century	St. Louis, Mo.
Nov. 1	Temple	Alton, Ill.
2	Chatterton Opera House	Springfield, Ill.
3	Grand Opera House	Peoria, Ill.
4	Grand Opera House	Bloomington, Ill.
5	Grand Opera House	Terre Haute, Ind.
6–7	English's Opera House	Indianapolis, Ind.
8–14	Lyric	Cincinnati, Ohio
15	Smith's Opera House	Hamilton, Ohio
16	Victoria	Dayton, Ohio
17	Fairbanks	Springfield, Ohio
18	Southern	Columbus, Ohio

	19	Court	Wheeling, W. Va.
	20	Cambria	Johnstown, Pa.
	21	Academy of Music	Hagerstown, Md.
	23–28	Ford's Opera House	Baltimore, Md.
Nov.	30–Dec. 5	National	Washington, D.C.
Dec.	7	York Opera House	York, Pa.
	8	Majestic	Harrisburg, Pa.
	9	Taylor Opera House	Trenton, N.J.
	10	Able Opera House	Easton, Pa.
	11	Nesbitt	Wilkes-Barre, Pa.
	12	Lyceum	Scranton, Pa.
	14	Lyceum	Elmira, N.Y.
	15	Harmanus Bleecker Hall	Albany, N.Y.
	16	Colonial	Pittsfield, Mass.
	17	Holyoke Opera House	Holyoke, Mass.
	18–24	(Christmas Lay-Off)	
	25–26	Court Square	Springfield, Mass.
	28	Poli's	Waterbury, Conn.
	29	Smith's Opera House	Bridgeport, Conn.
	30	Hyperion	New Haven. Conn.
	31	Poli's	Meriden, Conn.
1909	Jan. 1–2	Parsons'	Hartford, Conn.
	4–23	Globe	Boston, Mass.
	25	Bangor Opera House	Bangor, Maine
	26	Empire	Lewiston, Maine
	27	Jefferson	Portland, Maine
	28	Portsmouth	Portsmouth, N.H.
	29	Empire	Salem, Mass.
	30	Lawrence Opera House	Lawrence, Mass.
Feb.	1	Lowell Opera House	Lowell, Mass.
	2	Academy of Music	Havershill, Mass.
	3	City	Brockton, Mass.
	4	Academy of Music	Fall River, Mass.
	5	Cumings	Fitchburg, Mass.
	6	Worcester	Worcester, Mass.
	8–13	Majestic	Brooklyn, N.Y.
	15–20	Grand Opera House	Philadelphia, Pa.
	22–27	Grand Opera House	New York, N.Y.
March	1	Paterson Opera House	Paterson, N.J.
	2	New Brunswick O.H.	New Brunswick, N.J.
	3	Grand Opera House	Wilmington, Del.
	4	Academy of Music	Richmond, Va.
	5	Academy of Music	Newport News, Va.
	6	Academy of Music	Norfolk, Va.
	8	Academy of Music	Raleigh, N.C.
	9	Academy of Music	Charlotte, N.C.
	10	Auditorium	Asheville, N.C.
	11	Staub's	Knoxville, Tenn.
	12	Vendome	Nashville, Tenn.
	13	Shubert	Chattanooga, Tenn.
	15	Jefferson	Birmingham, Ala.

16–17	Grand Opera House	Atlanta, Ga.
18	Grand Opera House	Augusta, Ga.
19	Columbia	Columbia, S.C.
20	Academy of Music	Charleston, S.C.
22	New Savannah	Savannah, Ga.
23	Grand Opera House	Brunswick, Ga.
24	Airdome	Jacksonville, Fla.
25	Grand Opera House	Macon, Ga.
26	Grand Opera House	Montgomery, Ala.
27	Mobile	Mobile, Ala.
March 28–April 3	Crescent	New Orleans, La.

I. P. WILKERSON'S "MINSTRELS OF TODAY"

1909	April 25–May 9	American	San Francisco, Calif.

LEW DOCKSTADER'S MINSTRELS

1909	May 23–29	Grand Opera House	Kansas City, Mo.
	30–31	Century	St. Louis, Mo.
	June 1	Grand Opera House	Decatur, Ill.
	2	Grand Opera House	Danville, Ill.
	3	Nelson	Logansport, Ind.
	4	Majestic	Fort Wayne, Ind.
	5	Academy of Music	Kalamazoo, Mich.
	7–12	Powers'	Grand Rapids, Mich.
	14	Baird's Opera House	Lansing, Mich.
	15	Post	Battle Creek, Mich.
	16	Athenaeum	Jackson, Mich.
	17	Majestic	Port Huron, Mich.
	18	Grand Opera House	London, Ont.
	19	Grand Opera House	Brantford, Ont.
	21–23	Princess	Toronto, Ont.
	24	Grand Opera House	Hamilton, Ont.
	25	Grand Opera House	St. Catharines, Ont.
	26	International	Niagara Falls, N.Y.
	28	Lyric	Rome, N.Y.
	29	Darling	Gloversville, N.Y.
	30	Colonial	Peekskill, N.Y.
	July 1	Warburton	Yonkers, N.Y.
	2–3	Casino	Asbury Park, N.J.
	4	Madeline	Sea Isle City, N.J.
	5–10	Nixon's Apollo	Atlantic City, N.J.

AL JOLSON
UBO Vaudeville

1909	July 19–24	Fifth Avenue	New York, N.Y.
	July 26–Aug. 7	New Brighton	Brooklyn, N.Y.
	Aug. 9–14	Keith's	Philadelphia, Pa.

LEW DOCKSTADER'S MINSTRELS

1909	Aug. 24	Stone Opera House	Binghamton, N.Y.
	25		
	26–28	Teck	Buffalo, N.Y.
	Aug. 29–Sept. 4	Colonial	Cleveland, Ohio
	Sept. 6–11	Alvin	Pittsburgh, Pa.
	12–18	Lyric	Cincinnati, Ohio
	19–25	Garrick	St. Louis, Mo.
	Sept. 26–Oct. 2	Garrick	Chicago, Ill.
	Oct. 3–6	Lyric	Minneapolis, Minn.
	7–9	Burwood	Omaha, Neb.
	10–16	Sam S. Shubert	Kansas City, Mo.
	17–18	Tootle	St. Joseph, Mo.
	20	Burtis Opera House	Davenport, Iowa
	21	Galesburg Auditorium	Galesburg, Ill.
	22	Grand Opera House	Peoria, Ill.
	23–24	Chatterton Opera House	Springfield, Ill.
	25	Urbana Opera House	Urbana, Ill.
	26	Grand Opera House	Danville, Ill.
	27	Joliet	Joliet, Ill.
	28	Elgin Opera House	Elgin, Ill.
	29	Grand Opera House	Rockford, Ill.
	30	Racine	Racine, Wisc.
	Oct. 31–Nov. 6	Alhambra	Milwaukee, Wisc.
	Nov. 8–10	Masonic Auditorium	Louisville, Ky.
	11	Frankfort Opera House	Frankfort, Ky.
	12		
	13	Auditorium	Lexington, Ky.
	15–16	Colonial	Columbus, Ohio
	17	Colonial	Cambridge, Ohio
	18	Virginia	Wheeling, W. Va.
	19	Union Opera House	New Phila., Ohio
	20		
	22–24	National	Rochester, N.Y.
	25	Burtis Auditorium	Auburn, N.Y.
	26	Van Curler Opera House	Schenectady, N.Y.
	27	Harmanus Bleecker Hall	Albany, N.Y.
	Nov. 29–Dec. 1	Providence Opera House	Providence, R.I.
	Dec. 2–4	Hartford	Hartford, Conn.
	6–11	Auditorium	Baltimore, Md.
	13–18	Belasco	Washington, D.C.

AL JOLSON
UBO Vaudeville

Dec. 27–Jan. 1, 1910		Colonial	New York, N.Y.
1910	Jan. 3–8	Orpheum	Brooklyn, N.Y.
	10–15	Alhambra	New York, N.Y.

17–22	Hammerstein's Victoria	New York, N.Y.
24–29	Hammerstein's Victoria	New York, N.Y.
	Bronx	Bronx, N.Y.
Jan. 31–Feb. 5	Greenpoint	Brooklyn, N.Y.
Feb. 7–12	(Lay-Off)	
14–19	Keith's	Boston, Mass.
21–26	Keith's	Providence, R.I.
Feb. 28–Mar. 5	Fifth Avenue	New York, N.Y.
March 7–12	Shea's	Buffalo, N.Y.
14–19	Shea's	Toronto, Ont.
21–26	Orpheum	Montreal, Que.
March 28–April 2	Hammerstein's Victoria	New York, N.Y.
April 4–9	Trent	Trenton, N.J.
11–16	Chase's	Washington, D.C.
18–23	Maryland	Baltimore, Md.
April 25–May 7	Keith's	Philadelphia, Pa.
May 9–14	Colonial	New York, N.Y.
16–21	Orpheum	Brooklyn, N.Y.
23–28	Hammerstein's Victoria	New York, N.Y.
	Bronx	Bronx, N.Y.

Orpheum Circuit

1910 July 24–30	Orpheum	Spokane, Wash.
July 31–Aug. 6	Orpheum	Seattle, Wash.
Aug. 8–13	Orpheum	Portland, Ore.
14–20	(Travel)	
Aug. 21–Sept. 3	Orpheum	San Francisco, Calif.
Sept. 4–17	Orpheum	Oakland, Calif.
Sept. 19–Oct. 2	Orpheum	Los Angeles, Calif.
Oct. 3–5	Garrick	San Diego, Calif.
6–8	(Travel)	
9–15	Orpheum	Ogden, Utah
16–22	Orpheum	Salt Lake City, Utah
24–29	Orpheum	Denver, Colo.
Oct. 30–Nov. 5	(Travel)	
Nov. 6–12	Orpheum	Duluth, Minn.
13–19	Orpheum	Minneapolis, Minn.
13–19	Orpheum	Minneapolis, Minn.
20–26	Orpheum	St. Paul, Minn.
Nov. 27–Dec. 3	Orpheum	Des Moines, Iowa
Dec. 4–10	Orpheum	Kansas City, Mo.
11–17	Orpheum	Omaha, Neb.
19–24	Majestic	Milwaukee, Wisc.
26–31	Majestic	Chicago, Ill.
1911 Jan. 2–7	Grand Opera House	Indianapolis, Ind.
9–14	Mary Anderson	Louisville, Ky.

UBO Vaudeville

1911 Feb. 20–25	Hammerstein's Victoria	New York, N.Y.

LA BELLE PAREE

A Jumble of Jollity in two acts and eleven scenes. Book by Edgar Smith. Lyrics by Edward Madden. Music by Jerome Kern. Staged by J. C. Huffman and William J. Wilson.

Cast

George Ramsbotham	HARRY FISHER
Ezema Johnson	STELLA MAYHEW
La Duchesse	DOROTHY JARDON
Fifi Montmarte	MITZI HAJOS
La Sylphide	MLLE. DAZIE
Henri Dauber	EDGAR ATCHISON-ELY
Lady Guff Jordan	KITTY GORDON
Jack Ralston	PAUL NICHOLSON
Isadore Cohen	BARNEY BERNARD
Ike Skinheimer	LEE HARRISON
Toots Horner	FLORENCE TEMPEST
Susie Jenkins	MARION SUNSHINE
Susan Brown	MISS RAY COX
A Violinist	YVETTE
Bridgeeta McShane	ARTHUR CUNNINGHAM
Erastus Sparkler	AL JOLSON
Russian Dancers	HESS SISTERS
The Marquis de Champignon	HAROLD A. ROBE
Madame Clarice	JEAN AYLWIN
Mimi	GRACE STUDDIFORD
Fifine, a model	VIOLET BOWERS
Margot, a model	BESSIE FREWEN
Marcelle, a model	GRACE WASHBURN
Fifine	KATHERINE MCDONALD
Juliette	MAY ALLEN
A flower girl	SYLVIA CLARK
A Grisette	IDA KRAMER
Buck Lyons	RAY DODGE
A "Cook" Guide	LEW GUINN
A Cocher	MILBERRY RYDER

Ray Cox left the cast on March 25. Melissa Ten Eyck replaced Jean Aylwin on April 10. Doris Cameron replaced Melissa Ten Eyck on May 1. George White replaced Ray Dodge on April 17. Mitzi Hajos left the cast on April 15. Edgar Atchison-Ely and Lee Harrison left the cast on April 29. Kitty Gordon left the cast on May 27. Elsie Schumann played Fifine and Beatrice played Marcelle on tour.

Score

"I'm the Human Brush"
* "Paris Is a Paradise for Coons"
"Pretty Little Milliners"
"The Edinboro Wriggle"

"Sing Trovatore"
"The Goblins' Glide"

Jolson's Songs

"That Lovin' Traumerei" (Aubrey Stauffer)

March 20–June 10, 1911	Winter Garden	New York, N.Y.

AL JOLSON
Orpheum Circuit

1911 July 9–15	Orpheum	San Francisco, Calif.
July 16–30	(Lay-Off)	
July 31–Aug. 6	Orpheum	Los Angeles, Calif.

LA BELLE PAREE

Jolson's Songs

"Dat Lovin' Touch" (Leo Bennett-Sam M. Lewis)

1911 Sept. 11–16	Winter Garden	New York, N.Y.
18–23	Sam S. Shubert	Brooklyn, N.Y.
Sept. 25–Oct. 14	Sam S. Shubert	Boston, Mass.
Oct. 16–21	Providence Opera House	Providence, R.I.
Oct. 23–Nov. 4	Lyric	Philadelphia, Pa.

VERA VIOLETTA

A Musical Entertainment in two scenes. Book by Leonard Liebling and Harold Atteridge, adapted from the German of Leo Stein. Lyrics by Harold Atteridge. Music by Edmund Eysler. Staged by Lewis Morton, William J. Wilson, and Joseph C. Smith.

Cast

Manager of Skating Rink	EDWARD CUTLER
Claude, a waiter	AL JOLSON
Margot	DORIS CAMERON
Aristide de St. Cloche	VAN RENSSELAER WHEELER
Pierre, a waiter	ERNEST HARE
Prof. Otto von Gruenberg	JAMES B. CARSON
Mlle. Angelique	MAE WEST
Morris Cohen	BARNEY BERNARD
A Rounder	BILLEE TAYLOR
La Duchesse	FLORENCE DOUGLAS
Mme. von Gruenberg	JOSE COLLINS
Paul Voissen	MELVILLE ELLIS
Mme. Adelle de. St. Cloche	GABY DESLYS
Mme. Elise	STELLA MAYHEW

Andrew Mason	HARRY PILCER
M. Berton	HARRY FISCHER
Marquis de Tivoli	CLARENCE HARVEY
Ninon	MAIDIE BERKER
Lulu	FLORENCE DOUGLAS
Susanne	JANE LAURENCE
Count de Mokins	LEW QUINN
Signor de Skate	MEL RYDER

Kathleen Clifford replaced Mae West prior to the Broadway opening.

Score

"Paree, Gay Paree"
"Olga from the Volga"
"Vera Violetta"
"Come Back to Me"
"My Lou"
"I Wonder If It's True"

Jolson's Songs

"Rum Tum Tiddle" (Jean Schwartz-Edward Madden)
"That Haunting Melody" (George M. Cohan)

1911	Nov. 13–15	Harmanus Bleecker Hall	Albany, N.Y.
	16	Court Square	Springfield, Mass.
	17–18	Hyperion	New Haven, Conn.
Nov. 20–Feb. 29, 1912		Winter Garden	New York, N.Y.

THE WHIRL OF SOCIETY, preceded by A NIGHT WITH THE PIERROTS
A NIGHT WITH THE PIERROTS
Prologue

Cast

The Humpback	AL JOLSON
Sumurun	STELLA MAYHEW

Cast

Interlocutor	BILLEE TAYLOR
Bones	AL JOLSON
Tambo	BARNEY BERNARD

Stella Mayhew, Jose Collins, Blossom Seeley, Kathleen Clifford, Mildred Elaine, George White, Melissa Tan Eyck, Laura Hamilton, Courtney Sisters, Doris Cameron, Clarence Harvey, Ernest Hare, Edward Cutler, Cecil Ryan, Barney Thornton, Harry Wardell, Martin Brown, Florence Cable.

Kathleen Clifford left the cast on March 9. Blossom Seeley left the cast on March 16. Willie Weston replaced Barney Bernard on April 1. Willie and Eugene Howard joined the cast on April 8. Irene Claire joined the cast on May 6. George White and Melissa Ten Eyck left the cast on May 13, the same date that James Davis and Laura Hamilton joined it. Eugene Howard replace Billee

Taylor on May 27. Ernest Hare replaced Eugene Howard on June 17. Violet Colby joined the cast on June 24.

Jolson's songs:

"My Sumurun Girl" [prologue]
"The Villain Still Pursued Her"

THE WHIRL OF SOCIETY

A musical satire of up-to-date society. Book by Harrison Rhodes. Lyrics by Harold Atteridge. Music by Louis A. Hirsch. Staged by J. C. Huffman. Musical numbers staged by William J. Wilson.

Cast

Mrs. Dean	STELLA MAYHEW
Mr. Dean	CLARENCE HARVEY
Angela, their daughter	JOSE COLLINS
Gus, their butler	AL JOLSON
Archduke Frederich	LAWRENCE D'ORSAY
Archduchess	MILDRED ELAINE
Harry Courtfield	MELVILLE ELLIS
Franklyn Copeland	MARTIN BROWN
Mrs. Vandercrief	DORIS CAMERON
Mrs. Tatters	FLORENCE CABLE
Mlle. Eclatante	DOLLE DALNERT
Baron de Shine	BARNEY BERNARD

Score

"Hard Luck in Society"
"Which Shall I Choose?"
"Cinderella Waltz"

Jolson's Songs

"Snap Your Fingers"
"Row, Row, Row"
"Waiting for the Robert E. Lee"

1912	March 1–2	Harmanus Bleecker Hall	Albany, N.Y.
	March 5–June 29	Winter Garden	New York, N.Y.

Cast

Miss Vandercrief	FLORENCE CABLE
Mrs. Thatcher-Raypen	CLAUDIA CARLSTEDT
Sadie, a maid	FANNY BRICE
Mrs. J. Hemmingway Deane	ADA LEWIS
Angela Deane	LAURA HAMILTON
Gus, a butler at Deane's	AL JOLSON
Baron von Shine	WILLIE WESTON
Franklyn Copeland	OSCAR SCHWARTZ
J. Hemmingway Deane	CLARENCE HARVEY
A footman	HENRY DETTLOFF

Harry Courtfield	MELVILLE ELLIS
Earl of Pawtucket	LAWRENCE D'ORSAY
Countess of Pawtucket	BESSIE FREWEN
FLORENCE & FAY COURTNEY	
FLORENCE WALTON & MAURICE	

1912	Sept. 1–28	Lyric	Chicago, Ill.
	Sept. 29–Oct. 5	Sam S. Shubert	Kansas City, Mo.
	Oct. 6–12	Sam S. Shubert	St. Louis, Mo.
	13–19	Lyric	Cincinnati, Ohio
	21	Lexington Opera House	Lexington, Ky.
	22–23	Masonic Temple	Louisville, Ky.
	24–26	Murat	Indianapolis, Ind.
	Oct. 28–Nov. 2	Garrick	Detroit, Mich.
	Nov. 4–9	Colonial	Cleveland, Ohio
	11–16	Alvin	Pittsburgh, Pa.
	18–20	Auditorium	Baltimore, Md.
	21–23	Belasco	Washington, D.C.
	Nov. 25–Dec. 28	Lyric	Philadelphia, Pa.
	Dec. 30–Jan. 4, 1913	Princess	Montreal, Que.
1913	Jan. 6–11	Royal Alexandra	Toronto, Ont.
	13–15	Teck	Buffalo, N.Y.
	16	Majestic	Utica, N.Y.
	17	Van Curler Opera House	Schenectady, N.Y.
	18	Harmanus Bleecker Hall	Albany, N.Y.
	20–25	Majestic	Brooklyn, N.Y.

THE HONEYMOON EXPRESS

A Spectacular Farce with Music in two acts and six scenes. Book by Joseph W. Herbert. Lyrics by Harold Atteridge. Music by Jean Schwartz. Staged by Ned Wayburn.

Cast

Henri Dubonet	ERNEST GLENDINNING
Pierre, his friend	HARRY FOX
Baudry, a lawyer	HARRY PILCER
Gardonne, hotel keeper at Arignon	LOU ANGER
Gus, butler at Dubonet's	AL JOLSON
Doctor D'Zuvray	MELVILLE ELLIS
Achille	FRANK HOLMES
Eduard	ROBERT HASTINGS
Gautier	GERALD MCDONALD
Constant	JACK CARLETON
Paul	HENRY DYER
Guillaume	CLINT RUSSELL
Felix, a gateman	HARRY WARDELL
Alfonse	HARLAND DIXON
Gaston	JAMES DOYLE
Maurice, a poster painter	F. OWEN BAXTER

Yvonne, wife of Henri	GABY DESLYS
Mme. De Bressie, Yvonne's aunt	ADA LEWIS
Marguerite, Gardonne's daughter	YANSCI DOLLY
Marcelle, a domestic	FANNY BRICE
Marcus, a waiter	GILBERT WILSON
Noelie, a maid	MARJORIE LANE

Score

"That Is the Life for Me"
"When The Honeymoon Stops Shining"
"Syncopatia Land"
"You'll Call the Next Love the First"
"I Want the Strolling Good"
"The Ragtime Express"
* "That Gal of Mine"
* "Give Me the Hudson Shore"
"My Cocoa-Cola Belle"
"You Are the Someone"
"I Want a Toy Soldier Man"
"Our Little Cabaret Up Home"
"Bring Back Your Love"
"My Raggyadore"
* "My Yellow Jacket Girl"
"When Gaby Did the Gaby Glide"

Jolson's Songs

"The Spaniard That Blighted My Life" (Merson)

1913	Feb. 3–4	Hyperion	New Haven, Conn.
	Feb. 6–June 14	Winter Garden	New York, N.Y.

Major cast changes resulted in a "second edition" of *The Honeymoon Express* on April 28, 1913. Grace LaRue replaced Gaby Deslys, Ina Claire replaced Fanny Brice, and Charles King replaced Harry Pilcer. "Where the Red, Red Roses Grow" was added to the score. Jolson's songs for this second edition included "You Made Me Love You," "Good-Bye, Boys," "I Love Her (Oh! Oh! Oh!)," and "Down where the Tennesee Flows."

Juliette Dika played Yvonne on tour until March 2, 1914, when she was replaced by Marie Robson. Rae Samuels played Marcelle until February 1, 1914, when she was replaced by Marie Fenton. Earl Benham played Baudry until February 1, 1914, when he was replaced by Harry Wilcox. Donald MacDonald and Anna Wheaton played the roles of Pierre and Marguerite throughout the tour.

Jolson's songs:

"He'd Have To Get Under—Get Out and Get Under"
"I'm on My Way to Mandalay"
"Who Paid the Rent for Mrs. Rip Van Winkle?"
"While They Were Dancing Around"

1913	Sept. 18–20	Nixon's Apollo	Atlantic City, N.J.
	Sept. 22–Oct. 11	Lyric	Philadelphia, Pa.
	Oct. 13–18	Majestic	Brooklyn, N.Y.
	20–25	Belasco	Washington, D.C.
	27–28	Hyperion	New Haven, Conn.
	29	Court Square	Springfield, Mass.
	Oct. 30–Nov. 1	Providence Opera House	Providence, R.I.
	Nov. 3–29	Sam S. Shubert	Boston, Mass.
	Dec. 1–6	Princess	Montreal, Que.
	8–13	Royal Alexandra	Toronto, Ont.
	15–20	Teck	Buffalo, N.Y.
	22–27	Alvin	Pittsburgh, Pa.
	Dec. 29, Jan. 3, 1914	Garrick	Detroit, Mich.
1914	Jan. 4–31	Garrick	Chicago, Ill.
	Feb. 1–14	Sam S. Shubert	Kansas City, Mo.
	15–21	Sam S. Shubert	St. Louis, Mo.
	23–24	Murat	Indianapolis, Ind.
	25–26	Southern	Columbus, Ohio
	27–28	Valentine	Toledo, Ohio
	March 2–7	Colonial	Cleveland, Ohio
	8–14	Auditorium	Chicago, Ill.
	15–18	Davidson	Milwaukee, Wisc.
	19–21	(Lay-Off)	
	22–25	Broadway	Denver, Colo.
	26		
	27–28	Salt Lake	Salt Lake City, Utah
	March 30–April 5	Hamburger's Majestic	Los Angeles, Calif.
	April 6–11	(Holy Week Lay-Off)	
	12–25	Cort	San Francisco, Calif.
	26–30	MacDonough	Oakland, Calif.
	May 1	Clunie	Sacramento, Calif.
	2		
	3–9	Heilig	Portland, Oregon
	10–16	Moore	Seattle, Wash.
	18	Royal Victoria	Victoria, B.C.
	19	Tacoma	Tacoma, Wash.
	20–21	Auditorium	Spokane, Wash.
	22	Broadway	Butte, Mont.
	23		
	24–30	Metropolitan	Minneapolis, Minn.

DANCING AROUND

A musical spectacle in 12 scenes. Book and lyrics by Harold Atteridge. Music by Sigmund Romberg and Harry Carroll. Staged by J. C. Huffman. Dances by Jack Mason.

Cast

Lieutenant Larry	JAMES DOYLE
Lieutenant Tommy	HARLAND DIXON
Lieutenant Hartley	BERNARD GRANVILLE

Clarice	AIMEE DALMORES
Shirley	ELEANOR BROWN
Dora	OLGA HEMPSTONE
Pinky Roberts	KITTY DONER
Lt. Harry Graham	FRANK CARTER
Annette Truesdale	LUCY WESTON
Lieutenant Robert	EARL FOX
Tillie, a telephone operator	GEORGIE O'RAMEY
Clarence	CLIFTON WEBB
Gus, a man of many parts	AL JOLSON
Mlle. Mitzi, of the Frivolity	MARY ROBSON
Ethel	EILEEN MOLYNEUX
Beulah Elliot, prima donna	CECIL CUNNINGHAM
Lord Graham	FRED LESLIE
Fireman	PHIL BRANSON
Train Announcer	HAROLD ROBE
John Elliot	MELVILLE ELLIS
Messenger Boy	MABEL HILL
Patricia	MILDRED MANNING
Lucy	MAY DEALY
Butler	PHIL BRANSON
Miss Thames	EFFIE GRAHAM
Maid	GEORGIE O'RAMEY
Miss Gerard	KATHERINE HILL
Miss Social Leader	LUCY WESTON
Monsieur Jean	AL JOLSON

Many cast changes were made en tour. The parts played by Doyle & Dixon were dropped. Frank Carter replaced Bernard Granville. Harry Clarke took over Carter's role. Frank Holmes replaced Melville Ellis. The parts played by Mary Robson and Cecil Cunningham were combined into one and played by Zella Call. Lucy Weston's part was played by Wanda Lyon. Edith Day made her professional debut, replacing Eileen Molyneaux as Ethel in September 1915.

Score

"Never Trust a Soldier Man"
"When an Englishman Marries a Parisian"
"My Rainbow Beau"
"The Call of the Colors"
* "Venetia"
"By the Grand Canal"

Jolson's Songs

"I Want To Be in Norfolk"
"I'm Seeking for Siegfried"
"The Shuffling Shiveree"
"When the Grown Up Ladies Act Like Babies"
"Sister Susie's Sewing Shirts for Soldiers"
"Everybody Rag with Me"
"When I Leave the World Behind" [Chicago run]
"Bring Along Your Dancing Shoes"

1914	Sept. 28–Oct. 3	Hyperion	New Haven, Conn.
	Oct. 10, Feb. 13, 1915	Winter Garden	New York, N.Y.
1915	Feb. 15–March 6	Lyric	Philadelphia, Pa.
	March 8–20	Sam S. Shubert	Boston, Mass.
	22–27	Alvin	Pittsburgh, Pa.
	March 29–Apr. 3	Teck	Buffalo, N.Y.
	April 5–10	Colonial	Cleveland, Ohio
	12–17	Garrick	Detroit, Mich.
	April 18–May 29	Garrick	Chicago, Ill.
	May 30–June 1	(Lay-Off)	
	June 2–6	Tabor Grand O.H.	Denver, Colo.
	7	Colo. Springs O.H.	Colorado Springs, Colo.
	8	Capitol Avenue	Cheyenne, Wyo.
	9	Orpheum	Ogden, Utah
	10–12	Salt Lake	Salt Lake City, Utah
	14–19	Morosco	Los Angeles, Calif.
	20	White	Fresno, Calif.
	June 21–July 11	Cort	San Francisco, Calif.
	Aug. 8–14	Heilig	Portland, Ore.
	15–21	Moore	Seattle, Wash.
	22	Everett	Everett, Wash.
	23–24	Tacoma	Tacoma, Wash.
	25	Yakima	Yakima, Wash.
	26	Keylor Grand	Walla Walla, Wash.
	27–29	Auditorium	Spokane, Wash.
	30	Broadway	Butte, Mont.
	Aug. 31–Sept. 1	Grand Opera House	Great Falls, Mont.
	Sept. 2	Babcock	Billings, Mont.
	3	Auditorium	Bismarck, N.D.
	4	Jamestown Opera House	Jamestown, N.D.
	5–11	Metropolitan	Minneapolis, Minn.
	12–18	Metropolitan	St. Paul, Minn.
	19–25	Davidson	Milwaukee, Wisc.
	26	Majestic	Peoria, Ill.
	27	Burtis Opera House	Davenport, Iowa
	28	Greene Opera House	Cedar Rapids, Iowa
	29	Berchel	Des Moines, Iowa
	30	Auditorium	Sioux City, Iowa
	Oct. 1–2	Boyd	Omaha, Neb.
	3–9	Sam S. Shubert	Kansas City, Mo.
	10–16	Sam S. Shubert	St. Louis, Mo.
	17–23	Lyric	Cincinnati, Ohio
	24	Grand Opera House	Terre Haute, Ind.
	25–27	Murat	Indianapolis, Ind.
	28–30	Macauley's	Louisville, Ky.
	Nov. 1	Lexington Opera House	Lexington, Ky.
	2	Victoria	Dayton, Ohio
	3–4	Southern	Columbus, Ohio
	5–6	Valentine	Toledo, Ohio
	8–13	Royal Alexandra	Toronto, Ont.

15	Wieting Opera House	Syracuse, N.Y.
16–17	Harmanus Bleecker Hall	Albany, N.Y.
19–20	Parsons'	Hartford, Conn.
22–27	Academy of Music	Baltimore, Md.
Nov. 29–Dec. 4	Belasco	Washington, D.C.

ROBINSON CRUSOE, JR.

A Musical Extravaganza in Two Acts and Ten Scenes. Book by Harold Atteridge and Edgar Smith. Lyrics by Harold Atteridge. Music by Sigmund Romberg and James F. Hanley. Staged by J. C. Huffman. Musical Numbers Staged by Allan K. Foster.

Cast

Poindexter	LEE PHELPS
Frank Speed	FRANK HOLMES
Bob Van Astor	JOHNNY BERKES
Jack Jitney	FRANK GRACE
Gladys Brookville	LOUISE CONTI
Hiram Westbury	CLAUDE FLEMMING
Captain Chichester	LAWRENCE D'ORSAY
Diana Westbury	WANDA LYON
Suzie Westbury	KITTY DONER
Howell Louder	BARRY LUPINO
Leading Lady	JEAN FORBES
Soubrette	ELEANOR BROWN
Miss Reel	LOIS WHITNEY
Leading Man	HARRY WILCOX
Star Feature	MME. COMONT
Camera Man	BERT DUNLAP
Movie Actor	HARRY WARDELL
Dick Hunter	FRANK CARTER
Gus Jackson	AL JOLSON
First Constable	EDWARD BOWERS
Second Constable	ALFRED CROCKER
Third Constable	FRANK WALTERS

Score

"Simple Life"
"You'll Have To Gallop Some"
"When You're Starring for the Movies"
"Go Ahead and Dance a Little More"
"Pretty Little Mayflower Girl"
"Happy Hottentots"
"Voodoo Maiden"
"Don't Be a Sailor"
"My Pirate Lady"
"Robinson Crusoe"
* "Tillie Titwillow"
"Minstrel Days"

Jolson's Songs

"Down Where the Swanee River Flows"
"Now He's Got a Beautiful Girl"
"Yaaka Hula Hickey Dula"
"Where Did Robinson Crusoe Go with Friday on Saturday Night?"

| 1916 | Feb. 10–12 | Sam S. Shubert | New Haven, Conn. |
| | Feb. 17–June 10 | Winter Garden | New York, N.Y. |

Jolson's Songs
"Where the Black-Eyed Susans Grow"

1916	Aug. 28–Sept. 2	Globe	Atlantic City, N.J.
	Sept. 4–30	Lyric	Philadelphia, Pa.
	Oct. 2–7	Academy of Music	Baltimore, Md.
	9–14	Belasco	Washington, D.C.
	16–21	Alvin	Pittsburgh, Pa.
	23–28	Royal Alexandra	Toronto, Ont.
	Oct. 30–Nov. 4	Princess	Montreal, Que.
	Nov. 6–Dec. 2	Sam S. Shubert	Boston, Mass.
	4–9	Providence Opera House	Providence, R.I.
	11	Sam S. Shubert	New Haven, Conn.
	12–13	Parsons'	Hartford, Conn.
	14	Van Curler Opera House	Schenectady, N.Y.
	15–16	Harmanus Bleecker Hall	Albany, N.Y.
	18–23	Teck	Buffalo, N.Y.
	25–30	Colonial	Cleveland, Ohio
	Dec. 31–Feb. 24, 1917	Garrick	Chicago, Ill.
1917	Feb. 26–March 10	Garrick	Detroit, Mich.
	March 11–17	Lyric	Cincinnati, Ohio
	19–24	Alvin	Pittsburgh, Pa.
	25–31	Valentine	Toledo, Ohio
	April 2–7	Murat	Indianapolis, Ind.
	8–14	Southern	Columbus, Ohio
	15–21	Jefferson	St. Louis, Mo.
	22	Majestic	Evansville, Ind.
	23	Grand Opera House	Terre Haute, Ind.
	24	Wysor Grand	Muncie, Ind.
	25	Theatre Belvoir	Champaign, Ill.
	26	Chatterton	Springfield, Ill.
	27	Lincoln Square	Decatur, Ill.
	28	Chatterton	Bloomington, Ill.
	29–30	Majestic	Peoria, Ill.
	May 1	Orpheum	Galesburg, Ill.
	3	Grand Opera House	Burlington, Iowa
	4	Grand Opera House	Keokuk, Iowa
	5	Empire Hippodrome	Quincy, Ill.
	6–13	Sam S. Shubert	Kansas City, Mo.
	14	Lyceum	St. Joseph, Mo.
	15–16	Oliver	Lincoln, Neb.

17–19	Boyd	Omaha, Neb.
20–21	Auditorium	Sioux City, Iowa
22	Greene Opera House	Cedar Rapids, Iowa
23	Grand Opera House	Rockford, Ill.
24–26	Davidson	Milwaukee, Wisc.
June 7	Metropolitan	St. Paul, Minn.
8–9	Lyceum	Duluth, Minn.
10	Metropolitan	Minneapolis, Minn.
11	Auditorium	Bismarck, N.D.
12	Babcock	Billings, Mont.
13	Minicipal	Bozeman, Mont.
14–15	Broadway	Butte, Mont.
16	Margaret	Anaconda, Mont.
18	Missoula	Missoula, Mont.
19–20	Auditorium	Spokane, Wash.
21	Temple	Lewiston, Idaho
22	Keylor Grand	Walla Walla, Wash.
23	Yakima	Yakima, Wash.
24–27	Metropolitan	Seattle, Wash.
28–29	Tacoma	Tacoma, Wash.
30	Grand Opera House	Aberdeen, Wash.
July 1–4	Baker	Portland, Ore.
5	Page	Medford, Ore.
6	Clunie	Sacramento, Calif.
7	Yosemite	Stockton, Calif.
8–28	Cort	San Francisco, Calif.
29	White	Fresno, Calif.
July 30–Aug. 11	Mason Opera House	Los Angeles, Calif.
Sept. 2–3	Orpheum	Ogden, Utah
4–6	Salt Lake	Salt Lake City, Utah
7	Norris Opera House	Granger, Wyo.
8	Colo. Springs O.H.	Colorado Springs, Colo.
9–15	Broadway	Denver, Colo.
17	Oliver	Lincoln, Neb.
18–19	Auditorium	Sioux City, Iowa
20	Boyd	Omaha, Neb.
21–22	Berchel	Des Moines, Iowa
23	Odeon	Marshalltown, Iowa
24	Waterloo	Waterloo, Iowa
25	Greene Opera House	Cedar Rapids, Iowa
26	Englert	Iowa City, Iowa
27	Burtis Opera House	Davenport, Iowa
28	Clinton	Clinton, Iowa
29	Grand Opera House	Dubuque, Iowa
Oct. 1	Orpheum	Racine, Wisc.
2	Grand Opera House	Elgin, Ill.
3	Oliver	South Bend, Ind.
4		
5	Fuller	Kalamazoo, Mich.

6–7	(Lay-Off)	
8	Powers'	Grand Rapids, Mich.
9	Gladmer	Lansing, Mich.
10	Franklin	Saginaw, Mich.
11	Washington	Bay City, Mich.
12	Majestic	Flint, Mich.
13–14	(Lay-Off)	
15	Grand Opera House	Akron, Ohio
16	Grand Opera House	Canton, Ohio
17	Park	Youngstown, Ohio
18	Court	Wheeling, W. Va.
19	Robinson Grand	Clarksburg, W. Va.
20		
22	Academy of Music	Roanoke, Va.
23–24	Academy of Music	Richmond, Va.
25	Academy of Music	Newport News, Va.
26–27	Colonial	Norfolk, Va.
29	Rajah	Reading, Pa.
30	Fulton Opera House	Lancaster, Pa.
Oct. 31–Nov. 2	(Lay-Off)	
Nov. 3	Grand Opera House	Wilkes-Barre, Pa.
5	Academy of Music	Scranton, Pa.
6	Lyceum	Elmira, N.Y.
7	Armory	Binghamton, N.Y.
8	Lyceum	Ithaca, N.Y.
9–10	Lyceum	Rochester, N.Y.
12	Wieting Opera House	Syracuse, N.Y.
13	Colonial	Utica, N.Y.
14	Proctor's	Troy, N.Y.
15	Harmanus Bleecker Hall	Albany, N.Y.
16–17	Court Square	Springfield, Mass.

SINBAD

A Spectacular Extravaganza in two acts and fourteen scenes. Book and Lyrics by Harold Atteridge. Music by Sigmund Romberg and Al Jolson. Staged by J. C. Huffman.

Cast

Harriet	REBEKAH CAUBLE
Mildred	BESS HOBAN
Marcelle	WINONA WILKINS
Harry	FRANK HOLMES
Betty	GRACE LANGDON
Isabel	BETTY TOURAINE
Mack	JACK LAUGHLIN
Tony	HARRY KEARLEY
Patricia de Trait	HAZEL COX
Mrs. Van Decker	FRITZI VON BUSING
Stephen Gilwater	LAWRENCE D'ORSAY

Professor Graves   ERNEST HARE
Stubb Talmadge   KITTY DONER
Audrey Van Decker   VIRGINIA SMITH
Nan Van Decker   VIRGINIA FOX BROOKS
Jack Randall   FRANKLYN A. BATIE
Van Rennsellar Sinbad   FORREST HUFF
Jeanette Verdear   IRENE FARBER
Tessie Verdear   CONSTANCE FARBER
Gus   AL JOLSON
A Yogi   JOHN KEARNEY

Score

"On Cupid's Green"
"A Little Bit of Every Nationality"
"Our Ancestors"
"A Thousand and One Arabian Nights"
"Beauty and Beast"
"Bagdad"
"The Rag Lad of Bagdad"
"A Night in the Orient"
"I Hail from Cairo"
"Love Ahoy"
"The Bedalumbo"
"Isle of Youth"
"I'll Tell the World"
"It's Wonderful"
"Raz-Ma-Taz"

Jolson's Songs

"Rock-a-Bye Your Baby with a Dixie Melody"
"Why Do They All Take the Night Boat to Albany?"
"I Wonder Why She Kept On Saying 'Si, Si, Si, Si, Senor' "
"Cleopatra"
" 'N' Everything"

| 1918 | Feb. 4–9 | Sam S. Shubert | New Haven, Conn. |
| | Feb. 14–July 6 | Winter Garden | New York, N.Y. |

Jolson's Songs

"I'll Say She Does"
"On The Road to Calais"

1918	Sept. 2–Oct. 12	Century	New York, N.Y.
	Oct. 14–Nov. 9	Casino	New York, N.Y.
	Nov. 11–Feb. 8, 1919	Winter Garden	New York, N.Y.
1919	Feb. 10–March 29	Forty-Fourth Street	New York, N.Y.
	March 30–April 13	Poli's	Washington, D.C.
	April 14–19	Globe	Atlantic City, N.J.
	April 21–June 21	Boston Opera House	Boston, Mass.

Jolson's Songs
"By the Honeysuckle Vine"
"I Gave Her That"
"Chloe"
"Swanee"

1919	Sept. 11–Nov. 8	Sam S. Shubert	Philadelphia, Pa.
	Nov. 10–15	Auditorium	Baltimore, Md.
	17–29	Boston Opera House	Boston, Mass.
	Dec. 1–3	Parsons'	Hartford, Conn.
	4–6	Sam S. Shubert	New Haven, Conn.
	8–13	Shubert-Majestic	Providence, R.I.
	15–17	Worcester	Worcester, Mass.
	18–20	Court Square	Springfield, Mass.
	Dec. 22–Jan. 3, 1920	Crescent	Brooklyn, N.Y.
1920	Jan. 5–10	Broad Street	Newark, N.J.
	11–17	Poli's	Washington, D.C.
	19–24	Teck	Buffalo, N.Y.
	Jan. 25–March 6	Auditorium	Chicago, Ill.
	March 8–27	Shubert-Detroit	Detroit, Mich.
	March 29–Apr. 10	Alvin	Pittsburgh, Pa.

Jolson's Songs
"Avalon"

1920	Aug. 30–Sept. 4	His Majesty's	Montreal, Que.
	Sept. 6–8	Russell	Ottawa, Ont.
	9	Grand Opera House	Kingston, Ont.
	10–11	Grand Opera House	Hamilton, Ont.
	13–18	Royal Alexandra	Toronto, Ont.
	20–25	Shubert-Detroit	Detroit, Mich.
	27–29	Hartman	Columbus, Ohio
	Sept. 30–Oct. 2	Victory	Dayton, Ohio
	Oct. 3–23	Garrick	Chicago, Ill.
	24–30	Sam S. Shubert	Kansas City, Mo.
	Oct. 31–Nov. 6	Jefferson	St. Louis, Mo.
	Nov. 8–13	Lyric	Cincinnati, Ohio
	15–18	Murat	Indianapolis, Ind.
	19–20	Court	Wheeling, W. Va.
	Nov. 22–Dec. 4	Colonial	Cleveland, Ohio
	Dec. 6–11	Teck	Buffalo, N.Y.
	13–18	Auditorium	Baltimore, Md.
	Dec. 20–Jan. 1, 1921	Sam S. Shubert	Philadelphia, Pa.

Jolson's Songs
"My Mammy"
"Dixie Rose"

1921	Jan. 31–Feb. 2	Shubert-Majestic	Providence, R.I.
	Feb. 3–5	Court Square	Springfield, Mass.

7–9	Parsons'	Hartford, Conn.
10–12	Sam S. Shubert	New Haven, Conn.
14	Grand Opera House	Trenton, N.J.
15–16	Lyric	Allentown, Pa.
17–19	Playhouse	Wilmington, Del.
21–26	Colonial	Norfolk, Va.
Feb. 27–March 5	Belasco	Washington, D.C.
March 7–12	Colonial	Cleveland, Ohio
14–16	Hartman	Columbus, Ohio
17–19	Murat	Indianapolis, Ind.
20	Grand Opera House	Terre Haute, Ind.
21	Chatterton	Springfield, Ill.
22	Lincoln Square	Decatur, Ill.
23		
24	Majestic	Peoria, Ill.
25		
26	Grand Opera House	Burlington, Iowa
March 27–April 2	Sam S. Shubert	Kansas City, Mo.
April 3–4	Convention Hall	Tulsa, Ok.
5	Orpheum	Muskogee, Ok.
6	Busby	McAlester, Ok.
7–9	Orpheum	Oklahoma City, Ok.
11–17	Broadway	Denver, Colo.
18	City Auditorium	Pueblo, Colo.
19	Burns	Colorado Springs, Colo.
20	Princess	Cheyenne, Wyo.
21	Orpheum	Ogden, Utah
22–23	Salt Lake	Salt Lake City, Utah
25–30	Philharmonic Audtrm.	Los Angeles, Calif.
May 1	White	Fresno, Calif.
2–15	Curran	San Francisco, Calif.
16	Victory	San Jose, Calif.
17	T. & D.	Stockton, Calif.
18–19	Municipal Auditorium	Oakland, Calif.
20–21	Clunie	Sacramento, Calif.
22	Majestic	Chico, Calif.
23	Redding	Redding, Calif.
24	Page	Medford, Ore.
25		
26–28	Heilig	Portland, Ore.
May 29–June 1	Metropolitan	Seattle, Wash.
June 2		
3–4	Tacoma	Tacoma, Wash.
5–6	Auditorium	Spokane, Wash.
7	Wilma	Missoula, Mont.
8–9	Broadway	Butte, Mont.
10–11	Grand Opera House	Great Falls, Mont.
13	Marlow	Helena, Mont.
14	Ellen	Bozeman, Mont.

15	Orpheum	Livingston, Mont.
16	Babcock	Billings, Mont.
17	Auditorium	Bismarck, N.D.
18	Auditorium	Fargo, N.D.
19–22	Metropolitan	Minneapolis, Minn.
23–25	Metropolitan	St. Paul, Minn.

BOMBO

A Musical Extravaganza in Two Acts and Fourteen Scenes. Book and Lyrics by Harold Atteridge. Music by Sigmund Romberg. Staged by J. C. Huffman. Dances Staged by Allan K. Foster.

Cast

Harry	HARRY RAY
Elsa	DURYA RUDAC
Paul Marcus	FRANKLYN A. BATIE
Annabelle Downing	VERA BAYLES COLE
Jenkins	FRANK HOLMES
Bud Wilson	RUSSELL MACK
Hazel Downing	MILDRED KEATS
Jack Christopher	FORREST HUFF
Patricia Downing	GLADYS CALDWELL
Count Garibaldi	FRED HALL
Mrs. Downing	FRITZI VON BUSING
Elvira	ELIZABETH REYNOLDS
Inez	GRACE KEESHON
Mona Tessa	JANET ADAIR
Red	HARRY TURPIN
Louis	THE COURIER
Guisseppo	JACK KEARNS
Banditti	ERNEST MILLER
	DENNIS MURRAY
	WALTER WHITE
	HARRY SIEVERS
	EDWARD POOLEY
Text	THOMAS ROSS
Context	THEODORE HOFFMAN
Twinkle	IRENE HART
Twilight	BERNICE HART
Lois	JANETTE DIETRICH
Alfred	FRANK BERNARD
Sam Masterson	SAM CRITCHERSON
Mrs. Moore	ELIZABETH REYNOLDS
Gus	AL JOLSON
Rosie	VIVIENNE OAKLAND

Ann Mason replaced Vivienne Oakland in 1922.

Score

"Life Is a Gamble"
"Any Place Will Do with You"
"In the Way Off There"
"The Very Next Girl I See"
"In Old Grenada"
"Jazza-da-dadoo"
"No One Loves a Clown"
"Rose of Spain"
"I'm Glad I'm Spanish"
"In a Curio Shop"
"Wait Until My Ship Comes In"
"My Guiding Star"
"A Girl Has a Sailor in Every Port"
"Bylo Bay"
"Through the Mist"
"Wetona"

Jolson's Songs

"April Showers"
"That Barber in Seville"
"Give Me My Mammy"
"Down South"

1921	Sept. 28–Oct. 1	Globe	Atlantic City, N.J.
	Oct. 6–April 8, 1922	Jolson's 59th Street	New York, N.Y.
1922	April 10–15	Globe	Atlantic City, N.J.
	April 17–May 13	Sam S. Shubert	Philadelphia, Pa.

Jolson's Songs

"Toot, Toot, Tootsie!"
"Who Cares?"

1922	Sept. 15–16	Park	Youngstown, Ohio
	Sept. 17–Jan. 6, 1923	Apollo	Chicago, Ill.
1923	Jan. 8–13	Murat	Indianapolis, Ind.
	14–20	Jefferson	St. Louis, Mo.
	21–27	Sam S. Shubert	Kansas City, Mo.
	Jan. 28–Feb. 3	Grand Opera House	Cincinnati, Ohio
	Feb. 5–10	Alvin	Pittsburgh, Pa.
	11–17	Garrick	Detroit, Mich.
	18–24	Hanna	Cleveland, Ohio
	Feb. 26–March 3	Royal Alexandra	Toronto, Ont.
	March 5–10	Teck	Buffalo, N.Y.
	12–24	Sam S. Shubert	Philadelphia, Pa.
	25–31	(Holy Week Lay-Off)	
	April 2–7	Auditorium	Baltimore, Md.
	8–14	Poli's	Washington, D.C.

| April 16–May 12 | Sam S. Shubert | Boston, Mass. |
| May 14–June 9 | Winter Garden | New York, N.Y. |

Jolson's Songs
"Arcady"
"I'm Goin' South"
"California, Here I Come"

1923 Oct. 15–20	Capital	Albany, N.Y.
22–27	Sam S. Shubert	Newark, N.J.
Oct. 29–Nov. 3	Parsons'	Hartford, Conn.
Nov. 5–10	Court Square	Springfield, Mass.
12–17	Sam S. Shubert	New Haven, Conn.
19–24	Majestic	Brooklyn, N.Y.
Nov. 26–Dec. 1	Apollo	Atlantic City, N.J.
Dec. 3–5	Academy of Music	Norfolk, Va.
6–8	Academy of Music	Richmond, Va.
9–15	Belasco	Washington, D.C.
16–22	(Pre Christmas Lay-Off)	
24–29	Alvin	Pittsburgh, Pa.
Dec. 30–Jan. 5, 1924	Detroit Opera House	Detroit, Mich.
1924 Jan. 6–26	Apollo	Chicago, Ill.
Jan. 27–Feb. 2	Hanna	Cleveland, Ohio
Feb. 4	Park	Youngstown, Ohio
5–6	Grand Opera House	Canton, Ohio
7	Goodyear	Akron, Ohio
8–9	Court	Wheeling, W. Va.
10–16	Sam S. Shubert	Cincinnati, Ohio
17–20	Macauley's	Louisville, Ky.
21–23	Victory	Dayton, Ohio
Feb. 25–March 1	Hartman	Columbus, Ohio
March 3	Fairbanks	Springfield, Ohio
4	Faurot Opera House	Lima, Ohio
5	Majestic	Fort Wayne, Ind.
6–8	Murat	Indianapolis, Ind.
9–15	Jefferson	St. Louis, Mo.
16–22	Sam S. Shubert	Kansas City, Mo.
23–24	Lyceum	St. Joseph, Mo.
25–26	Orpheum	Lincoln, Neb.
27–29	Berchel	Des Moines, Iowa
30	Auditorium	Sioux City, Iowa
March 31–April 3	Brandeis	Omaha, Neb.
April 6–12	Broadway	Denver, Colorado
13–19	(Holy Week Lay-Off)	
21	City Auditorium	Pueblo, Colo.
22	Avalon	Grand Junction, Colo.
23	Orpheum	Ogden, Utah
24–26	Salt Lake	Salt Lake City, Utah
April 27–May 10	Mason Opera House	Los Angeles, Calif.
May 11–12	Spreckels	San Diego, Calif.

13	Loring	Riverside, Calif.
14	San Bernardino O.H.	San Bernardino, Calif.
15	Hoyt's	Long Beach, Calif.
16		
17	Potter	Santa Barbara, Calif.
18–31	Curran	San Francisco, Calif.

BIG BOY

A musical comedy in two acts and twelve scenes. Book by Harold Atteridge. Lyrics by Bud DeSylva. Music by James F. Hanley and Joseph Meyer. Staged by J. C. Huffman. Dialogue directed by Alexander Leftwich. Dances by Seymour Felix and Larry Ceballos.

Cast

Mrs. Ella Bedford	MAUDE TURNER GORDON
Phyllis Carter	EDYTHE BAKER
Joe Warren	HUGH BANKS
Tessie Forbes	FLO LEWIS
Annabelle Bedford	PATTI HARROLD
Jack Bedford	FRANK BEASTON
Coley Reid	RALPH WHITEHEAD
Doc Wilbur	LEO DONNELLY
Jim Redding	FRANKLYN A. BATIE
Judkins	GEORGE GILDAY
Steve Leslie	COLIN CAMPBELL
Gus	AL JOLSON
Caroline Purdy	EDITH ROSE-SCOTT
Bully John Bagby	WILLIAM L. THORNE
Silent Ransom	GEORGE SPELVIN
Tucker	FRANKLYN A. BATIE
Manager	L. C. SHERMAN
Wainwright	WILLIAM L. THORNE
Legrande	WILLIAM BONELLI
Danny	IRVING CARTER
Mr. Gray	CHARLES MORAN
Dolly Graham	FRANKIE JAMES
Tout	CHARLES MORAN
Dancers	GEORGE ANDRE
	DOROTHY RUDAC

Score

"Welcome Home"
"Born and Bred in Old Kentucky"
"Lead 'Em On"
"The Day I Rode Half Fare"
* "Hello, 'Tucky"
"True Love"
* "As Long as I've Got My Mammy"
"Tap the Toe"

"Come On and Play"
"The Dance from Down Yonder"
"Something for Nothing"
"Lackawanna"
* "Who Was Chasing Paul Revere?"
"Cookies and Bookies"
"The Race Is Over"

Jolson's Songs
"Keep Smiling at Trouble"
"If You Knew Susie"

1924	Nov. 24–29	Alvin	Pittsburgh, Pa.
	Nov. 30–Dec. 6	Hanna	Cleveland, Ohio
	Dec. 8–13	Teck	Buffalo, N.Y.
	14–20	Sam S. Shubert	Cincinnati, Ohio
	Dec. 21–Jan. 3, 1925	Detroit Opera House	Detroit, Mich.
1925	Jan. 7–24	Winter Garden	New York, N.Y.
	Jan. 26–Feb. 7	(Lay-Off)	
	Feb. 9–Mar. 14	Winter Garden	New York, N.Y.

Doris Eaton replaced Edythe Baker in November, 1925.

Jolson's Songs
"Miami"
"Nobody But Fanny"

1925	Aug. 17–22	Nixon's Apollo	Atlantic City, N.J.
	Aug. 24–Dec. 5	Forty-fourth Street	New York, N.Y.
	Dec. 7–12	Sam S. Shubert	Newark, N.J.
	14–19	Alvin	Pittsburgh, Pa.
	20–23	(Pre-Christmas Lay-Off)	
	Dec. 24–Jan. 26, 1926	Apollo	Chicago, Ill.

Jolson's Songs
"It All Depends on You"
"One O'Clock Baby"

1926	Sept. 10–11	Playhouse	Wilmington, Del.
	Sept. 13–Nov. 6	Sam S. Shubert	Boston, Mass.
	Nov. 8–13	Parsons'	Hartford, Conn.
	15–20	Sam S. Shubert	New Haven, Conn.
	22–27	Majestic	Brooklyn, N.Y.
	Nov. 29–Dec. 4	Nixon's Apollo	Atlantic City, N.J.
	Dec. 6–11	Auditorium	Baltimore, Md.
	12–18	Poli's	Washington, D.C.
	19–24	(Christmas Lay-Off)	
	Dec. 25–Jan. 22, 1927	Sam S. Shubert	Philadelphia, Pa.
1927	Jan. 24–29	Teck	Buffalo, N.Y.
	Jan. 31–Feb. 5	Princess	Montreal, Que.

Feb. 7–12	Royal Alexandra	Toronto, Ont.
13–26	Shubert-Detroit	Detroit, Mich.
Feb. 27–March 5	Hanna	Cleveland, Ohio
March 6–12	Sam S. Shubert	Cincinnati, Ohio
14–19	Brown	Louisville, Ky.
21–23	Hartman	Columbus, Ohio
24–26	English's Opera House	Indianapolis, Ind.
March 27–April 2	Shubert-Rialto	St. Louis, Mo.
April 3–9	Sam S. Shubert	Kansas City, Mo.
10–16	(Holy Week Lay-Off)	
April 17–May 14	Apollo	Chicago, Ill.
May 16–21	Broadway	Denver, Colo.
May 23–June 11	Biltmore	Los Angeles, Calif.
June 13–July 2	Curran	San Francisco, Calif.
Dec. 1–3	Wieting Opera House	Syracuse, N.Y.

AL JOLSON—WORLD CONCERT TOUR

1930 Jan. 18	Liberty Hall	El Paso, Texas
20	Forum	Wichita, Kansas
22	Coliseum	Tulsa, Ok.
23	Coliseum	Oklahoma City, Ok.
25	Dallas Auditorium	Dallas, Texas
27	Municipal Auditorium	San Antonio, Texas
28	City Auditorium	Houston, Texas
30	New Auditorium	New Orleans, La.

THE WONDER BAR

A Continental Novelty of European Night Life in two sections. Book by Irving
Caesar, based on Aben Kandel's adaptation of the German "Vunderbar" of
Geta Herczeg and Karl Farkas. Lyrics by Irving Caesar. Music by Robert Katscher
and Rowland Leigh. Staged by William Mollison.

Cast

Richard	GUSTAV ROLLAND
Marcel	AUGUSTE ARMINI
Prince Nikolos Engalitcheff	NIKOLOS ENGALITCHEFF
Mary Evans	JEAN NEWCOMBE
Elmer Evans	C. JAY WILLIAMS
Sonya	ANTONINA FECHNER
Billie	DAGMAR OAKLAND
Rosette	ANDRIANA DORI
Martha	ELVIRA TRABERT
Helen Brown	LAURA PIERPONT
Edgar Banks	HENRY CROSBY
Monsieur Al Wonder	AL JOLSON
Inez	TRINI
Ramon Colmano	REX O'MALLEY
Lord Cauldwell	ARTHUR TREACHER

Françqis Vale	STUART CASEY
Oscar Wayne	CLARENCE HARVEY
Liane Duval	WANDA LYON
Pierre Duval	VERNON STEELE
A Gendarme	ROMAN ARNOLDOFF
Monsieur Simon	ADRIAN ROSLEY
Electra Pivonka	PATSY KELLY
Charlie	AL SIEGAL
A Rajah	MOHAMMED IBRAHIM
Count Rugtoffsky	MICHAEL DAIMATOFF
Signora Medea Columbara	MEDEA COLUMBARA
Benno Bondy	HUGO BRUCKEN
Mrs. Solomon	BERTHA WALDEN
Sam Solomon	LEO HOYT
Pascal	ARMAND CROTEZ
Baroness Rosseau	MARIE HUNT

Score

* "Good Evening, Friends"
* "Oh, Donna Clara"
  "I'm Falling in Love"
* "Ma Mere"
* "Lenox Avenue"
* "Elizabeth, My Queen"
  "Something Seems To Tell Me"

Jolson's Songs
"A Chazend'l Ohf Shabbes"

1931	March 5–7	Belasco	Washington, D.C.
	9–14	Sam S. Shubert	New Haven, Conn.
	March 17–May 30	Nora Bayes	New York, N.Y.

Major cast changes for tour: Claire Windsor played Lianne Duval. Lina Basquette played Inez. Edward Ranquello played Ramon Colmano. Akim Tamiroff played Monsieur Simon. Henry Morrell played François Vale.

1931	Sept. 28–Oct. 3	Sam S. Shubert	Newark, N.J.
	Oct. 5–17	Sam S. Shubert	Boston, Mass.
	Oct. 19–Nov. 7	Sam S. Shubert	Philadelphia, Pa.
	Nov. 9–14	Auditorium	Baltimore, Md.
	15–21	Belasco	Washington, D.C.
	23–28	Alvin	Pittsburgh, Pa.
	Nov. 29–Dec. 5	Sam S. Shubert	Cincinnati, Ohio
	Dec. 6–12	Cass	Detroit, Mich.
	14–19	Hanna	Cleveland, Ohio
	20–24	(Christmas Lay-Off)	
	Dec. 25–Jan. 30, 1932	Apollo	Chicago, Ill.
1932	Jan. 31–Feb. 6	Davidson	Milwaukee, Wisc.
	Feb. 8–10	National	Louisville, Ky.

11–13	English's Opera House	Indianapolis, Ind.
14–20	Shubert-Rialto	St. Louis, Mo.
21	Masonic Temple	Davenport, Iowa
22	Shrine Temple	Cedar Rapids, Iowa
23	Shrine Auditorium	Des Moines, Iowa
24	Coliseum	Sioux Falls, S.D.
25	Auditorium	Sioux City, Iowa
26	City Auditorium	Omaha, Neb.
27	Coliseum	Lincoln, Neb.
Feb. 28–March 5	Sam S. Shubert	Kansas City, Mo.
March 6	Memorial Hall	Joplin, Mo.
7	Convention Hall	Tulsa, Ok.
8	Forum	Wichita, Ks.
9	Shrine Auditorium	Oklahoma City, Ok.
10	Municipal Auditorium	Amarillo, Texas
11	Memorial Auditorium	Wichita Falls, Texas
12	State Fair Auditorium	Dallas, Texas
14	Municipal Auditorium	Shreveport, La.
15	City Auditorium	Houston, Texas
16	Auditorium	San Antonio, Texas
17	Liberty Hall	El Paso, Texas
18	Fox	Phoenix, Ariz.
19	Fox California	San Diego, Calif.
20–26	(Holy Week Lay-Off)	
March 27–April 2	Biltmore	Los Angeles, Calif.
April 3–9	Curran	San Francisco, Calif.

HOLD ON TO YOUR HATS

A musical comedy in two acts and thirteen scenes. Book by Guy Bolton, Matt Brooks, and Eddie Davis. Lyrics by E. Y. Harburg. Music by Burton Lane. Staged by Edgar J. MacGregor. Dances by Catherine Littlefield.

Cast

Sierra	MARGARET IRVING
Slim	GIL LAMB
Lon	GEORGE CHURCH
Pete	JACK WHITING
Mamie	MARTHA RAYE
First Dudette	JINX FALKENBURG
Second Dudette	JOYCE MATTHEWS
Third Dudette	THEA PINTO
Sheriff	LEW ECCLES
Fernando	ARNOLD MOSS
The Lone Rider	AL JOLSON
Radio Announcer	JOHN RANDOLPH
Shep Martin	JOE STONER
Old Man Hawkins	MARTY DRAKE
Concho	BERT GORDON
Sound Effects	GEORGE MARAN

Dinky	RUSS BROWN
Shirley	RUBY KEELER
Luis	SID CASSEL
Pedro	WILL KULUVA
Rita	JINX FALKENBURG
Tanner Sisters	BETTY TANNER
	MARTHA TANNER
	MICKIE TANNER
Radio Aces	MARTY DRAKE
	JOE STONER
	LOU STONER
Ranchettes	MARGIE GREENE
	ANITA JAKOBI
	IRIS WAYNE
	JANIE WILLIAMS

Eunice Healey replaced Ruby Keeler on July 29, 1940.

Score

"Way Out West Where the East Begins"
"Hold On to Your Hats"
* "Walkin' Along, Mindin' My Business"
"The World Is in My Arms"
* "Would You Be So Kindly?"
"Life Was Pie for the Pioneer"
* "Don't Let It Get You Down"
* "There's a Great Day Coming Manana"
"Then You Were Never in Love"
* "Down on the Old Dude Ranch"
* "She Came, She Saw, She Can-Canned"
* "Old Timer"

1940	June 30–July 13	Cass	Detroit, Mich.
	July 15–Aug. 24	Grand Opera House	Chicago, Ill.
	Aug. 27–Sept. 7	Forrest	Philadelphia, Pa.
	Sept. 11–Feb. 1, 1941	Sam S. Shubert	New York, N.Y.

Cast

Hitch Hiker	JACQUELINE GATELEY
Sierra	JEAN CLEVELAND
Slim	HERMAN TIMBERG, JR.
Shorty	GEORGE MORAN
Pete	LEE DIXON
Mamie	COLETTE LYONS
First Dudette	BUNNY WATERS
Second Dudette	BETTY JANE HESS
Third Dudette	JEAN CAMPBELL
Sheriff	BEN ROBERT
Fernando	JOSEPH VITALE
The Lone Rider	AL JOLSON
Radio Announcer	MARION MOORE

Shep Martin	JOE STONER
Old Man Hawkins	MARTY DRAKE
Concho	SID MARION
Sound Effects	GEORGE MARAN
Dinky	MURRAY LEONARD
Shirley	EUNICE HEALEY
Luis	SID CASSEL
Pedro	FRANK SANTORI
Rita	BUNNY WATERS
Radio Aces	MARTY DRAKE
	JOE STONER
	LOU STONER
Ranchettes	MARGIE GREENE
	MARJORIE JANE
	VIVIEN NEWELL

1941	Aug. 27–30	Garden Pier	Atlantic City, N.J.
	Sept. 1–20	Sam S. Shubert	Boston, Mass.
	22	Metropolitan	Providence, R.I.
	23–24	Bushnell Auditorium	Hartford, Conn.
	25–27	Sam S. Shubert	New Haven, Conn.
	Sept. 28–Oct. 4	National	Washington, D.C.
	Oct. 6–11	Nixon	Pittsburgh, Pa.
	13–18	Hanna	Cleveland, Ohio
	20–25	Royal Alexandra	Toronto, Ont.
	27–29	Masonic Auditorium	Rochester, N.Y.
	Oct. 30–Nov. 1	Erlanger	Buffalo, N.Y.
	Nov. 2–5	Taft Auditorium	Cincinnati, Ohio
	6–8	Hartman	Columbus, Ohio

LOEW'S THEATRES

1949	Aug. 10	8:00	Yonkers	Yonkers, N.Y.
		8:30	175th Street	Bronx, N.Y.
		9:00	Paradise	Bronx, N.Y.
		9:30	Fairmont	Bronx, N.Y.
		10:00	National	New York, N.Y.
		10:30	Victoria	New York, N.Y.
	Aug. 11	8:00	Coney Island	Brooklyn, N.Y.
		8:30	Oriental	Brooklyn, N.Y.
		9:00	Kings	Brooklyn, N.Y.
		9:30	Metropolitan	Brooklyn, N.Y.
		10:00	Commodore	New York, N.Y.
		10:30	Orpheum	New York, N.Y.
	Aug. 12	8:00	Triboro	Astoria, N.Y.
		8:30	Prospect	Flushing, N.Y.
		9:00	Valencia	Jamaica, N.Y.
		9:30	Gates	Brooklyn, N.Y.
		10:00	Premier	Brooklyn, N.Y.
		10:30	Pitkin	Brooklyn, N.Y.

Filmography

This filmography includes three early silent subjects, all of Jolson's sound feature films, and *Al Jolson in a Plantation Act,* a one-real sound short made in 1926. Composers and lyricists for each song are given, in parentheses, where the writers differ from those listed in the credits. This is done for Warner Bros. films only; Rodgers and Hart wrote all the songs in *Hallelujah, I'm a Bum,* while the Fox and Columbia films were made up primarily of standards.

This filmography does not include *Oh, You Beautiful Doll* (Twentieth Century–Fox, 1949), to which Jolson contributed his off-screen speaking voice.

Songs marked with an asterisk (*) were sung by Jolson.

THE HONEYMOON EXPRESS
(Messrs. Shubert, 1913)

Production: Jan. 21, 1913, outskirts of New York, N.Y.
Premiere: Feb. 3, 1913, Hyperion Theatre, New Haven, Conn.
Length: Approximately one-quarter of a reel.

Cast

Gus	AL JOLSON
Baudry	HARRY PILCER
Yvonne	GABY DESLYS
Mme. De Bressie	ADA LEWIS

[The final scene of Act I of *The Honeymoon Express* consisted of a frantic race between an automobile driven by Gus, with Baudry, Yvonne, and Mme. De Bressie as passengers, and a train traveling to Rouen on which Henry Dubonet (Ernest Glendinning) is supposedly a passenger. This film, which depicted the chase, ended with the car and train about to pull into Rouen at the same time. On the stage, the screen was raised, the lights came on, and the orchestra struck its final notes as both the car and train were shown beside each other at the Rouen station. This was the finale of Act I.]

HUNTING THE FEROCIOUS AND EXTINCT CUCKOO
(Calif. Motion Picture Corp.)

Production: April 1914, Los Angeles, Calif.

356

[This short subject, a burlesque of silent movie acting featuring Al Jolson in whiteface, was shown from February 20 to December 4, 1915 in the California Building at the Panama-Pacific International Exposition in San Francisco.]

UNTITLED (1918)

[Produced by Vitagraph for the benefit of the Patrolman's Benevolent Association's fund for the children of policemen killed in service. Jolson and thirty-five motorcycle policemen filmed a chase sequence in Bronx Park on May 6th. A follow-up scene, in which Jolson, in blackface, listens to a lecture from a judge about the dangers of speeding and sobs "Make it a year" when he is sentenced to a day in jail, was filmed at the Magistrate House on May 9th. Only one screening of the film was held: during a special "police performance" of *Sinbad* at the Winter Garden on Saturday evening, May 11, 1918. Jolson made this film with the understanding that the PBA fund was to receive all profits. When he found out that Vitagraph was to receive 60 percent of the profits and the PBA only 40 he ordered the film confiscated. It was never shown commercially.]

AL JOLSON IN A PLANTATION ACT
(Warner Bros., 1926)

Production: Sept. 6, 1926, Manhattan Opera House
Premiere: Oct. 7, 1926, Colony Theatre, New York
Length: One reel.

Producer: Robert Green
Director: Philip Roscoe
Conductor: Al Goodman

Cast

AL JOLSON

Songs

* "Rock-A-Bye your Baby with a Dixie Melody"
* "When the Red, Red Robin Comes Bob, Bob, Bobbin' Along"
* "April Showers"

THE JAZZ SINGER
(Warner Bros., 1927)

Production: July 11–Sept. 3, 1927, Los Angeles, Calif.
Premiere: Oct. 6, 1927, Warner Theatre, New York
Length: Nine reels.

Director: Alan Crosland
Scenario: Alfred A. Cohn
Source: Based on the play by Samson Raphaelson
Captions: Jack Jarmuth
Photography: Hal Mohr
Conductor: Louis Silvers

Cast

Jakie Rabinowitz	AL JOLSON
Mary Dale	MAY MCAVOY
Cantor Rabinowitz	WARNER OLAND
Sara Rabinowitz	EUGENIE BESSERER
Moshe Yudelson	OTTO LEDERER
Cantor Josef Rosenblatt	CANTOR ROSENBLATT
Jakie Rabinowitz (13 years old)	BOBBY GORDON
Harry Lee	RICHARD TUCKER
Levi	NAT CARR
Buster Billings	WILLIAM DEMAREST
Randolph Dillings	ANDERS RANDOLF
Doctor	WILL WALLING
First Chorus Girl	MYRNA LOY
Second Chorus Girl	AUDREY FERRIS

Songs

"My Gal Sal" (Paul Dresser)
"Waiting for the Robert E. Lee" (Muir-Gilbert)
* "Dirty Hands, Dirty Face" (Monaco-Jolson-Clarke-Leslie)
* "Toot, Toot, Tootsie! (Goo' Bye)" (Erdman-Russo-Kahn)
"Yahrzeit" [traditional]
* "Blue Skies" (Irving Berlin)
* "Mother of Mine, I Still Have You" (Silvers-Clarke)
* "Kol Nidre" [traditional]
* "My Mammy" (Walter Donaldson-Sam M. Lewis-Joe Young)

Joseph Diskay dubbed for Warner Oland.
Bert Fiske played the piano for Al Jolson.

THE SINGING FOOL
(Warner Bros., 1928)

Production:	June–Aug., 1928, Los Angeles, Calif.
Premier:	Sept. 19, 1928, Winter Garden, New York.
Length:	Eleven reels

Director:	Lloyd Bacon
Scenario:	C. Graham Baker
Source:	A story by Leslie S. Barrows
Photography:	Byron Haskin

Cast

Al Stone	AL JOLSON
Grace Farrell	BETTY BRONSON
Molly Winton	JOSEPHINE DUNN
Sonny Boy	DAVEY LEE
John Perry	REED HOWES
Marcus	EDWARD MARTINDEL
Blackie Joe	ARTHUR HOUSEMAN
Billy Cline	ROBERT EMMETT O'CONNOR

Maid	HELEN LYNCH
Chorus Girl	AGNES FRANEY

Songs

* "It All Depends on You" (DeSylva-Brown-Henderson)
* "I'm Sitting on Top of The World" (Henderson)
* "The Spaniard That Blighted My Life" (Merson)
* "There's A Rainbow 'Round My Shoulder" (Dreyer)
* "Golden Gate" (Dreyer-Meyer-Jolson-Rose)
* "Sonny Boy" (Jolson-DeSylva-Brown-Henderson)
* "Keep Smiling at Trouble" (Gensler-Jolson-DeSylva)

SAY IT WITH SONGS
(Warner Bros., 1929)

Production:	March–April, 1929, Los Angeles, Calif.
Premiere:	Aug. 6, 1929, Warner Theatre, New York
Length:	Ten reels

Director:	Lloyd Bacon
Screenplay:	Joseph Jackson
Source:	A story by Darryl Zanuck and Harvey Gates
Songs:	Jolson, DeSylva, Brown & Henderson
Conductor:	Louis Silvers

Cast

Joe Lane	AL JOLSON
Little Pal	DAVEY LEE
Katherine Lane	MARIAN NIXON
Dr. Robert Merrill	HOLMES HERBERT
Arthur Phillips	KENNETH THOMSON
Joe Lane's cellmate	FRED KOHLER

Songs

* "Back in Your Own Back Yard" (Dreyer-Jolson-Rose)
* "I'm 'Ka-razy' for You" (Dreyer-Jolson-Rose)
* "Used to You"
* "Little Pal"
* "I'm in Seventh Heaven"
* "Why Can't You?"
* "(Mem'ries of) One Sweet Kiss" (Dreyer-Jolson)

MAMMY
(Warner Bros., 1930)

Production:	Sept.–Nov. 1929
Premiere:	March 26, 1930, Warner Theatre, New York
Length:	Eighty-four minutes

Director:	Michael Curtiz
Screenplay:	Gordon Rigby, Joseph Jackson

Source: A story by Irving Berlin
Songs: Irving Berlin
Conductor: Louis Silvers

Cast

Al Fuller	AL JOLSON
Nora Meadows	LOUIS MORAN
Al's mother	LOUISE DRESSER
Westy	LOWELL SHERMAN
Tonopah Red	NOAH BEERY
Mr. Meadows	HOBART BOSWORTH
Slats	TULLY MARSHALL
Tambo	MITCHELL LEWIS
Flat Feet	LEE MORAN
The Sheriff	JACK CURTIS
Pig Eyes	STANLEY FIELDS
Props	RAY COOKE

Songs

* "Knights of the Road"
* "Let Me Sing and I'm Happy"
* "Who Paid the Rent for Mrs. Rip Van Winkle?" (Fisher)
  "When You And I Were Young, Maggie" (Butterfield)
* "Yes, We Have No Bananas" [operatic parody]
* "My Mammy" (Walter Donaldson-Sam M. Lewis-Joe Young)
* "Across the Breakfast Table Looking at You"
  "Here We Are"
  "Oh, Dem Golden Slippers" (James A. Bland)
  "In the Morning"
* "The Call of the South"
* "Why Do They All Take the Night Boat to Albany?"
  (Jean Schwartz-Sam M. Lewis-Joe Young)
* "To My Mammy"

BIG BOY
(Warner Bros., 1930)

Production: April–May 1930, Los Angeles, Calif.
Premiere: Sept. 11, 1930, Winter Garden, New York
Length: Nine reels

Director: Alan Crosland
Screenplay: William J. Wells, Perry Vekroff, Rex Taylor
Source: Based on the musical comedy by Harold Atteridge
Conductor: Louis Silvers

Cast

Gus	AL JOLSON
Annabelle Bedford	CLAUDIA DELL

Mrs. Bedford	LOUISE CLOSSER HALE
Jack Bedford	LLOYD HUGHES
Coley Reed	EDDIE PHILLIPS
Doc Wilbur	LEW HARVEY
Steve Leslie	GEORGE HARRIS
Jim Redding	FRANKLYN A. BATIE
Joe Warren	JOHN HARRON
Tucker	TOM WILSON
Bully John Bagby	NOAH BEERY

THE MONROE JUBILEE SINGERS

Songs

* "Liza Lee" (Sam H. Stept-Bud Green)
* "Little Sunshine" (George W. Meyer–Gottler-Mitchell)
  "Dixie's Land" (Daniel D. Emmett)
* "All God's Children Got Shoes" [traditional]
* "Go Down, Moses" [traditional]
* "Tomorrow Is Another Day" (Stept–Green)
* "Hooray for Baby and Me" (Meyer–Gottler–Mitchell)

HALLELUJAH, I'M A BUM
(United Artists, 1933)

Production:	Oct.–Nov. 1932, Los Angeles, Calif.
Premiere:	Feb. 8, 1933, Rivoli Theatre, New York
Length:	Nine reels
Director:	Lewis Milestone
Screenplay:	S. N. Behrman
Source:	A story by Ben Hecht
Music:	Richard Rodgers
Lyrics:	Lorenz Hart
Conductor:	Alfred Newman

Cast

Bumper	AL JOLSON
June Marcher	MADGE EVANS
Mayor Hastings	FRANK MORGAN
Egghead	HARRY LANGDON
Sunday	CHESTER CONKLIN
Acorn	EDGAR CONNOR
Mayor's secretary	TYLER BROOKE
Orlando	TAMMANY YOUNG
John	BERT ROACH
The General	VICTOR POTEL
Apple Mary	DOROTHEA WOLBERT
Ma Sunday	LOUISE CARVER
Bank Teller	LORENZ HART
Assistant Photographer	RICHARD RODGERS

Songs

* "I Gotta Get Back to New York"
  "My Pal Bumper"
* "Hallelujah, I'm a Bum" [first song]
  "Laying the Cornerstone"
* "Sleeping Beauty" (cut from release print)
* "Dear June"
  "Bumper Found a Grand"
* "What Do You Want with Money?"
* "Hallelujah, I'm a Bum" [second song]
  "Kangaroo Court"
* "I'd Do It Again"
* "You Are Too Beautiful"

Note: An earlier version of this film, directed by Chester Erskin, was shot during July–Sept. 1932, with songs by Irving Caesar and Roland Young in the role of Mayor Hastings. Erskin replaced Harry D'Arrast, who withdrew from the assignment after one day's shooting due to arguments with Jolson.

WONDER BAR
(Warner Bros., 1934)

Production: Nov. 13–Dec. 11, 1933, Burbank, Calif.
("Goin' To Heaven on a Mule" sequence shot in January 1934)
Premiere: Feb. 28, 1934, Strand Theatre, New York
Length: Ten reels

Director: Lloyd Bacon
Choreography: Busby Berkeley
Screenplay: Earl Baldwin
Source: The continental musical by Herczeg and Farkas
Music: Harry Warren
Lyrics: Al Dubin
Conductor: Leo F. Forbstein

Cast

Al Wonder	AL JOLSON
Liane Renaud	KAY FRANCIS
Inez	DOLORES DEL RIO
Harry	RICARDO CORTEZ
Tommy	DICK POWELL
Mr. Simpson	GUY KIBBEE
Mrs. Simpson	RUTH DONNELLY
Mr. Pratt	HUGH HERBERT
Mrs. Pratt	LOUISE FAZENDA
Dancer	HAL LEROY
Mitzi	FIFI D'ORSAY
Claire	MERNA KENNEDY
Capt. Van Ferring	ROBERT BARRAT
Mr. Renaud	HENRY KOLKER

Songs

* "Vive La France"
"Don't Say Good-Night"
* "Dark Eyes" [folk song]
"Why Do I Dream Those Dreams?"
"Wonder Bar"
* "Goin' to Heaven on a Mule"

GO INTO YOUR DANCE
(Warner Bros., 1935)

Production:	Nov. 1934–Feb. 1935, Burbank, Calif.
Premiere:	May 2, 1935, Capitol Theatre, New York
Length:	Ten reels
Director:	Archie Mayo
Choreographer:	Bobby Connolly
Screenplay:	Earl Baldwin
Source:	The novel by Bradford Ropes
Music:	Harry Warren
Lyrics:	Al Dubin
Conductor:	Leo F. Forbstein

Cast

Al Howard	AL JOLSON
Dorothy Wayne	RUBY KEELER
Molly Howard	GLENDA FARRELL
Luana Bell	HELEN MORGAN
The Duke	BARTON MACLANE
Irma	PATSY KELLY
Nellie, the blonde	SHARON LYNNE
Nellie's husband	WARD BOND
Mexican	AKIM TAMIROFF
Customer at bar	BENNY RUBIN
Eddie Rio	PHIL REGAN
Fred	GORDON WESTCOTT
McGee	WILLIAM DAVIDSON
Show Girl	JOYCE COMPTON
Jackson	JOSEPH CREGAN
Englishman	ARTHUR TREACHER
Snowflake	FRED TOONES
Harry	HARRY WARREN
Al	AL DUBIN
Rehearsal pianist	MARTIN FRIED

Songs

* "Celito Lindo" (Elpidio Fernandez)
"A Good Old Fashioned Cocktail"
* "Mammy, I'll Sing About You"
* "About a Quarter to Nine"

"The Little Things You Used To Do"
* "Casino de Paree"
* "She's a Latin from Manhattan"
* "Go into Your Dance"

THE SINGING KID
(Warner Bros., 1936)

Production:	Nov. 11, 1935–Jan. 28, 1936, Burbank, Calif.
Premiere:	April 3, 1936, Strand Theatre, New York
Length:	Ten reels

Director:	William Keighley
Choreographer:	Bobby Connolly
Screenplay:	Warren Duff, Pat C. Flick
Source:	A story by Robert Lord
Photography:	George Barnes
Music:	Harold Arlen
Lyrics:	E. Y. Harburg
Conductor:	Leo F. Forbstein

Cast

Al Jackson	AL JOLSON
Ruth Haines	BEVERLY ROBERTS
Sybil Haines	SYBIL JASON
Davenport Rogers	EDWARD EVERETT HORTON
Joe Eddy	ALLEN JENKINS
Bob Carey	LYLE TALBOT
Dope	FRANK MITCHELL
Barney Hammond	WILLIAM DAVIDSON
Potter	EDWARD KEANE
Singer	WINI SHAW
Babe	JACK DURANT
Dr. May	JOSEPH KING
Fulton	JOSEPH CREGAN
Dana Lawrence	CLAIRE DODD
Mary Lou	KAY HUGHES
Dr. Brown	JOHN HALE
Maid	HATTIE MCDANIEL

THE FOUR YACHT CLUB BOYS

CAB CALLOWAY AND HIS BAND

Songs

* "My Mammy" (Walter Donaldson-Lewis-Young)
* "Swanee" (George Gershwin-Irving Caesar)
* "Rock-a-Bye Your Baby with a Dixie Melody" (Schwartz)
* "California, Here I Come" (J. Meyer-Jolson-DeSylva)
* "April Showers" (Louis Silvers-Bud DeSylva)
* "About a Quarter to Nine" (Harry Warren-Al Dubin)
* "Sonny Boy (Jolson-DeSylva-Brown-Henderson)

* "I Love to Sing-A"
  "Keep That Hi-De-Ho in Your Soul" (Calloway-Mills)
* "Who's the Swingin'est Man in Town?"
* "Save Me, Sister"
* "Here's Looking at You"
  "My, How This Country's Changed"
* "You're the Cure for What Ails Me"

ROSE OF WASHINGTON SQUARE
(Twentieth Century–Fox, 1939)

Production:	Jan.–Feb. 1939, Los Angeles, Calif.
Premiere:	May 5, 1939, Roxy Theatre, New York
Length:	7,768 ft.

Director:	Gregory Ratoff
Dances:	Seymour Felix
Producer:	Darryl Zanuck
Screenplay:	Nunnally Johnson
Source:	A story by John Larkin, Jerry Horwin
Photography:	Karl Freund
Conductor:	Louis Silvers

Cast

Bart Clinton	TYRONE POWER
Rose Sargent	ALICE FAYE
Ted Cotter	AL JOLSON
Harry Long	WILLIAM FRAWLEY
Peggy	JOYCE COMPTON
Whitey Boone	HOBART CAVANAUGH
Buck Russell	MORONI OLSEN
Barouche Driver	E. E. CLIVE
Bandleader	LUIS PRIMA
Mike Cavanaugh	CHARLES WILSON
Chumps	HAL DAWSON
	PAUL BURNS
Tony	BEN WALDEN
Irving	HORACE MACMAHON
District Attorney	PAUL STANTON
Mrs. Russell	WINIFRED HARRIS
Judge	JOHN HAMILTON
Jim	ADRIAN MORRIS
Sam Kress	CHARLES LANE
Dexter	HARRY HAYDEN
Mr. Mok	MAURICE CASS

Songs

* "Pretty Baby"
  "I'm Sorry I Made You Cry"
  "Ja-Da"

"The Vamp"
* "Rock-a-Bye Your Baby with a Dixie Melody"
* "Toot, Toot, Tootsie (Goo' Bye)"
"I'm Just Wild About Harry"
"The Curse of an Aching Heart"
* "California, Here I Come"
"I Never Knew Heaven Could Speak"
* "April Showers"
* "Avalon"
"Rose of Washington Square"
"My Mammy"
"My Man"

HOLLYWOOD CAVALCADE
(Twentieth Century–Fox, 1939)

Production: Jolson sequence filmed on July 6, 1939
Premiere: Oct. 13, 1939, Roxy Theatre, New York
Length: 9,048 ft.

Director: Irving Cummings
Producer: Darryl Zanuck
Screenplay: Ernest Pascal
Source: A story by Hilary Lynn and Brown Holmes

Cast

Molly Adair	ALICE FAYE
Michael Linnett Connors	DON AMECHE
Dave Springold	EDWARD BROMBERG
Nicky Hayden	ALAN CURTIS
Pete Tinney	STUART IRWIN
Chief of Police	JED PROUTY
Buster Keaton	BUSTER KEATON
Lyle P. Stout	DONALD MEEK
Englishman	GEORGE GIVOT
Keystone Cops	EDDIE COLLINS
	HANK MANN
	HEINIE CONKLIN
	JAMES FINLAYSON
Assistant Director	CHICK CHANDLER
Henry Potter	ROBERT LOWERY
Roberts	RUSSELL HICKS
Agent	BEN WALDEN
Valet	WILLIE FUNG
Wilson	PAUL STANTON
Bartender	BEN TURPIN
Sheriff	CHESTER CONKLIN
Mack Sennett	MACK SENNETT
Telephone Operator	MARJORIE BEEBE
Thomas	FREDERICK BURTON

Lee Duncan	LEE DUNCAN
Rin Tin Tin	RIN TIN TIN, JR.
Al Jolson	AL JOLSON

Songs

* "Kol Nidre" [sung in Aramaic]

SWANEE RIVER
(Twentieth Century–Fox, 1939)

Production:	Sept.–Oct. 1939, Los Angeles, Calif.
Premiere:	Dec. 29, 1939, Roxy Theatre, New York
Length:	6,894 ft.

Director:	Sidney Lanfield
Choreographers:	Nick Castle, Geneva Sawyer
Producer:	Darryl Zanuck
Screenplay:	John Taintor Foote, Philip Dunne
Source:	The life of Stephen Foster
Photography:	Bert Glenner
Conductor:	Louis Silvers

Cast

Stephen Foster	DON AMECHE
Jane McDowell	ANDREA LEEDS
E. P. Christy	AL JOLSON
Henry Kleber	FELIX BROSSART
Bones	CHICK CHANDLER
Tambo	AL HERMAN
Andrew McDowell	RUSSELL HICKS
Joe	GEORGE REED
Tom Harper	RICHARD CLARKE
Marion Foster	DIANE FISHER
Ambrose	GEORGE BREAKSTONE
Mr. Foster	CHARLES TWOBRIDGE
Mrs. Foster	LEORA ROBERTS
Henry Foster	GEORGE MEEKER
Morrison Foster	CHARLES TANNEN
Mrs. McDowell	NELLA WALKER
Erwin	HARRY HAYDEN
Mrs. Griffin	CLARA BLANDICK
Temperance Woman	ESTHER DALE

THE HALL JOHNSON CHOIR

Songs

* "Oh! Susanna"
  "Boom! (Merry Minstrel Men)"
* "De Camptown Races"
* "My Old Kentucky Home"
  "Old Black Joe"

"Ring De Banjo"
"I Dream of Jeanie with the Light Brown Hair"
* "Old Folks at Home (Swanee River)"

RHAPSODY IN BLUE
(Warner Bros., 1945)

Production: Jolson sequence filmed in Dec. 1943
Premiere: June 27, 1945, Hollywood Theatre, New York
Length: 139 minutes.

Director: Irving Rapper
Producer: Jesse Lasky
Choreographer: LeRoy Prinz
Screenplay: Howard Koch, Elliott Paul
Source: A story by Sonya Levien, based on the life of George Gershwin
Conductor: Leo F. Forbstein

Cast

George Gershwin	ROBERT ALDA
Julie Adams	JOAN LESLIE
Christine Gilbert	ALEXIS SMITH
Max Dreyfus	CHARLES COBURN
Lee Gershwin	JULIE BLAHOE
Ira Gershwin	HERBERT RUDLEY
Professor Frank	ALBERT BASSERMAN
Mr. Gershwin	MORRIS CARNOVSKY
Mrs. Gershwin	ROSEMARY DECAMP
Buddy DeSylva	EDDIE MARR
Ravel	OSCAR LORAINE
Walter Damrosch	HUGO KIRVHOFFER
George Gershwin (as a boy)	MICKEY ROTH
Ira Gershwin (as a boy)	DARRYL HICKMAN
Mr. East	CHARLES HALTON
Mr. Million	ANDREW TOMBES
Mr. Katzman	GREGORY GOLLIBEFF
Foley	THEO. VON ELTZ
Herbert Stone	BILL KENNEDY
American Man	ROBERT SHAYNE
Dancer	JOHNNY DOWNS
Otto Kahn	ERNEST GULM
Heifitz	MARTIN NOBLE
Rachmaninoff	WILL WRIGHT

The following portrayed themselves: Oscar Levant, Paul Whiteman, Al Jolson, George White, Hazel Scott, Anne Brown, Tom Paricola, John B. Hughes, Elsa Maxwell

THE WARNER CHORAL SINGERS

Score
* "Swanee"

The remainder of the score was made up of George Gershwin standards.

THE JOLSON STORY
(Columbia, 1946)

Production: Oct. 1945–March 1946
Premiere: Oct. 10, 1946, Radio City Music Hall, N.Y.
Length: Fourteen reels; 128 minutes

Director: Alfred E. Green
Producer: Sidney Skolsky
Screenplay: Stephen Longstreet
Choreographer: Jack Cole
Conductor: Morris Stoloff

Cast

Al Jolson	LARRY PARKS
Julie Benson	EVELYN KEYES
Steve Martin	WILLIAM DEMAREST
Tom Baron	BILL GOODWIN
Cantor Yoelson	LUDWIG DONATH
Mama Yoelson	TAMARA SHAYNE
Lew Dockstader	JOHN ALEXANDER
Ann Murray	JO CARROLL DENNISON
Dick Glenn	WILLIAM FORREST
Father McGee	ERNEST COSSART
Al Jolson (as a boy)	SCOTTY BECKETT
Ann Murray (as a girl)	ANN TODD
Oscar Hammerstein I	EDWIN MAXWELL
Jonesy	EMMETT VOGAN
Henry	ERIC WILTON
Movie patron	WILL WRIGHT

THE MITCHELL "BOYCHOIR"

Rudy Wissler dubbed the songs for Scotty Beckett
Al Jolson dubbed the songs for Larry Parks

Songs
* "Let Me Sing and I'm Happy"
"Banks of the Wabash"
"Ave Maria"
"When You Were Sweet Sixteen"
"After the Ball"
"By the Light of the Silvery Moon"
"Blue Bell"
* "American Patrol"

* "Ma Blushin' Rosie"
* "I Want a Girl"
* "My Mammy"
* "I'm Sitting on Top of the World"
* "You Made Me Love You"
* "Swanee"
* "Toot, Toot, Tootsie! (Goo' Bye)"
* "The Spaniard That Blighted My Life"
* "April Showers"
* "California, Here I Come"
* "Liza (All the Clouds'll Roll Away)"
* "There's a Rainbow 'Round My Shoulder"
* "Avalon"
  "She's a Latin from Manhattan"
* "About a Quarter to Nine"
* "Anniversary Song"
* "Waiting for the Robert E. Lee"
* "Rock-a-Bye Your Baby with a Dixie Melody"

Notes: First part of "Blue Bell" sung by Rudy Wissler/lip synched by Scotty Beckett; second part whistled by Al Jolson/lip synched by Scotty Beckett.

"American Patrol" whistled by Al Jolson/lip synched by Scotty Beckett and Larry Parks for transition scene showing Jolson growing to adulthood.

JOLSON SINGS AGAIN
(Columbia, 1949)

Production: Oct. 1948–April 1949
Premiere: Aug. 10, 1949, Loew's State Theatre, New York
Length: 96 minutes

Director: Henry Levin
Producer: Sidney Buchman
Screenplay: Sidney Buchman
Conductor: Morris Stoloff

Cast

Al Jolson	LARRY PARKS
Ellen Clark	BARBARA HALE
Steve Martin	WILLIAM DEMAREST
Cantor Yoelson	LUDWIG DONATH
Tom Baron	BILL GOODWIN
Ralph Bryant	MYRON MCCORMICK
Mama Yoelson	TAMARA SHAYNE
Henry	ERIC WILTON
Charlie	ROBERT EMMETT KEANE

Al Jolson dubbed the songs for Larry Parks

Songs
* "Is It True What They Say About Dixie"
* "For Me and My Gal"

* "Back in Your Own Back Yard"
* "I'm Looking Over a Four-Leaf Clover"
* "When the Red, Red Robin Comes Bob, Bob, Bobbin' Along"
* "Give My Regards to Broadway"
* "Chinatown, My Chinatown"
* "I'm Just Wild About Harry"
* "Baby Face"
* "After You've Gone"
* "I Only Have Eyes for You"
* "Sonny Boy"
* "Pretty Baby"
* "Carolina in the Morning"
* "Rock-a-Bye Your Baby with Dixie Melody"

Radiography

Time slot:	Fridays, 10:00–10:30 p.m.
Sponsor:	General Motors
Announcer:	Howard Claney
Conductor:	Louis Silvers

Broadcast from San Francisco:
  Nov. 18, 1932
Broadcast from Los Angeles:
  Nov. 25, 1932
  Dec. 2, 1932
Broadcast from New York:
  Dec. 9, 1932
  Dec. 16, 1932
  Dec. 23, 1932
Broadcast from Chicago:
  Dec. 30, 1932
  Jan. 6, 1933

Broadcast from New York:
  Jan. 13, 1933
  Jan. 20, 1933
Broadcast from Miami Beach:
  Jan. 27, 1933
  Feb. 3, 1933
Broadcast from New York:
  Feb. 10, 1933
  Feb. 17, 1933
  Feb. 24, 1933

Total broadcasts: 15

Kraft Music Hall (N.B.C.)

Time slot:	Thursdays, 10:00–11:00 p.m.
Sponsor:	Kraft-Phoenix Cheese Corp.
Announcer:	Howard Claney
M.C.:	Deems Taylor
Conductor:	Paul Whiteman

Broadcast from New York: Aug. 3, 1933–Oct. 12, 1933 (11)
  Feb. 8, 1934–Apr. 12, 1934 (10)
  July 19, 1934–Aug. 16, 1934 (5)

Total broadcasts: 26

Shell Chateau (N.B.C.)

Time slot:	Saturdays, 9:30–10:30 p.m.
Sponsor:	Shell Union Oil Corp.

Announcer: John McIntyre
Conductor: Victor Young

Broadcast from New York: April 6, 1935–Sept. 28, 1935 (26)
Broadcast from Los Angeles: Jan. 4, 1936–March 28, 1936 (13)

Total broadcasts: 39

Cafe Trocadero (C.B.S.)

Time slot: Tuesdays, 8:30–9:00 p.m.
Sponsor: Lever Brothers Co.
Announcer: Tiny Ruffner
Conductor: Victor Young (1936–38)
             Lud Gluskin (1938–39)

Broadcast from Los Angeles: Dec. 22, 1936–June 29, 1937 (28)
                            Sept. 7, 1936–July 12, 1938 (45)
                            Sept. 20, 1938–Oct. 18, 1938 (5)
Broadcast from New York: Oct. 25, 1938–Nov. 15, 1938 (4)
Broadcast from Los Angeles: Nov. 22, 1938–March 14, 1939 (17)

Total broadcasts: 99

Al Jolson (C.B.S.)

Time slot: Tuesdays, 8:30–8:55 p.m.
Sponsor: Colgate-Palmolive-Peet Co.
Announcer: Fred Uttal (New York),
             Carlton Cardell (Los Angeles)
Conductor: Ray Bloch (New York),
             Gordon Jenkins (Los Angeles)

Broadcast from New York: Oct. 6, 1942–March 23, 1943 (25)
Broadcast from Los Angeles: March 30, 1943–June 29, 1943 (14)

Total broadcasts: 39

Kraft Music Hall (N.B.C.)

Time slot: Thursdays, 9:00–9:30 p.m.
Sponsor: Kraft Foods Co.
Announcer: Ken Carpenter
Conductor: Lou Bring

Broadcast from Los Angeles: Oct. 2, 1947–Feb. 19, 1948 (21)
Broadcast from Palm Springs: Feb. 26, 1948–March 4, 1948 (2)
Broadcast from Los Angeles: March 11, 1948–April 29, 1948 (8)
Broadcast from New York: May 6, 1948–May 20, 1948 (3)
Broadcast from Chicago: May 27, 1948 (1)
Broadcast from Los Angeles: June 3, 1948–June 10, 1948 (2)
Broadcast from Los Angeles: Sept. 30, 1948–Dec. 23, 1948 (13)
Broadcast from Palm Springs: Dec. 30, 1948–Jan. 6, 1949 (2)
Broadcast from Los Angeles: Jan. 13, 1949–March 24, 1949 (11)
Broadcast from Los Angeles: April 7, 1949–May 26, 1949 (8)

Total broadcasts: 71

Note: There was no Kraft Music Hall on March 31, 1949, due to NBC's broadcast of
Winston Churchill's speech at the Massachusetts Institute of Technology.

GUEST RADIO APPEARANCES
(Principal Network Broadcasts)

Mississippi Valley Flood Appeal (N.B.C.) Apr. 30, 1927 Chicago
Dodge Victory Hour (N.B.C.) Jan. 4, 1928 New Orleans
Warner Bros. Vitaphone Jubilee (C.B.S.) Sept. 17, 1928 New York
           March 4, 1929 Los Angeles
Pure Oil Band (N.B.C.) Oct. 15, 1929 Los Angeles
Kraft Music Hall (N.B.C.) June 26, 1933 New York
Rudy Vallee Show (N.B.C.) Dec. 21, 1933 Los Angeles
Hollywood Hotel (C.B.S.) Nov. 23, 1934 Los Angeles
      June 11, 1937 Los Angeles
Ben Bernie Show (C.B.S.) Jan. 1, 1935 Los Angeles
      Sept. 18, 1937 Los Angeles
      Jan. 21, 1940 New York
Hollywood Studios Opening (N.B.C.) Dec. 7, 1935 Los Angeles
Lux Radio Theatre (C.B.S.) June 15, 1936 Los Angeles
      Aug. 10, 1936 Los Angeles
      April 2, 1945 Los Angeles
      April 7, 1947 Los Angeles
      June 2, 1947 Los Angeles
      Feb. 16, 1948 Los Angeles
      May 22, 1950 Los Angeles
Texaco Star Theatre (C.B.S.) Jan. 3, 1937 Los Angeles
Gershwin Memorial Concert (C.B.S.) Sept. 8, 1937 Hollywood
Burns & Allen Grape Nuts Show (N.B.C.) Nov. 1, 1937 Los Angeles
Alexander's Ragtime Band (C.B.S.) Aug. 3, 1938 Los Angeles
Screen Actors' Guild Broadcast (N.B.C.) June 26, 1939 Hollywood
Kate Smith Show (C.B.S.) Dec. 29, 1939 New York
It's Time to Smile (N.B.C.) June 4, 1941 New York
Star Spangled Theatre (N.B.C.) Aug. 10, 1941 New York
Star Spangled Vaudeville (N.B.C.) Aug. 16, 1942 New York
Stage Door Canteen (C.B.S.) Dec. 24, 1942 New York
Soldiers in Greasepaint (N.B.C.) Nov. 25, 1943 New York
Night Clubs for Victory (C.B.S.) Jan. 20, 1944 New York
Radio Hall of Fame (N.B.C.) May 28, 1944 Philadelphia
Your All-Time Hit Parade (N.B.C.) July 23, 1944 New York
Let Yourself Go (C.B.S.) June 6, 1945 New York
Amos 'n' Andy (N.B.C.) Dec. 17, 1946 Los Angeles
Philco Radio Time (A.B.C.) Jan. 15, 1947 Los Angeles
      March 5, 1947 Los Angeles
      April 2, 1947 Los Angeles
      May 7, 1947 Los Angeles
      Dec. 3, 1947 Los Angeles
Maxwell House Coffee Time (N.B.C.) Feb. 20, 1947 Los Angeles

Pabst Blue Ribbon Show (N.B.C.) March 6, 1947 Los Angeles
                           Jan. 8, 1948 Los Angeles
                           June 8, 1948 Los Angeles
                           Jan. 7, 1949 Los Angeles

Bob Hope Show (N.B.C.) April 8, 1947 Los Angeles

Jack Benny Show (N.B.C.) May 18, 1947 New York

Operation Nightmare (C.B.S.) June 9, 1947 Los Angeles
                        April 10, 1948 Los Angeles

Jimmy Durante Show (N.B.C.) Jan. 21, 1948 Los Angeles
                        March 4, 1949 Los Angeles
                        Nov. 11, 1949 Los Angeles

Chase & Sanborn Hour (N.B.C.) Jan. 25, 1948 Los Angeles
                        Jan. 15, 1950 Los Angeles

This is Your Life (N.B.C.) Nov. 23, 1948 Los Angeles

Elgin Two Hours of Stars (N.B.C.) Dec. 25, 1948 Los Angeles

Operation Dawn (N.B.C.) May 22, 1949 Los Angeles

Bing Crosby Show (C.B.S.) Nov. 30, 1949 Los Angeles
                        Dec. 28, 1949 Los Angeles
                        Jan. 4, 1950 Los Angeles
                        Feb. 15, 1950 Los Angeles
                        May 3, 1950 Los Angeles

Leave it to Joan (C.B.S.) Jan. 20, 1950 Los Angeles

Burns & Allen Show (C.B.S.) Feb. 1, 1950 Los Angeles
                        March 29, 1950 Los Angeles

Jack Benny Program (C.B.S.) April 2, 1950 Los Angeles

GUEST RADIO APPEARANCES
(Principal Non-Network Broadcasts)

*Westinghouse Wireless Broadcast Feb. 5, 1922 Newark, N.J.

Lambs' Gambol April 26, 1925 New York

Jack Rose Benefit April 18, 1926 New York

Salute to K.N.X. and K.S.F.O. Jan. 2, 1937 Los Angeles

Musical Tribute to George Gershwin July 12, 1937 Los Angeles

Hold on to Your Hats Aug. 1, 1940 Chicago

Command Performance, U.S.A. May 13, 1942 Cleveland

Barry Gray Show (W.O.R.) Oct. 27, 1946 New York

Steve Allen Show (K.N.X.) Oct. 26, 1949 Los Angeles

* This was Jolson's radio debut. Singing into a "broadcasting wireless telephone" at the Westinghouse plant in Newark, he was heard throughout most of the eastern United States—particularly in hospitals housing wounded soldiers, where his voice was received and relayed by "loud speaking telephone devices" in the wards.

Discography

(Recordings made for direct sale to the public)

Feb. 9, 1910. New York, N.Y.
With Edison Orchestra.

	"Come Along My Mandy"	UNISSUED
	(Jack Norworth-Nora Bayes)	
	"That Mesmereizing Mendelssohn Tune"	UNISSUED
	(Irving Berlin)	

Dec. 22, 1911. Camden, N.J.
With Victor Orchestra under direction of Walter B. Rogers.

B-11409	"That Haunting Melody"	Victor
	(George M. Cohan)	17037 (2)
B-11410	"Rum Tum Tiddle"	Victor
	(Jean Schwartz-Edward Madden)	17037 (3)
B-11411	"Asleep in the Deep" [parody]	Victor
	(Arthur Lamb-H. W. Petrie)	17915 (1)

March 15, 1912. Camden, N.J.
With Victor Orchestra under direction of Walter B. Rogers.

B-11730	"The Villain Still Pursued Her"	UNISSUED
	(Harry von Tilzer-William Jerome)	
B-11731	"My Sumurun Girl"	UNISSUED
	(Louis A. Hirsch-Al Jolson)	
B-11732	"Snap Your Fingers"	Victor
	(Harry von Tilzer-Wiliam Jerome)	17075
B-11733	"Brass Band Ephraham Jones"	Victor
	(George W. Meyer-Joe Goodwin)	17068

April 17, 1912. Camden, N.J.
With Victor Orchestra under direction of Walter B. Rogers.
Matrix B-11886 is a whistling solo.

B-11883	"Ragging the Baby to Sleep"	Victor
	(Lewis F. Muir-L. Wolfe Gilbert)	17081
B-11884	"That Lovin' Traumerei"	Victor
	(Aubrey Stauffer)	17119 (2)

B-11885 "Movin' Man, Don't Take My Baby Grand"   Victor
         (Ted Snyder-Bert Kalmar)   17081
B-11886 "Uncle Sammy" (March And Two-Step)   UNISSUED
         (Abe Holzman-F. Henri Klickman)

March 7, 1913. Camden, N.J.
With Victor Orchestra under direction of Walter B. Rogers.

B-12971 "My Yellow Jacket Girl"   Victor
         (Jean Schwartz-Harold Atteridge)   17318 (1)
B-12972 "The Spaniard That Blighted My Life"   Victor
         (Billy Merson)   17318 (1)

June 4, 1913. New York, N.Y.
With Columbia Orchestra under direction of Charles A. Prince.

38901   "Pullman Porters on Parade"   Columbia
         (Irving Berlin-Maurice Abrahams)   A1374 (1)
38902   "You Made Me Love You"   Columbia
         (Joseph McCarthy-James V. Monaco)   A1374 (1)
38903   "That Little German Band"   Columbia
         (Fred Fisher-Joe Godwin-Joseph McCarthy)   A1356 (2)
38904   "Everybody Snap Your Fingers with Me"   Columbia
         (Harry Puck-Bert Kalmar)   A1356 (1)

Sept. 19, 1914. New York, N.Y.
With Columbia Orchestra under direction of Charles A. Prince.

39567   "Back to the Carolina You Love"   Columbia
         (Jean Schwartz-Grant Clarke)   A1621 (1, 8)
39568   "Revival Day"   Columbia
         (Irving Berlin)   A1621 (1, 5)

Dec. 3, 1914. New York, N.Y.
With Columbia Orchestra under direction of Charles A. Prince.

39664   "Sister Susie's Sewing Shirts for Soldiers"   Columbia
         (Hermann Darewski-R. P. Weston)   A1671
                                                      (1, 5, 6, 8)
39665   "When the Grown Up Ladies Act Like Babies (I've   Columbia
         Gotta Love 'Em, That's All)"   A1671 (1, 2)
         (Maurice Abrahams-Edgar Leslie-Joe Young)

Jan. 14, 1916. New York, N.Y.
With Columbia Orchestra under direction of Charles A. Prince.

46335   "There's a Broken Heart for Every Light on   UNISSUED
         Broadway"
         (Fred Fisher-Howard Johnson)
46336   "Eeny Meany Miney Moe"   UNISSUED
         (Authorship Unknown)
46337   "Yaaka Hula Hickey Dula"   Columbia
         (Pete Wendling-E. Ray Goetz-Joe Young)   A-1956 (1)

Feb. 28, 1916. New York, N.Y.
With Columbia Orchestra under direction of Charles A. Prince.

46459	"Where Did Robinson Crusoe Go with Friday on Saturday Night?" (George W. Meyer-Sam M. Lewis-Joe Young)	Columbia A-1976 (1)
46460	"Down Where the Swanee River Flows" (Albert von Tilzer-Charles S. Alberte-Charles McCarron)	Columbia A-2007 (1)
46463	"Now He's Got a Beautiful Girl" (Ted Snyder-Edgar Leslie-Grant Clarke)	Columbia A-2080 (1)

May 17, 1916. New York, N.Y.
With Columbia Orchestra under direction of Charles A. Prince.

46786	"I Sent My Wife to the Thousand Isles" (Harry von Tilzer-Ed P. Moran-Andrew B. Sterling)	Columbia A-2021 (1)
46787	"You're a Dangerous Girl" (James V. Monaco-Grant Clarke)	Columbia A-2041 (2)

June 9, 1916. New York, N.Y.
With Columbia Orchestra under direction of Charles A. Prince.

46820	"I'm Saving Up the Means To Get to New Orleans" (Harry DeCosta-Howard Johnson)	Columbia A-2064 (1)

Sept. 19, 1916. New York, N.Y.
With Columbia Orchestra under direction of Charles A. Prince.

47029	"Someone Else May Be There While I'm Gone" (Irving Berlin)	Columbia A-2124 (1)
47030	"I'm Down in Honolulu Looking Them Over" (Irving Berlin)	UNISSUED
47031	"Don't Write Me Letters" (Bert Grant)	Columbia A-2106 (1)

Nov. 26, 1916. New York, N.Y.
With Columbia Orchestra under direction of Charles A. Prince.

47191	"A Broken Doll" (Clifford Harris-Joseph W. Tate)	Columbia A-2154 (1)
47192	"Ev'ry Little While" (Ernie Golden-Joseph W. Tate)	Columbia A-2181 (2)

Dec. 11, 1916. New York, N.Y.
With Columbia Orchestra under direction of Charles A. Prince.

47217	"Pray for Sunshine" (Maurice Abrahams-Sam M. Lewis-Joe Young)	Columbia A-2169 (3)
47218	"From Here to Shanghai" (Irving Berlin)	Columbia A-2224 (3)

May 29, 1917. New York, N.Y.
With Columbia Orchestra under direction of Charles A. Prince.

77079 "Tillie Titwillow"   Columbia
       (Phil Schwartz-Harold Atteridge)   A-2296 (1, 2, 3)

Dec. 13, 1917. New York, N.Y.
With Columbia Orchestra under direction of Charles A. Prince.

77571 "Wedding Bells"   Columbia
       (Jean Schwartz-Sam M. Lewis-Joe Young)   A-2512 (4, 6)

77572 "I'm All Bound 'Round with the Mason-Dixon   Columbia
       Line"   A-2478 (1, 2)
       (Jean Schwartz-Lewis-Young)

Dec. 27, 1917. New York, N.Y.
With Columbia Orchestra under direction of Charles A. Prince.

77602 " 'N' Everything"   Columbia
       (Al Jolson-Bud DeSylva-Gus Kahn)   A-2519 (1, 2, 3)

77603 "There's A Lump of Sugar Down in Dixie"   Columbia
       (Albert Gamble-Jack Yellen-Alfred Bryan)   A-2491 (1, 2)

March 13, 1918. New York, N.Y.
With Columbia Orchestra under direction of Charles A. Prince.

77720 "Rock-a-Bye Your Baby with a Dixie Melody"   Columbia
       (Jean Schwartz-Lewis-Young)   A-2560 (2)

April 3, 1918. New York, N.Y.
With Columbia Orchestra under direction of Charles A. Prince.

77753 "Hello Central, Give Me No Man's Land"   Columbia
       (Jean Schwartz-Lewis-Young)   A-2542 (1, 2)

Sept. 10, 1918. New York, N.Y.
With Columbia Orchestra under direction of Charles A. Prince.

78046 "Tell That to the Marines"   Columbia
       (Jean Schwartz-Al Jolson-Harold Atteridge) A-2657 (1, 2)

78047 "I Wonder Why She Kept On Saying 'Si, Si, Si,   Columbia
       Si, Senor' "   A-2671 (1)
       (Ted Snyder-Lewis-Young)

Oct. 24, 1918. New York, N.Y.
With Columbia Orchestra under direction of Charles A. Prince.

78153 "I'll Say She Does"   Columbia
       (Al Jolson-Gus Kahn-Bud DeSylva)   A-2746 (3)

Dec. 6, 1918. New York, N.Y.
With Columbia Orchestra under direction of Charles A. Prince.

78193 "On the Road to Calais"   Columbia
       (Jean Schwartz-Al Jolson-Alfred Bryan)   A-2690 (1)

Dec. 13, 1918. New York, N.Y.
With Columbia Orchestra under direction of Charles A. Prince.

78201 "Don't Forget the Boys"   UNISSUED
       (Fred E. Ahlert-Al Jolson-Harold Atteridge)

July 23, 1919. New York, N.Y.
With Columbia Orchestra under direction of Charles A. Prince.

78593   "Some Beautiful Morning"   Columbia
        (Al Jolson-Cliff Friend)   A-2940 (1, 4)
78594   "Who Played Poker with Pocahontas?"   Columbia
        (Fred E. Ahlert-Sam M. Lewis-Joe Young)   A-2787 (1)

July 25, 1919. New York, N.Y.
With Columbia Orchestra under direction of Charles A. Prince.

78600   "Her Danny"   UNISSUED
        (Chris Schonberg-Hale N. Byers)

Sept. 14, 1919. New York, N.Y.
With Columbia Orchestra under direction of Charles A. Prince.

78652   "I've Got My Captain Working for Me Now"   Columbia
        (Irving Berlin)   A-2794 (2, 5)

Sept. 21, 1919. New York, N.Y.
With Columbia Orchestra under direction of Charles A. Prince.

78684   "You Ain't Heard Nothing Yet"   Columbia
        (Al Jolson-Gus Kahn-Bud DeSylva)   A-2836 (1, 2)
78685   "I Gave Her That"   Columbia
        (Al Jolson-Bud DeSylva)   A-2835 (1, 2)

Oct. 3, 1919. New York, N.Y.
With Columbia Orchestra under direction of Charles A. Prince.

78722   "Tell Me (Why Nights Are Lonely)"   Columbia
        (Max Kortlander-J. Will Callahan)   A-2821 (1, 2, 3)

Oct. 19, 1919. New York, N.Y.
With Columbia Orchestra under direction of Charles A. Prince.

78743   "Chloe"   Columbia
        (Al Jolson-Bud DeSylva)   A-2861 (2)

Jan. 8, 1920. New York, N.Y.
With Columbia Orchestra under direction of Charles A. Prince.

78916   "That Wonderful Kid from Madrid"   Columbia
        (Nat Osborne-Ballard MacDonald)   A-2898 (2, 3)
78917   "Swanee"   Columbia
        (George Gershwin-Irving Caesar)   A-2884 (2)

April 30, 1920. New York, N.Y.
With Columbia Orchestra under direction of Charles A. Prince.

79152   "In Sweet September"   Columbia
        (Pete Wendling-James V. Monaco-Edgar Leslie)   A-2946 (2, 3)

Aug. 16, 1920. New York, N.Y.
With Columbia Orchestra under direction of Charles A. Prince.

79371   "Avalon"   Columbia
        (Vincent Rose-Al Jolson-Bud DeSylva)   A-2995

Dec. 12, 1920. New York, N.Y.
With Columbia Orchestra under direction of Charles A. Prince.

79568 "O-HI-O"   Columbia
       (Abe Olman-Jack Yellen)   A-3361 (1, 2)

Jan. 4, 1921. New York, N.Y.
With Columbia Orchestra under direction of Charles A. Prince.

79624 "Ding-A-Ring A-Ring"   Columbia
       (Ira Schuster-Irving Bibo-Al Wilson)   A-3375 (3)

Feb. 14, 1921. New York, N.Y.
With Columbia Orchestra under direction of Charles A. Prince.

79726 "Scandinavia"   Columbia
       (Ray Perkins)   A-3382

July 19, 1921. New York, N.Y.
With Columbia Orchestra under direction of Charles A. Prince.

79953 "She Knows It"   UNISSUED
       (Clarence J. Marks-Jack Stern)

Oct. 21, 1921. New York, N.Y.
With Columbia Orchestra under direction of Charles A. Prince.

80041 "April Showers"   Columbia
       (Louis Silvers-Bud DeSylva)   A-3500 (2)
80042 "Give Me My Mammy"   Columbia
       (Walter Donaldson-Bud DeSylva)   A-3540 (2)

Nov. 7, 1921. New York, N.Y.
With Columbia Orchestra under direction of Charles A. Prince.

80052 "Yoo-Hoo"   Columbia
       (Al Jolson-Bud DeSylva)   A-3513 (1)

Jan. 17, 1922. New York, N.Y.
With Columbia Orchestra under direction of Charles A. Prince.

80140 "Angel Child"   Columbia
       (Abner Silver-Georgie Price-Benny Davis)   A-3568 (3)

March 10, 1922. New York, N.Y.
With Columbia Orchestra under direction of Charles A. Prince.

80232 "Oogie Oogie Wa Wa"   Columbia
       (Archie Gottler-Edgar Leslie-Grant Clarke)   A-3588 (2, 10)

April 24, 1922. New York, N.Y.
With Columbia Orchestra under direction of Charles A. Prince.

80317 "Coo-Coo"   Columbia
       (Al Jolson-Bud DeSylva)   A-3626 (2)

Aug. 4, 1922. New York, N.Y.
With Columbia Orchestra under direction of Charles A. Prince.

80500 "I'll Stand Beneath Your Window Tonight And   Columbia
          Whistle"   A-3694 (2, 3)
       (Jimmy McHugh-Georgie Price-Jerry Benson)

Sept. 9, 1922. New York, N.Y.
With Columbia Orchestra under direction of Charles A. Prince.

80532	"Toot, Toot, Tootsie! (Goo' Bye)"	Columbia
	(Gus Kahn-Ernie Erdman-Dan Russo)	A-3705 (3)
80533	"Do I? (Do I? Do I Love Her?)"	UNISSUED
	(Harry Akst-Sam M. Lewis-Joe Young)	

Oct. 10, 1922. Chicago, Ill.
With Frank Westphal Orchestra.

80593	"Lost: A Wonderful Girl"	Columbia
	(James F. Hanley-Benny Davis)	A-3744 (1)

Nov. 10, 1922. Chicago, Ill.
With Frank Westphal Orchestra.

80609	"Some of These Days"	UNISSUED
	(Shelton Brooks)	

Nov. 13, 1922. Chicago, Ill.
With Paul Biese and his Edgewater Beach Hotel Orchestra.

80631	"Who Cares?"	UNISSUED:
	(Milton Ager-Jack Yellen)	REJECTS

Dec. 5, 1922. Chicago, Ill.
With Paul Biese and his Edgewater Beach Hotel Orchestra.

80631	"Who Cares?"	Columbia
	(Milton Ager-Jack Yellen)	A-3779 (8)

Jan. 4, 1923. Chicago, Ill.
With Frank Westphal Orchestra.

80761	"Coal Black Mammy"	Columbia
	(Ivy St. Helier-Laddie Cliff)	A-3854 (2)
80762	"Wanita"	Columbia
	(Sam Coslow-Al Sherman)	A-3812 (1)

March 31, 1923. New York, N.Y.
With Columbia Orchestra.

80929	"Morning Will Come"	UNISSUED:
	(Con Conrad-Al Jolson-Bud DeSylva)	REJECTS

April 15, 1923. New York, N.Y.
With Columbia Orchestra.

80929	"Morning Will Come"	Columbia
	(Con Conrad-Al Jolson-Bud DeSylva)	A-3880 (6)

May 15, 1923. New York, N.Y.
With Columbia Orchestra.

81016	"Stella"	Columbia
	(Harry Akst-Al Jolson-Benny Davis)	A-3913 (1)

June 12, 1923. New York, N.Y.
With Columbia Orchestra.

81072	"Waitin' for the Evenin' Mail"	Columbia
	(Billy Baskette)	A-3933 (2, 3)

July 27, 1923. New York, N.Y.
With Columbia Orchestra.

81152	"That Big Blond Mama"	Columbia
	(James V. Monaco-Billy Rose)	A-3968 (1)

Sept. 7, 1923. New York, N.Y.
With Columbia Orchestra.

81201	"You've Simply Got Me Cuckoo"	Columbia
	(Jesse Greer-Walter Hirsch)	A-3984 (1)

Oct. 13, 1923. New York, N.Y.
With Columbia Orchestra.

81281	"Mama Loves Papa"	UNISSUED
	(Abel Baer-Cliff Friend)	

Nov. 23, 1923. New York, N.Y.
With Columbia Orchestra.

81368	"Arcady"	Columbia
	(Al Jolson-Bud DeSylva)	43-D (1)

Dec. 18, 1923. New York, N.Y.
With Columbia Orchestra.

81423	"I'm Goin' South"	Columbia
	(Harry Woods-Abner Silver)	61-D (1)

Dec. 20, 1923. New York, N.Y.
With Columbia Orchestra.

81429	"Twelve O'Clock at Night"	Columbia
	(Lou Handman-Roy Turk)	79-D (3)

Jan. 17, 1924. Chicago, Ill.
With Isham Jones and his Orchestra.

C-20	"I'm Goin' South"	Brunswick
C-21	(Harry Woods-Abner Silver)	2569-A
C-22		
C-23	"Never Again"	Brunswick
C-24	(Isham Jones-Gus Kahn)	2611-B
C-25		
C-26	"California, Here I Come"	Brunswick
C-27	(Joseph Meyer-Al Jolson-Bud DeSylva)	2569-B
C-28	"The One I Love Belongs to Somebody Else"	Brunswick
C-29	(Isham Jones-Gus Kahn)	2567-A

Jan. 18, 1924. Chicago, Ill.
With Isham Jones and his Orchestra.

C-41	"Steppin' Out"	Brunswick
C-42	(Con Conrad-Richard Howard)	2567-B
C-43	"Feeling The Way I Do"	Brunswick
C-44	(Walter Donaldson-Bud DeSylva)	2611-A

Feb. 24, 1924. Chicago, Ill.
With Isham Jones and his Orchestra.

C-81	"Mr. Radio Man"	UNISSUED
C-82	(Ira Schuster-William Wilfred-Cliff Friend)	
C-83	"Home in Pasadena"	UNISSUED
C-84	(Harry Warren-Grant Clarke-Edgar Leslie)	

March 13, 1924. Chicago, Ill.
With Gene Rodemich and his Orchestra.

C-95	"My Papa Doesn't Two Time No Time"	Brunswick
C-96	(Walter Donaldson)	2595-B
C-97		
C-98		
C-99	"Lazy"	Brunswick
C-100	(Irving Berlin)	2595-A
C-101		
C-102		

March 14, 1924. Chicago, Ill.
With Isham Jones and his Orchestra.

C-106	"Mr. Radio Man"	Brunswick
C-107	(Ira Schuster-William Wilfred-Cliff Friend)	2582-A
C-108	"Home in Pasadena"	Brunswick
C-109	(Harry Warren-Grant Clarke-Edgar Leslie)	2582-B
C-110		

July 2, 1924. New York, N.Y.
With Abe Lyman's California Orchestra.

13472	"Mandalay"	Brunswick
13473	(Abe Lyman-Gus Arnheim-Earl Burtnett)	2650-A
13474		

July 3, 1924. New York, N.Y.
With Brunswick Orchestra.

13475	"*Il Barbiere di Siviglia*"	UNISSUED
13476	(G. Rossini)	
13477		
13478	"I, Pagliacci"	UNISSUED
13479	(R. Leonca Vallo)	
13480		

July 18, 1924. New York, N.Y.
With Abe Lyman's California Orchestra.

13566	"Who Wants a Bad Little Boy?"	UNISSUED:
13567	(Fred Fisher-Joe Burke)	REJECTS
13568		
13569		

July 25, 1924. New York, N.Y.
With Abe Lyman's California Orchestra.

| 13617 | "Who Wants a Bad Little Boy?" | Brunswick |
| 13618 | (Fred Fisher-Joe Burke) | 2650-B |

Aug. 6, 1924. New York, N.Y.
With Carl Fenton and his Orchestra.

13686	"Follow the Swallow"	Brunswick
13687	(Ray Henderson-Billy Rose-Mort Dixon)	2671-A
13688		
13689	"I Wonder What's Become of Sally"	Brunswick
13690	(Milton Ager-Jack Yellen)	2671-B
13691		

Oct. 2, 1924. New York, N.Y.
With Ray Miller and his Orchestra.

13864	"All Alone"	Brunswick
13865	(Irving Berlin)	2743-A
13866		
13867		

Oct. 15, 1924. New York, N.Y.
With Ray Miller and his Orchestra.

13954	"I'm Gonna Tramp! Tramp! Tramp!"	Brunswick
13955	(Harry Woods-Bud DeSylva)	2743-B
13956		

Nov. 14, 1924. New York, N.Y.
With Carl Fenton and his Orchestra.

14206	"Hello, 'Tucky!"	UNISSUED:
14207	(James F. Hanley-Joseph Meyer-Bud DeSylva)	REJECTS
14208	"Keep Smiling at Trouble"	UNISSUED:
14209	(Lewis Gensler-Al Jolson-Bud DeSylva)	REJECTS
14210		

Nov. 19, 1924. New York, N.Y.
With Carl Fenton and his Orchestra.

14264	"Keep Smiling at Trouble"	Brunswick
14265	(Lewis Gensler-Al Jolson-Bud DeSylva)	2763-A
14266	"Hello, 'Tucky!"	Brunswick
14267	(James F. Hanley-Joseph Meyer-Bud DeSylva)	2763-B
14268		

Oct. 22, 1925. New York, N.Y.
With Orchestra under direction of Alfred Newman.

E-16744	"Nobody But Fanny"	UNISSUED
E-16745	(Con Conrad-Al Jolson-Bud DeSylva)	
E-16746	"Miami"	UNISSUED
E-16747	(Con Conrad-Al Jolson-Bud DeSylva)	

Oct. 30, 1925. New York, N.Y.
With Orchestra under direction of Alfred Newman.

E-16807	"Miami"	UNISSUED
E-16808	(Con Conrad-Al Jolson-Bud DeSylva)	
E-16809	"Nobody But Fanny"	UNISSUED
E-16810	(Con Conrad-Al Jolson-Bud DeSylva)	

Dec. 21, 1925. New York, N.Y.
With Carl Fenton and his Orchestra.

E-17172	"I'm Sitting on Top of the World"	Brunswick
E-17173	(Ray Henderson-Lewis-Young)	3014-A
E-17174	"You Forgot To Remember"	Brunswick
E-17175	(Irving Berlin)	3013-B
E-17176	"You Flew Away from the Nest"	Brunswick
E-17177	(Harry Ruby-Bert Kalmar)	3014-B
E-17178	"Miami"	Brunswick
E-17179	(Con Conrad-Al Jolson-Bud DeSylva)	3013-A

April 23, 1926. New York, N.Y.
With Carl Fenton and his Orchestra.

E-18852	"I Wish I Had My Old Gal Back Again"	Brunswick
E-18853	(Milton Ager-Lew Pollack-Jack Yellen)	3183-A
E-18854		
E-18855	"(I'd Climb the Highest Mountain) If I Knew I'd	Brunswick
E-18856	Find You"	3183-B
E-18857	(Sidney Clare-Lew Brown)	

May 3, 1926. New York, N.Y.
With Carl Fenton and his Orchestra.

E-18982	"At Peace with the World"	Brunswick
E-18983	(Irving Berlin)	3196-A
E-18984	"Tonight's My Night with Baby"	Brunswick
E-18985	(Joseph Meyer-Bobby Buttenuth-Irving Caesar)	3196-B
E-18986		

June 1, 1926. New York, N.Y.
With Carl Fenton and his Orchestra.

E-19418	"When the Red, Red Robin Comes Bob, Bob,	Brunswick
E-19419	Bobbin' Along"	3222-A
E-19420	(Harry Woods)	
E-19421	"Here I Am"	Brunswick
E-19422	(B. G. DeSylva-Lew Brown-Ray Henderson)	3222-B
E-19423		

Nov. 11, 1927. New York, N.Y.
With William F. Wirges and his Orchestra.

E-25183	"Mother of Mine, I Still Have You"	Brunswick
E-25184	(Louis Silvers-Al Jolson-Grant Clarke)	3719-A
E-25185		
E-25186	"Blue River"	Brunswick
E-25187	(Joseph Meyer-Alfred Bryan)	3719-B
E-25188		
E-25189		

Jan. 13, 1928. New York, N.Y.
With William F. Wirges and his Orchestra.

E-26010	"Four Walls"	Brunswick
E-26011	(Dave Dreyer-Al Jolson-Billy Rose)	3775-B

E-26012	"Golden Gate"	Brunswick
E-26013	(Dave Dreyer-Joseph Meyer-Al Jolson-Billy Rose)	3775-A
E-26014		

March 8, 1928. New York, N.Y.
With William F. Wirges and his Orchestra.

E-26879	"Ol' Man River"	Brunswick
E-26880	(Jerome Kern-Oscar Hammerstein II)	3867-A
E-26881		
E-26882	"Back in Your Own Back Yard"	Brunswick
E-26883	(Dave Dreyer-Al Jolson-Billy Rose)	3867-B
E-26884		

March 31, 1928. New York, N.Y.
With Abe Lyman's California Orchestra.

C-1832	"Dirty Hands, Dirty Face" (James V. Monaco-Al Jolson-Grant Clarke-Edgar Leslie)	Brunswick 3912 (A)(B)(C)
C-1833	"My Mammy" (Walter Donaldson-Sam M. Lewis-Joe Young)	Brunswick 3912 (A)(B)(C)

Aug. 20, 1928. Los Angeles, Calif.
With Vitaphone Orchestra under direction of Louis Silvers.

LAE-249	"There's a Rainbow 'Round My Shoulder" (Dave Dreyer-Al Jolson-Billy Rose)	Brunswick 4033 (A)(B)(C)
LAE-250	"Sonny Boy" (Al Jolson-DeSylva-Brown-Henderson)	Brunswick 4033 (A)(B)

April 7, 1929. Los Angeles, Calif.
With Vitaphone Orchestra under direction of Louis Silvers.

LAE-446	"I'm in Seventh Heaven" (Al Jolson-DeSylva-Brown-Henderson)	Brunswick 4400 (A)(B)
LAE-447	"Little Pal" (Al Jolson-DeSylva-Brown-Henderson)	Brunswick 4400 (A)(B)(C)
LAE-448	"Used to You" (Al Jolson-DeSylva-Brown-Henderson)	Brunswick 4401 (A)(B)
LAE-449	"Why Can't You?" (Al Jolson-DeSylva-Brown-Henderson)	Brunswick 4401 (A)(B)
LAE-450	"(Mem'ries of) One Sweet Kiss" (Dave Dreyer-Al Jolson)	Brunswick 4402 (A)(B)

July 25, 1929. New York, N.Y.
With Brunswick Orchestra under direction of Robert Haring.

E-30576	"Liza" (George Gershwin-Ira Gershwin-Gus Kahn)	Brunswick 4402 (A)(B)

Jan. 10, 1930. Los Angeles, Calif.
With Vitaphone Orchestra under direction of Louis Silvers.

LAE-685	"Let Me Sing and I'm Happy" (Irving Berlin)	Brunswick 4721 (A)(B)

LAE-686   "To My Mammy"   Brunswick 4722
          (Irving Berlin)   (A)(B)

LAE-687   "Looking at You"   Brunswick 4721
          (Irving Berlin)   (A)(B)

LAE-688   "When the Little Red Roses Get the Blues for   Brunswick 4722
              You"   (A)(B)
          (Joe Burke-Al Dubin)

Dec. 20, 1932. New York, N.Y.
With Brunswick Orchestra under direction of Victor Young.

B-12760   "A Chazend'l Ohf Shabbes"   Brunswick 6501
          (Arranged by A. W. Binder)

B-12761   "Hallelujah, I'm a Bum"   Brunswick 6500
          (Richard Rodgers-Lorenz Hart)

B-12762   "You Are Too Beautiful"   Brunswick 6500
          (Richard Rodgers-Lorenz Hart)

Dec. 20, 1932. New York, N.Y.
With Guy Lombardo and his Royal Canadians.

B-12763   "April Showers"   Brunswick 6502
          (Louis Silvers-Bud DeSylva)

B-12764   "Rock-A-Bye Your Baby with a Dixie Melody"   Brunswick 6502
          (Jean Schwartz-Lewis-Young)

Aug. 10, 1945. Los Angeles, Calif.
With Orchestra under direction of Carmen Dragon.

L-3912   "Swanee"   Decca 23470-A
          (George Gershwin-Irving Caesar)

L-3913   "April Showers"   Decca 23470-B
          (Louis Silvers-Bud DeSylva)

March 20, 1946. Los Angeles, Calif.
With Orchestra under direction of Morris W. Stoloff.

L-4126   "Ma Blushin' Rosie"   Decca 23613-B
          (John Stromberg-Edgar Smith)

L-4127   "My Mammy"   Decca 23614-B
          (Walter Donaldson-Lewis-Young)

L-4128   "You Made Me Love You"   Decca 23613-A
          (James V. Monaco-Joseph McCarthy)

March 27, 1946. Los Angeles, Calif.
With Orchestra under direction of Morris W. Stoloff.

L-4140   "Rock-a-Bye Your Baby with a Dixie Melody"   Decca 23612-B
          (Jean Schwartz-Lewis-Young)

L-4141   "California, Here I Come"   Decca 23612-A
          (Joseph Meyer-Al Jolson-Bud DeSylva)

L-4142   "Sonny Boy"   Decca 23614-A
          (Al Jolson-DeSylva-Brown-Henderson)

Aug. 21, 1946. Los Angeles, Calif.
With Orchestra under direction of Morris W. Stoloff.

L-4269   "Avalon"   Decca 23714-A
         (Vincent Rose-Al Jolson-Bud DeSylva)

L-4270   "Anniversary Song"   Decca 23714-B
         (Al Jolson-Saul Chaplin)

March 25, 1947. Los Angeles, Calif.
With Bing Crosby.
With Orchestra under direction of Morris W. Stoloff.

L-4386   "Alexander's Ragtime Band"   Decca 40038-A
         (Irving Berlin)

L-4387   "The Spaniard That Blighted My Life"   Decca 40038-B
         (Billy Merson)

May 19, 1947. New York, N.Y.
With Orchestra under direction of Jay Blackton.

73916   "All My Love"   Decca 23953-A
         (Harry Akst-Al Jolson-Saul Chaplin)

73917   "Keep Smiling at Trouble"   Decca 23953-B
         (Lewis Gensler-Al Jolson-Bud DeSylva)

June 9, 1947. Los Angeles, Calif.
With Orchestra under direction of Morris W. Stoloff.

L-4440   "Back in Your Own Back Yard"   Decca 24108-B
         (Dave Dreyer-Al Jolson-Billy Rose)

L-4441   "I'm Sitting on Top of the World"   Decca 24107-B
         (Ray Henderson-Sam M. Lewis-Joe Young)

L-4442   "Where the Black-Eyed Susans Grow"   Decca 24398-B
         (Richard A. Whiting-Dave Radford)

L-4443   "Toot, Toot, Tootsie! (Goo' Bye)   Decca 24108-A
         (Gus Kahn-Ernie Erdman-Dan Russo)

June 11, 1947. Los Angeles, Calif.
With Orchestra under direction of Morris W. Stoloff.

L-4444   "Carolina in the Morning"   Decca 24109-A
         (Walter Donaldson-Gus Kahn)

L-4445   "Liza"   Decca 24109-B
         (George Gershwin-Ira Gershwin-Gus Kahn)

L-4446   "For Me and My Gal"   Decca 24399-A
         (George W. Meyer-E. Ray Goetz-Edgar Leslie)

June 18, 1947. Los Angeles, Calif.
With Orchestra under direction of Morris W. Stoloff.

L-4456   "About A Quarter to Nine"   Decca 24400-B
         (Harry Warren-Al Dubin)

L-4457   "Waiting for the Robert E. Lee"   Decca 24106-A
         (Lewis F. Muir-L. Wolfe Gilbert)

L-4458   "Golden Gate"   Decca 24107-A
         (Dave Dreyer-Joseph Meyer-Al Jolson-Billy Rose)

L-4459   "When You Were Sweet Sixteen"   Decca 24106-B
         (James Thornton)

Nov. 21, 1947. Los Angeles, Calif.
With Orchestra under direction of Morris W. Stoloff.

L-4569	"There's a Rainbow 'Round My Shoulder" (Dave Dreyer-Al Jolson-Billy Rose)	Decca 24400-A
L-4570	"If I Only Had a Match" (George W. Meyer-Arthur Johnson-Lee Morris)	Decca 24296-A
L-4571	"Let Me Sing and I'm Happy" (Irving Berlin)	Decca 24196-B

Nov. 28, 1947. Los Angeles, Calif.
With Orchestra and Male Quartet under direction of Morris W. Stoloff.

L-4584	"I Want a Girl (Just Like the Girl That Married Dear Old Dad)" (Harry von Tilzer-Will Dillon)	Decca 24397-A
L-4585	"By the Light of the Silvery Moon" (Gus Edwards-Edward Madden)	Decca 24518-A

Dec. 5, 1947. Los Angeles, Calif.
With Orchestra under direction of Morris W. Stoloff.

L-4620	"I Wish I Had a Girl" (Gus Kahn-Grace LeBoy)	Decca 24518-B
L-4621	"When I Leave the World Behind" (Irving Berlin)	Decca 24399-B
L-4622	"Someone Else May Be There While I'm Gone" (Irving Berlin)	Decca 24398-A
L-4623	"When the Red, Red Robin Comes Bob, Bob, Bobbin' Along" (Harry Woods)	Decca 24398-B

Dec. 19, 1947. Los Angeles, Calif.
With Orchestra and Choir under direction of Lou Bring.

L-4698	"Kol Nidre" (Traditional)	Decca 29251-A
L-4699	"A Chazend'l Ohf Shabbes" (Arranged by A. W. Binder)	Decca 29251-B

May 24, 1948. New York, N.Y.
With Simon Rady Chorus.

74539	"Hatikvoh" (Nahtali Herz Imber)	Decca 24456-A
74540	"Israel" (Al Jolson-Benee Russell)	Decca 24456-B

Dec. 8, 1948. Los Angeles, Calif.
With The Mills Brothers.

L-4845	"Down Among the Sheltering Palms" (Abe Olman-James Brockman)	Decca 24534-A
L-4846	"Is It True What They Say About Dixie?" (Irving Caesar-Sammy Lerner-Gerald Marks)	Decca 24534-B

Feb. 16, 1949. Los Angeles, Calif.
With Orchestra under direction of Morris W. Stoloff.

L-4899	"I'm Crying Just for You"	Decca 27410
	(James V. Monaco-Joseph McCarthy)	
L-4900	"I Only Have Eyes for You"	Decca 24601-B
	(Harry Warren-Al Dubin)	
L-4901	"That Wonderful Girl of Mine"	Decca 24601-A
	(Sammy Gallop-Jacob Jacobs-Alexander Olsha-netsky)	
L-4902	"In Our House"	Decca 27410
	(Al Jolson-Benee Russell-Martin Fried)	

May 17, 1949. Los Angeles, Calif.
With Orchestra under direction of Morris W. Stoloff.

L-5017	"Pretty Baby"	Decca 24681-A
	(Egbert Van Alstyne-Tony Jackson-Gus Kahn)	
L-5018	Medley:	Decca 24681-B
	"I'm Looking Over a Four-Leaf Clover"	
	(Harry Woods-Mort Dixon)	
	"Baby Face" (Harry Akst-Benny Davis)	
L-5019	"It All Depends on You"	UNISSUED:
	(B. G. DeSylva-Lew Brown-Ray Henderson)	REJECT

May 23, 1949. Los Angeles, Calif.
With Matty Malneck's Orchestra and Four Hits & A Miss.

L-5020	"Chinatown, My Chinatown"	Decca 24683-B
	(Jean Schwartz-William Jerome)	
L-5021	"After You've Gone"	Decca 24683-A
	(Henry Creamer-J. Turner Layton)	

May 24, 1949. Los Angeles, Calif.
With Orchestra under direction of Morris W. Stoloff.
Matrices L-5024 and L-5026 with Lee Gordon Singers.

L-5019	"It All Depends on You"	Decca 24667-B
(remade)	(B. G. DeSylva-Lew Brown-Ray Henderson)	
L-5024	"Give My Regards to Broadway"	Decca 24682-A
	(George M. Cohan)	
L-5025	"Is It True What They Say About Dixie?"	Decca 24684-B
	(Irving Caesar-Sammy Lerner-Gerald Marks)	
L-5026	"I'm Just Wild About Harry"	Decca 24682-A
	(Noble Sissle-Eubie Blake)	

May 31, 1949. Los Angeles, Calif.
With Orchestra under direction of Victor Young.

L-5029	"(Just One Way To Say) 'I Love You' "	Decca 24665-A
	(Irving Berlin)	
L-5030	"Paris Wakes Up and Smiles"	Decca 24665-B
	(Irving Berlin)	

L-5031   "Some Enchanted Evening"   Decca 24667-A
         (Richard Rodgers-Oscar Hammerstein II)

Jan. 23, 1950. Los Angeles, Calif.
With Orchestra and Chorus under direction of Vic Schoen.

L-5345   "Let's Go West Again"   Decca 24905
         (Irving Berlin)

L-5346   "God's Country"   Decca 24905
         (Haven Gillespie-Beasley Smith)

L-5347   "Remember Mother's Day"   Decca 24971
         (Harry Akst-Ben Ryan-Solly Violinsky)

L-5348   "My Mother's Rosary"   UNISSUED
         (George W. Meyer-Sam M. Lewis)

March 28, 1950. Los Angeles, Calif.
With Orchestra and Chorus under direction of Gordon Jenkins.

L-5418   "My Mother's Rosary"   Decca 24971
         (George W. Meyer-Sam M. Lewis)

April 18, 1950. Los Angeles, Calif.
With The Andrew Sisters.
With Orchestra under direction of Vic Schoen.

L-5554   "The Old Piano Roll Blues"   Decca 27024
         (Cy Coben)

L-5555   " 'Way Down Yonder in New Orleans"   Decca 27024
         (Henry Creamer-J. Turner Layton)

April 28, 1950. Los Angeles, Calif.
With Orchestra and Chorus under direction of Gordon Jenkins.

L-5583   "Are You Lonesome Tonight?"   Decca 27043
         (Roy Turk-Lou Handman)

L-5584   "No Sad Songs for Me"   Decca 27043
         (Harry Akst-Al Jolson)

July 13, 1950. Los Angeles, Calif.
With Orchestra and Chorus under direction of Gordon Jenkins.

L-5731   "Old Black Joe"   Decca 27364
         (Stephen Foster)

L-5732   "My Old Kentucky Home"   Decca 27365
         (Stephen Foster)

L-5733   "Beautiful Dreamer"   Decca 27363
         (Stephen Foster)

L-5734   "Massa's in De Cold, Cold Ground"   Decca 27365
         (Stephen Foster)

July 17, 1950. Los Angeles, Calif.
With Orchestra and Chorus under direction of Gordon Jenkins.

L-5741   "Old Folks at Home"   Decca 27363
         (Stephen Foster)

L-5742   "I Dream of Jeanie with the Light Brown Hair"   Decca 27364
         (Stephen Foster)

L-5743 "Oh! Susanna" Decca 27181
      (Stephen Foster)

L-5744 "De Camptown Races" Decca 27181
      (Stephen Foster)

Index